Sorcerer Hunters

Book 7

Sorcerer Hunters

Book 7

by Satoru Akahori & Ray Omishi

TOKYOPOP
Manga

TOKYOPOP Presents
Sorcerer Hunters 7 by Satoru Akahori & Ray Omishi
TOKYOPOP Manga Premium Edition is an imprint of Mixx Entertainment, Inc.
ISBN: 1-892213-87-7
First Printing December 2001

10   9   8   7   6   5   4   3   2   1

Translator - Anita Sengupta. Retouch Artists - Ryan Caraan, Roselyn Santos.
Graphic Assistant - Dao Sirivisal. Graphic Designer - Akemi Imafuku. Cover Design - Thea Willis.
Assistant Editor - Katherine Kim. Editor - Michael Schuster.
Senior Editor - Jake Forbes. Production Assistant - Rachel Udin.
Production Manager - Fred Lui. Vice President of Production - Ron Klamert.

Email: editor@Press.TOKYOPOP.com
Come visit us at www.TOKYOPOP.com

TOKYOPOP
LOS ANGELES - TOKYO

Contents

Seaside Days in the Springtime of Youth

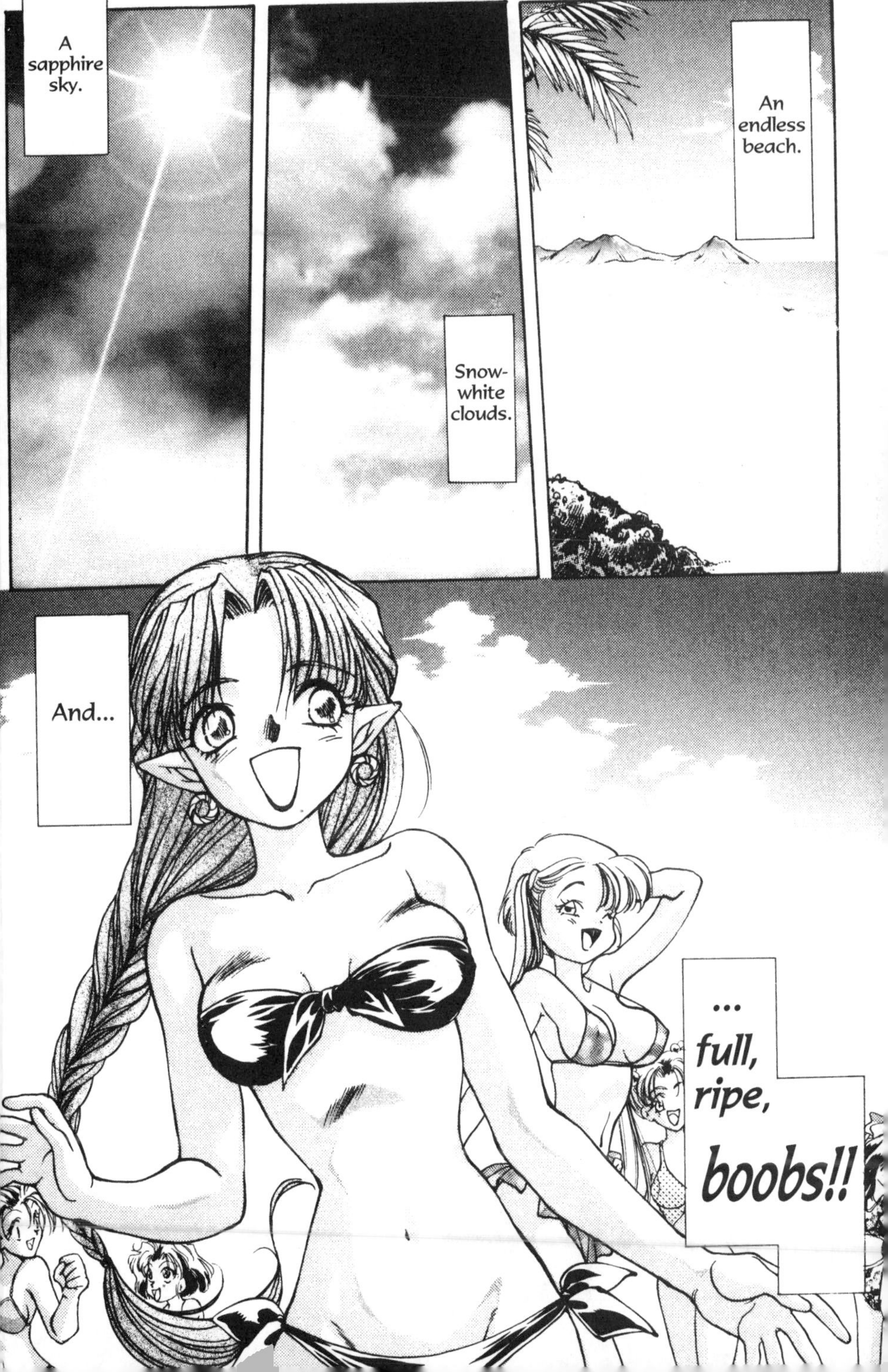
A sapphire sky.
Snow-white clouds.
An endless beach.
And...
... full, ripe, boobs!!

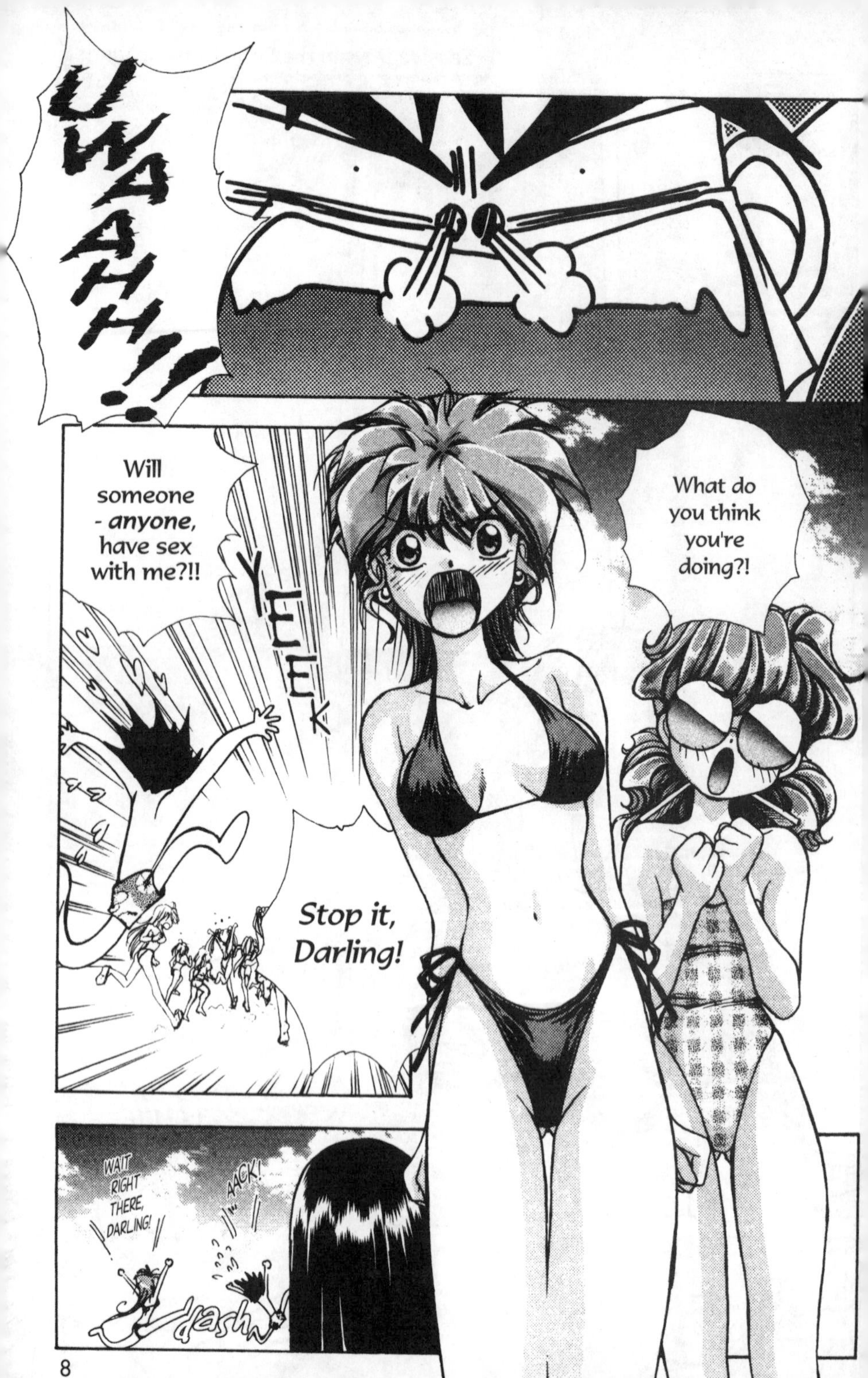
UWAHH!!
Will someone - *anyone*, have sex with me?!!
YEEEK
What do you think you're doing?!
Stop it, Darling!
WAIT RIGHT THERE, DARLING!
AACK!
dash

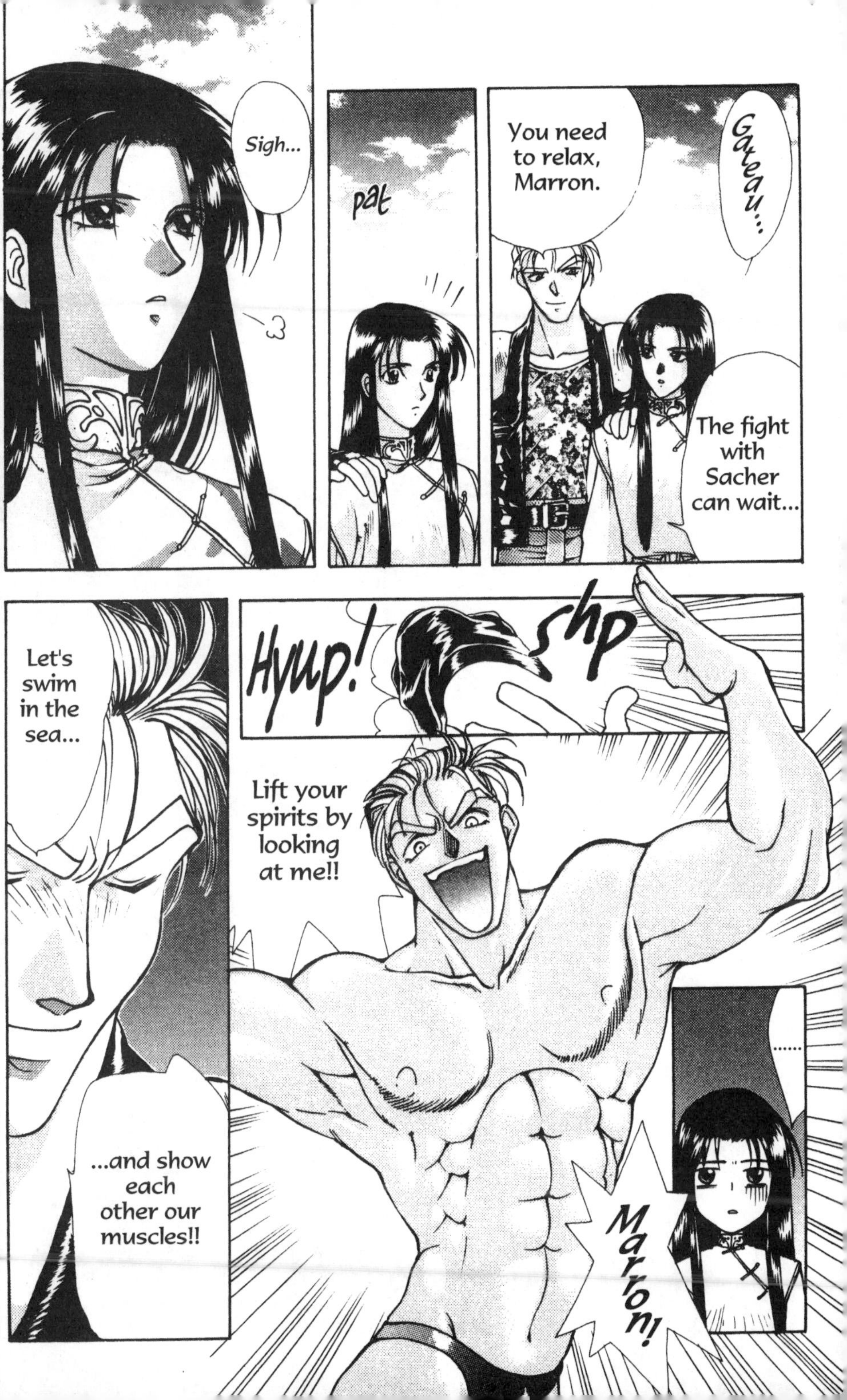
Sigh...
pat
You need to relax, Marron.
Gateau...
The fight with Sacher can wait...
Let's swim in the sea...
...and show each other our muscles!!
Hyup!
shp
Lift your spirits by looking at me!!
......
Marron!

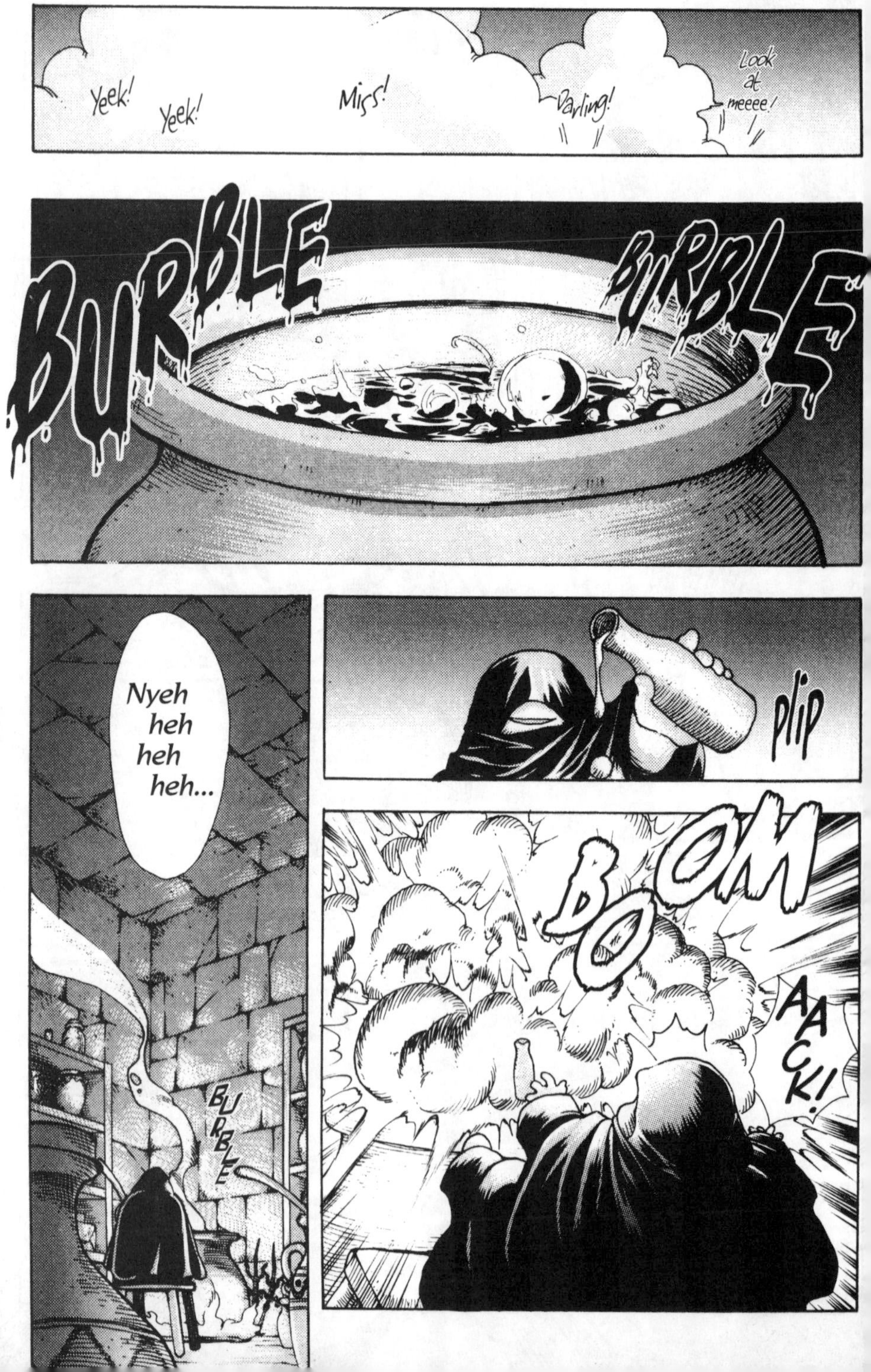
Yeek!
Yeek!
Miss!
Darling!
Look at meeee!
BURBLE
BURBLE
Nyeh heh heh heh...
BURBLE
plip
BOOM
AACK!

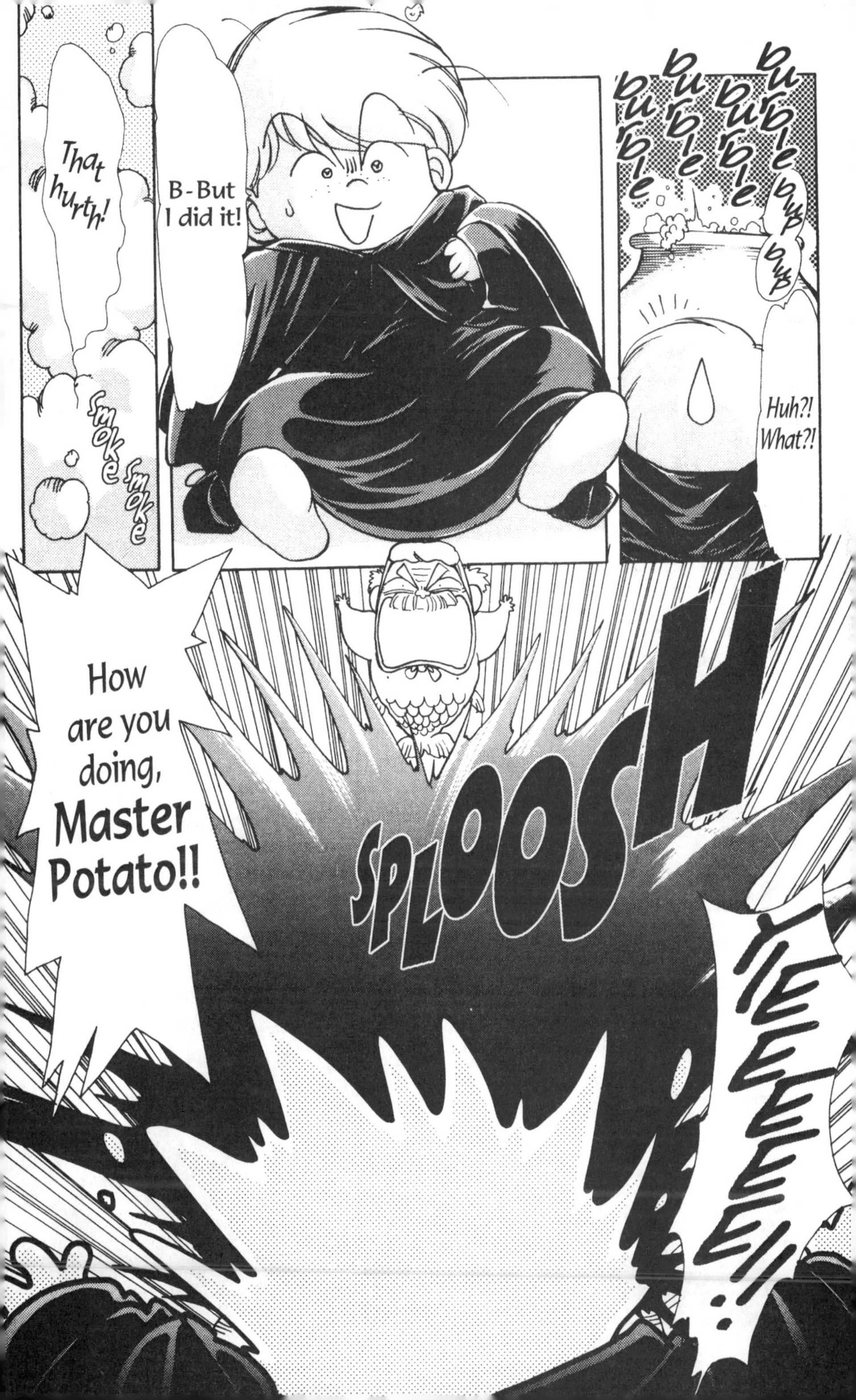
That hurth!
smoke smoke
B-But I did it!
durble durble durble durble bwp bwp
Huh?! What?!
How are you doing, Master Potato!!
SPLOOSH
YEEEEEE!!

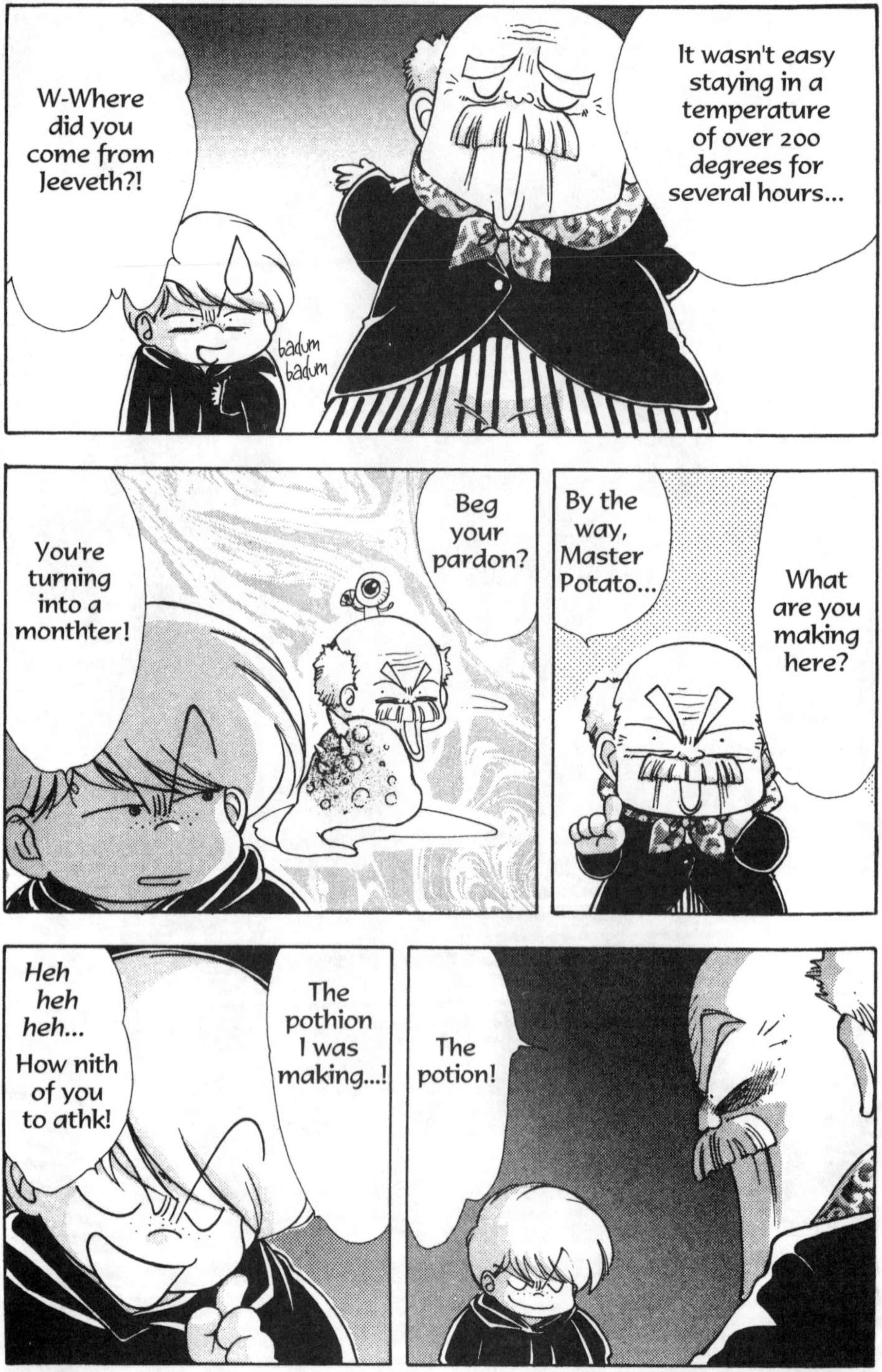
W-Where did you come from Jeeveth?!
It wasn't easy staying in a temperature of over 200 degrees for several hours...
badum badum
You're turning into a monthter!
Beg your pardon?
By the way, Master Potato...
What are you making here?
Heh heh heh... How nith of you to athk!
The pothion I was making...!
The potion!

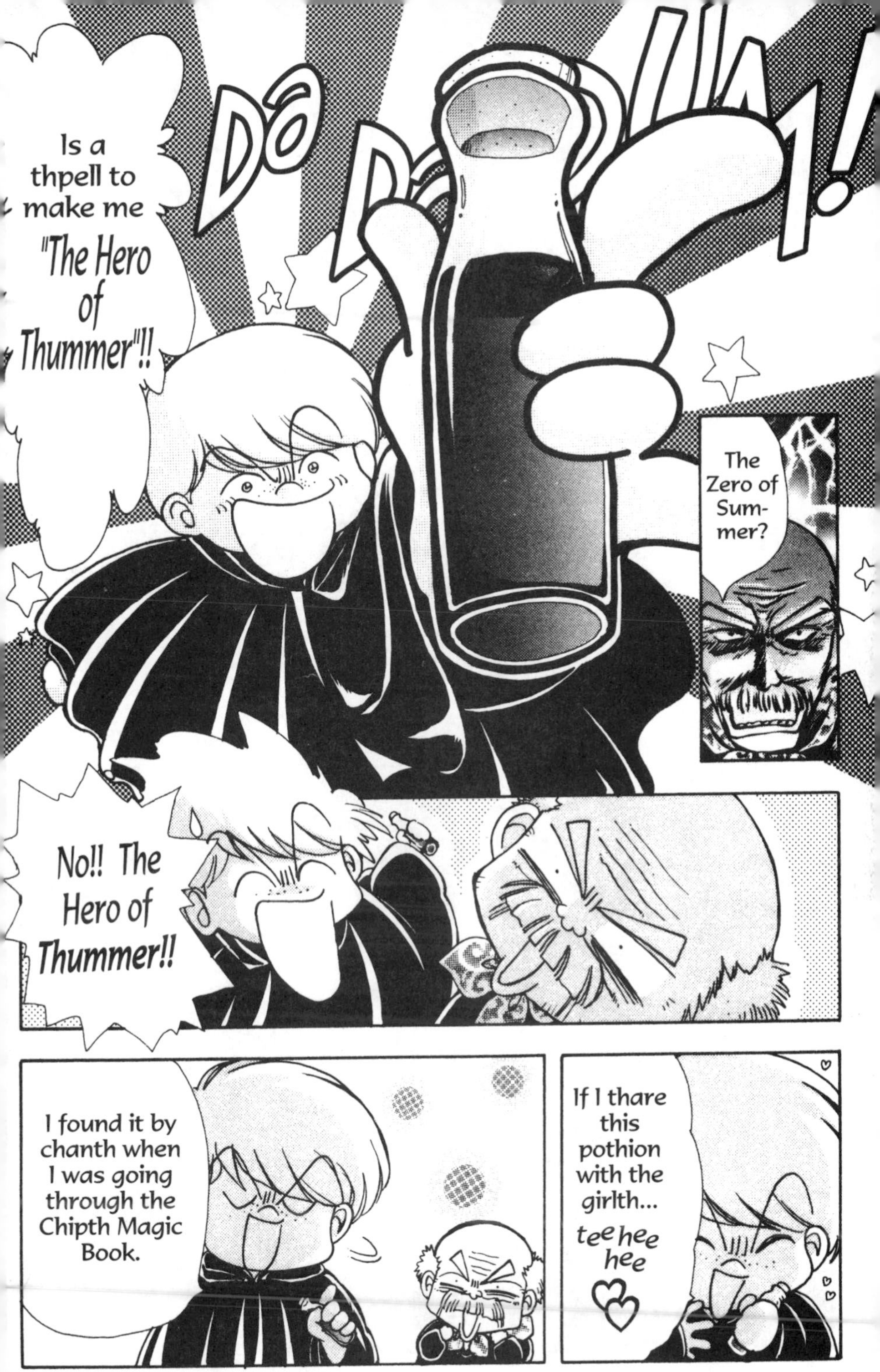

Is a thpell to make me "The Hero of Thummer"!!
The Zero of Sum-mer?
No!! The Hero of Thummer!!
I found it by chanth when I was going through the Chipth Magic Book.
If I thare this pothion with the girlth...
tee hee hee

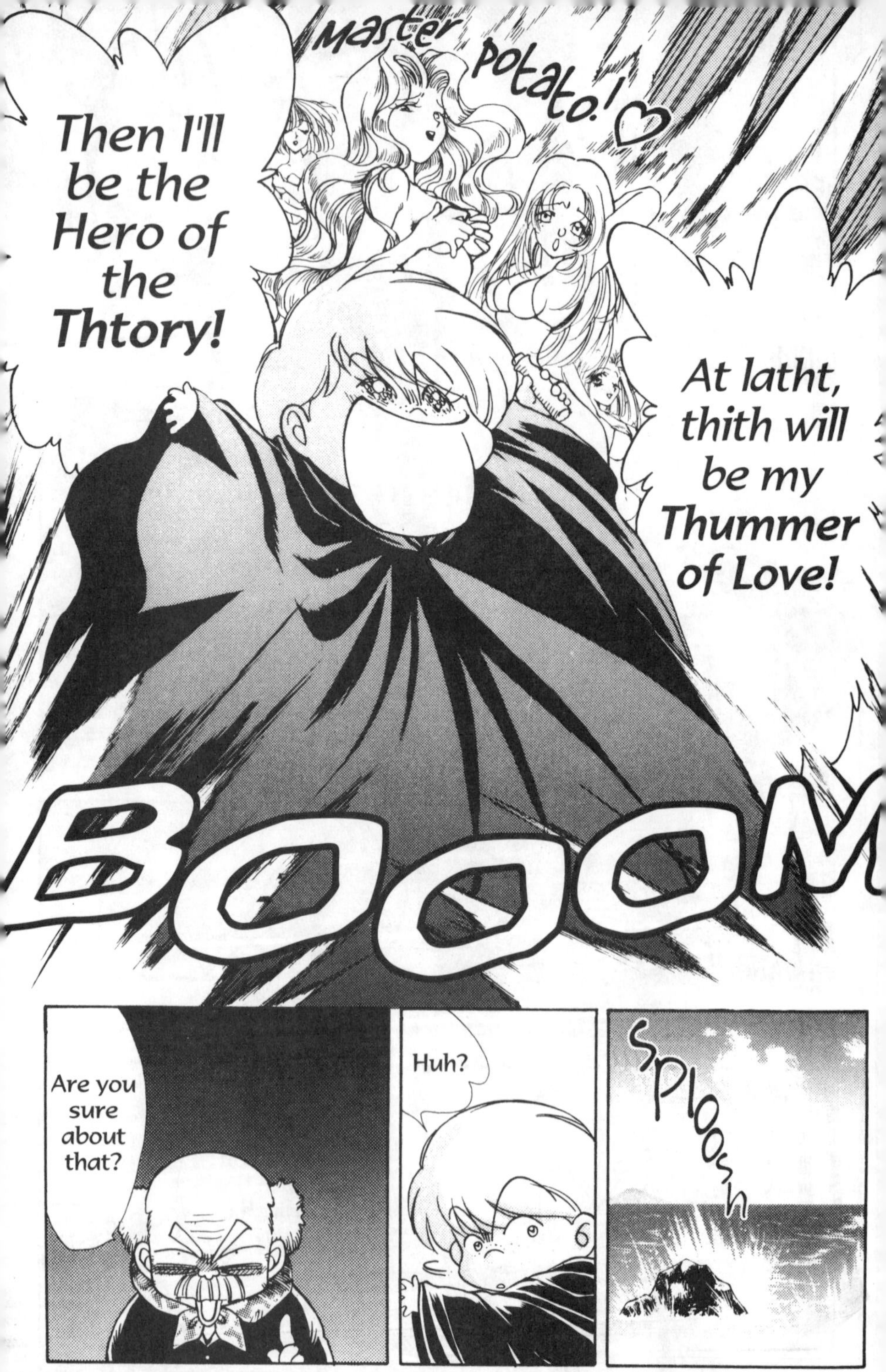
Master Potato!♥
Then I'll be the Hero of the Thtory!
At latht, thith will be my Thummer of Love!
BOOOM
Are you sure about that?
Huh?
Sploosh

Love potions always have some sort of catch.

Ith that tho?

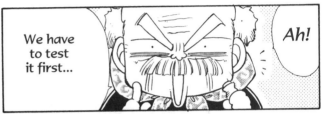

We have to test it first...

Ah!

Nyee hee hee... It looks like the perfect lab rats have arrived.

You're thkaring me, Jeeveth.

Darling! Stop!

Gaah! Lemme alone already!!

I'll never be able to get the babes this way!

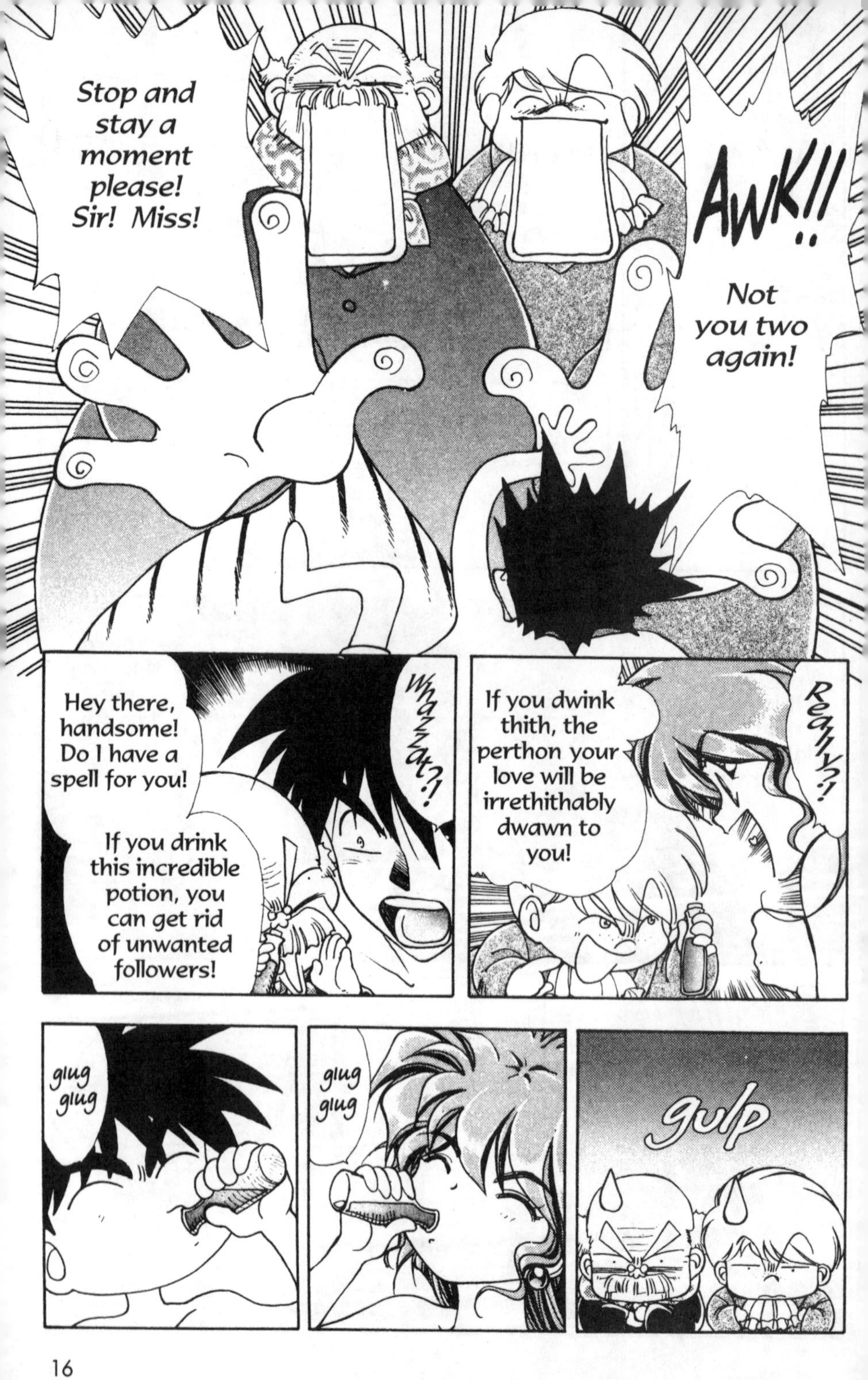
Stop and stay a moment please! Sir! Miss!
AWK!!
Not you two again!
Hey there, handsome! Do I have a spell for you!
Whazzat?!
If you drink this incredible potion, you can get rid of unwanted followers!
If you dwink thith, the perthon your love will be irrethithably dwawn to you!
Really?!
glug glug
glug glug
gulp

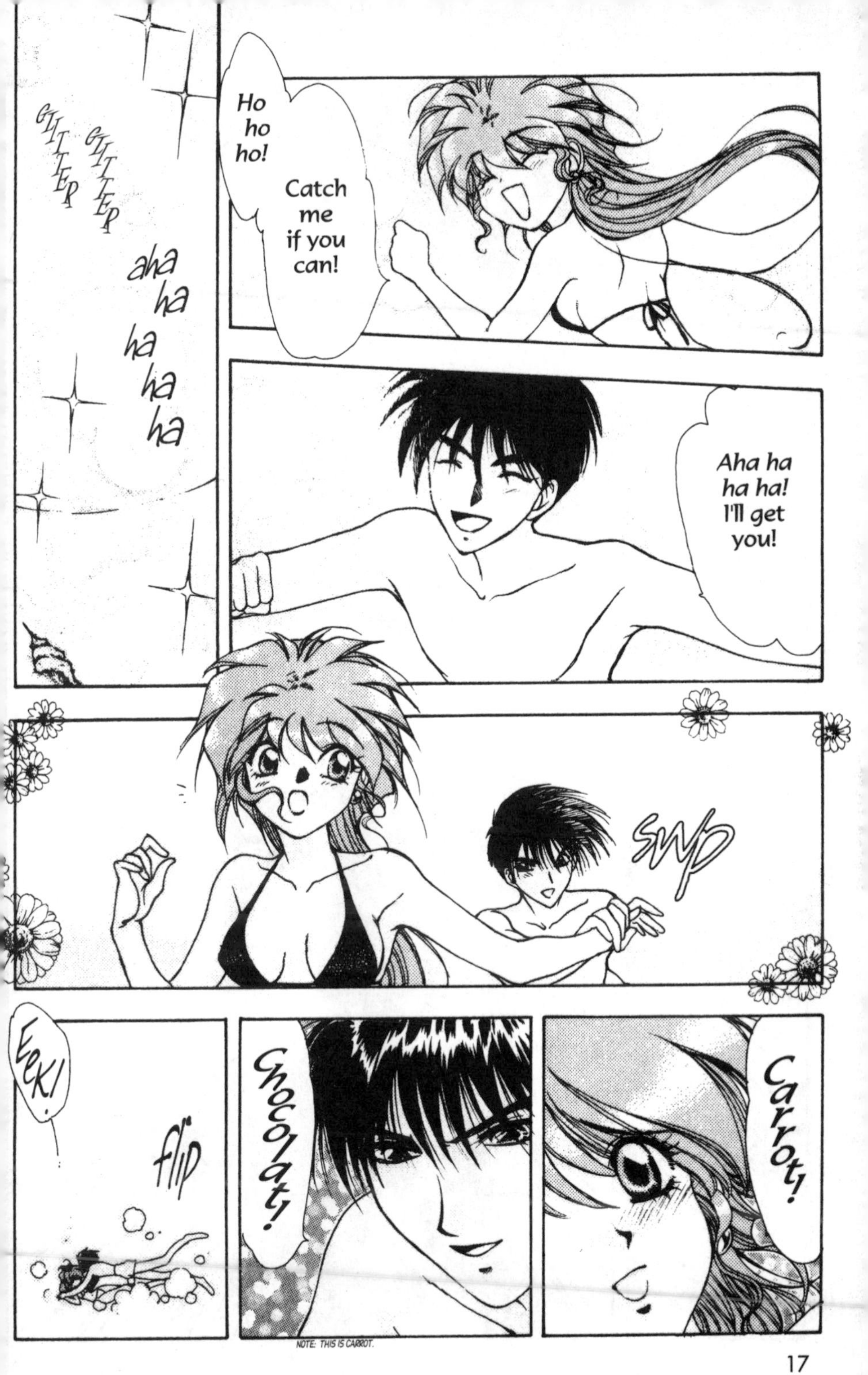
GLITTER GLITTER
aha ha ha ha ha
Ho ho ho! Catch me if you can!
Aha ha ha ha! I'll get you!
SNP
Eeek!
flip
Chocolat!
Carrot!

NOTE: THIS IS CARROT.

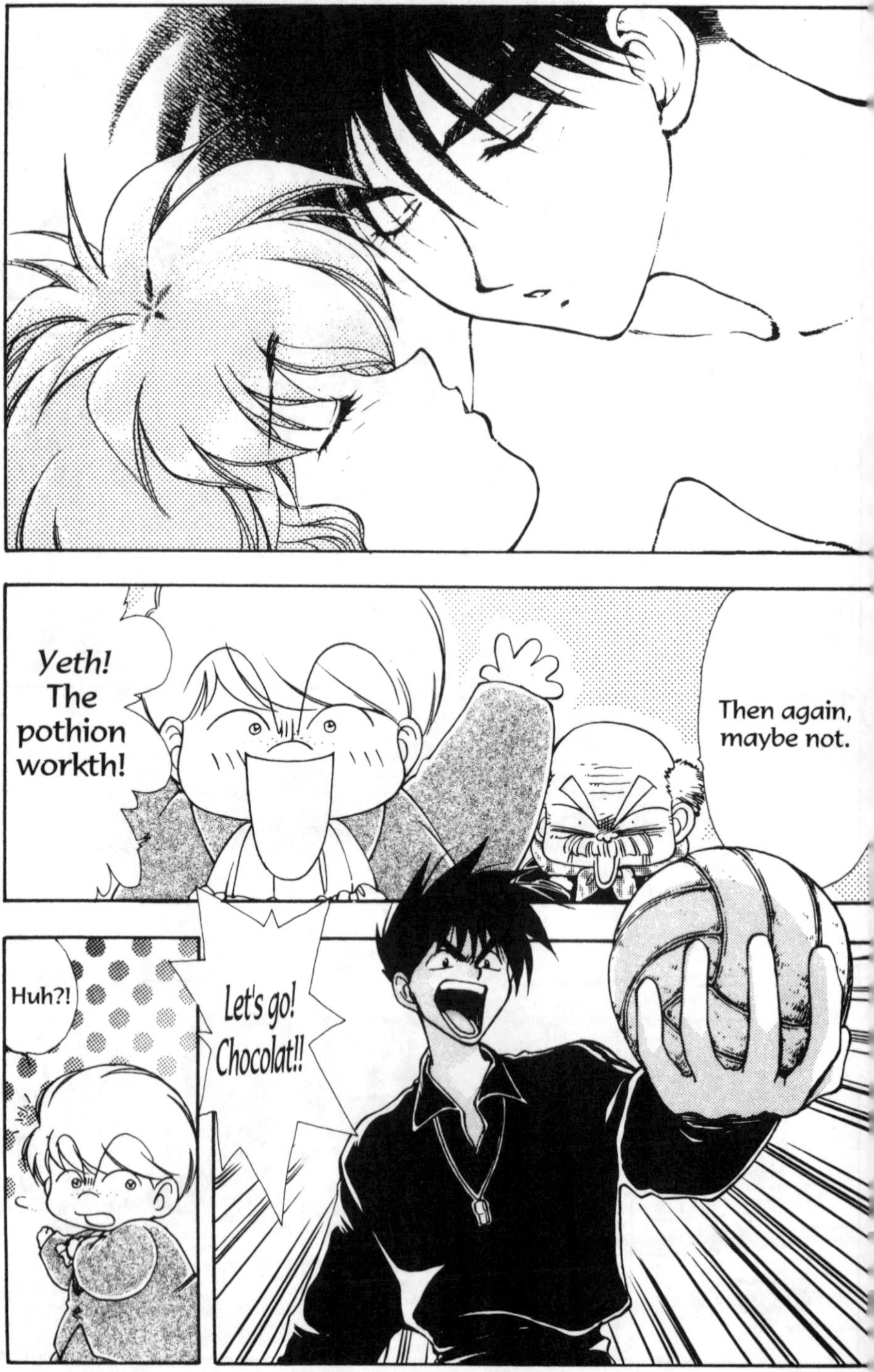
Yeth! The pothion workth!
Then again, maybe not.
Huh?!
Let's go! Chocolat!!

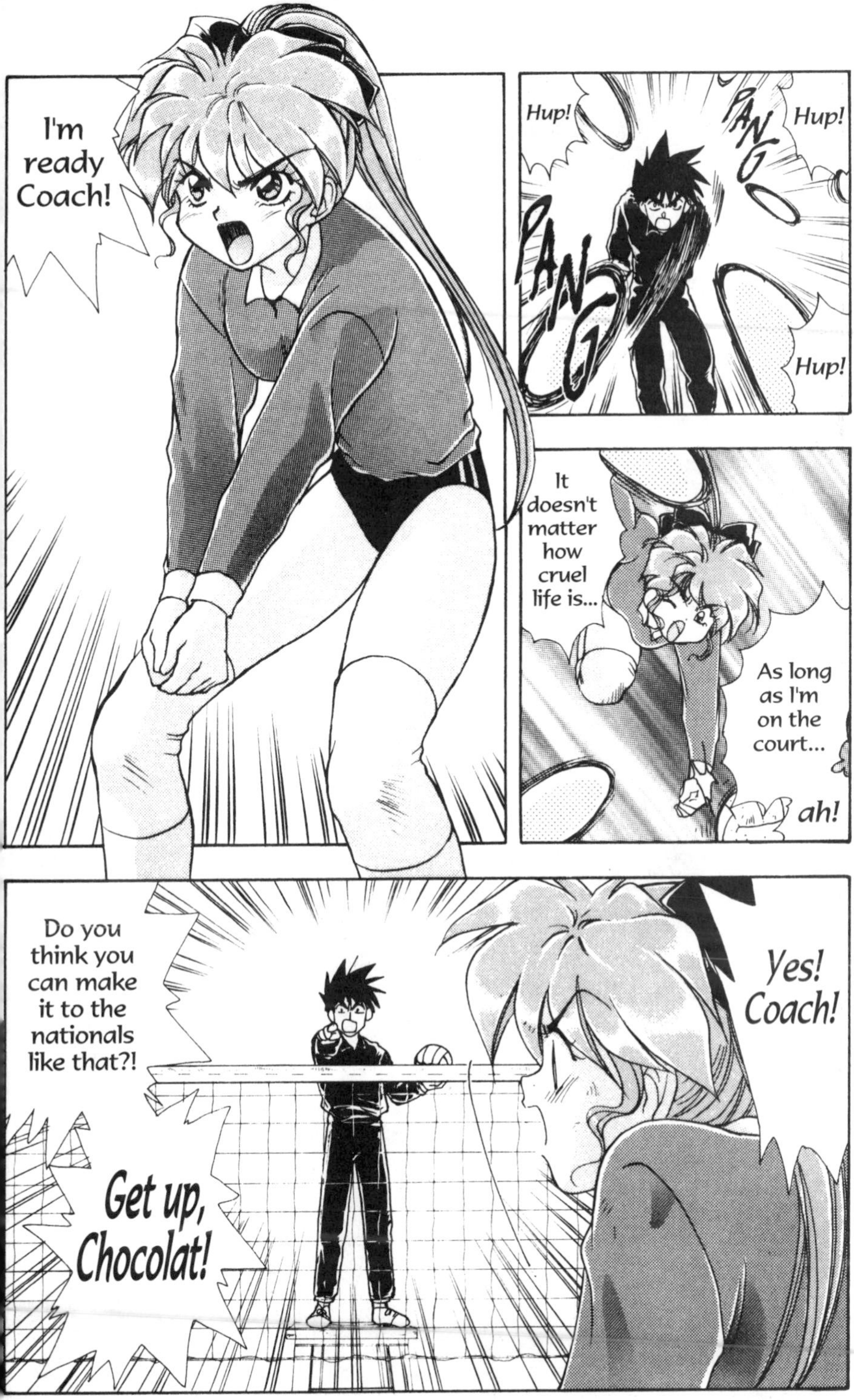
I'm ready Coach!
Hup!
PANG
Hup!
PANG
Hup!
It doesn't matter how cruel life is...
As long as I'm on the court...
ah!
Do you think you can make it to the nationals like that?!
Yes! Coach!
Get up, Chocolat!

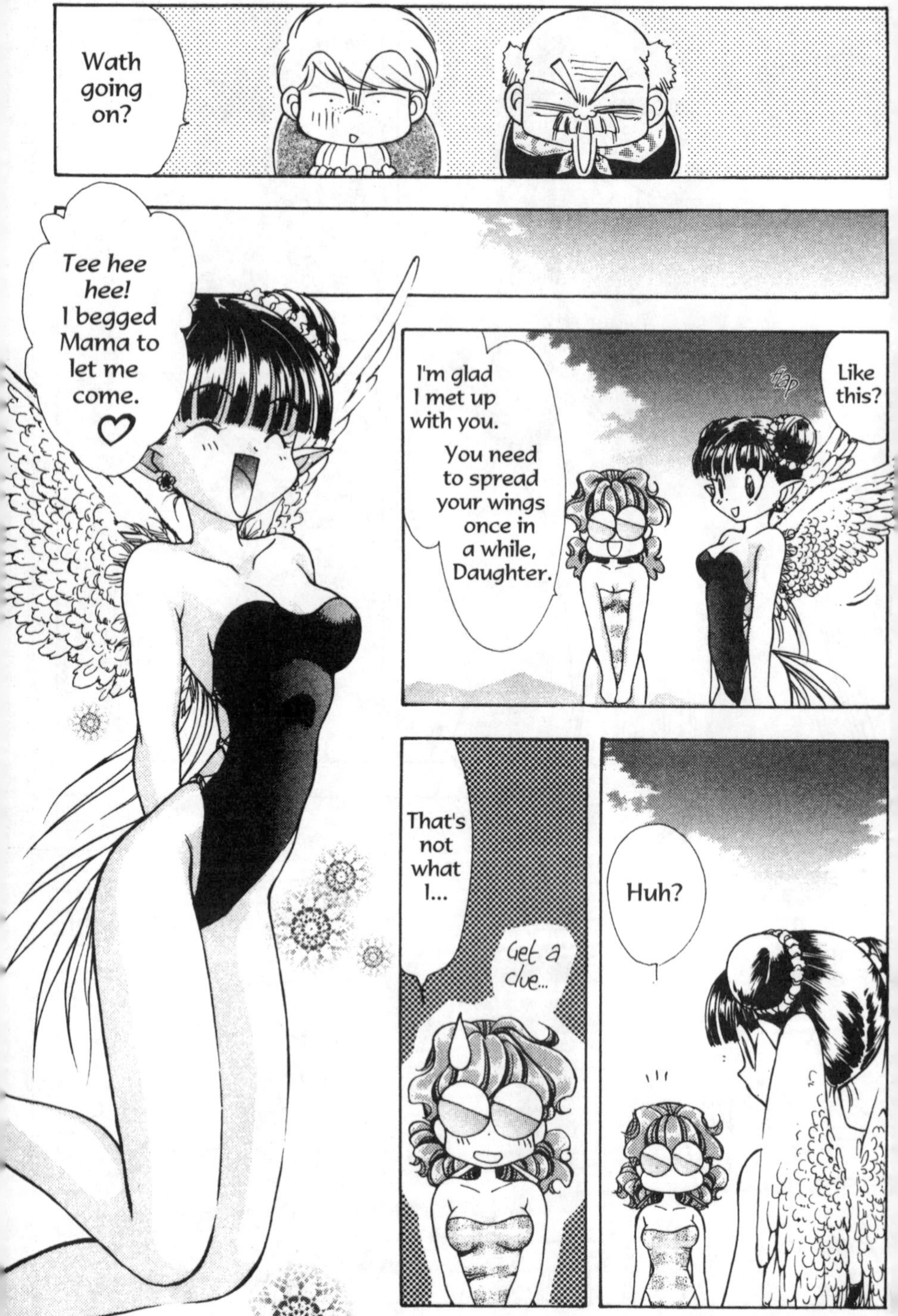

Wath going on?
Tee hee hee! I begged Mama to let me come. ♡
I'm glad I met up with you.
You need to spread your wings once in a while, Daughter.
flap
Like this?
That's not what I...
Get a clue...
Huh?

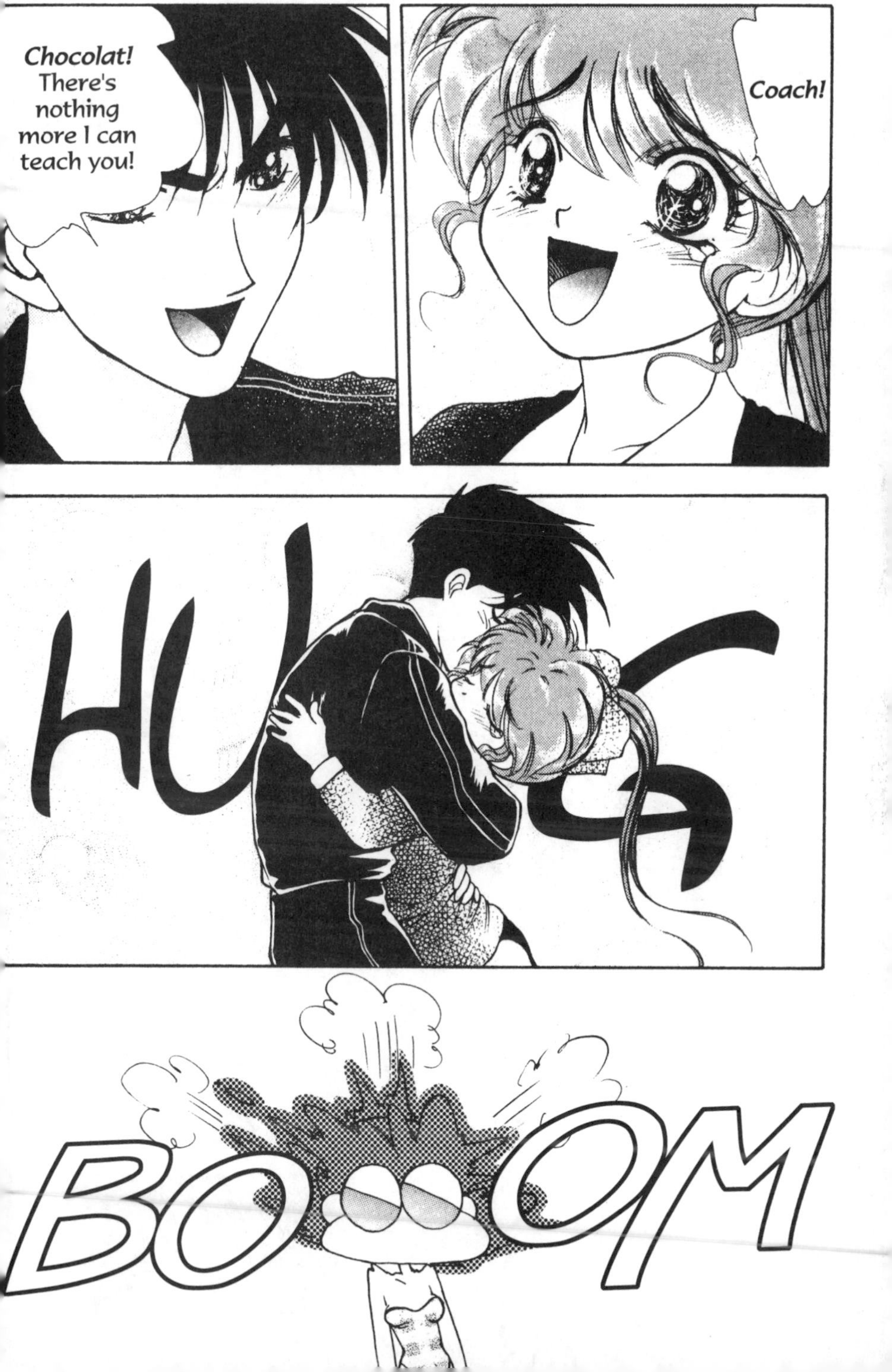
Chocolat! There's nothing more I can teach you!
Coach!
HUG
BOOOM

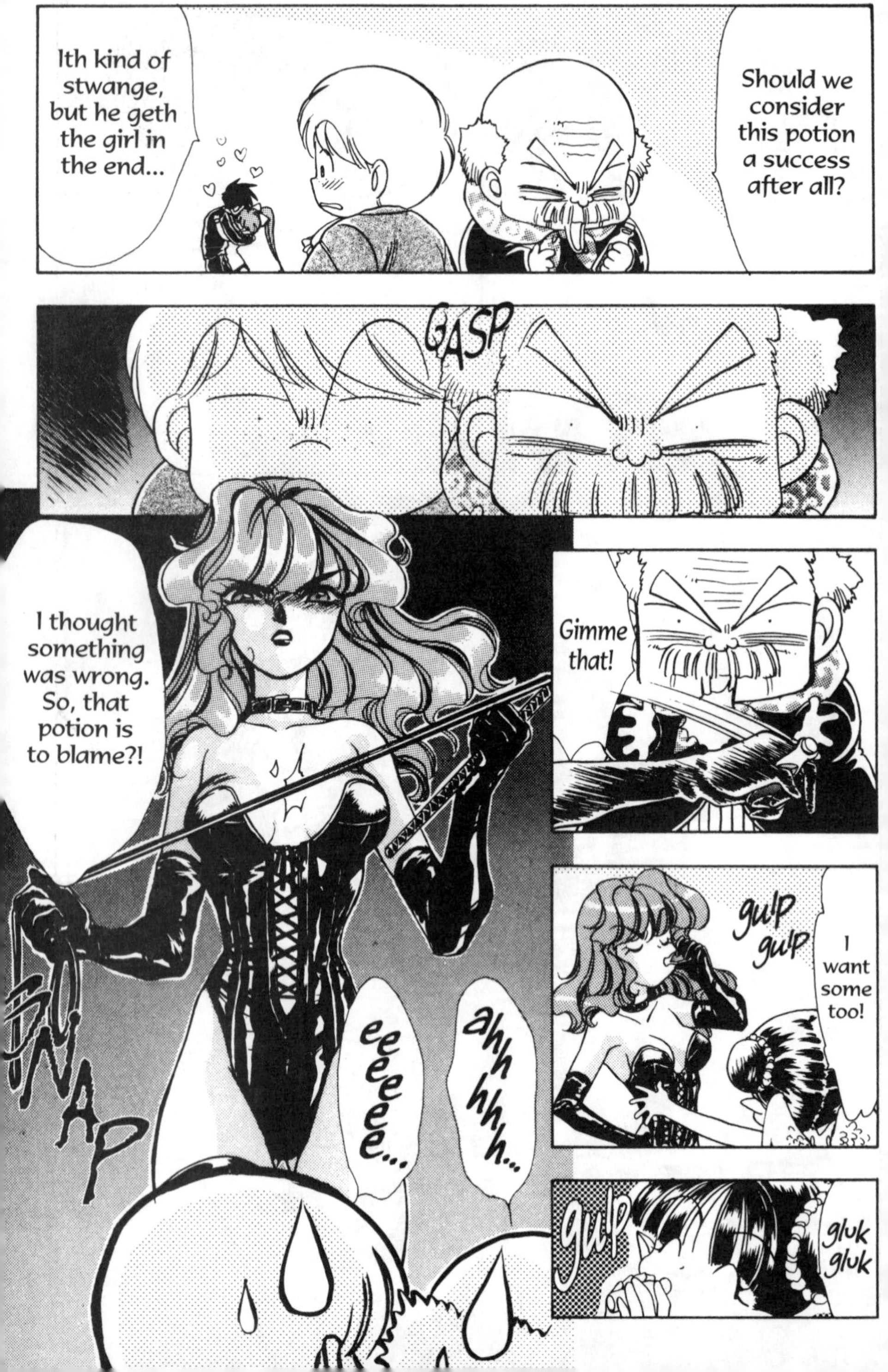

Ith kind of stwange, but he geth the girl in the end...
Should we consider this potion a success after all?
GASP
I thought something was wrong. So, that potion is to blame?!
SNAP
eeeeee...
ahhhhh...
Gimme that!
gulp gulp
I want some too!
gulp
gluk gluk

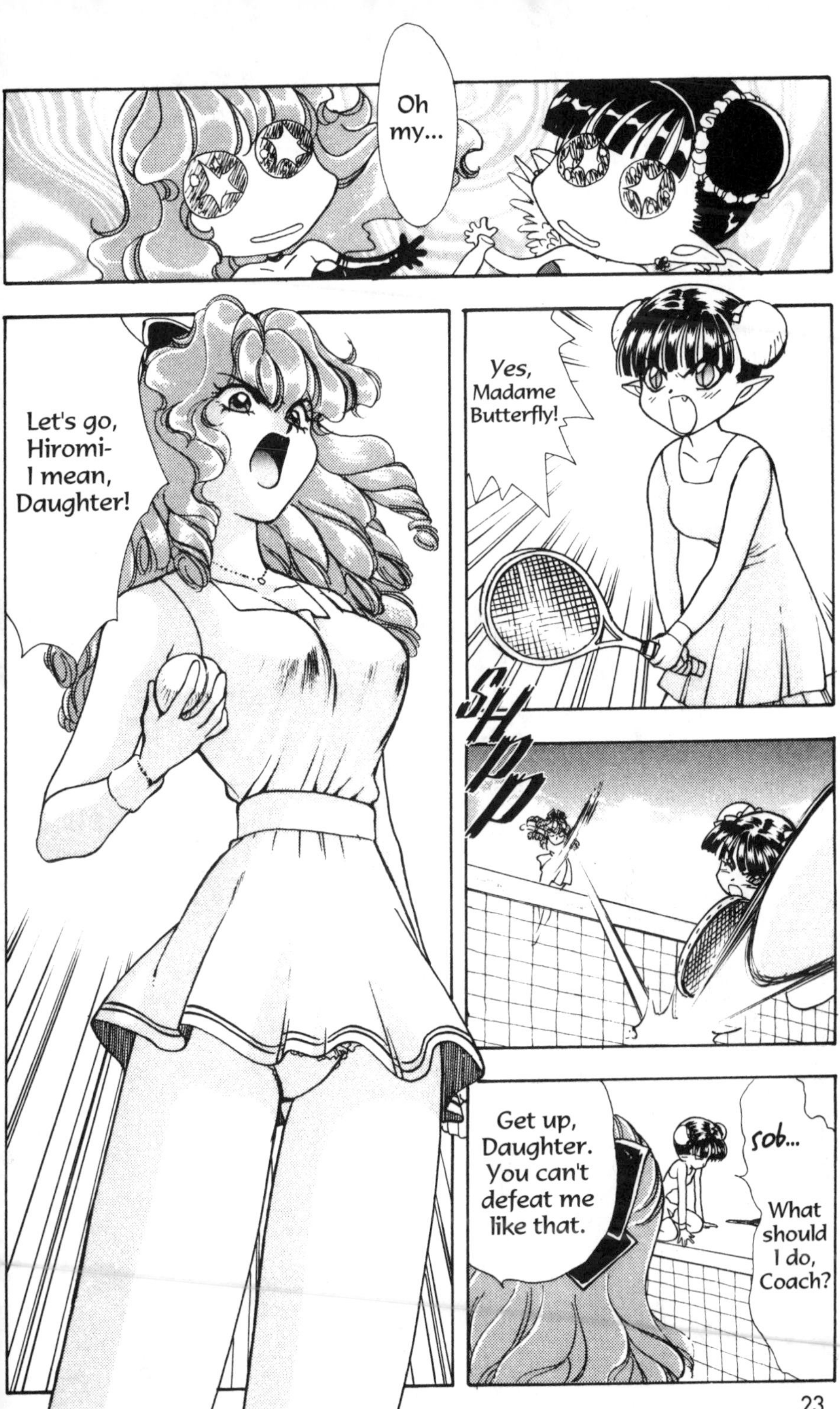
Oh my...
Let's go, Hiromi- I mean, Daughter!
Yes, Madame Butterfly!
SHPP
Get up, Daughter. You can't defeat me like that.
sob...
What should I do, Coach?

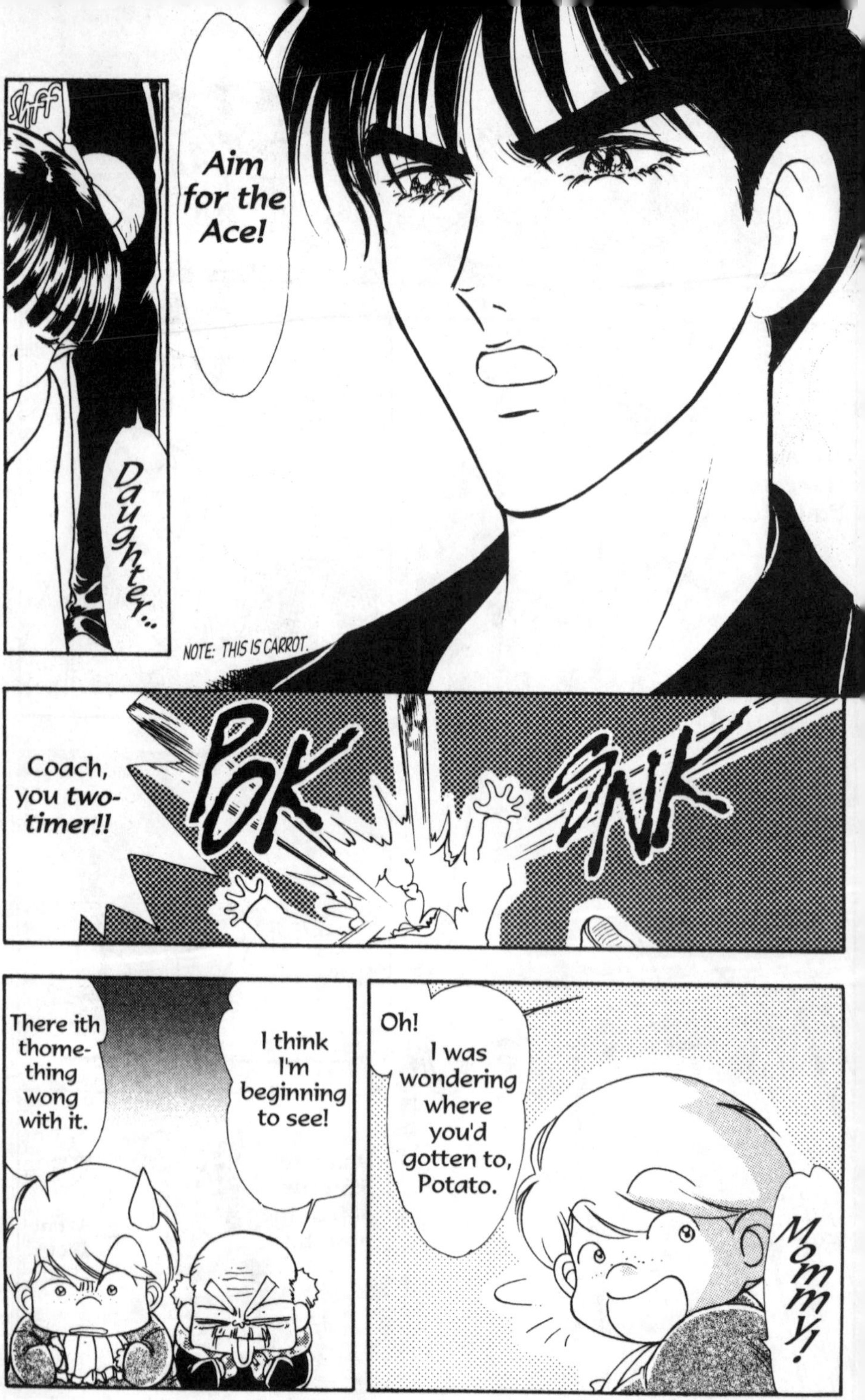
Shiff
Daughter...
Aim for the Ace!
NOTE: THIS IS CARROT.
Coach, you two-timer!!
POK
SNK
There ith thome-thing wong with it.
I think I'm beginning to see!
Oh!
I was wondering where you'd gotten to, Potato.
Mommy!

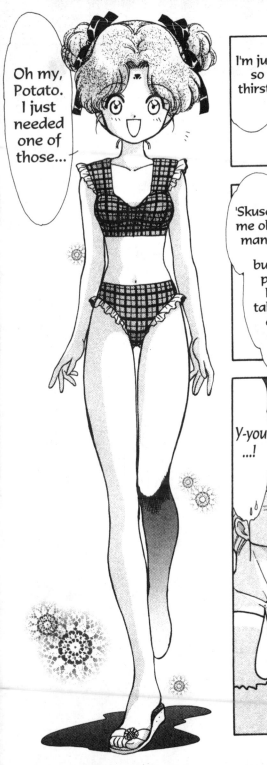

Oh my, Potato. I just needed one of those...

I'm just so thirsty.

gup gup gup

M-m-Mommy!

'Skuse me old man,

but I'm just parched. Lemme take a swig of that.

y-you ...!

gup gup

O-oh my...

W-what...

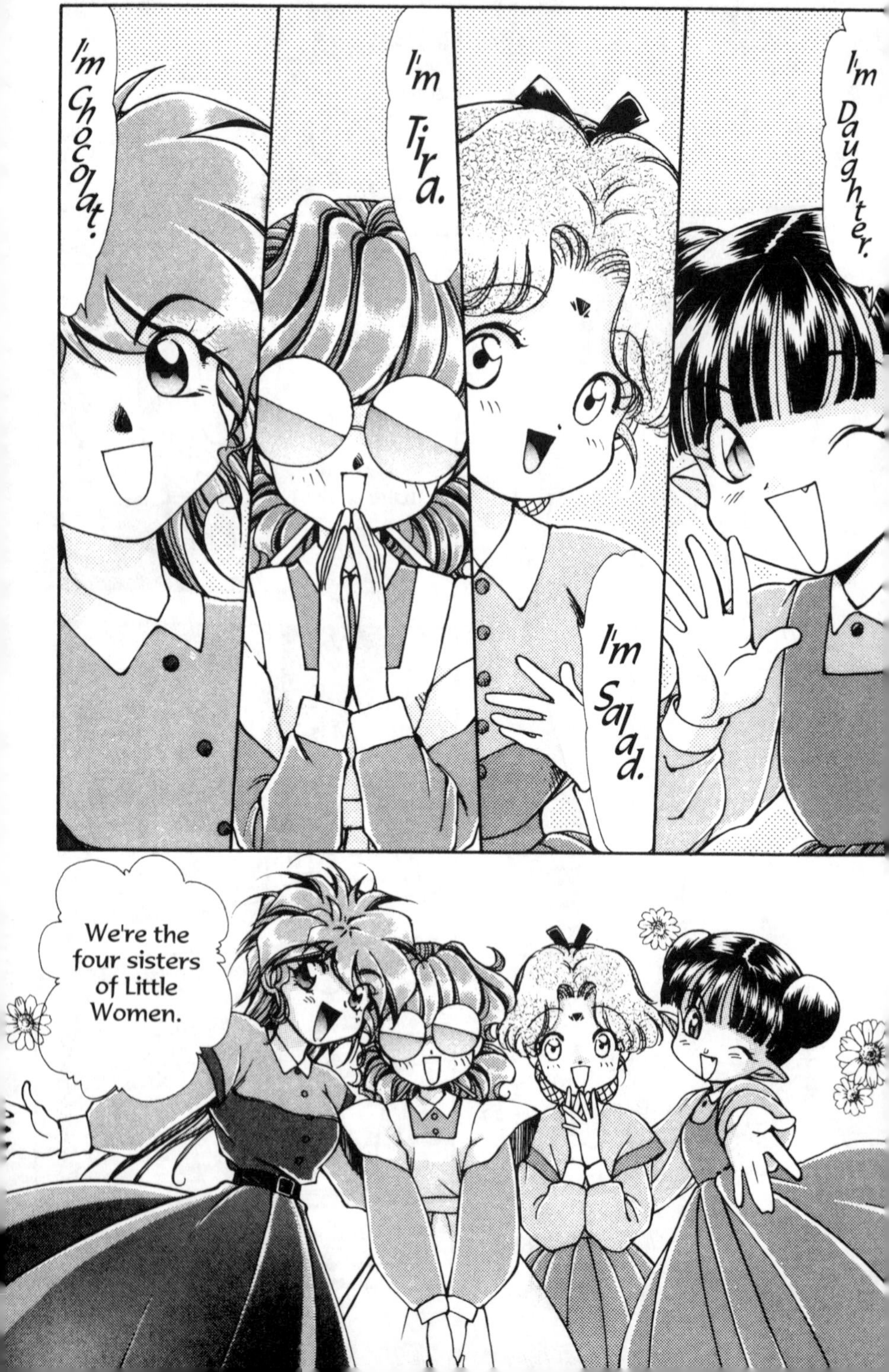

I'm Chocolat.
I'm Tira.
I'm Salad.
I'm Daughter.
We're the four sisters of Little Women.

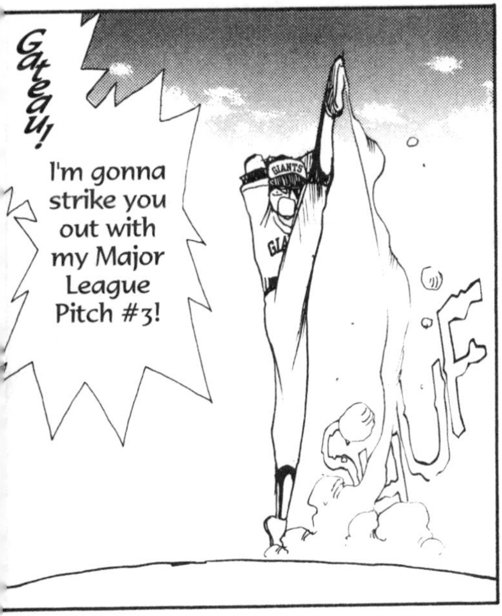
Gateau!
I'm gonna strike you out with my Major League Pitch #3!
GIANTS

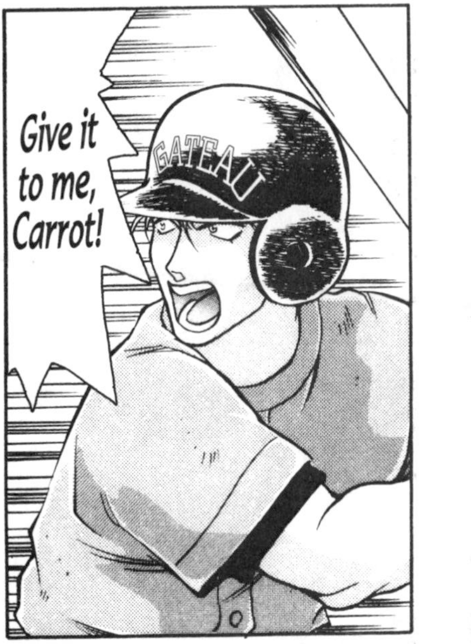
Give it to me, Carrot!
GATEAU

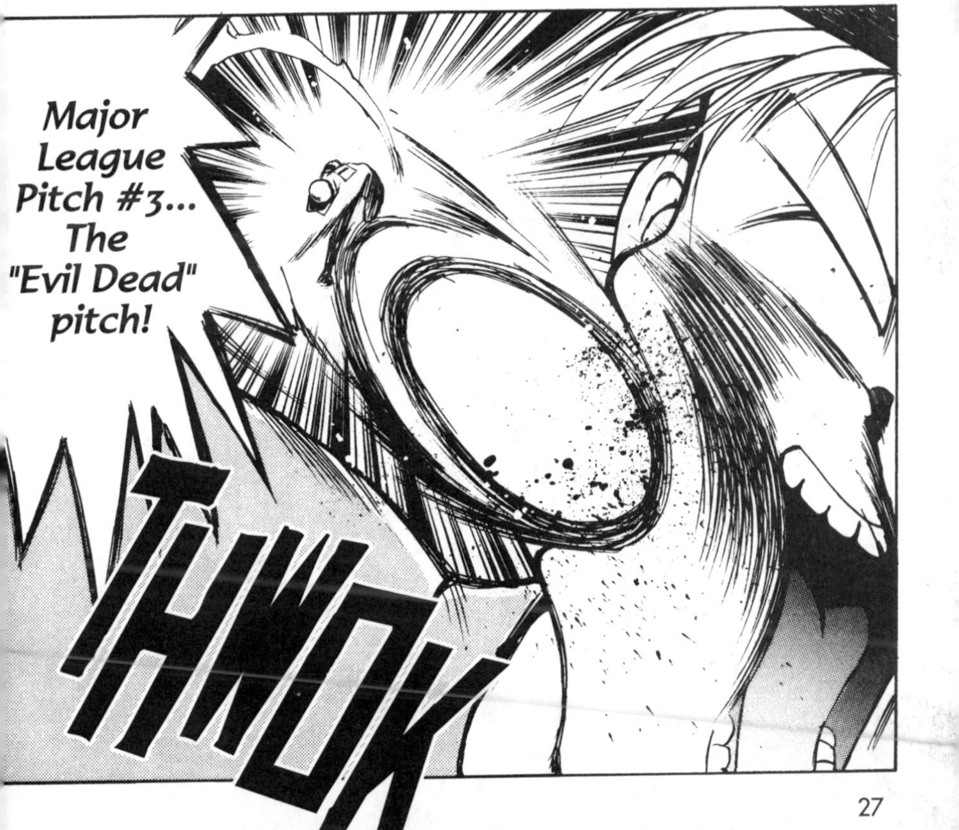
Major League Pitch #3... The "Evil Dead" pitch!
THWOK

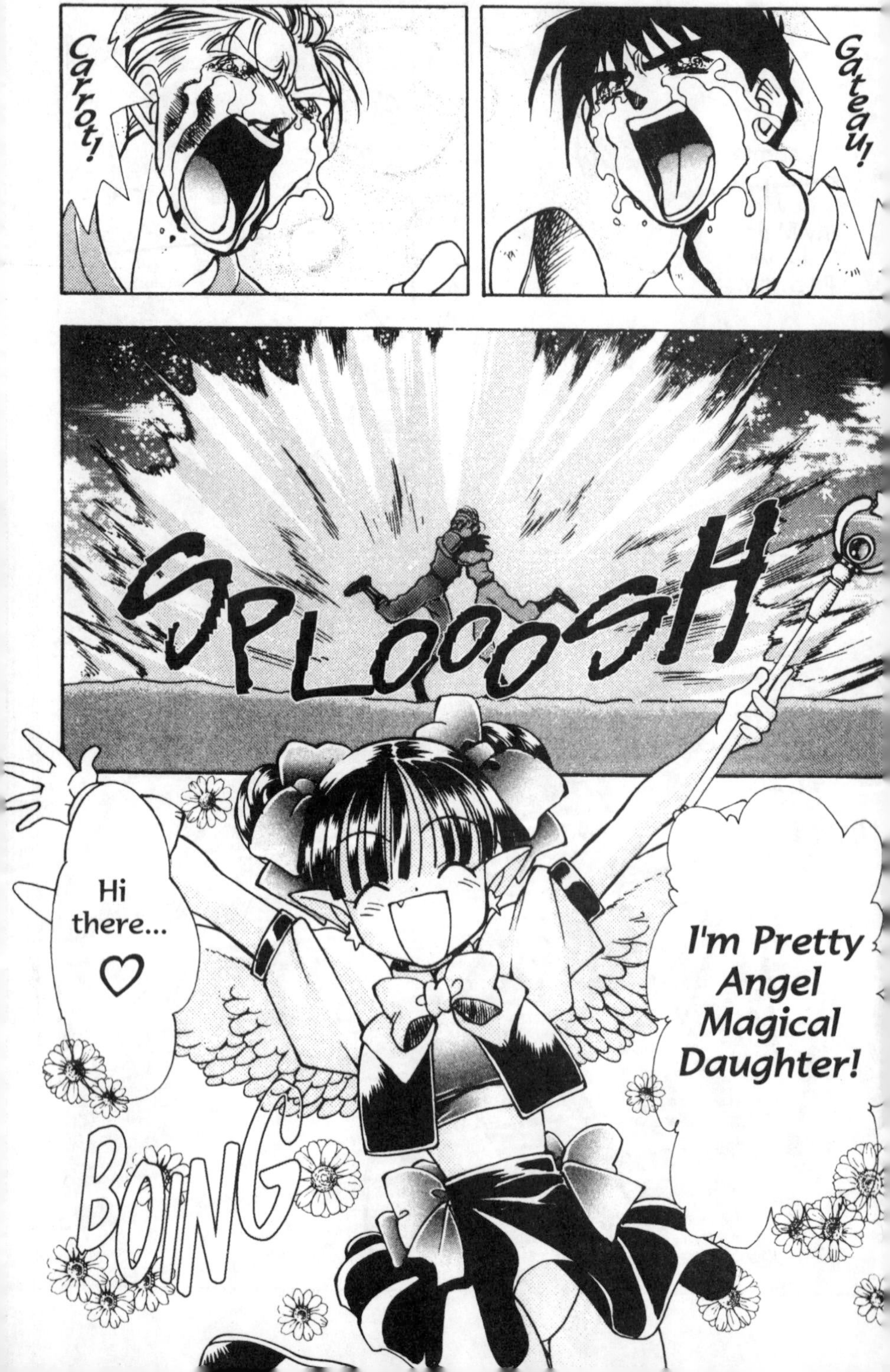
Carrot!
Gateau!
SPLOOOSH
Hi there... ♡
I'm Pretty Angel Magical Daughter!
BOING

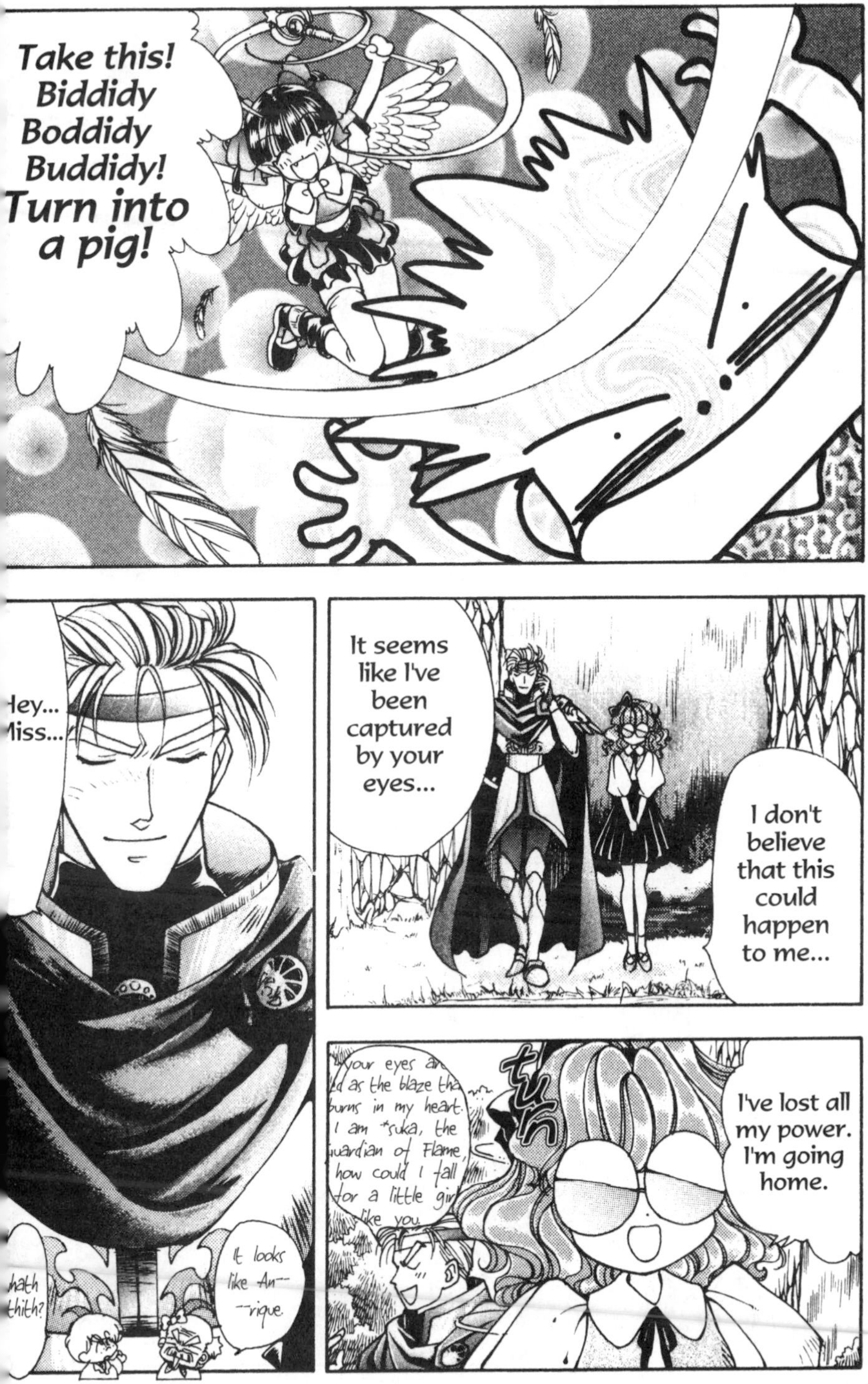
Take this! Biddidy Boddidy Buddidy! Turn into a pig!
ley... liss...
hath thith?
It looks like An--rique.
It seems like I've been captured by your eyes...
I don't believe that this could happen to me...
Your eyes ar ed as the blaze tha burns in my heart. I am *suka, the uardian of Flame, how could I fall for a little gir like you.
tun
I've lost all my power. I'm going home.

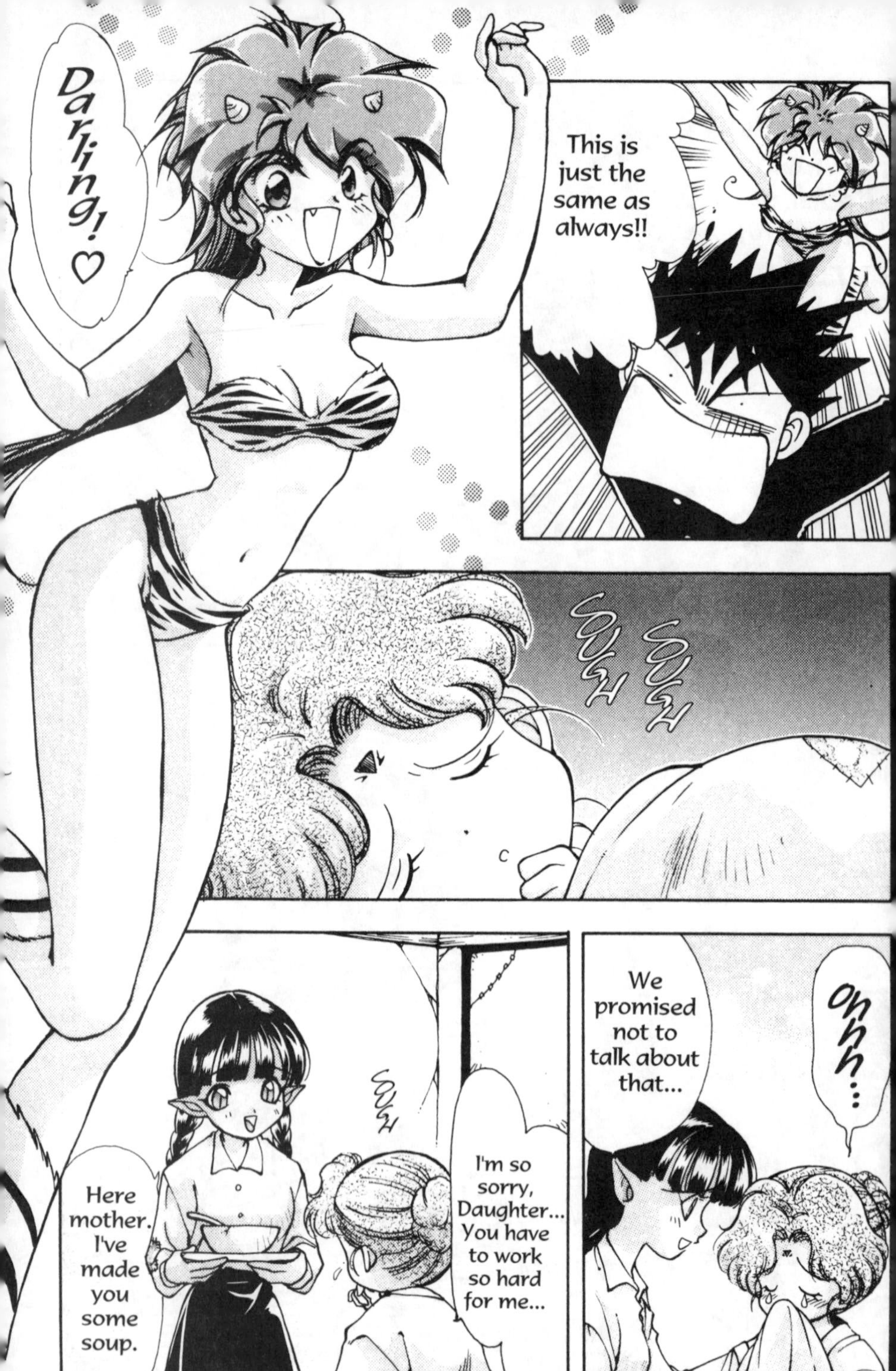
Darling! ♡
This is just the same as always!!
COUGH COUGH
COUGH
Here mother. I've made you some soup.
I'm so sorry, Daughter... You have to work so hard for me...
We promised not to talk about that...
Ohhh...

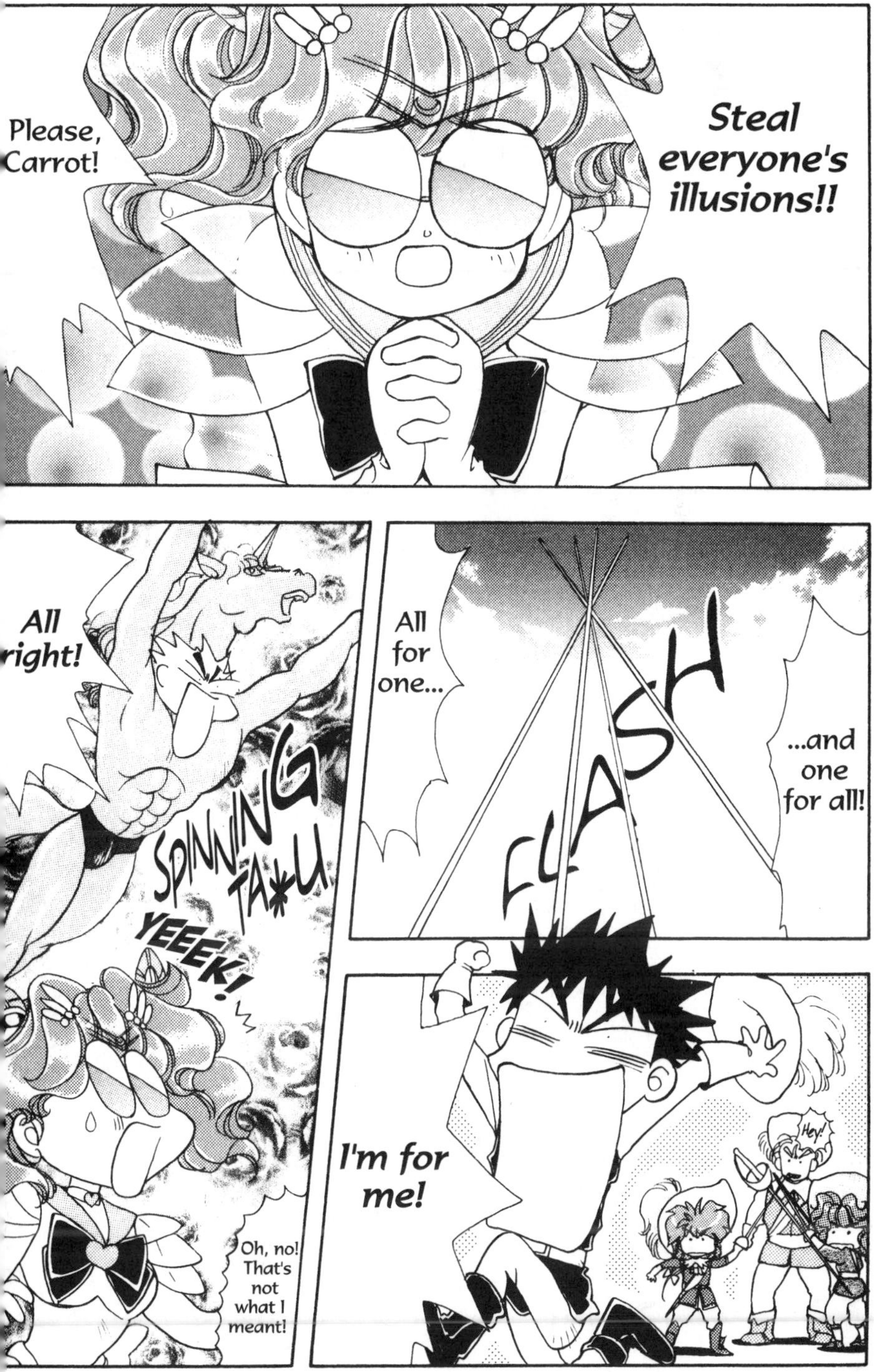
Please, Carrot!
Steal everyone's illusions!!
All right!
SPINNING TA*U
YEEEK!
Oh, no! That's not what I meant!
All for one...
CLASH
...and one for all!
I'm for me!
Hey!

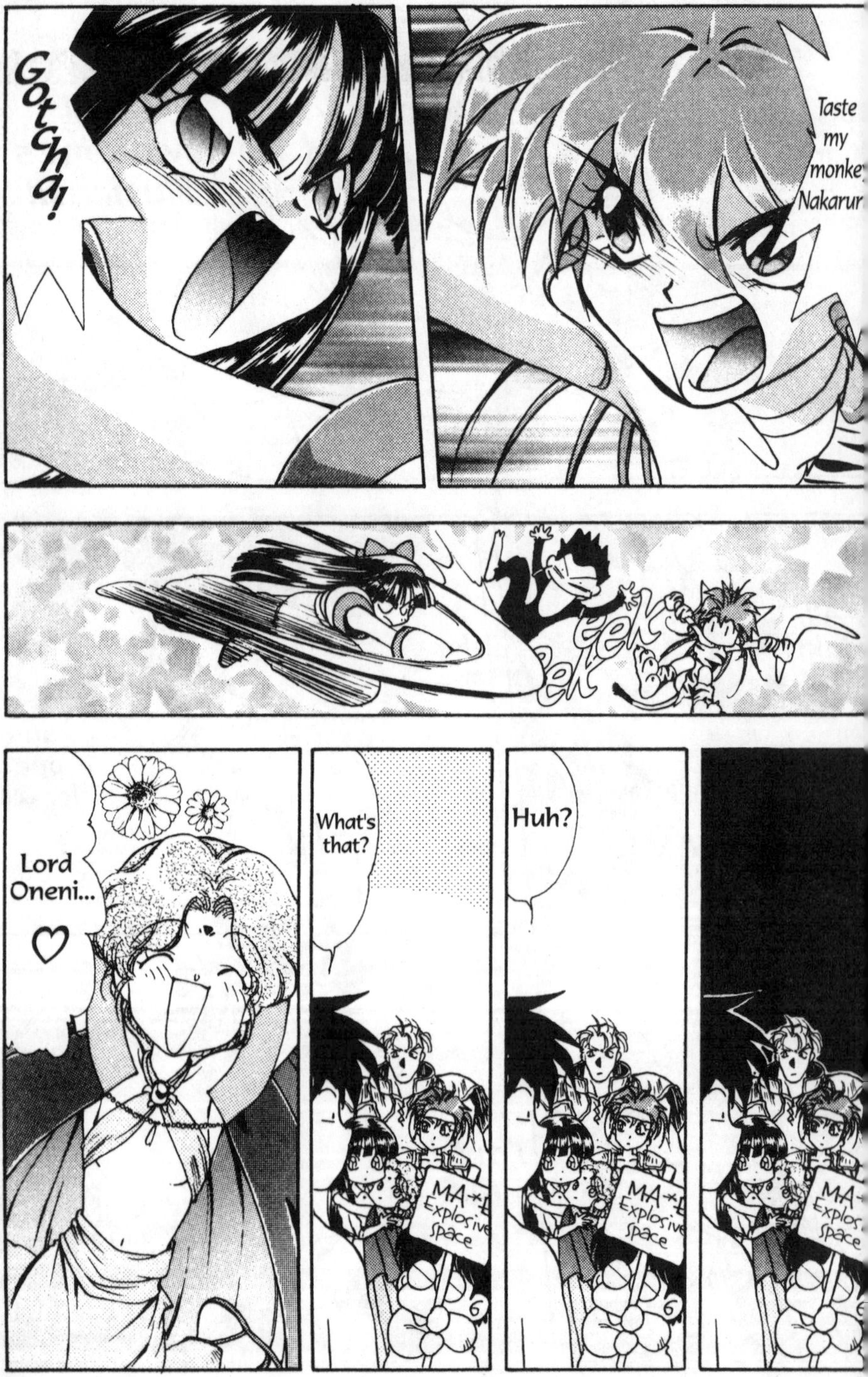
Gotcha!
Taste my monke Nakarur
eek eek
Lord Oneni...
♡
What's that?
Huh?
MA-E Explosive space

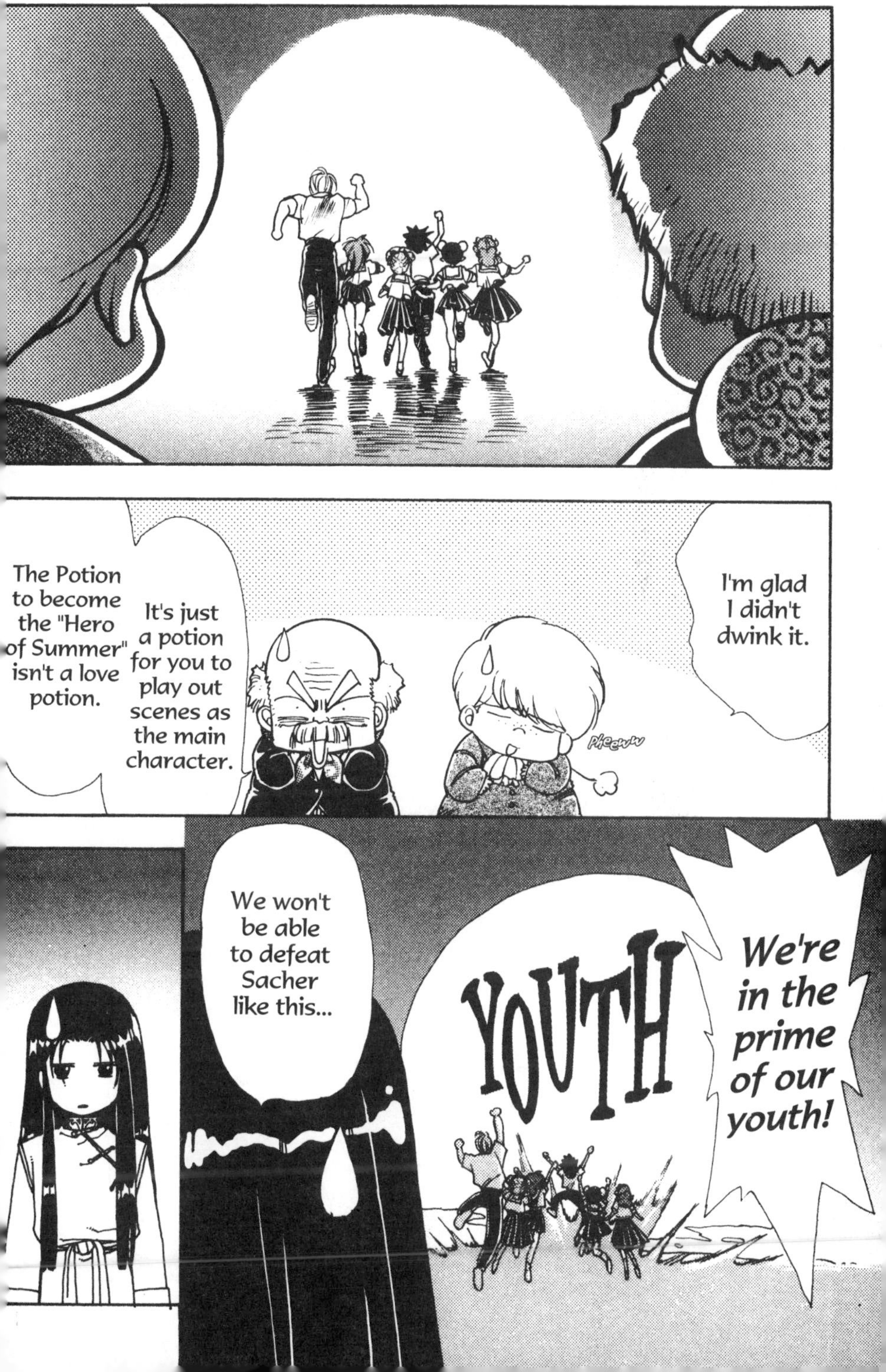

The Potion to become the "Hero of Summer" isn't a love potion.
It's just a potion for you to play out scenes as the main character.
Pheeww
I'm glad I didn't dwink it.
We won't be able to defeat Sacher like this...
YOUTH
We're in the prime of our youth!

The Last Guardian Spirit?!

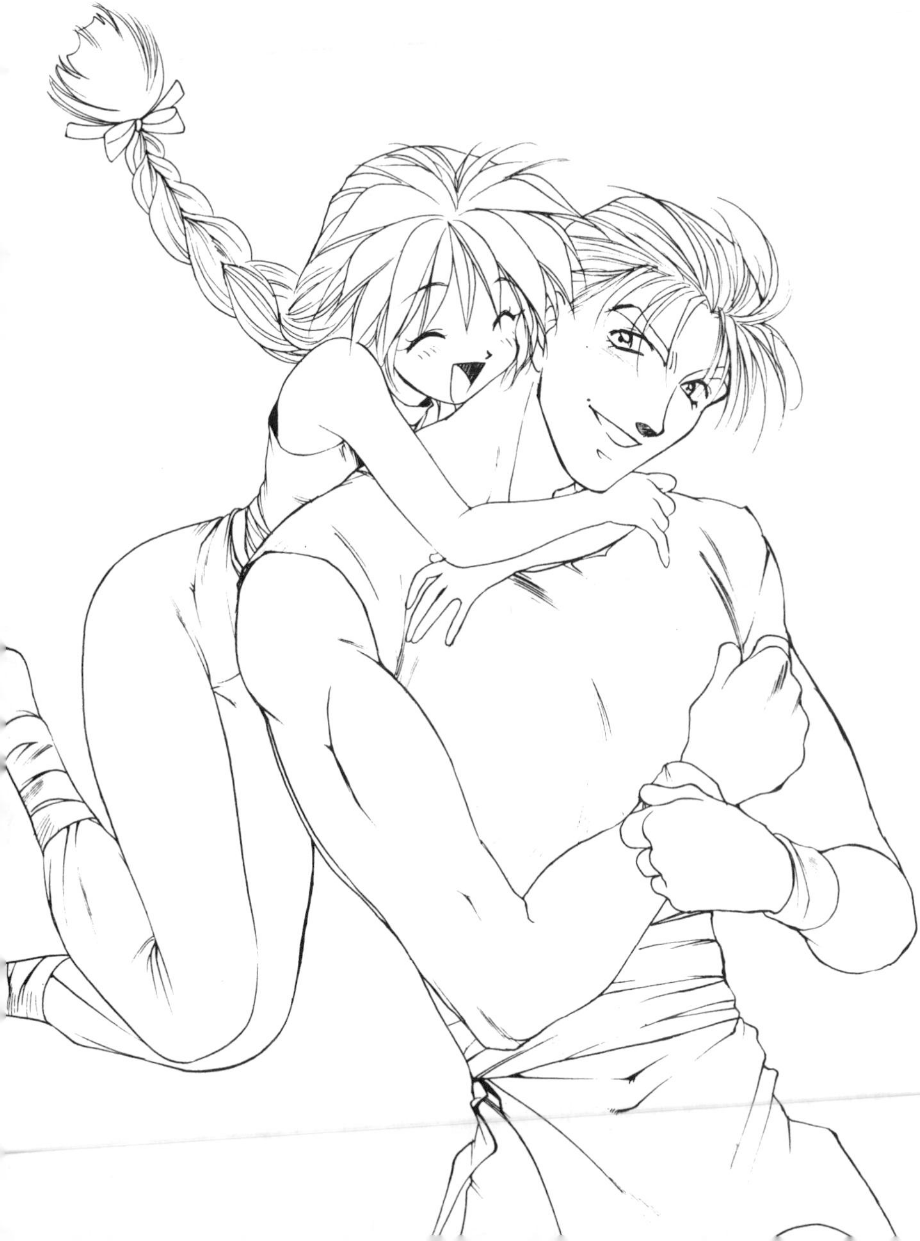

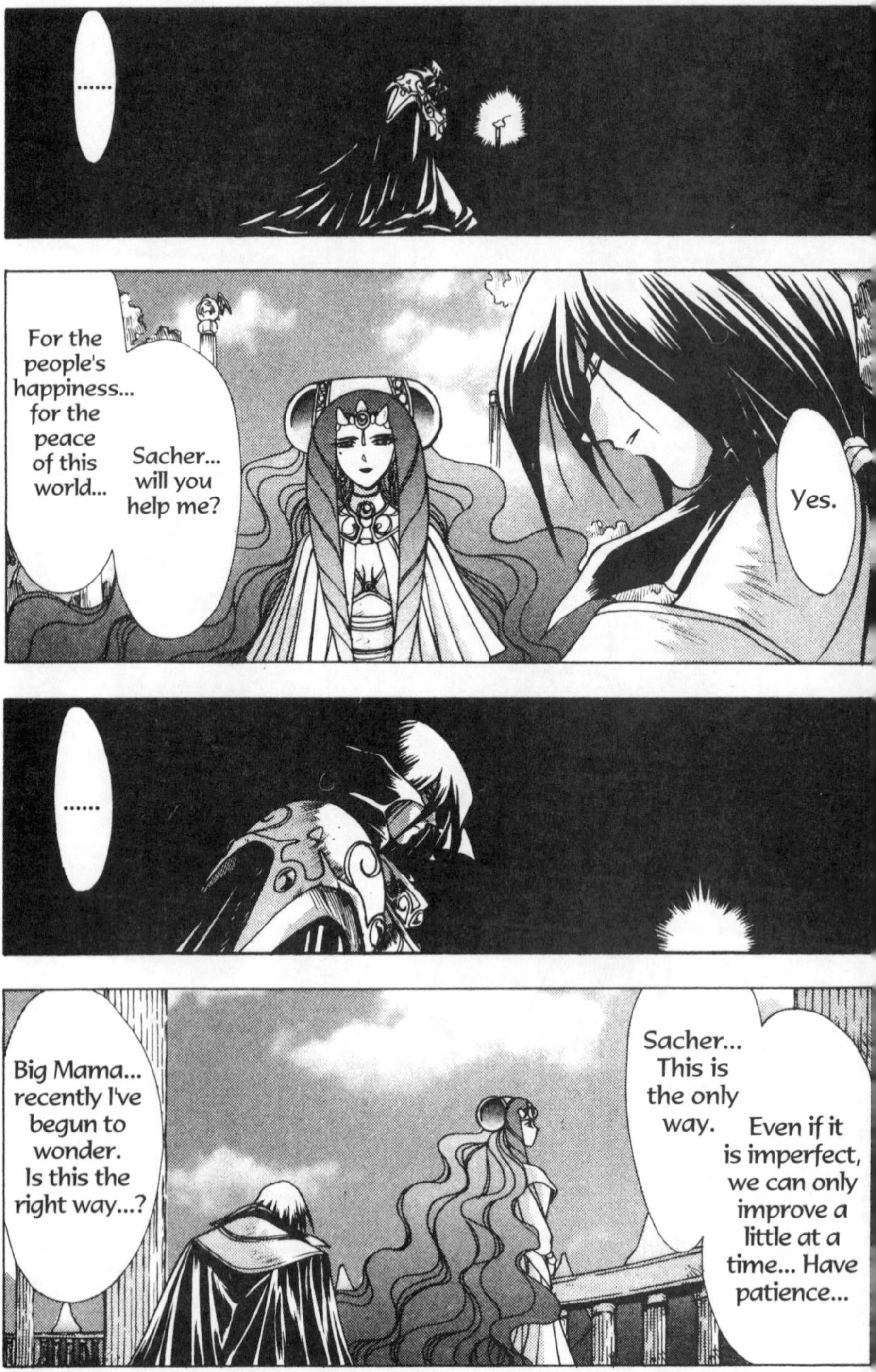
......
For the people's happiness... for the peace of this world...
Sacher... will you help me?
Yes.
......
Big Mama... recently I've begun to wonder. Is this the right way...?
Sacher... This is the only way.
Even if it is imperfect, we can only improve a little at a time... Have patience...

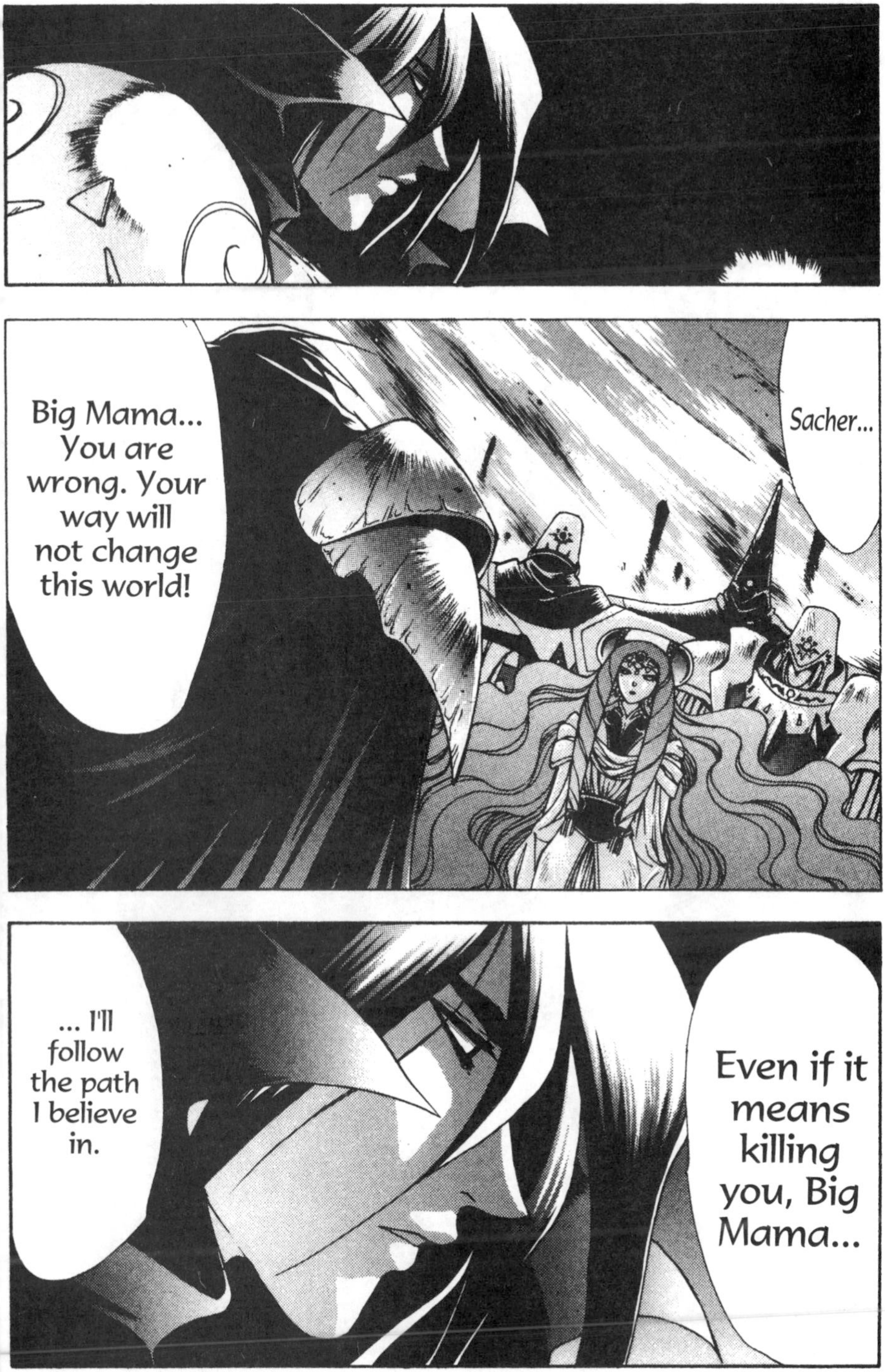
Big Mama... You are wrong. Your way will not change this world!
Sacher...
... I'll follow the path I believe in.
Even if it means killing you, Big Mama...

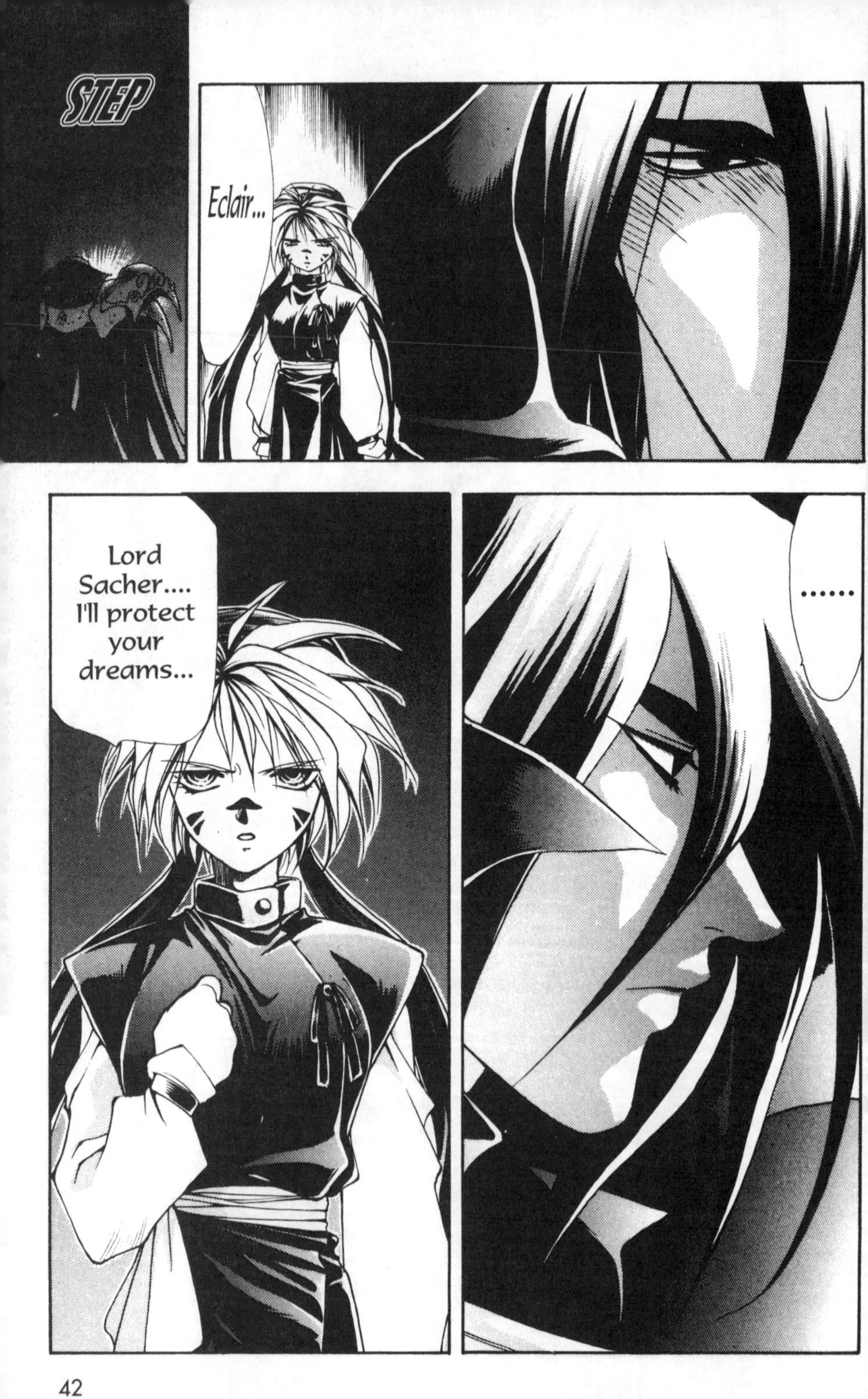
STEP
Eclair...
Lord Sacher.... I'll protect your dreams...
......

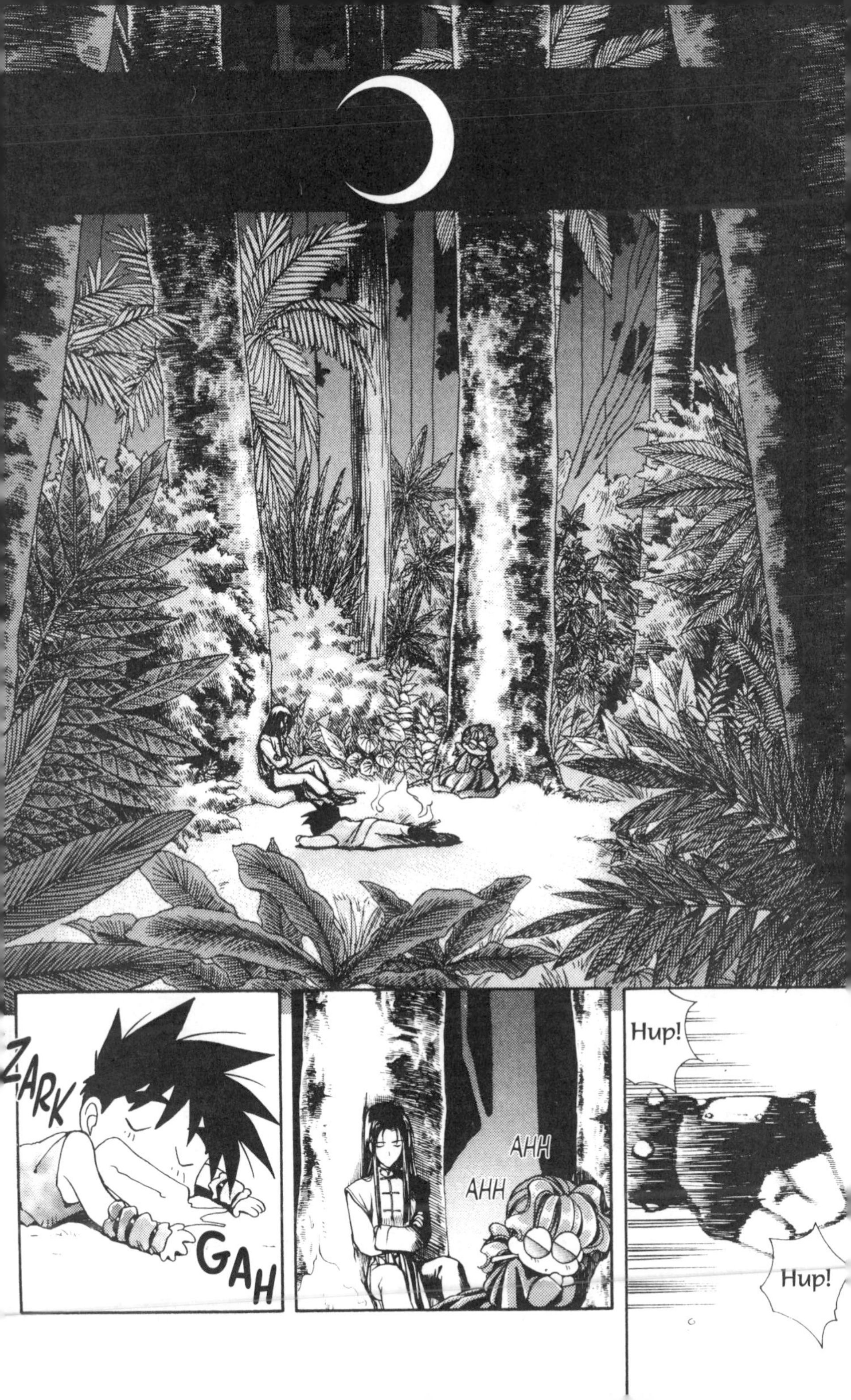

ZARK
GAH
AHH
AHH
Hup!
Hup!

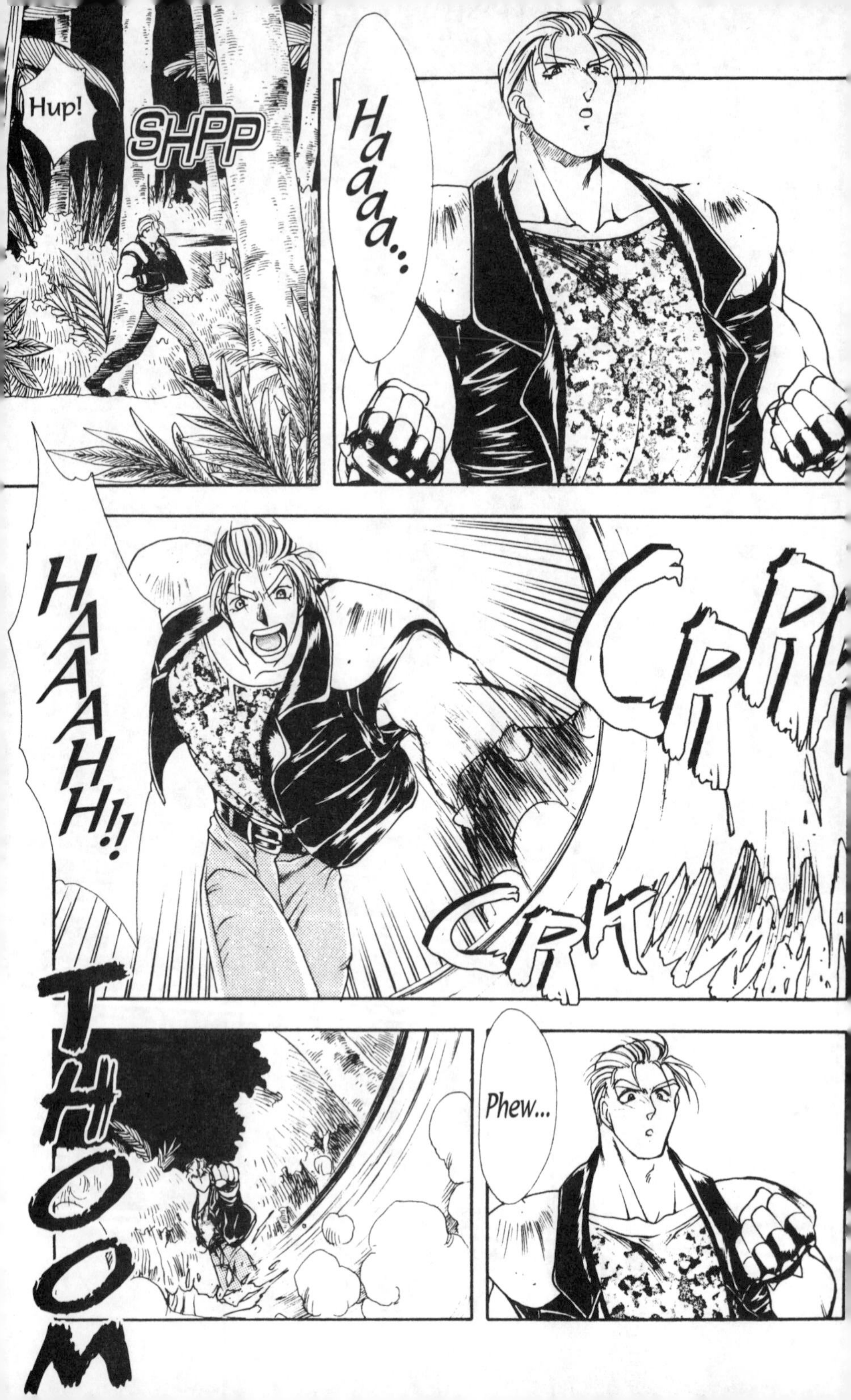
Hup!
SHPP
Haaaa...
HAAAHH!!
CRRK
CRK
THOOM
Phew...

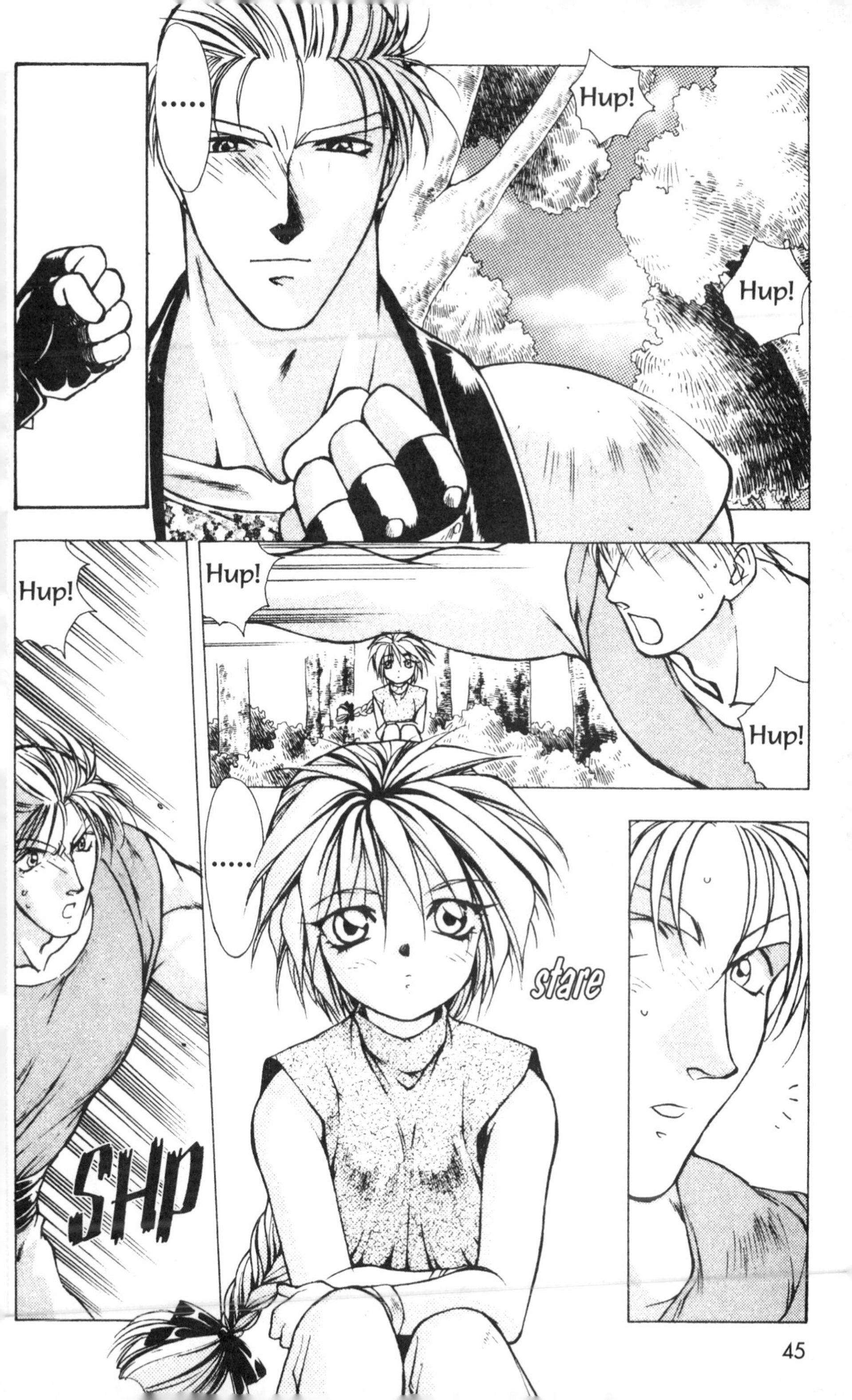
.....
Hup!
Hup!
Hup!
Hup!
Hup!
SHP
.....
stare

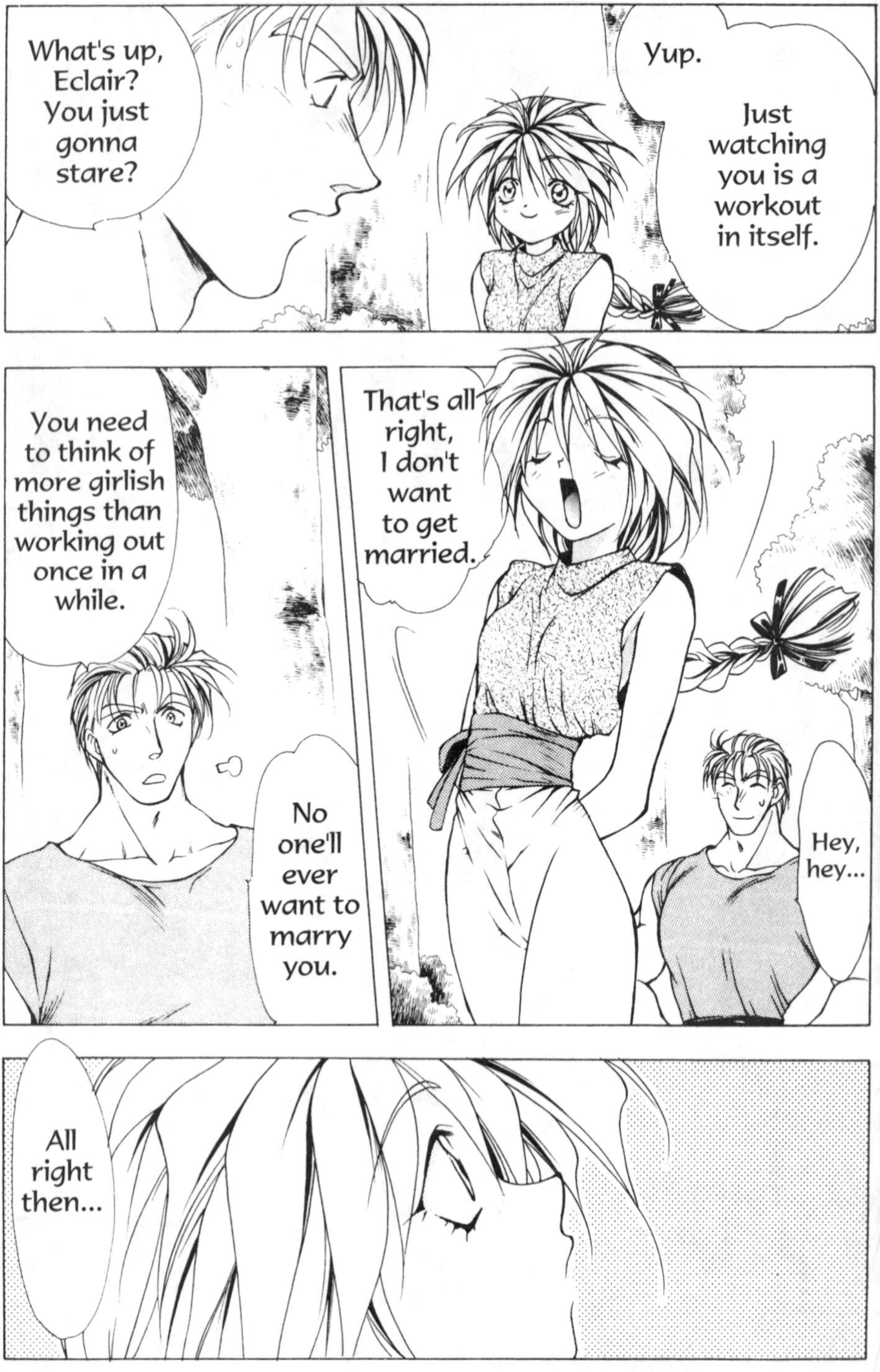
What's up, Eclair? You just gonna stare?
Yup.
Just watching you is a workout in itself.
You need to think of more girlish things than working out once in a while.
No one'll ever want to marry you.
That's all right, I don't want to get married.
Hey, hey...
All right then...

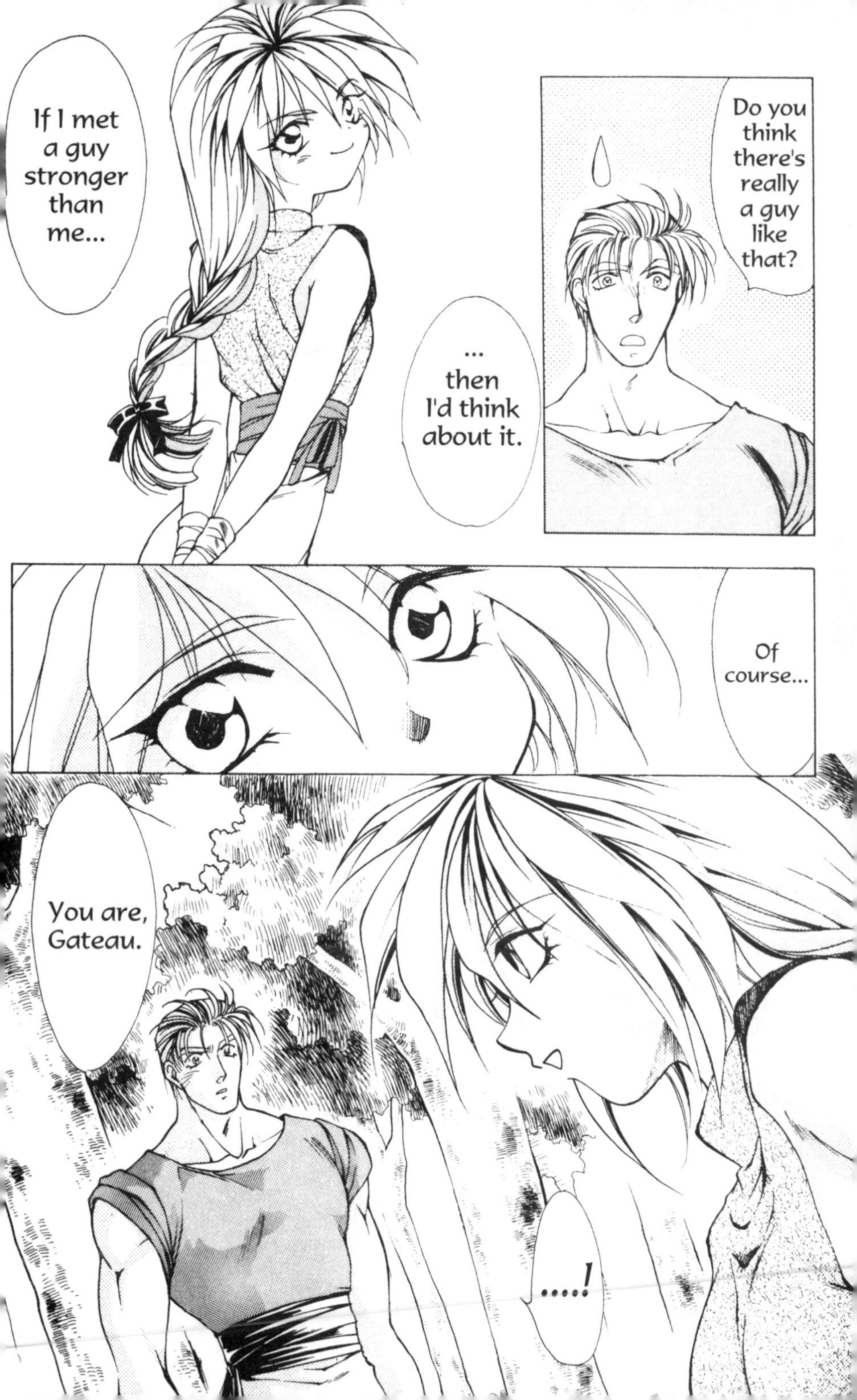
If I met a guy stronger than me...
... then I'd think about it.
Do you think there's really a guy like that?
Of course...
You are, Gateau.
....!

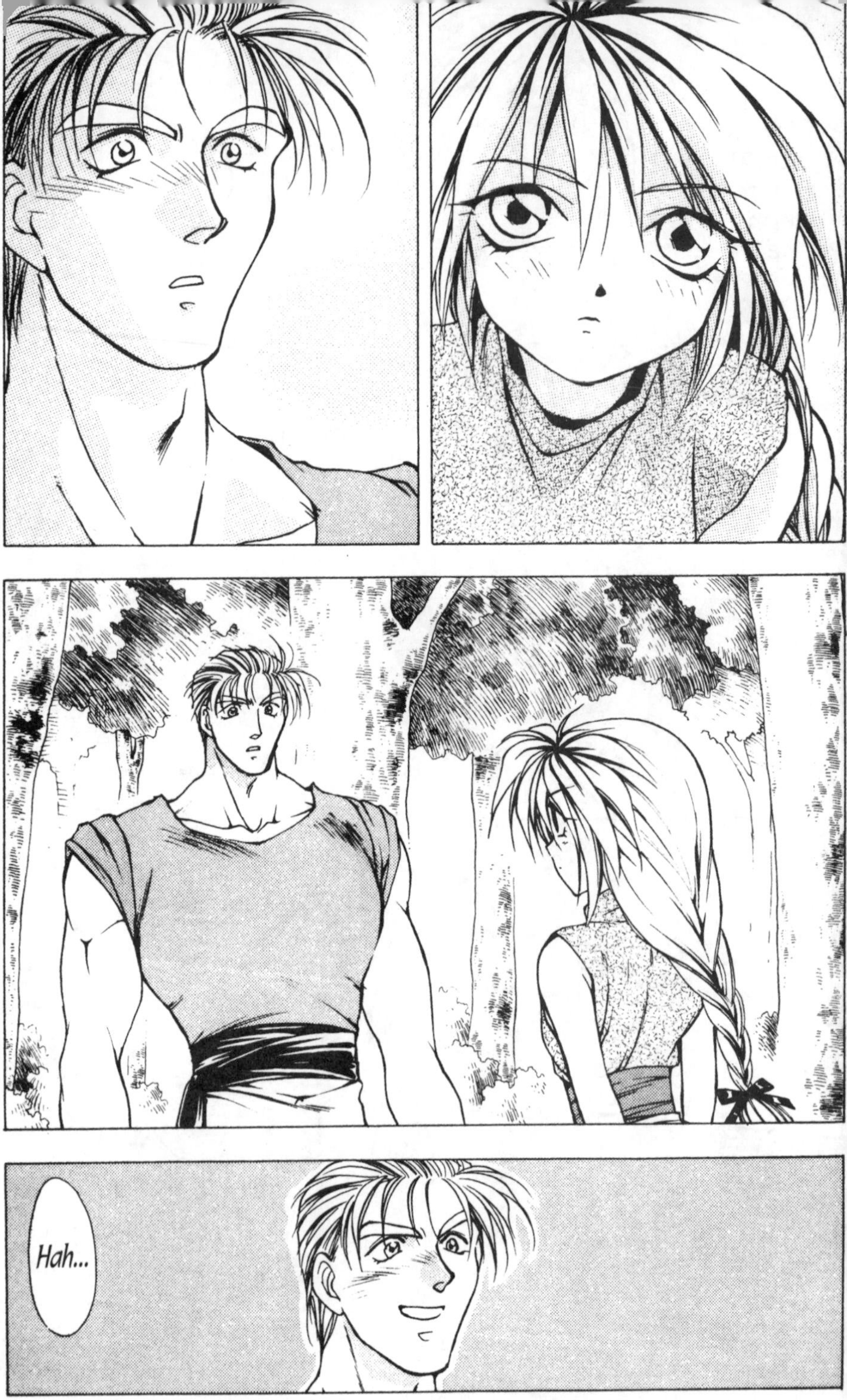
Hah...

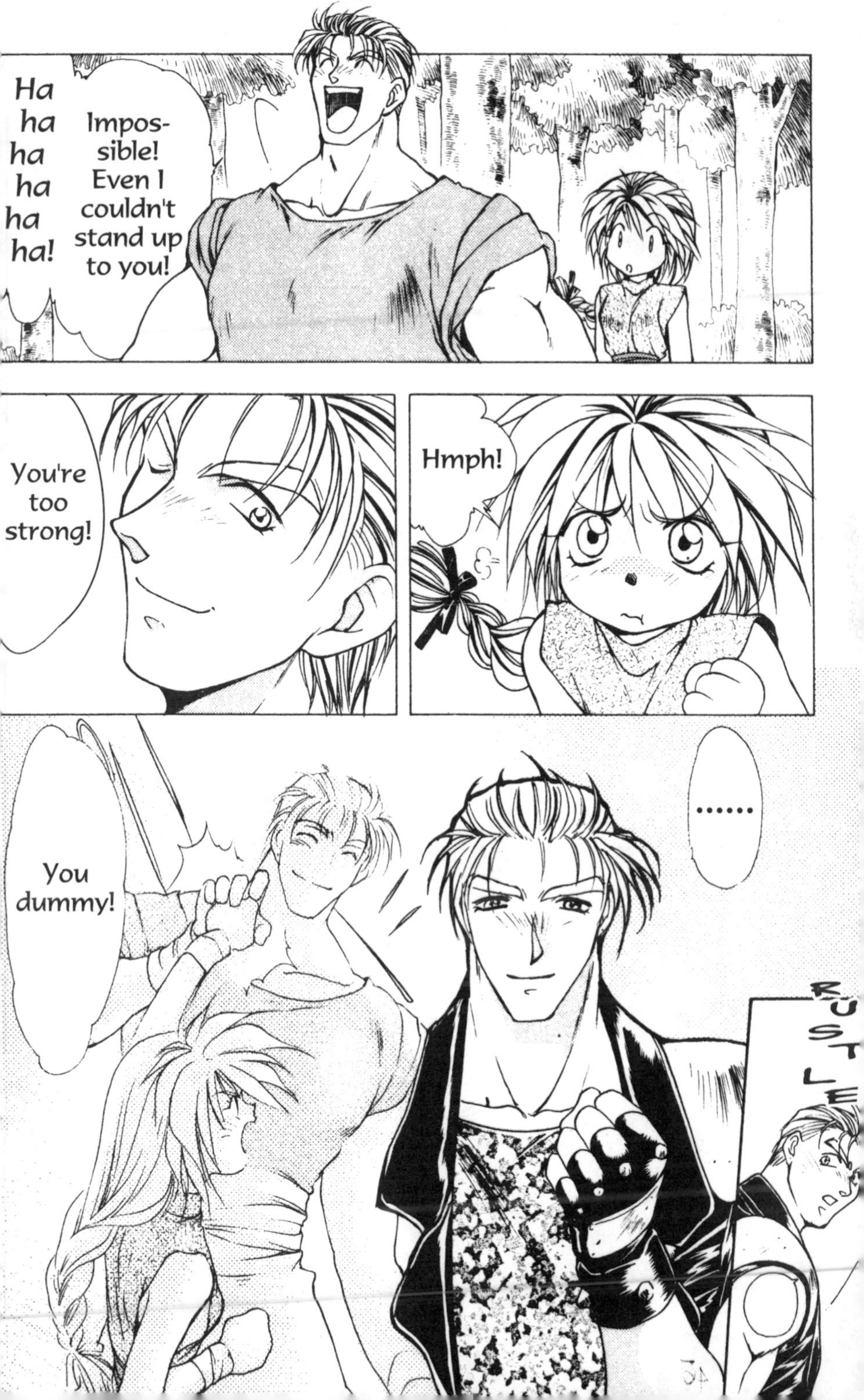
Ha ha ha ha ha ha!
Impos-sible! Even I couldn't stand up to you!
You're too strong!
Hmph!
You dummy!
......
RUSTLE

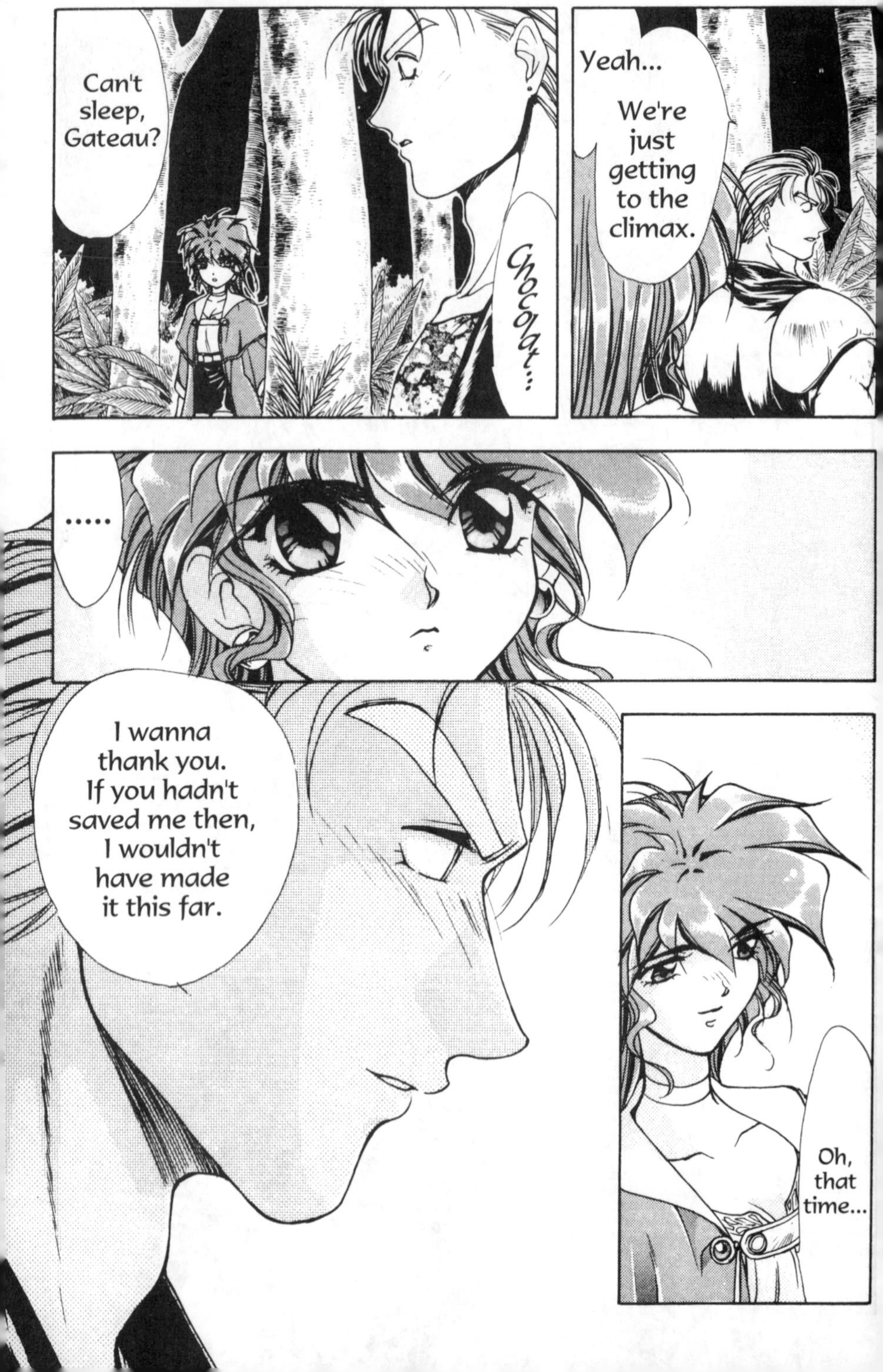
Can't sleep, Gateau?
Chocolat...
Yeah...
We're just getting to the climax.
.....
I wanna thank you. If you hadn't saved me then, I wouldn't have made it this far.
Oh, that time...

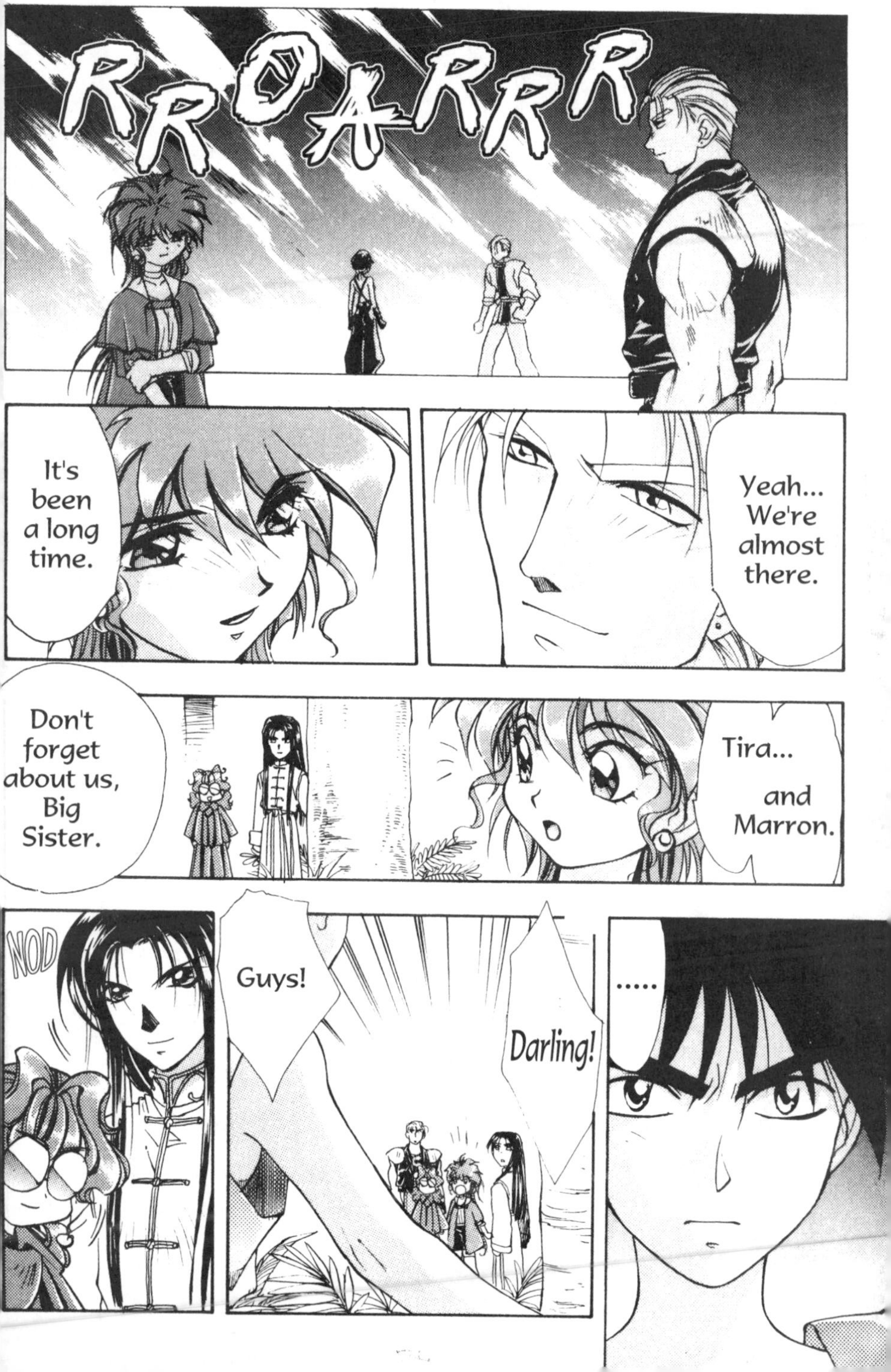
RROARRR
It's been a long time.
Yeah... We're almost there.
Don't forget about us, Big Sister.
Tira... and Marron.
NOD
Guys!
Darling!
.....

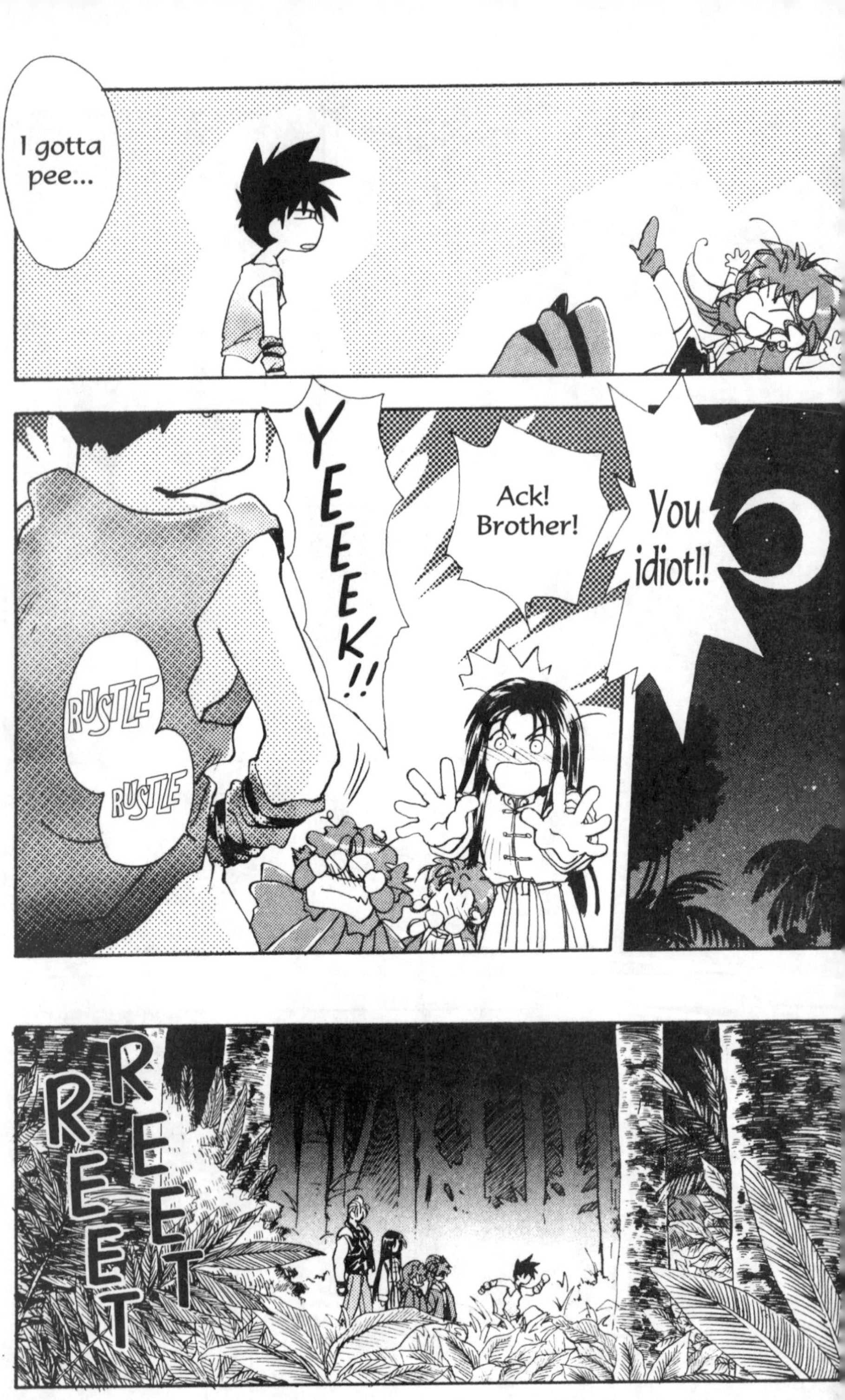
I gotta pee...
YEEEK!!
RUSTLE
RUSTLE
Ack! Brother!
You idiot!!
REEET
REEET

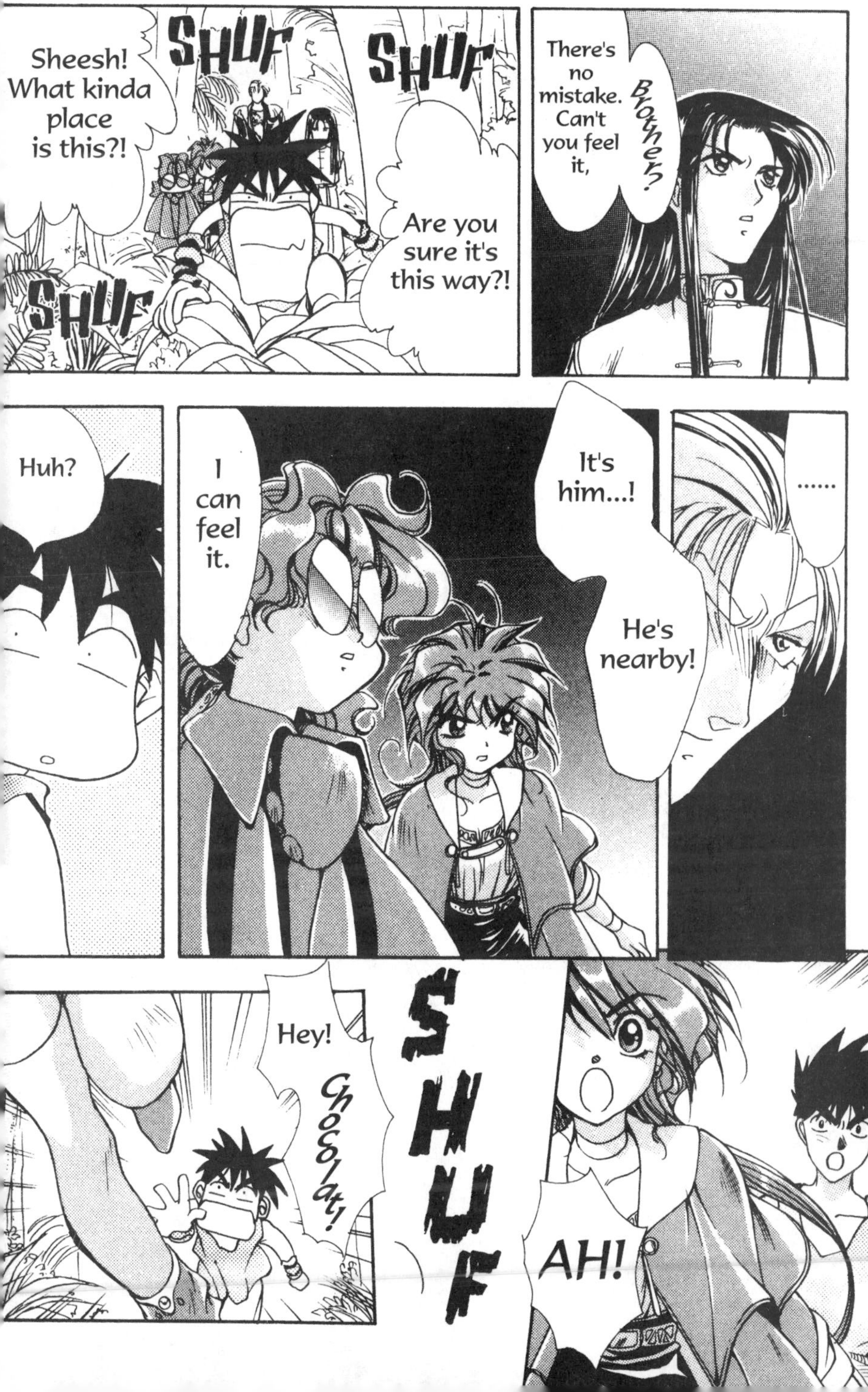
Sheesh! What kinda place is this?!
SHUF
SHUF
SHUF
Are you sure it's this way?!
There's no mistake. Can't you feel it,
Brother?
Huh?
I can feel it.
It's him...!
He's nearby!
......
Hey!
Chocolat!
SHUF
AH!

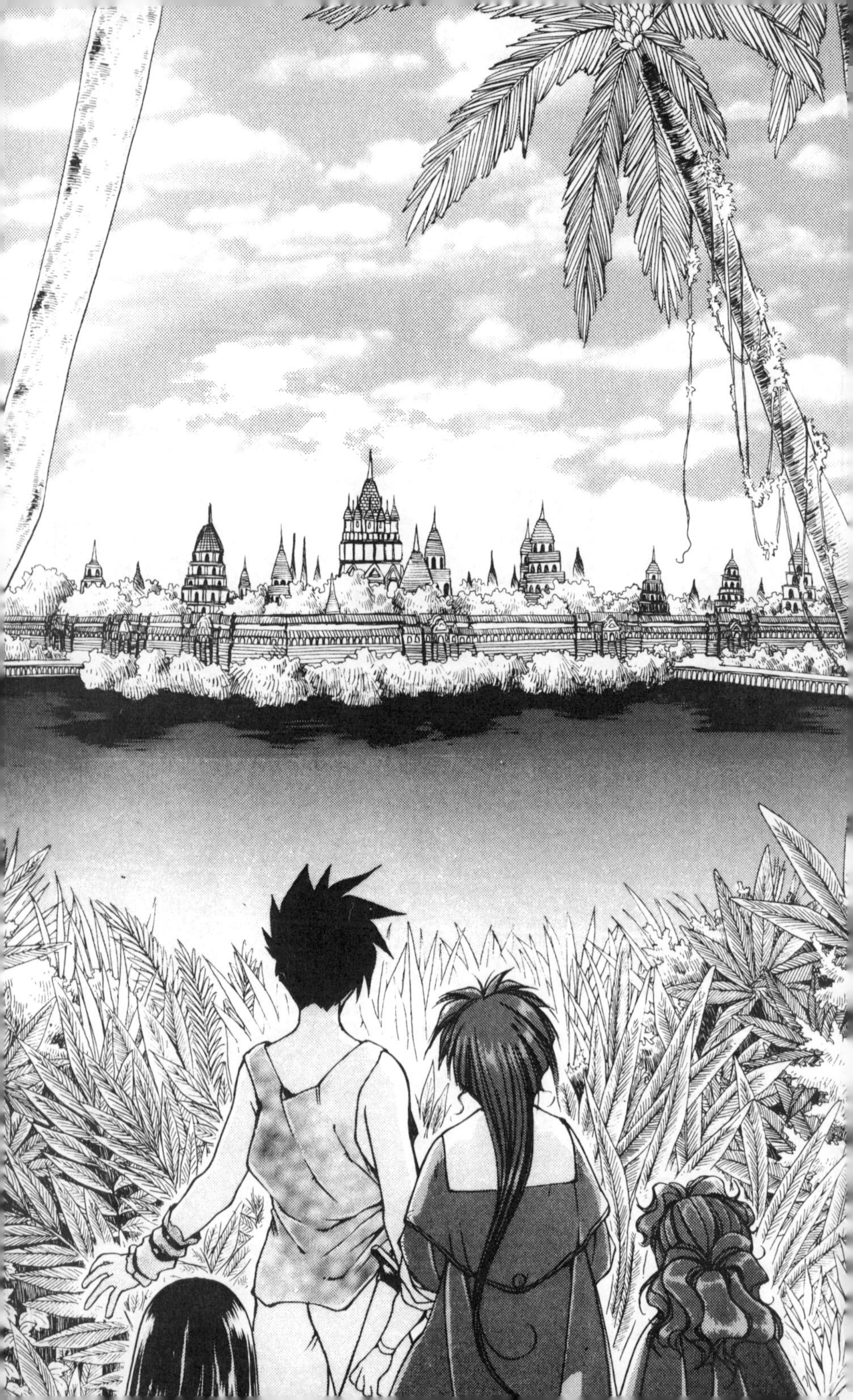

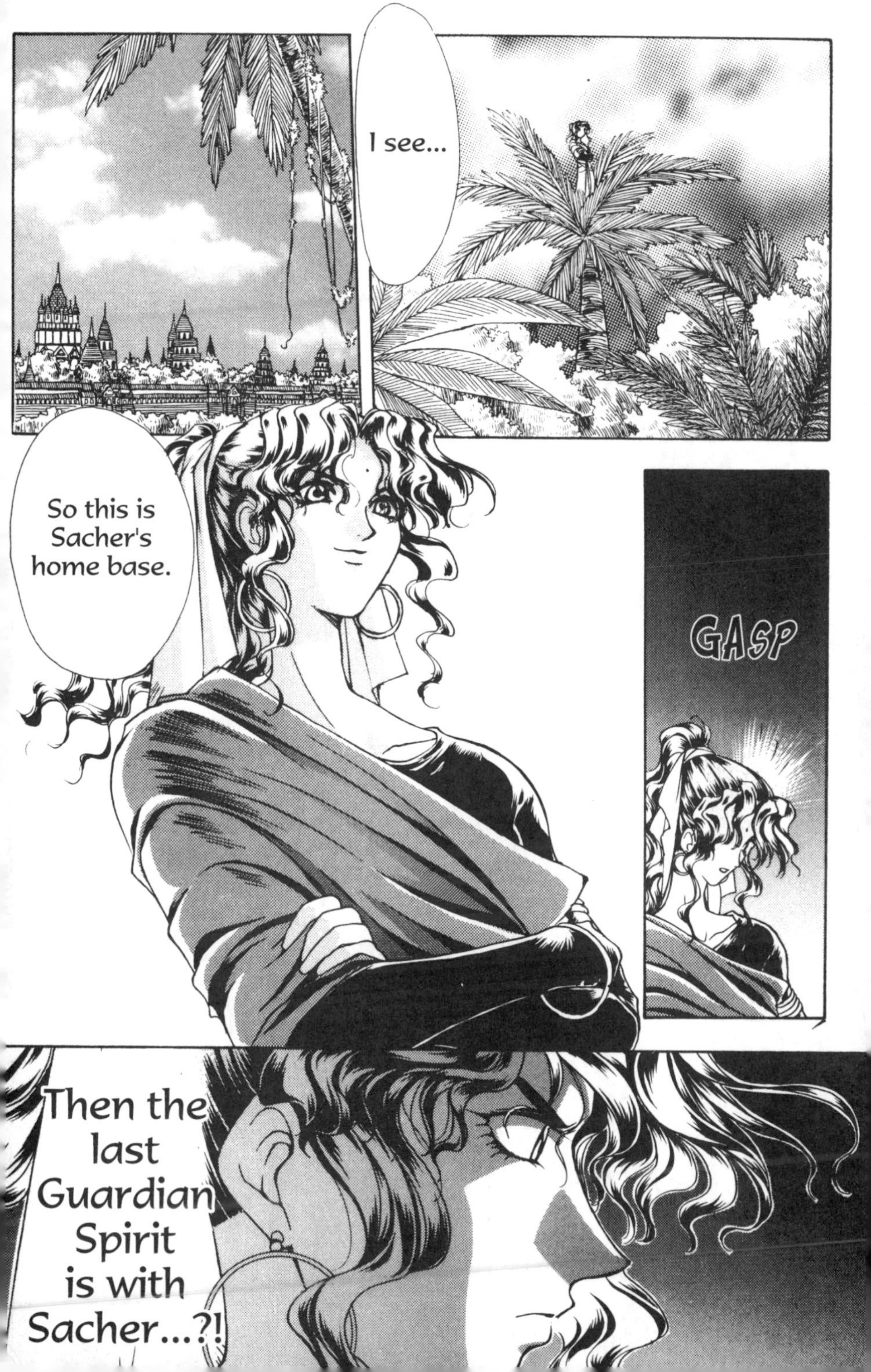
I see...
So this is Sacher's home base.
GASP
Then the last Guardian Spirit is with Sacher...?!

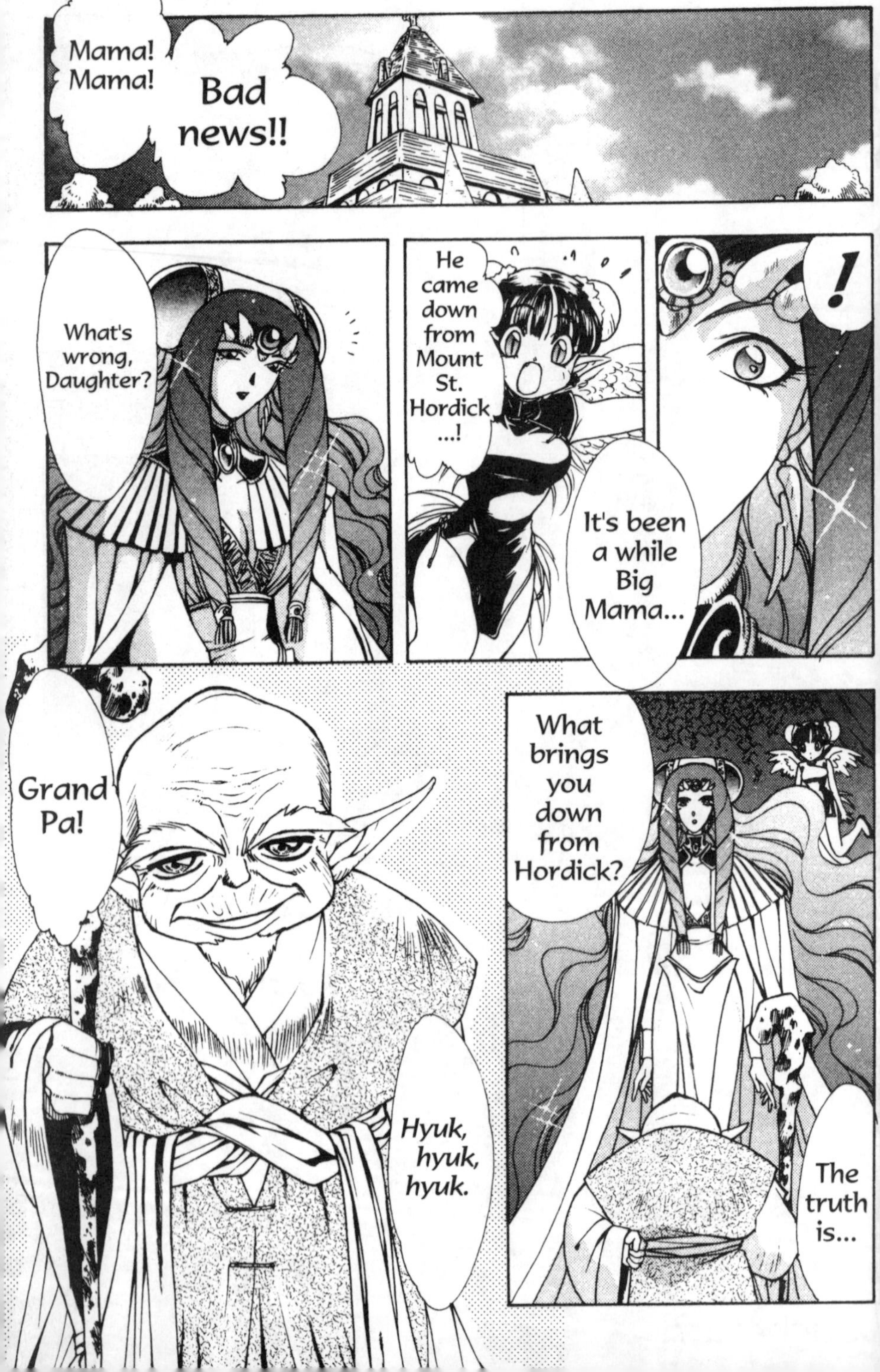
Mama! Mama!
Bad news!!
What's wrong, Daughter?
He came down from Mount St. Hordick ...!
!
It's been a while Big Mama...
Grand Pa!
Hyuk, hyuk, hyuk.
What brings you down from Hordick?
The truth is...

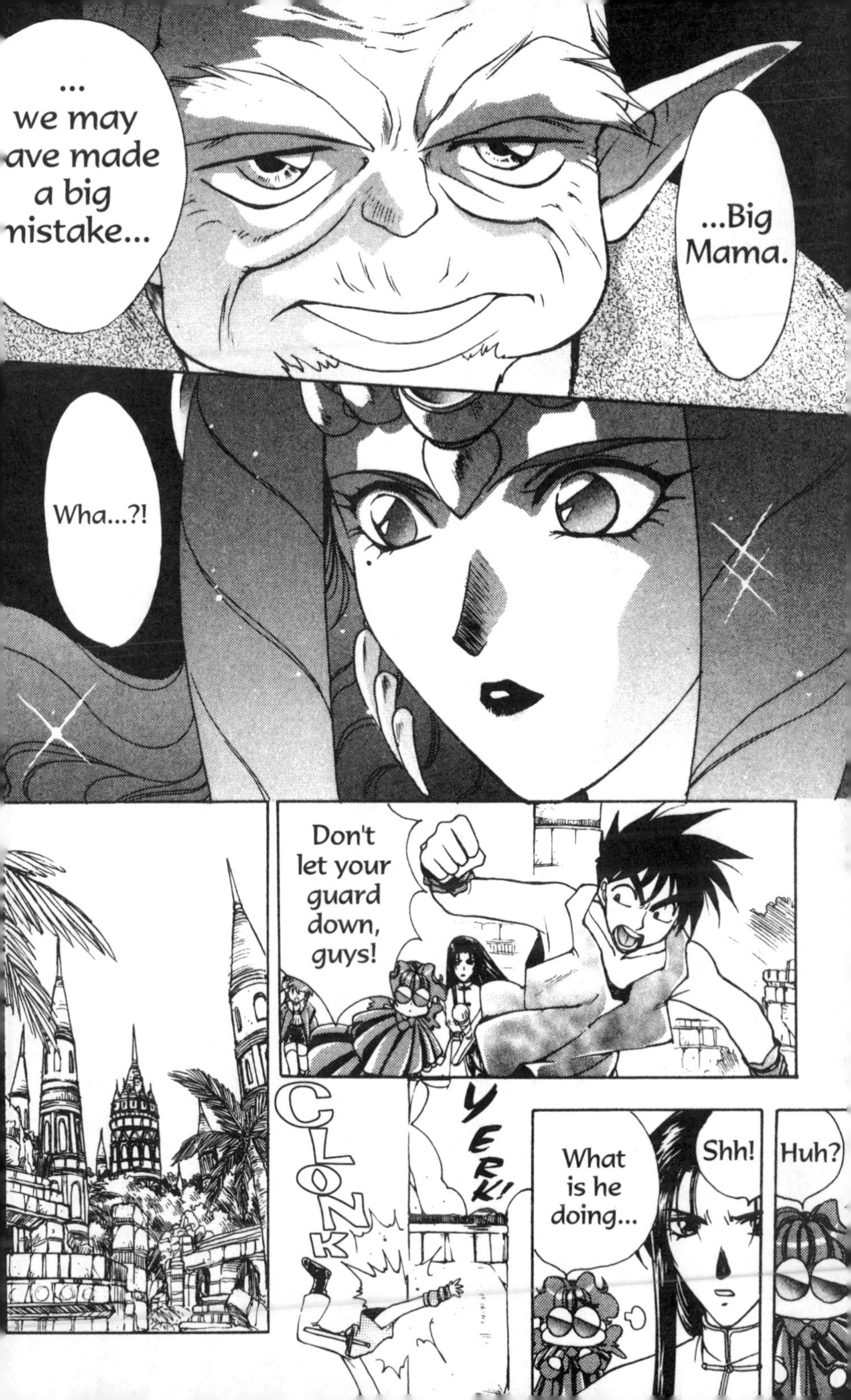

... we may ave made a big nistake...
...Big Mama.
Wha...?!
Don't let your guard down, guys!
CLONK
YERK!
What is he doing...
Shh!
Huh?

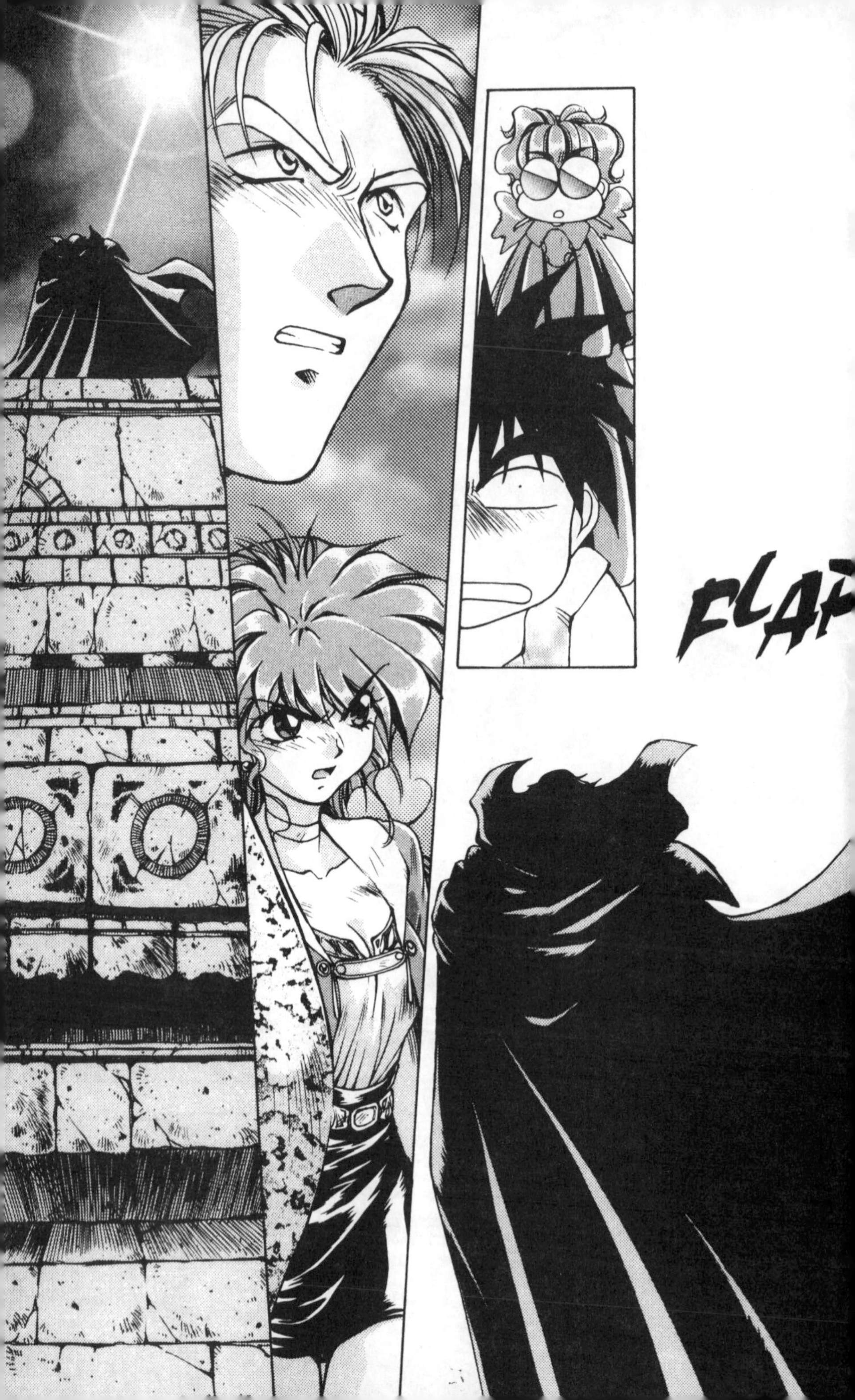
FLAP

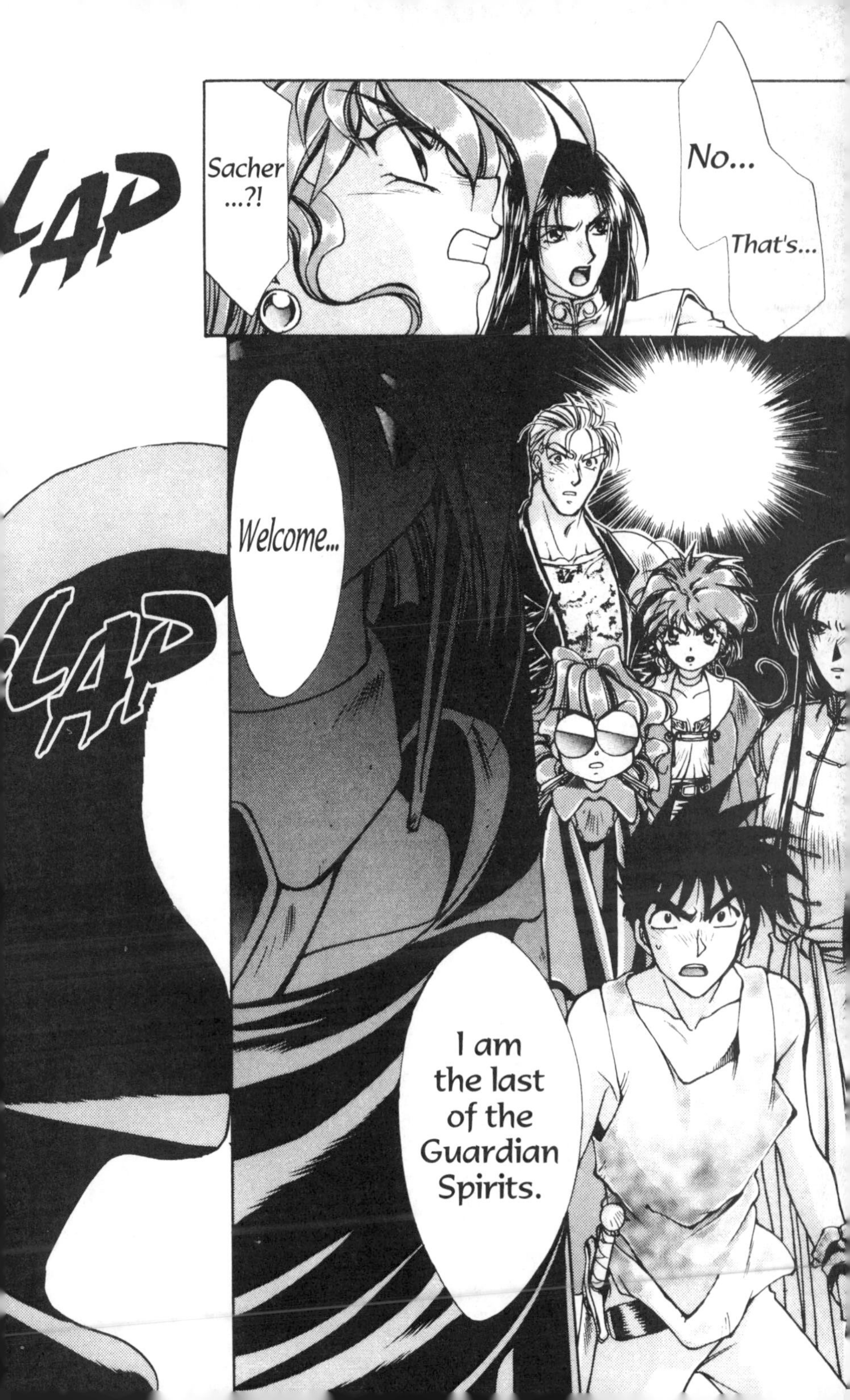

LAP
Sacher ...?!
No...
That's...
Welcome...
LAP
I am the last of the Guardian Spirits.

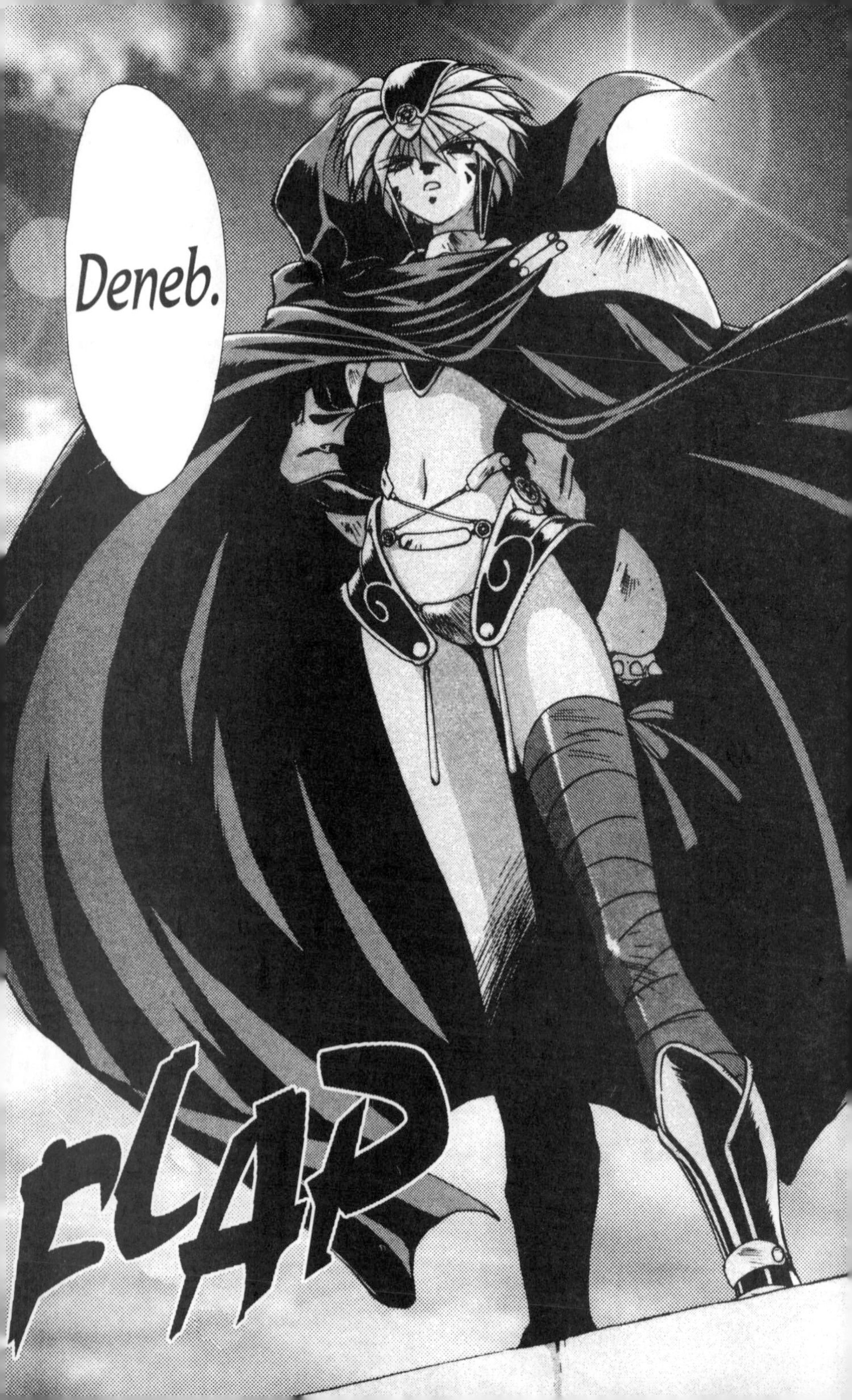
Deneb.
FLAP

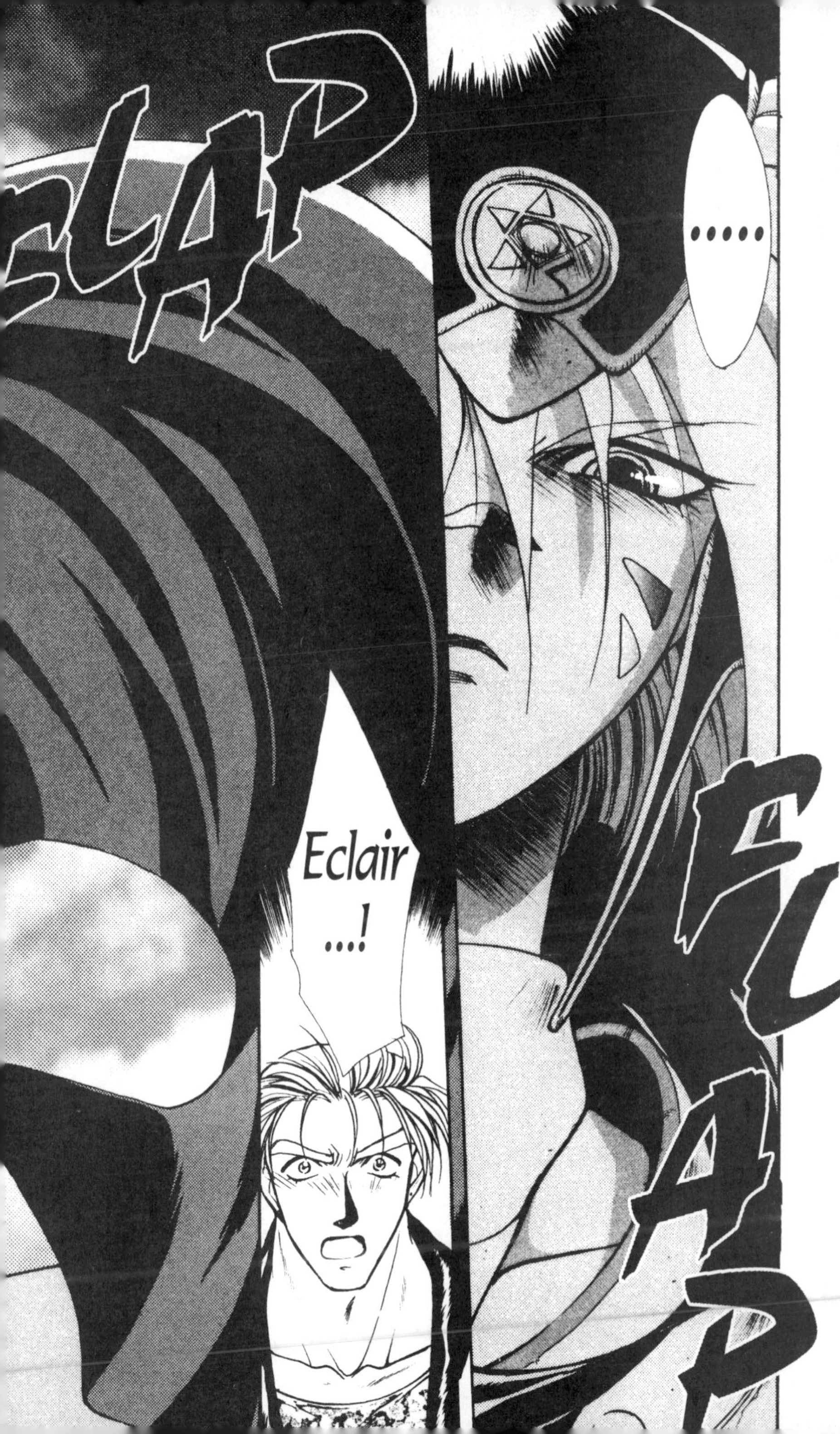
CLAP
Eclair ...!
.....
CLAP

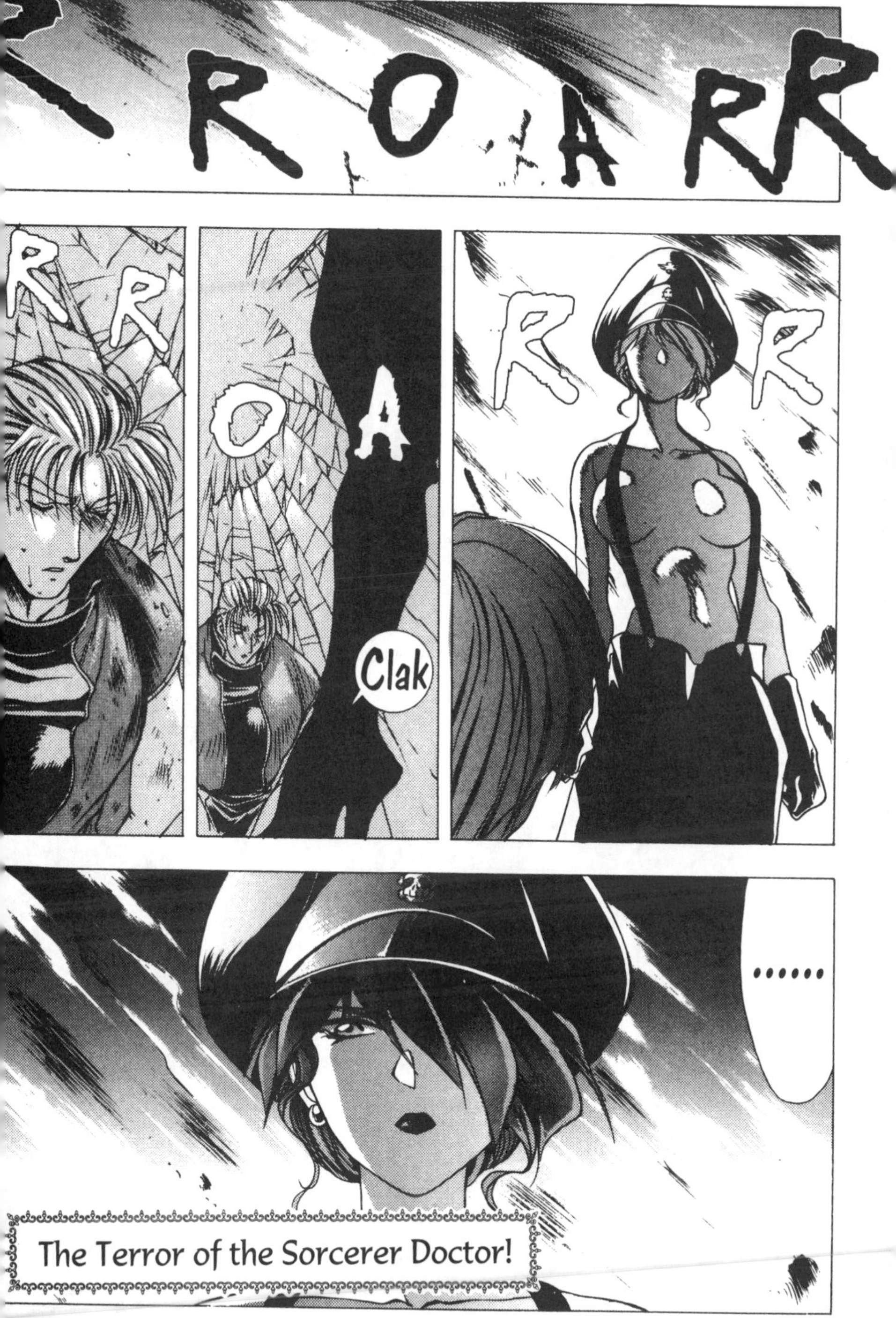
RROARR
RR
O
A
Clak
RR
......
The Terror of the Sorcerer Doctor!

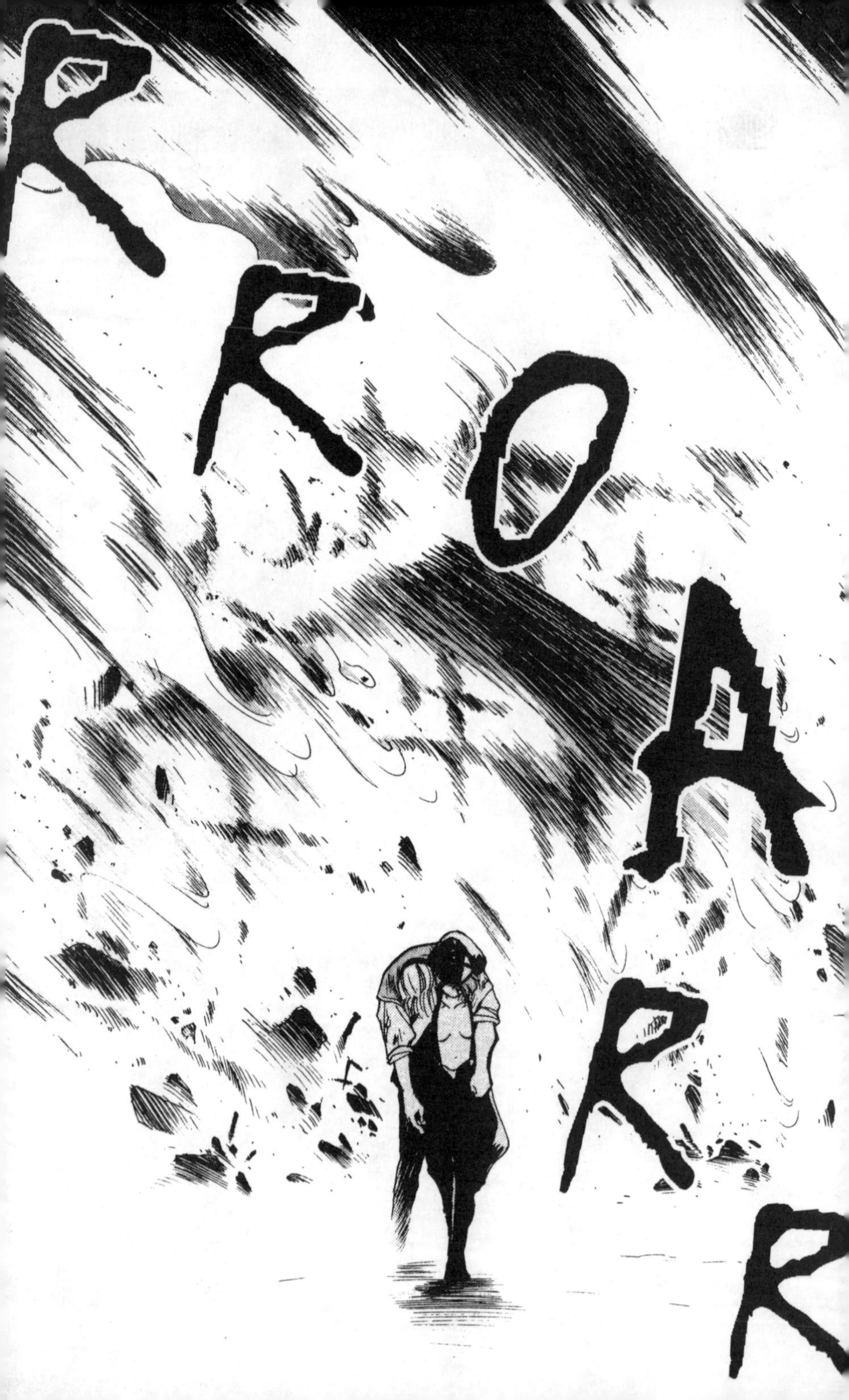
RROARR

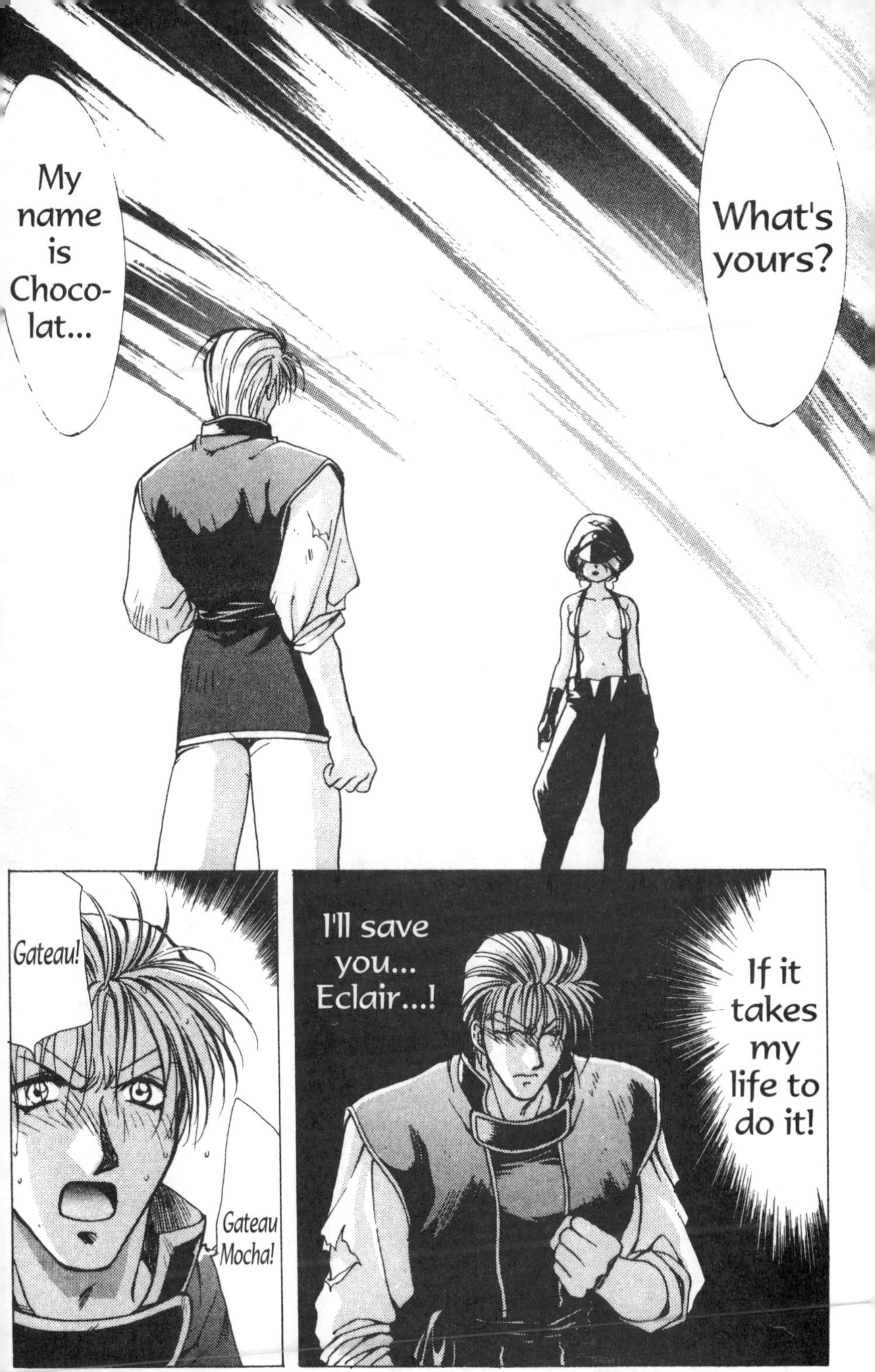
My name is Choco-lat...
What's yours?
Gateau!
Gateau Mocha!
I'll save you... Eclair...!
If it takes my life to do it!

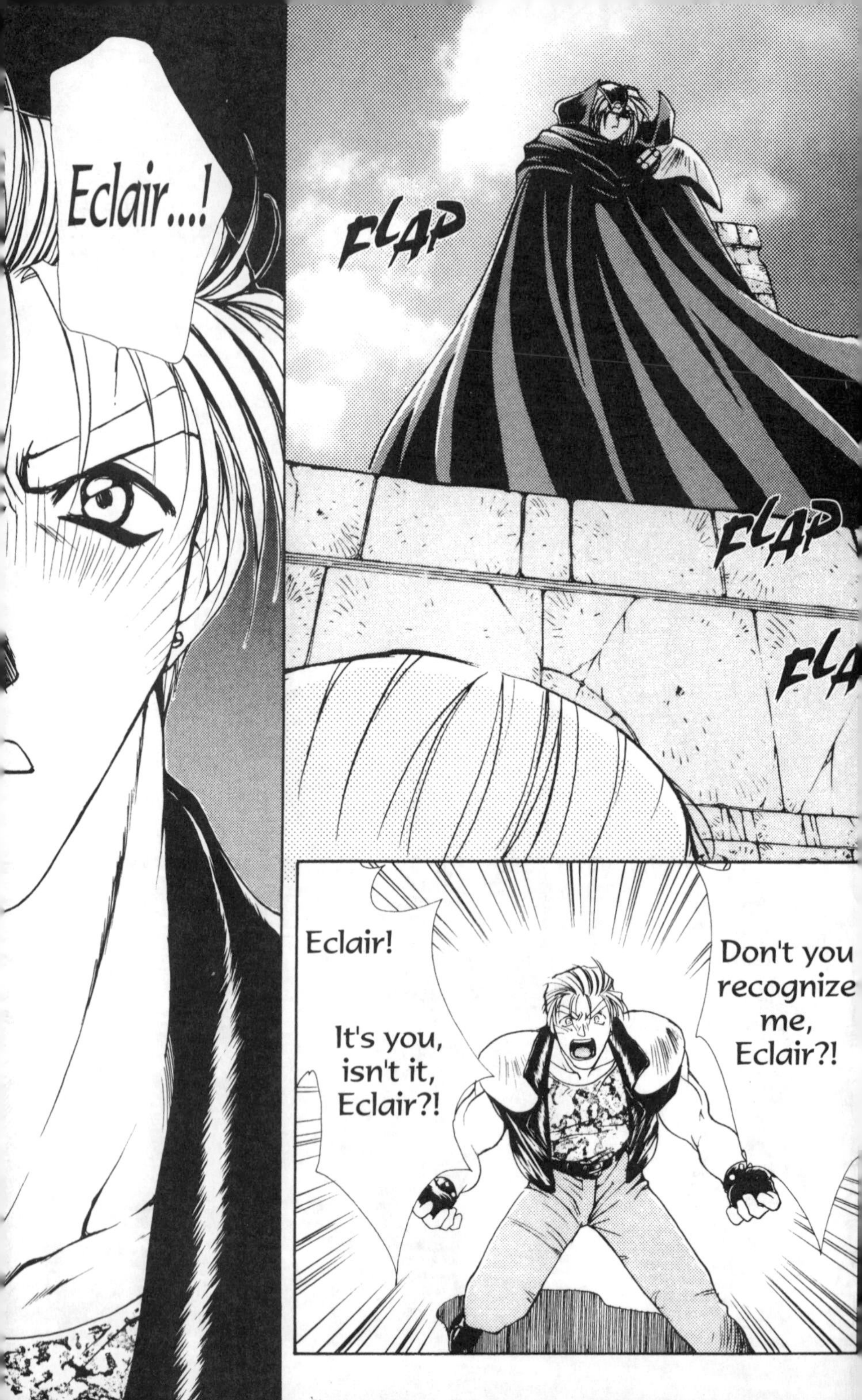
Eclair...!
FLAP
FLAP
FLA
Eclair!
It's you, isn't it, Eclair?!
Don't you recognize me, Eclair?!

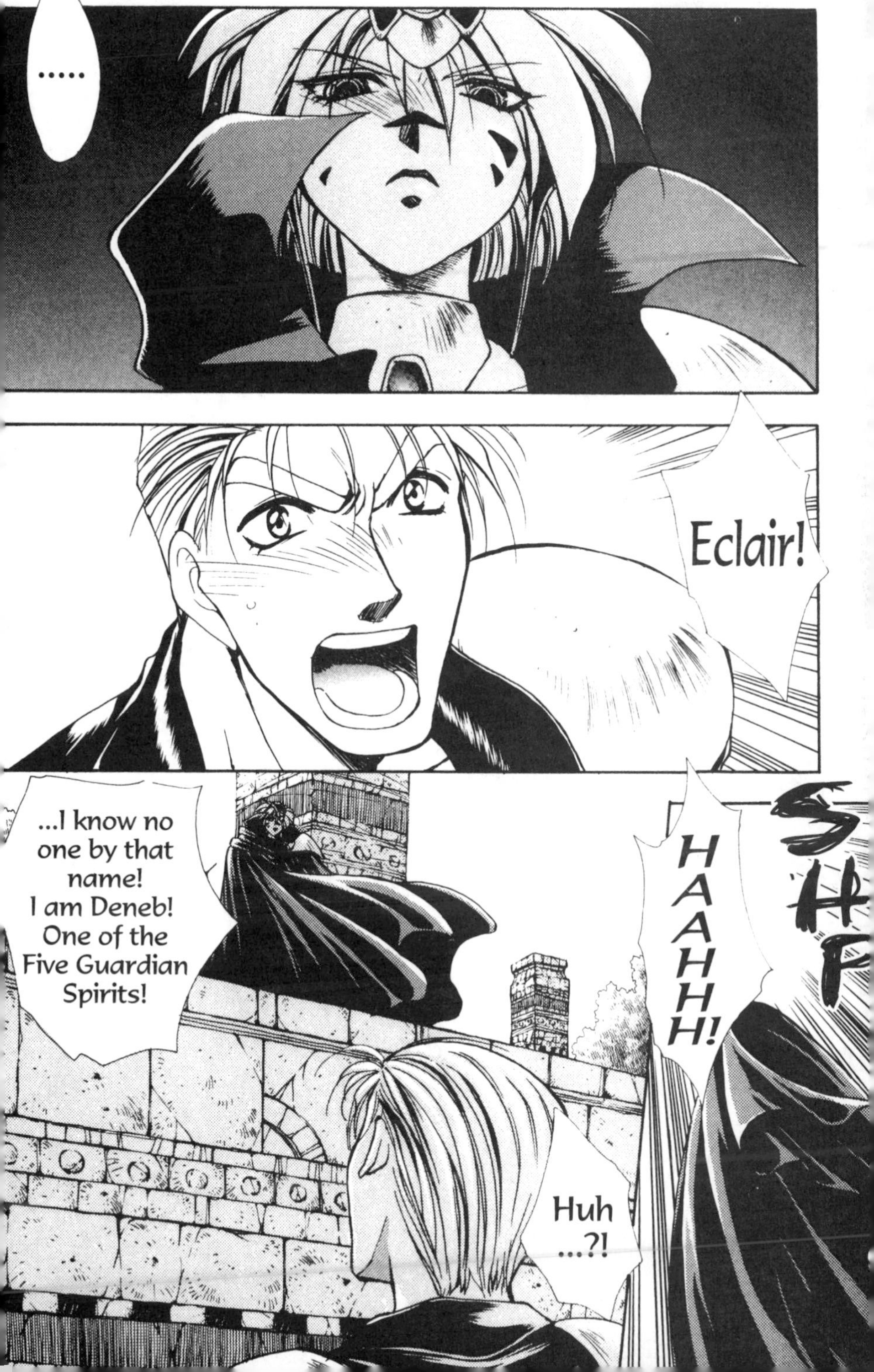
......
Eclair!
...I know no one by that name! I am Deneb! One of the Five Guardian Spirits!
SHF
HAAHHH!
Huh ...?!

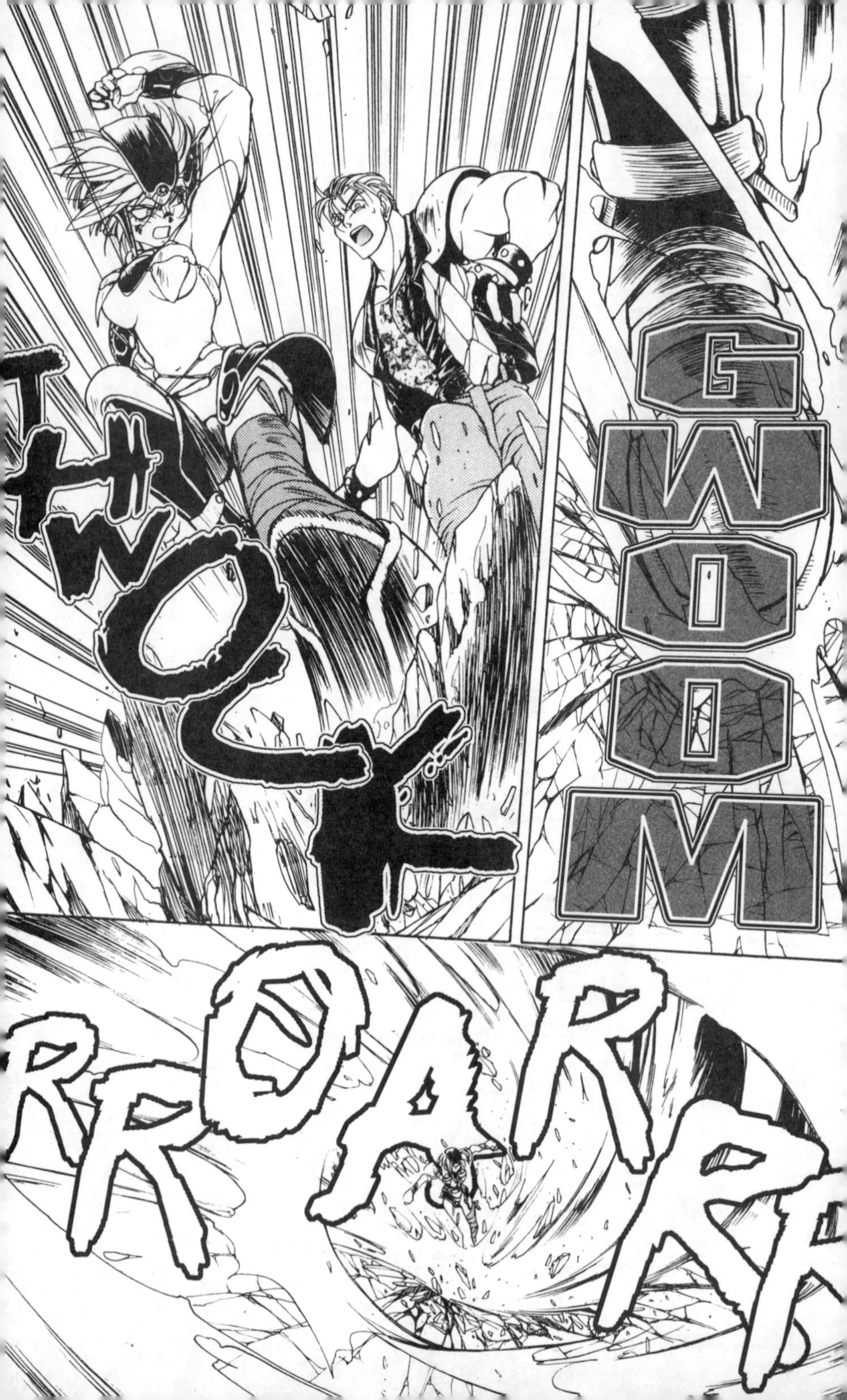
GWOOM
RROARRR

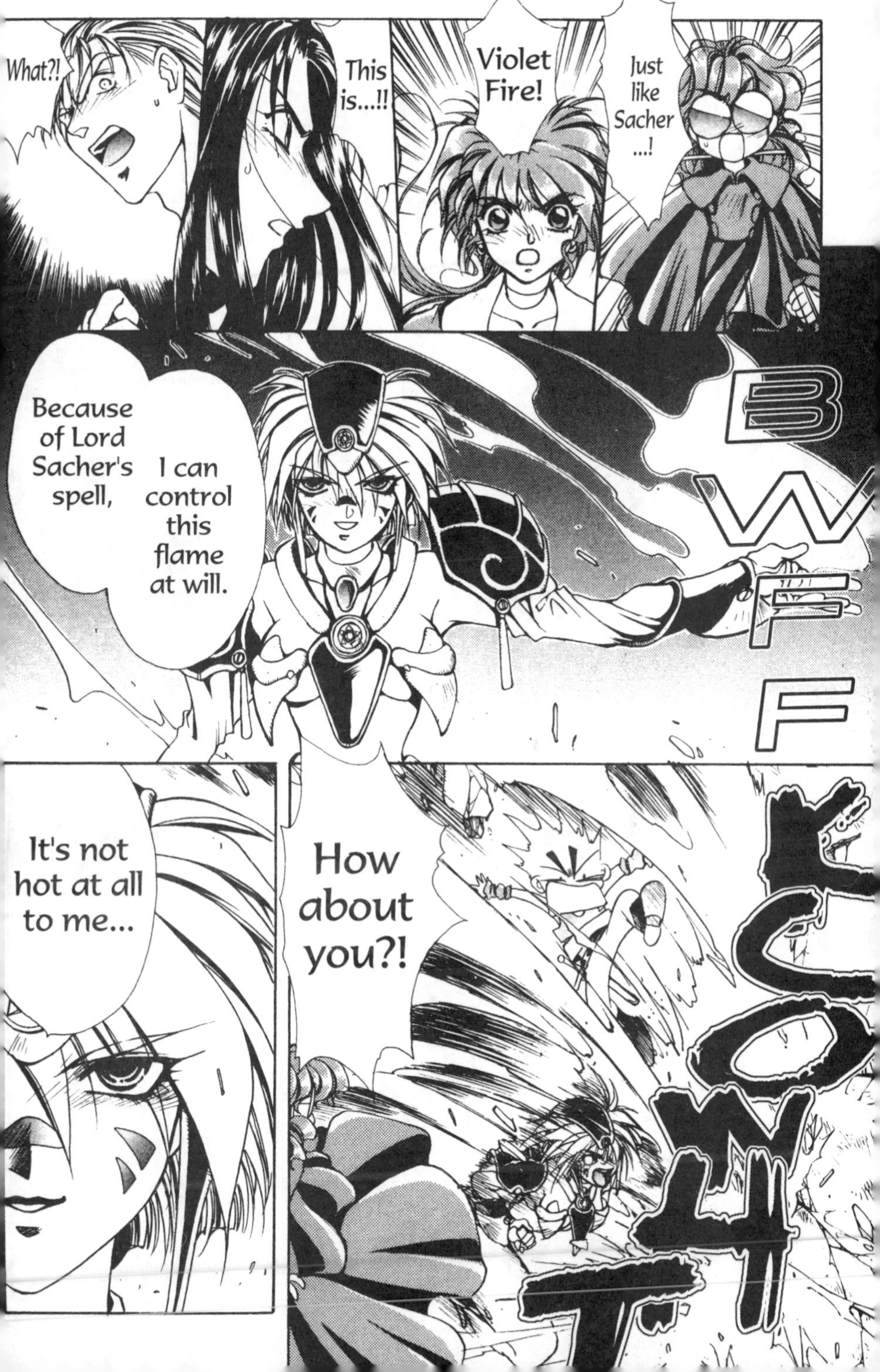
What?!
This is...!!
Violet Fire!
Just like Sacher ...!
Because of Lord Sacher's spell,
I can control this flame at will.
BWFF
It's not hot at all to me...
How about you?!

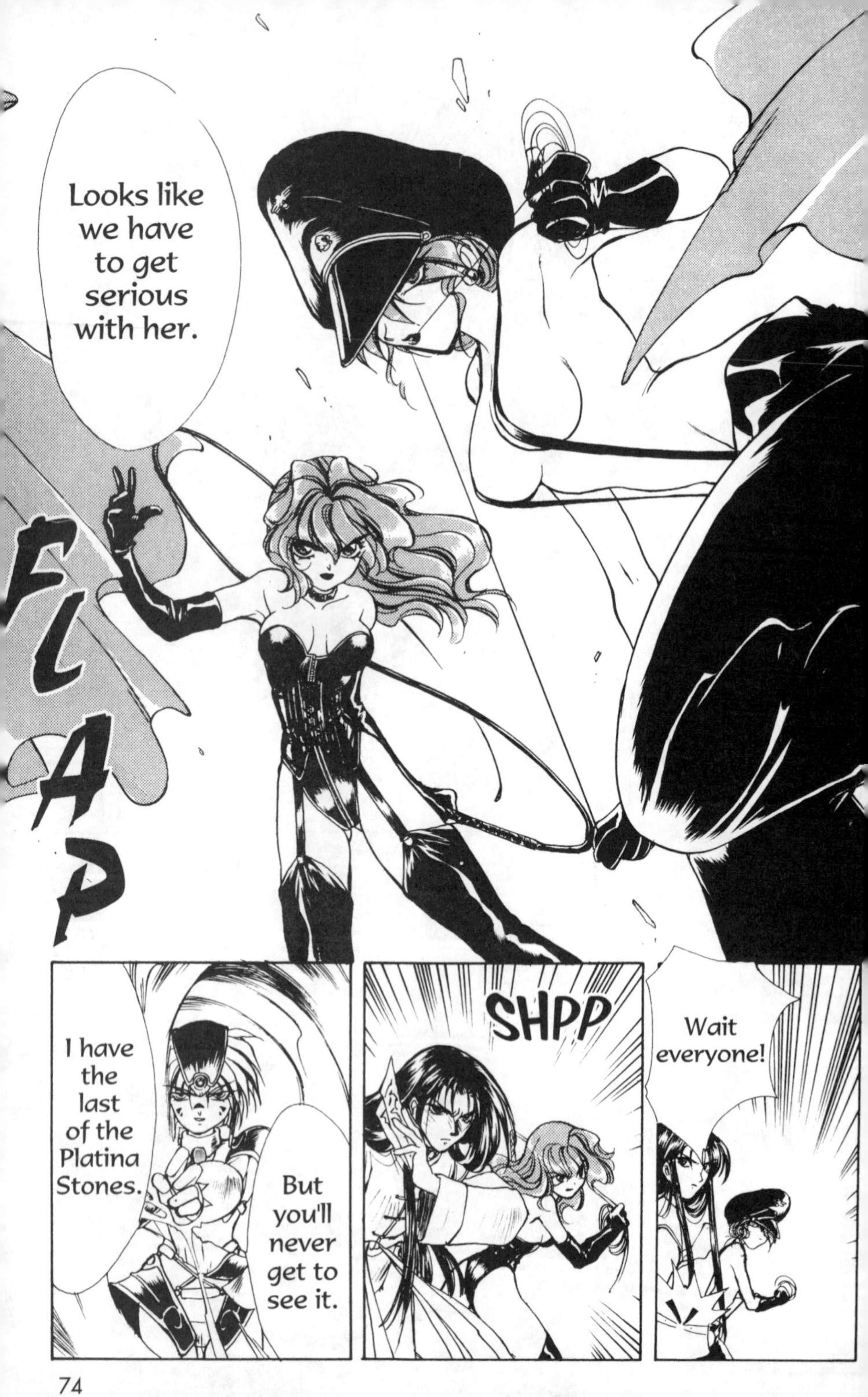

Looks like we have to get serious with her.
FLAP
I have the last of the Platina Stones.
But you'll never get to see it.
SHPP
Wait everyone!

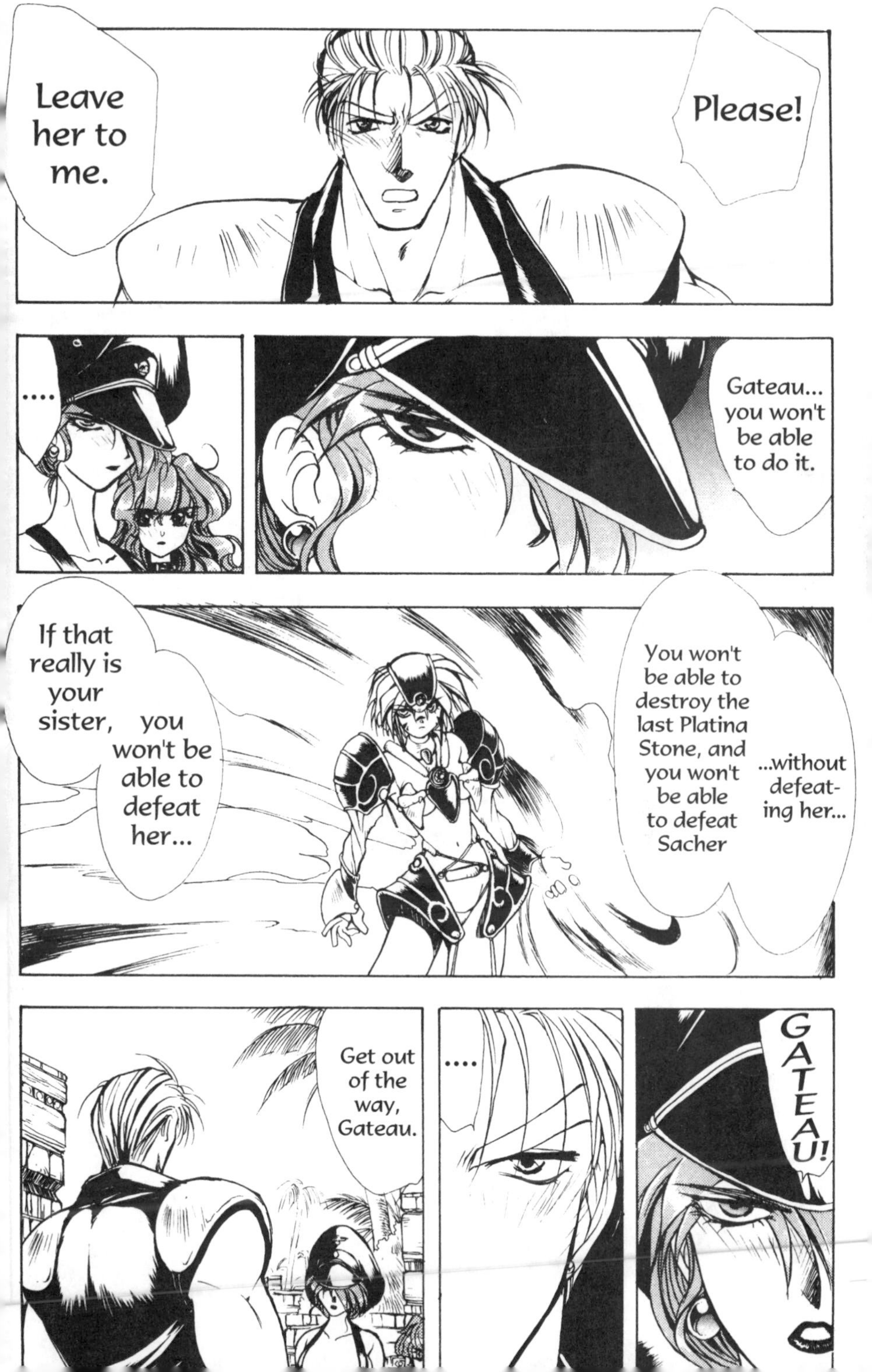
Leave her to me.
Please!
....
Gateau... you won't be able to do it.
If that really is your sister,
you won't be able to defeat her...
You won't be able to destroy the last Platina Stone, and you won't be able to defeat Sacher
...without defeating her...
Get out of the way, Gateau.
....
GATEAU!

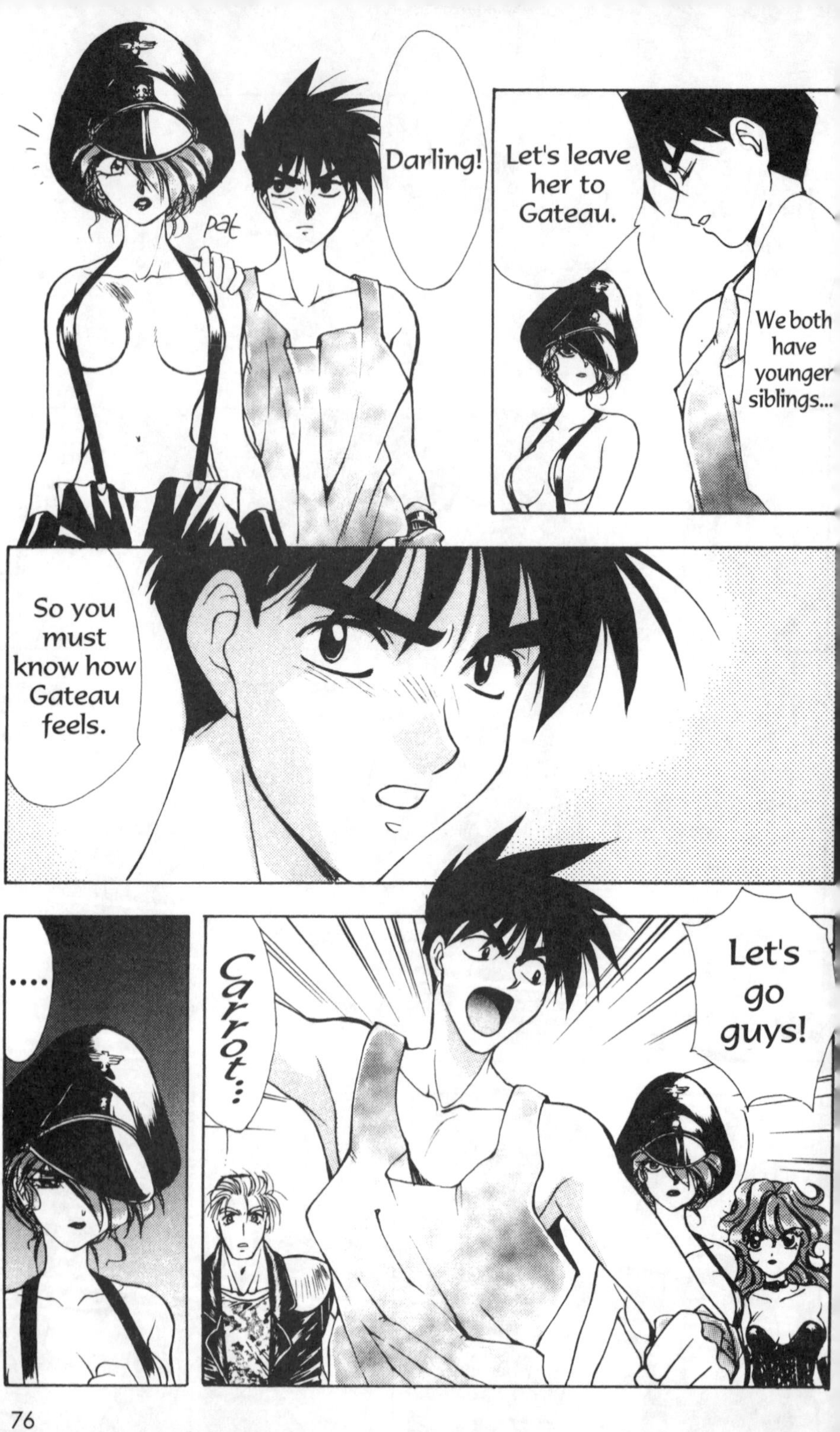

pat
Darling!
Let's leave her to Gateau.
We both have younger siblings...
So you must know how Gateau feels.
....
Carrot...
Let's go guys!

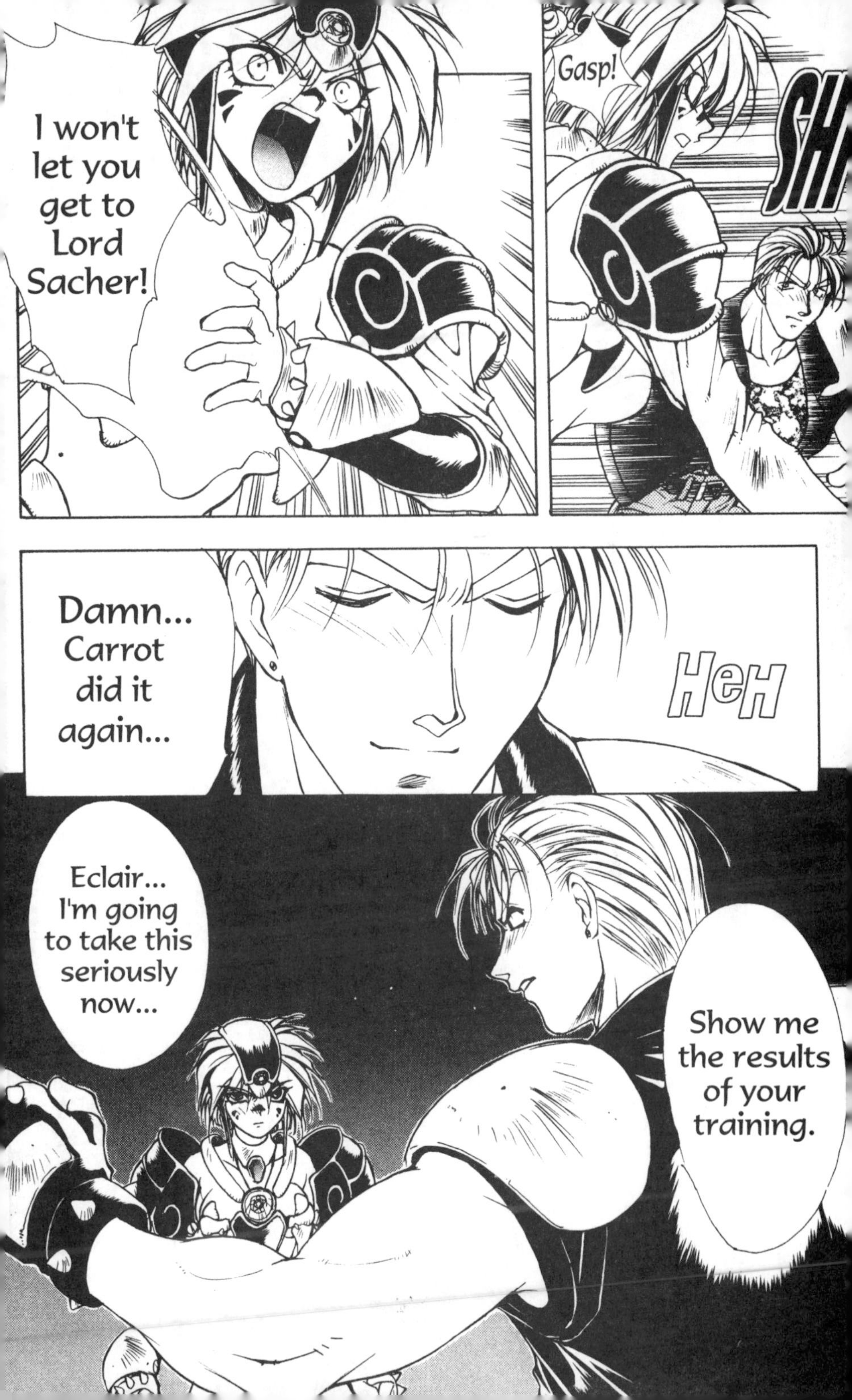
I won't let you get to Lord Sacher!
Gasp!
SH
Damn... Carrot did it again...
HeH
Eclair... I'm going to take this seriously now...
Show me the results of your training.

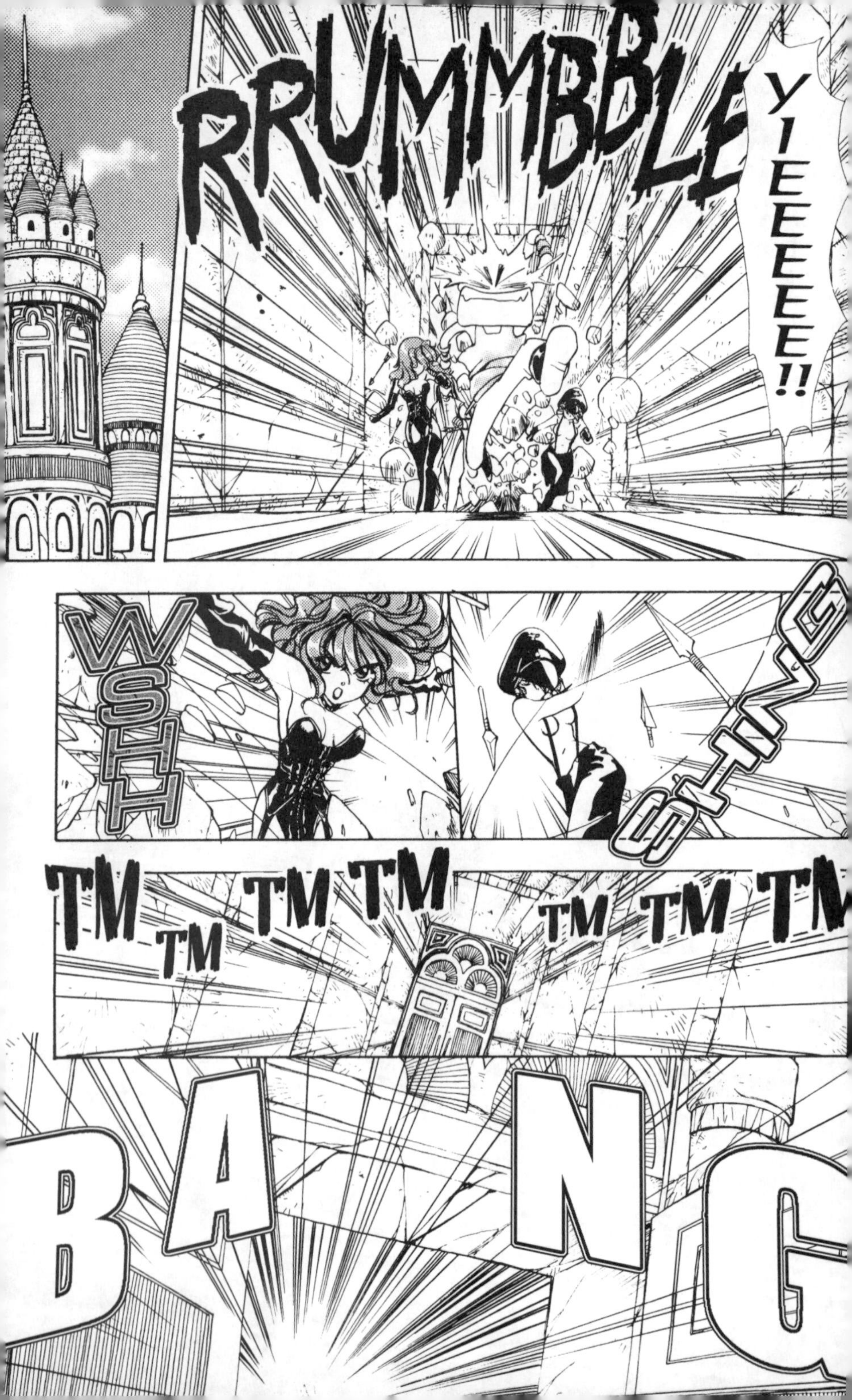
RRUMMBBLE
YIEEEEEE!!
WSHH
SHING
TM TM TM TM TM TM TM
BANG

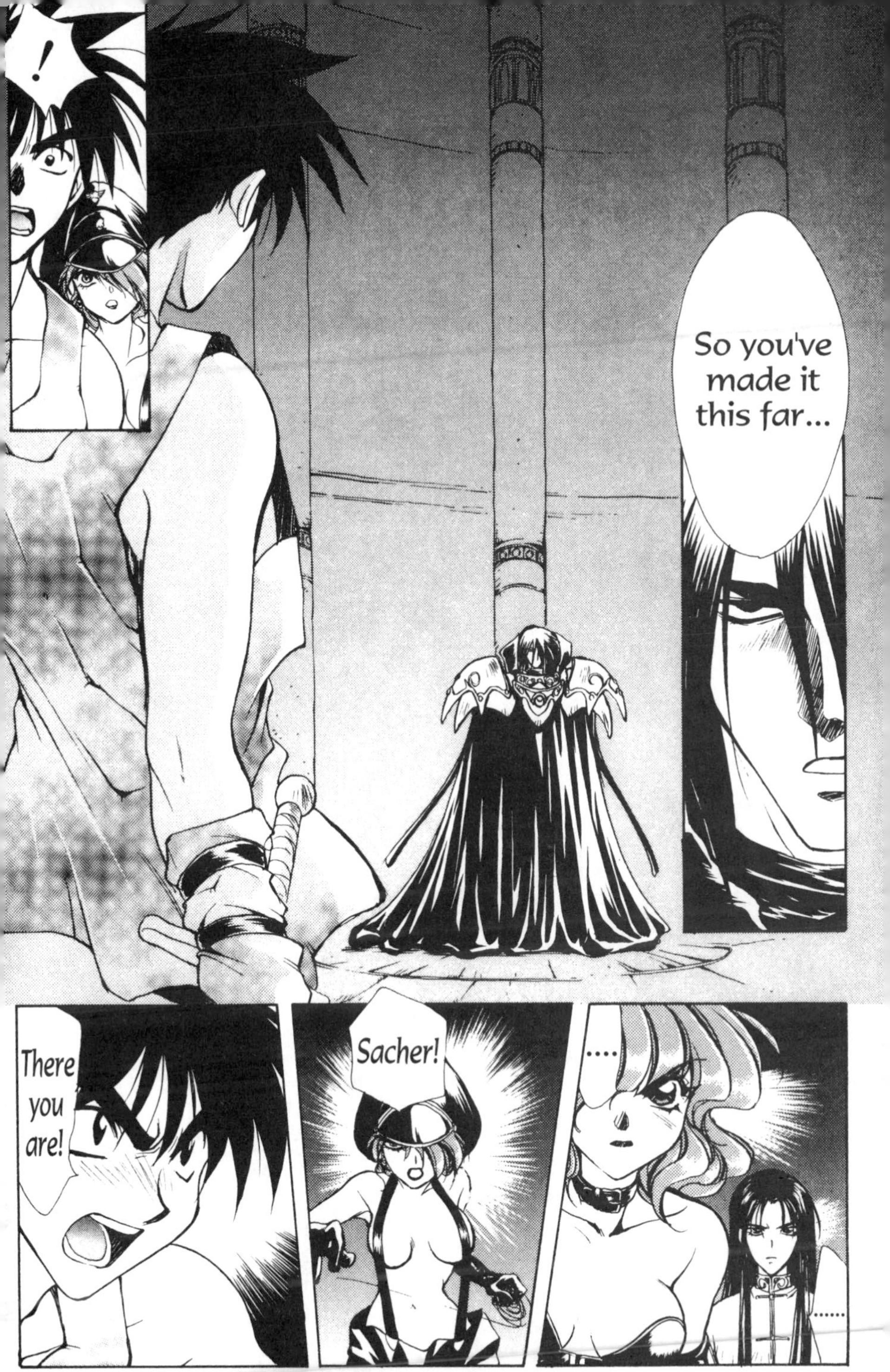
!
So you've made it this far...
There you are!
Sacher!
....
......

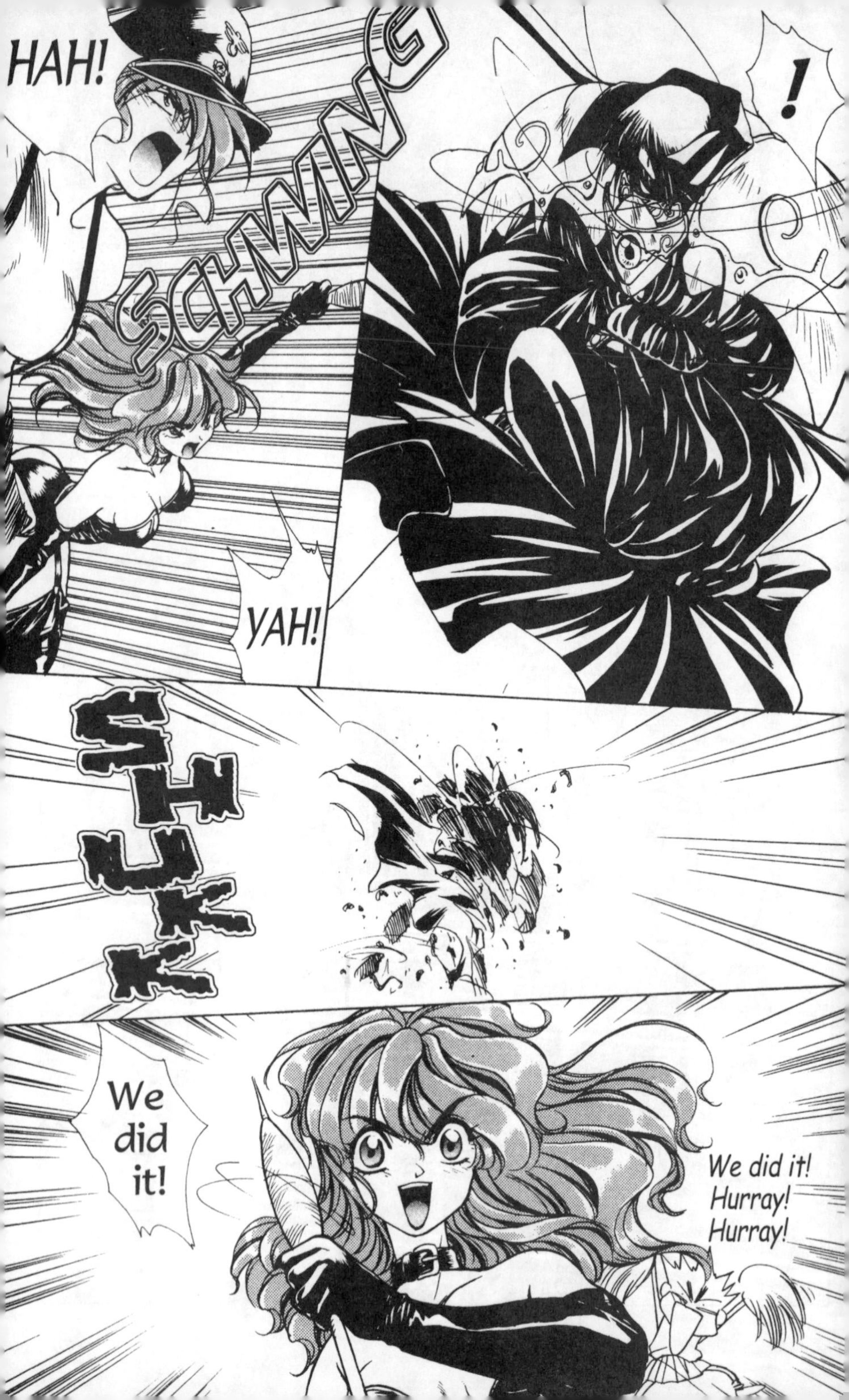
HAH!
SCHWING
YAH!
!
SHUKK
We did it!
We did it! Hurray! Hurray!

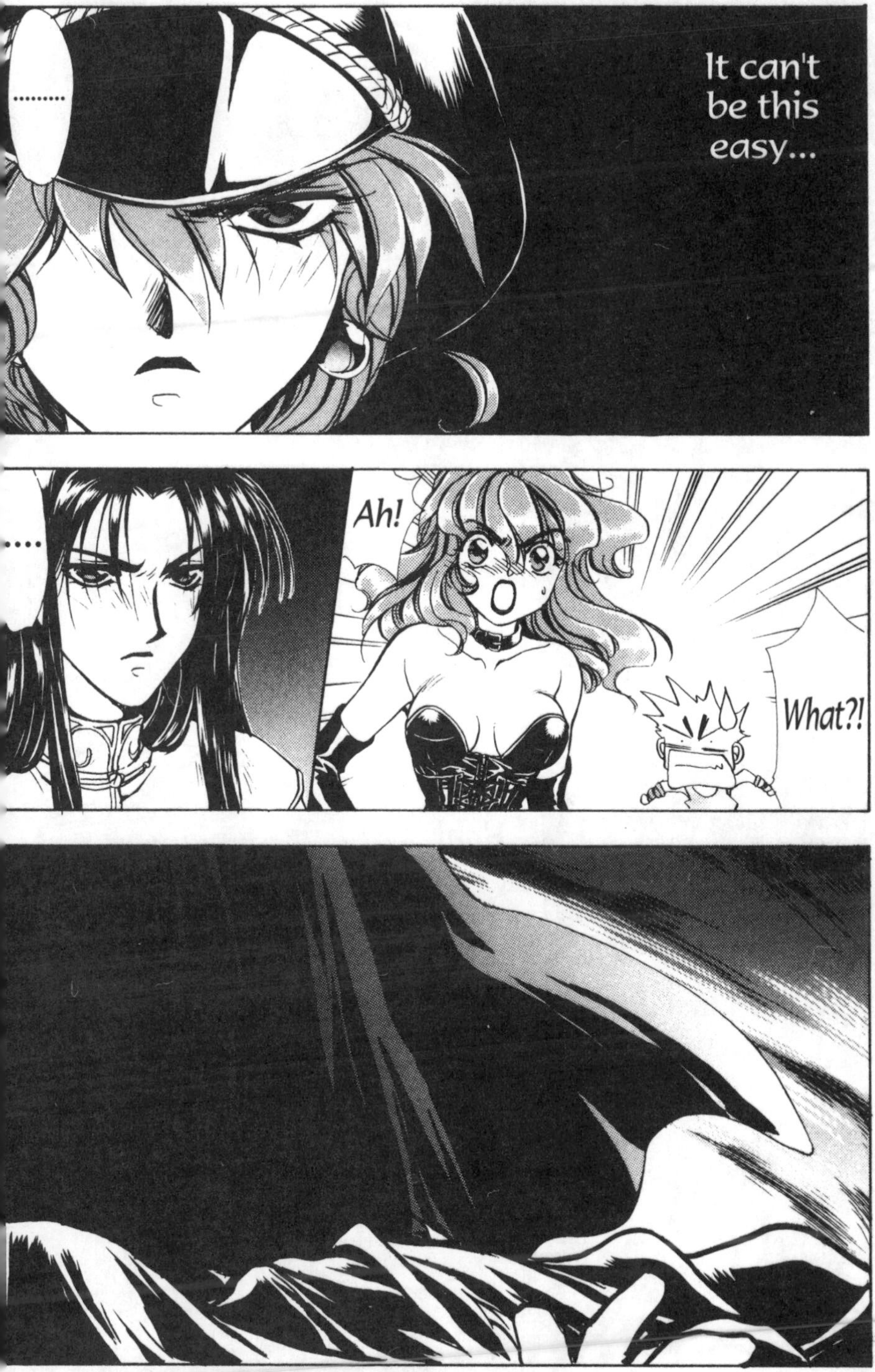
....
It can't be this easy...
....
Ah!
What?!

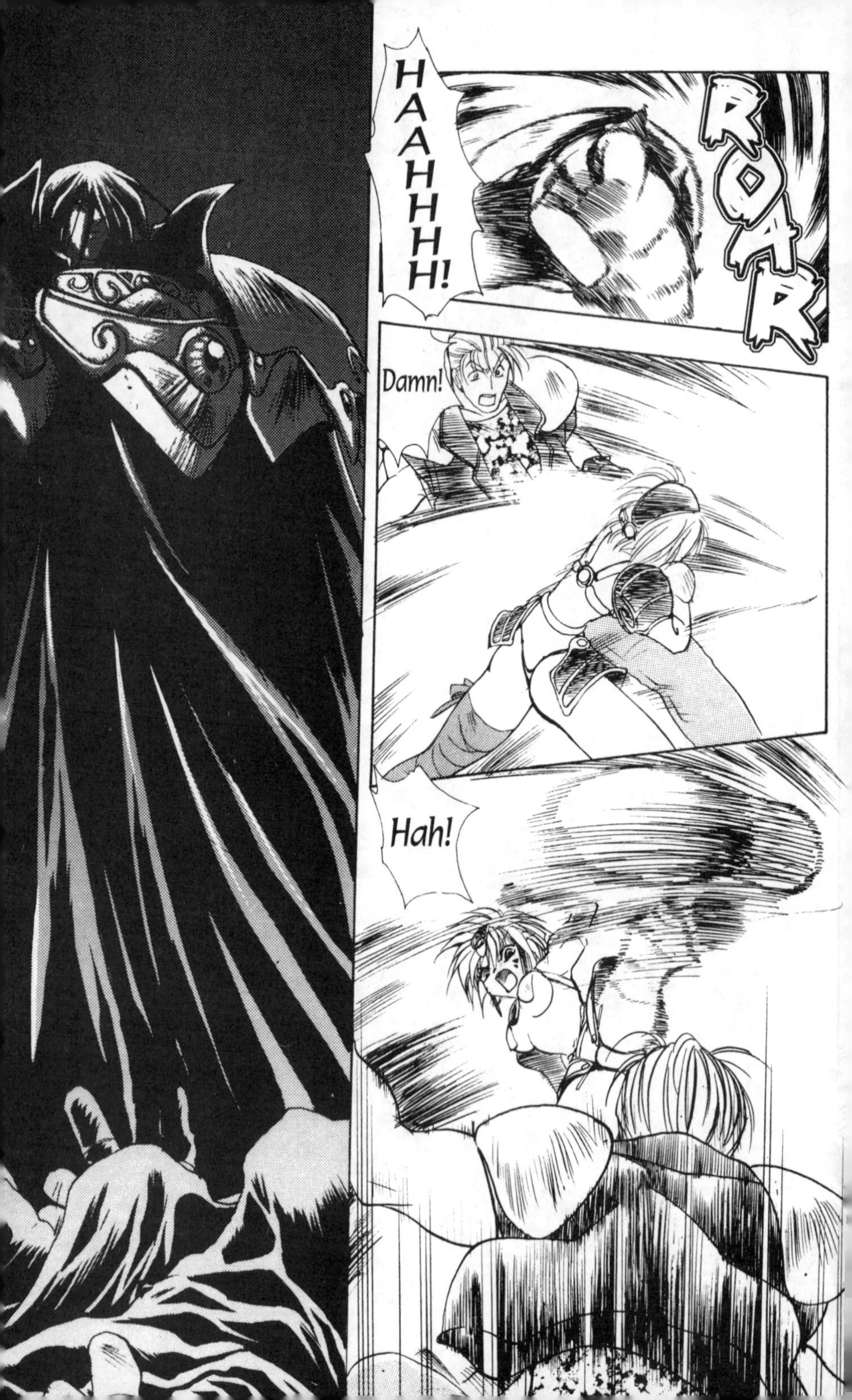
HAAAHHHH!
ROAR
Damn!
Hah!

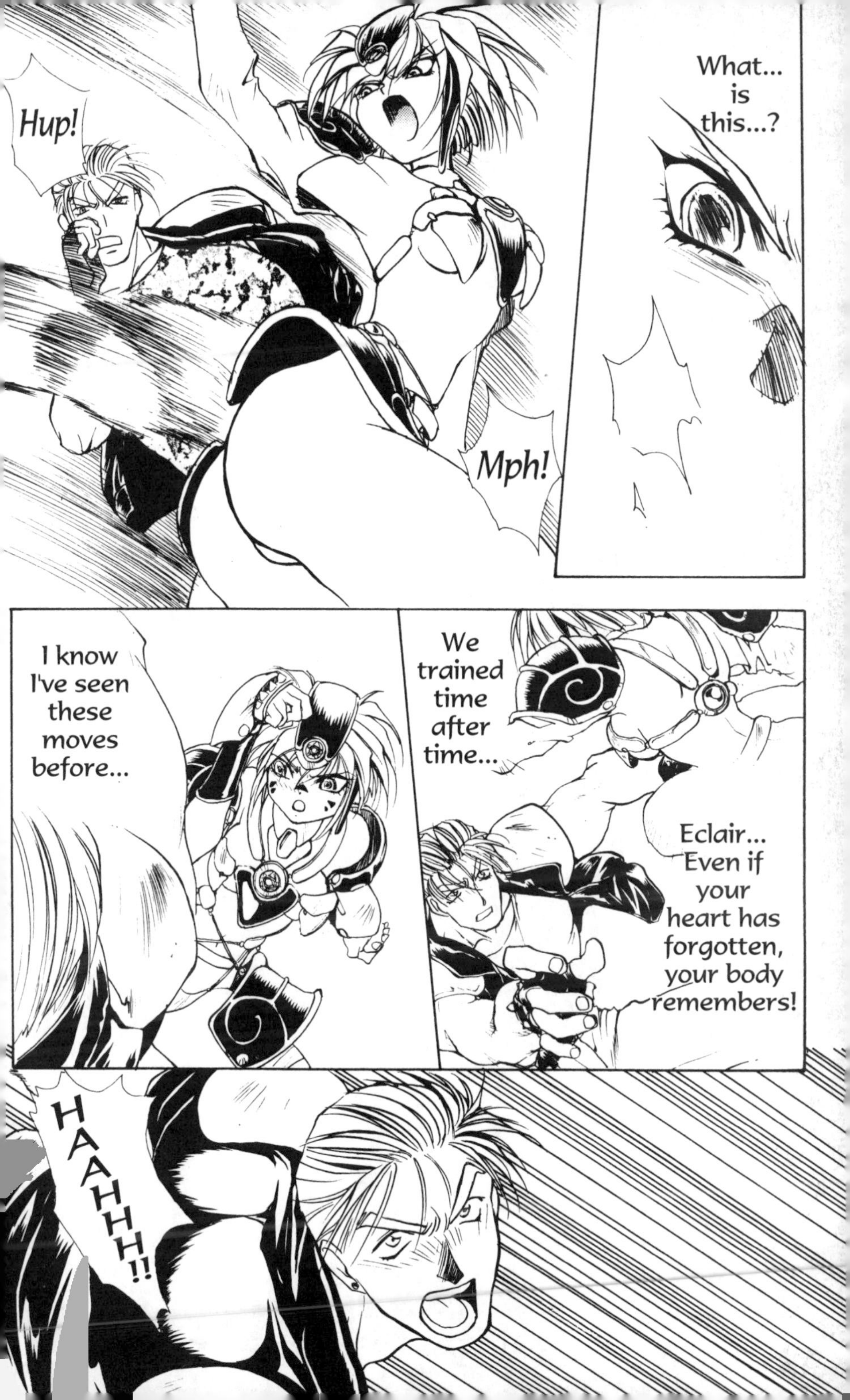
Hup!
Mph!
What... is this...?
I know I've seen these moves before...
We trained time after time...
Eclair... Even if your heart has forgotten, your body remembers!
HAAHHH!!

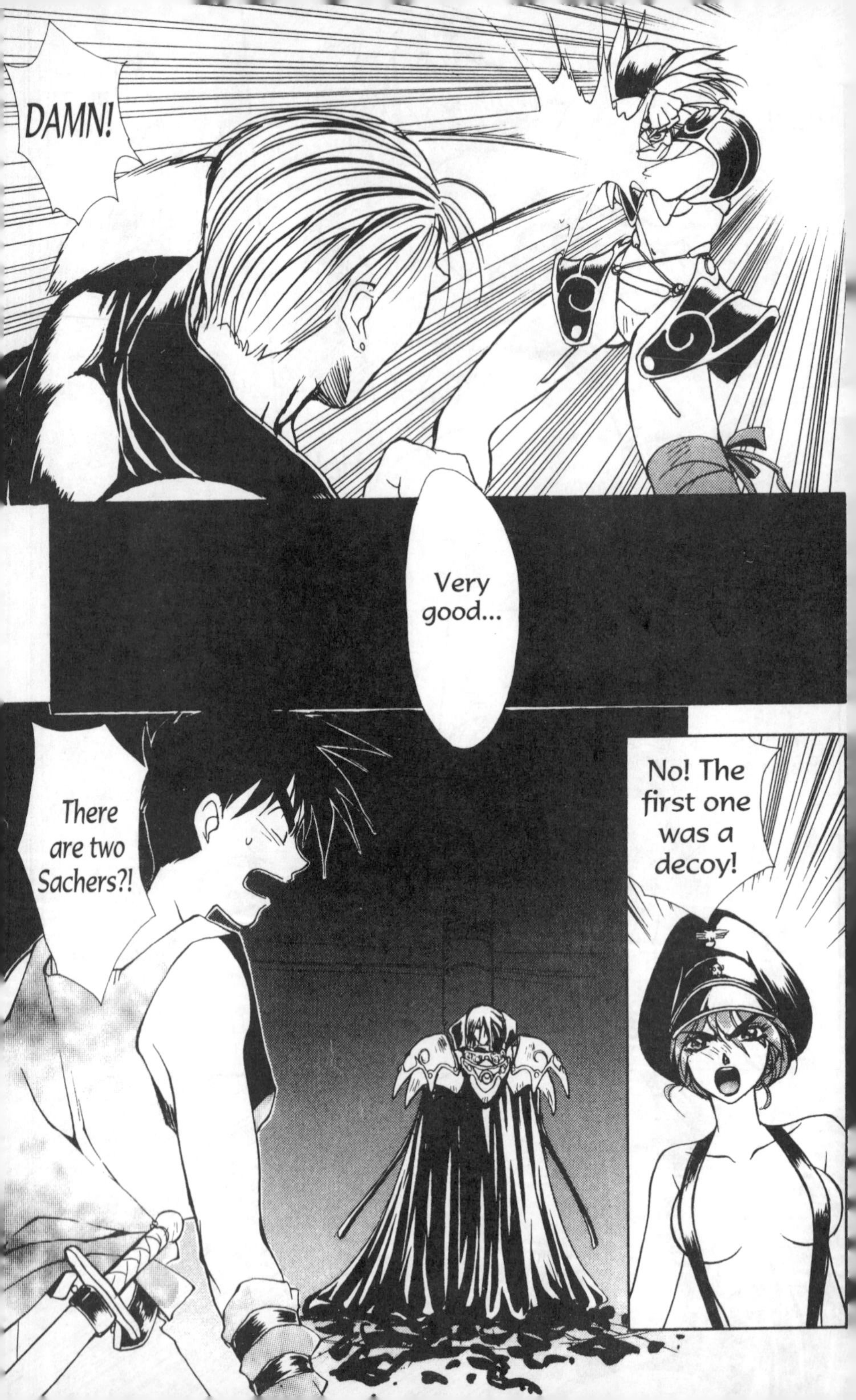
DAMN!
Very good...
There are two Sachers?!
No! The first one was a decoy!

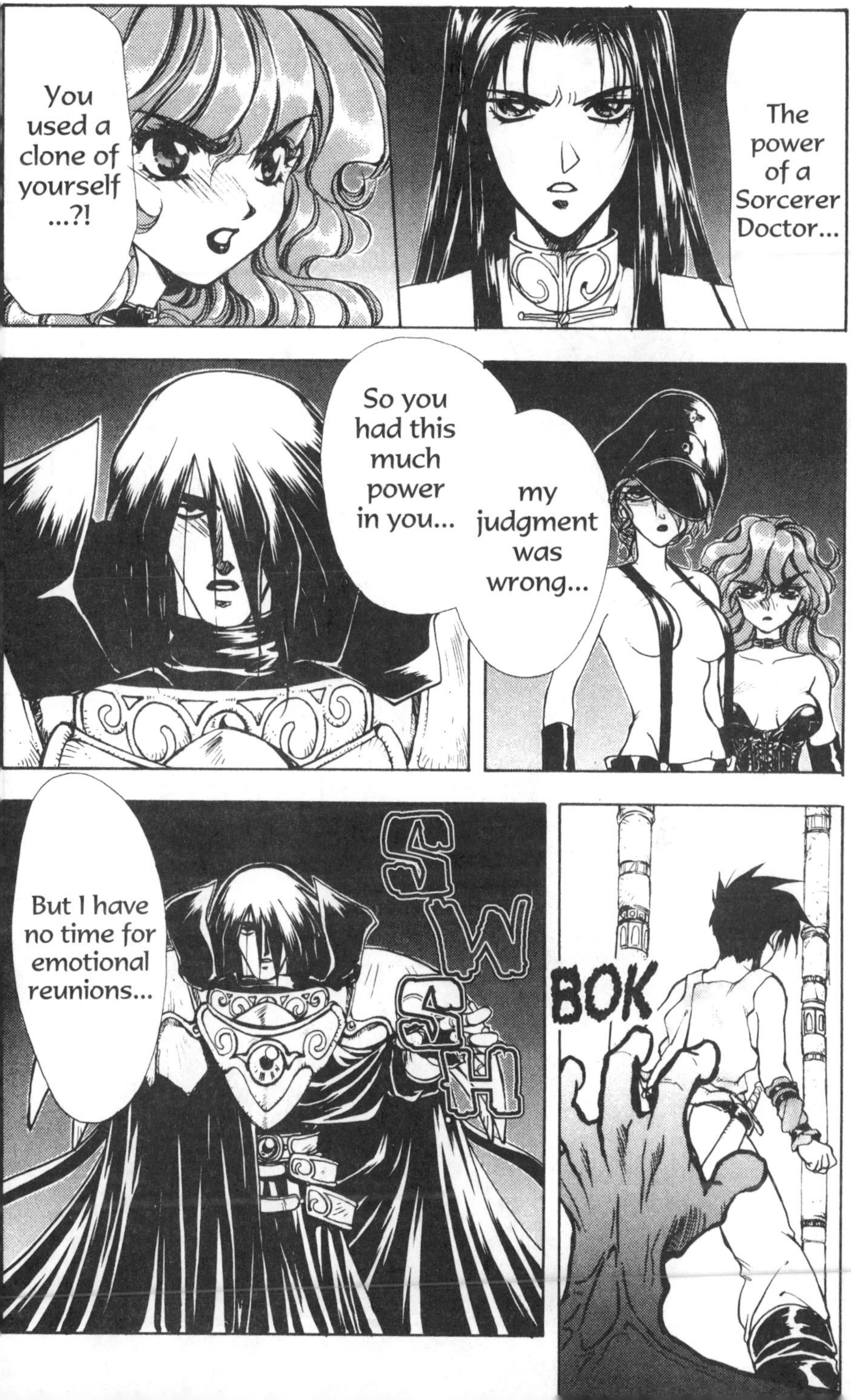
You used a clone of yourself ...?!
The power of a Sorcerer Doctor...
So you had this much power in you...
my judgment was wrong...
But I have no time for emotional reunions...
SWSSH
BOK

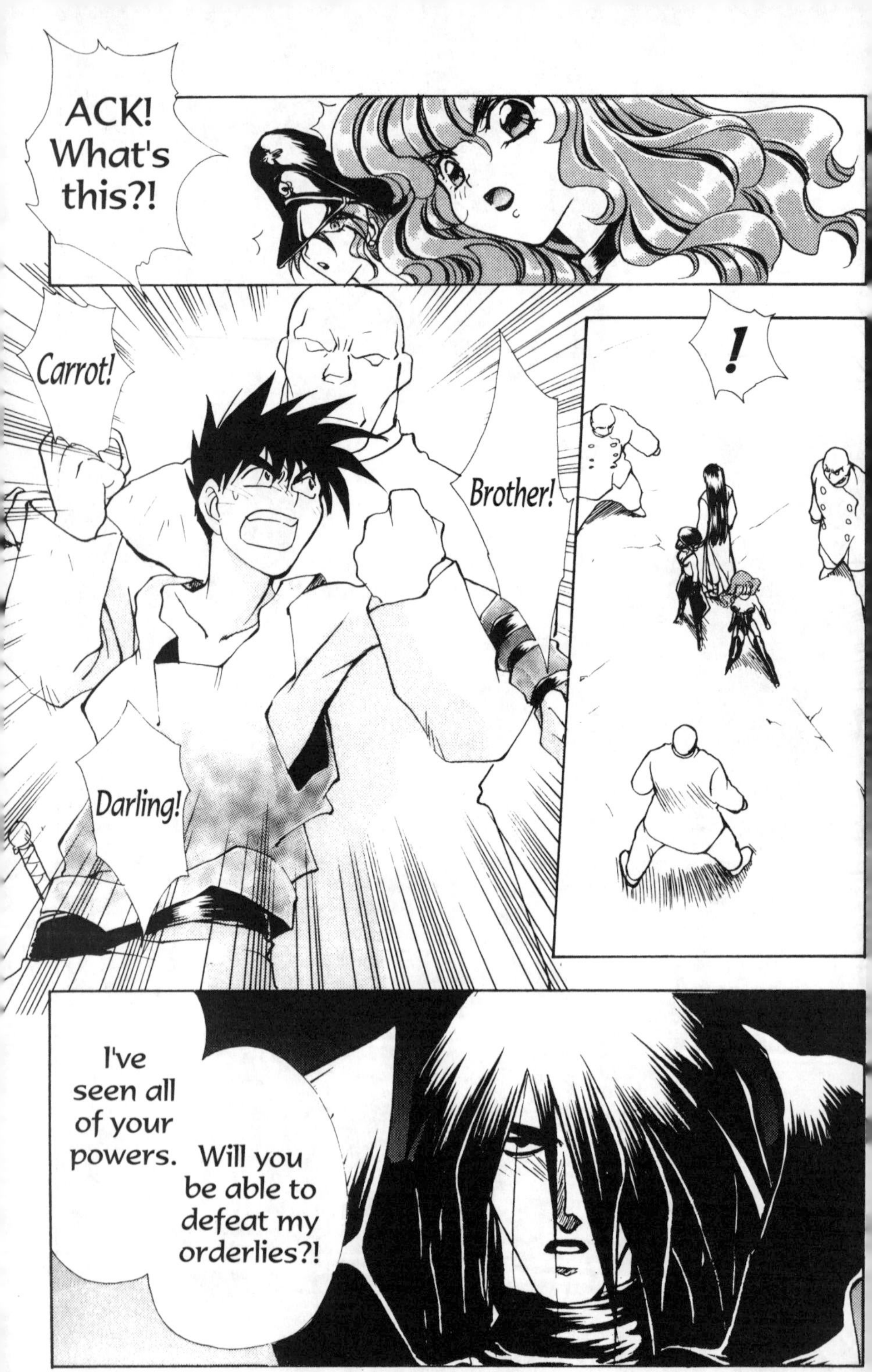
ACK! What's this?!
Carrot!
Brother!
Darling!
!
I've seen all of your powers.
Will you be able to defeat my orderlies?!

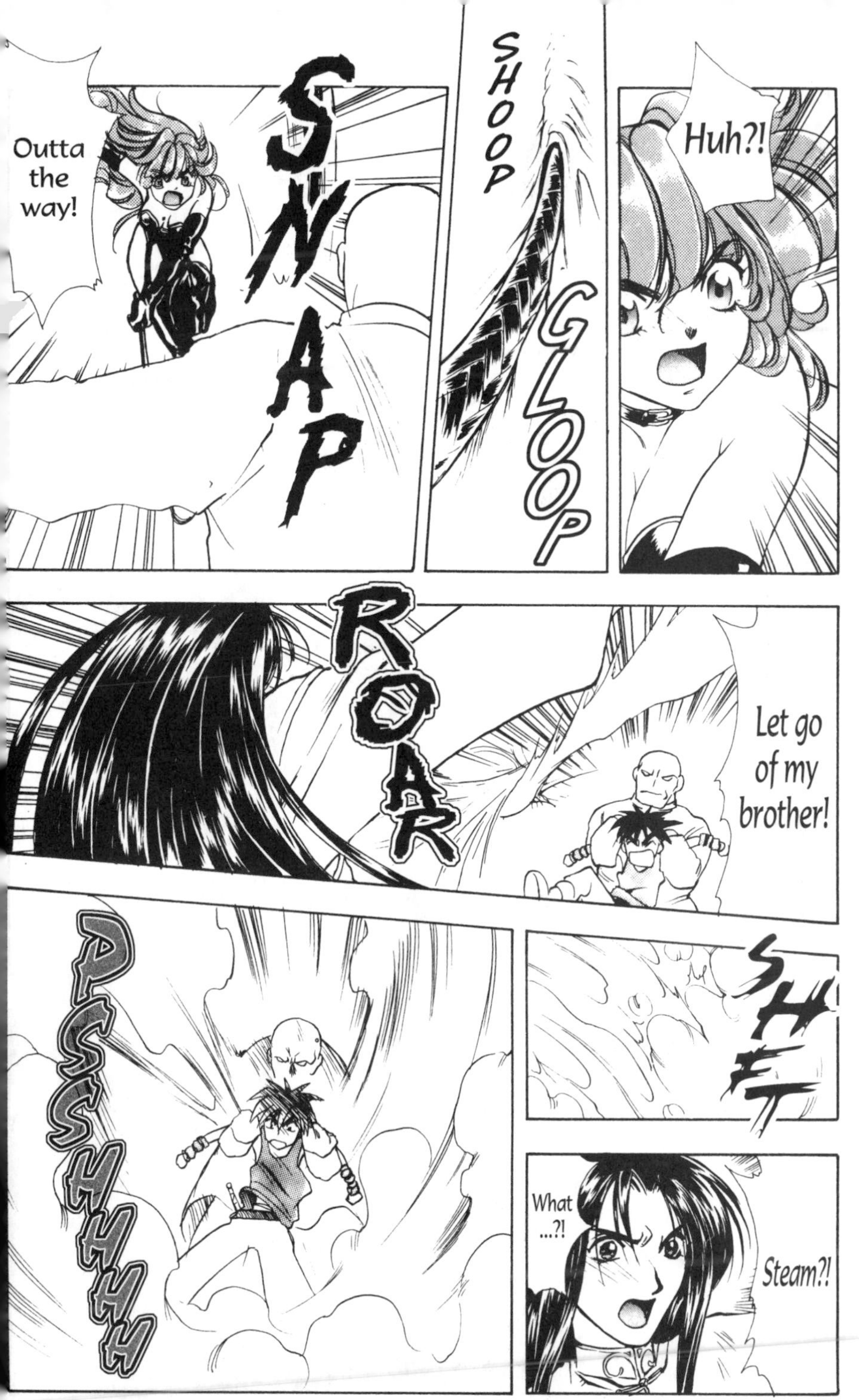
Outta the way!
SNAP
SHOOP
GLOOP
Huh?!
ROAR
Let go of my brother!
PSHHHH
SHFT
What ...?!
Steam?!

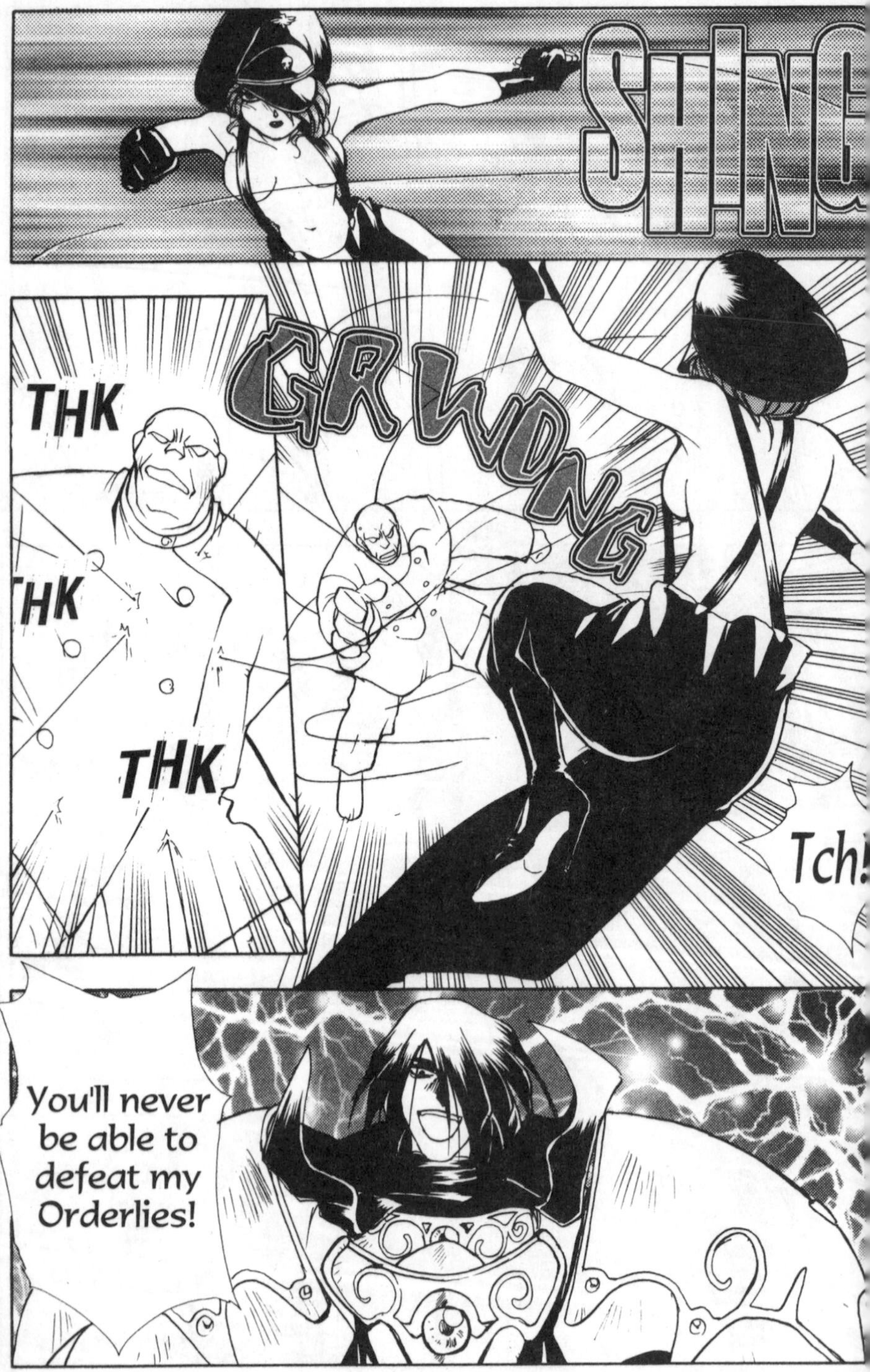
SHING
THK
THK
THK
GRWONG
Tch!
You'll never be able to defeat my Orderlies!

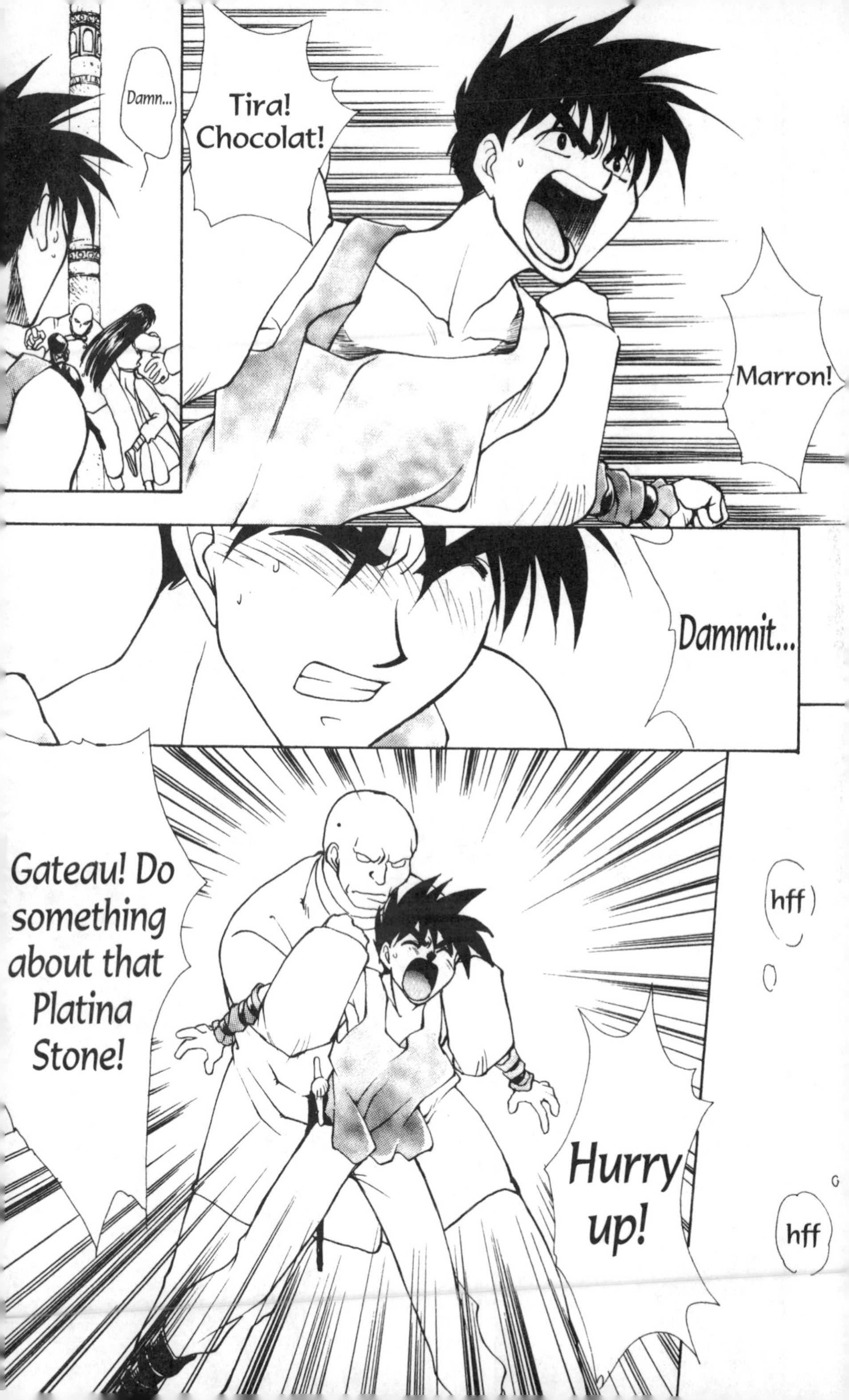
Tira! Chocolat!
Marron!
Damn...
Dammit...
hff
Gateau! Do something about that Platina Stone!
Hurry up!
hff

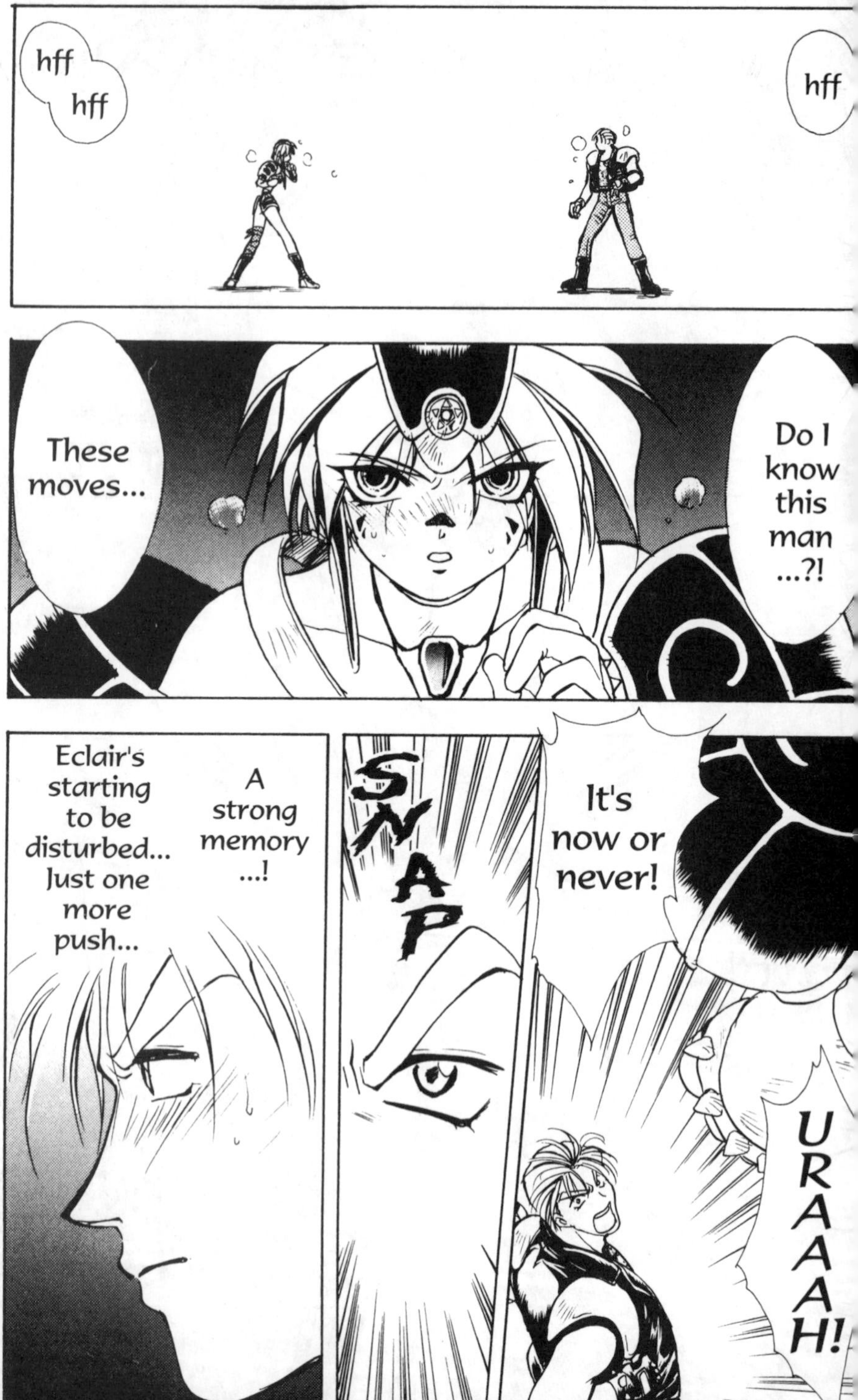
hff
hff
hff
These moves...
Do I know this man ...?!
Eclair's starting to be disturbed... Just one more push...
A strong memory ...!
SNAP
It's now or never!
URAAAAH!

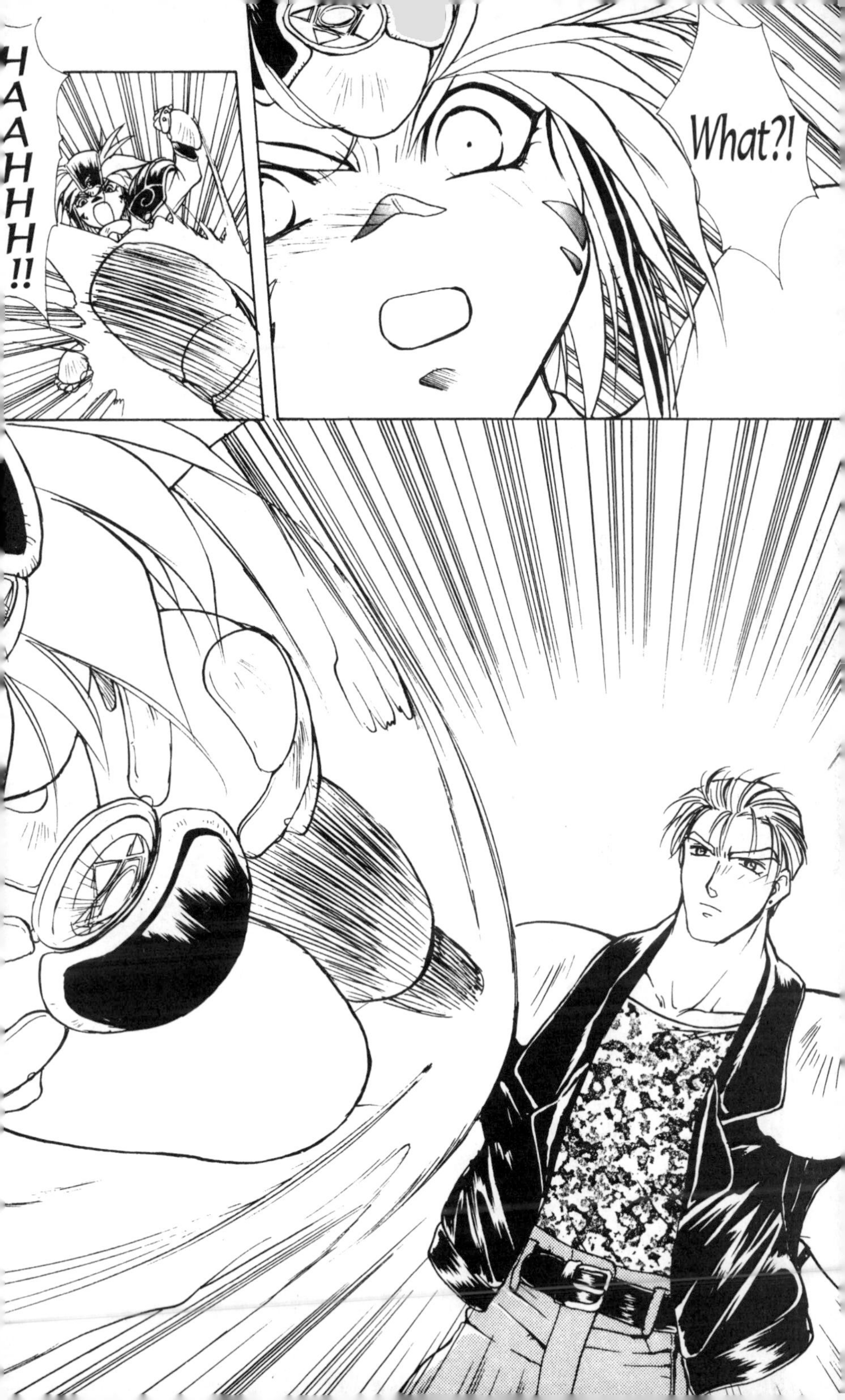
HAAAHHHH!!
What?!

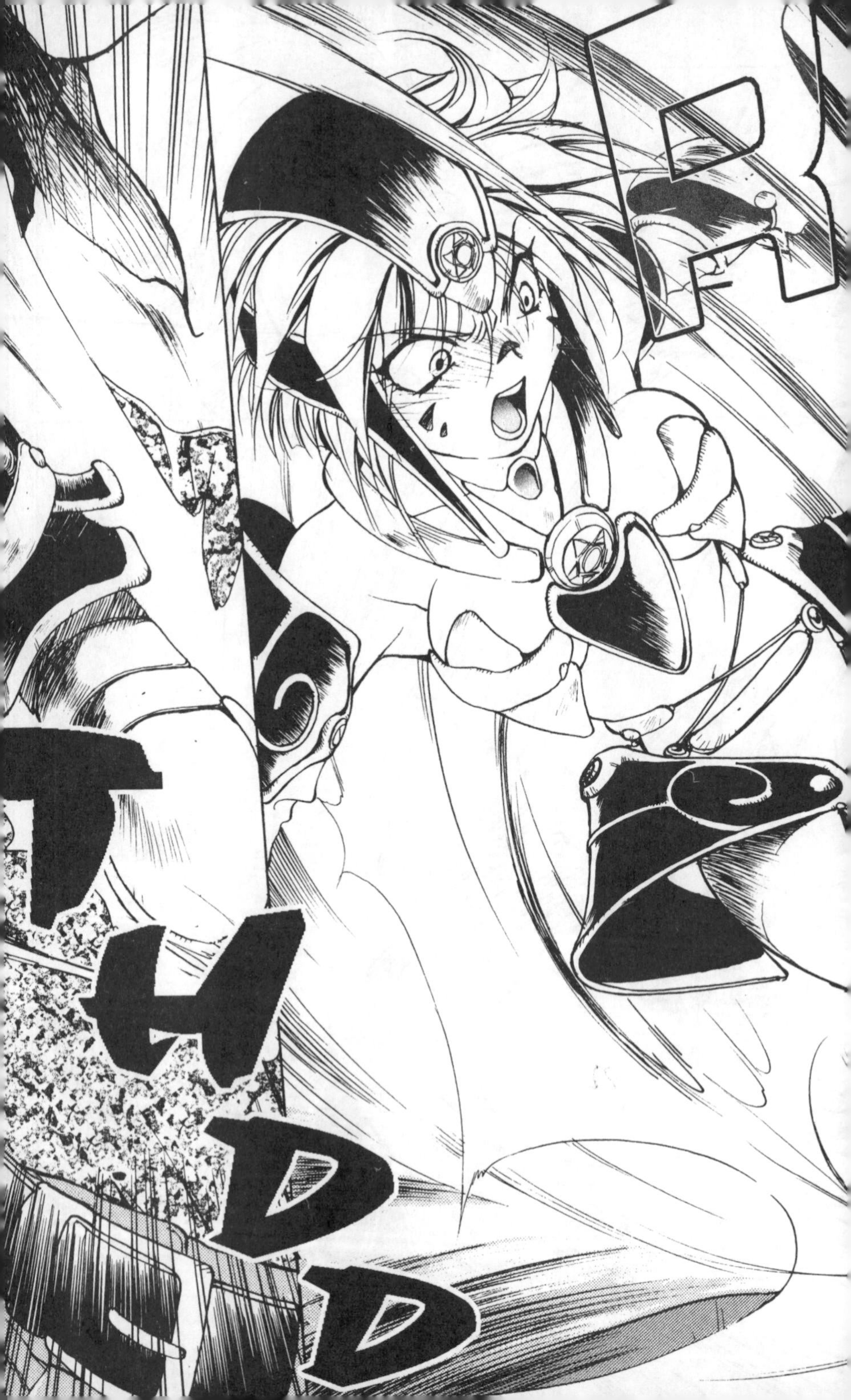

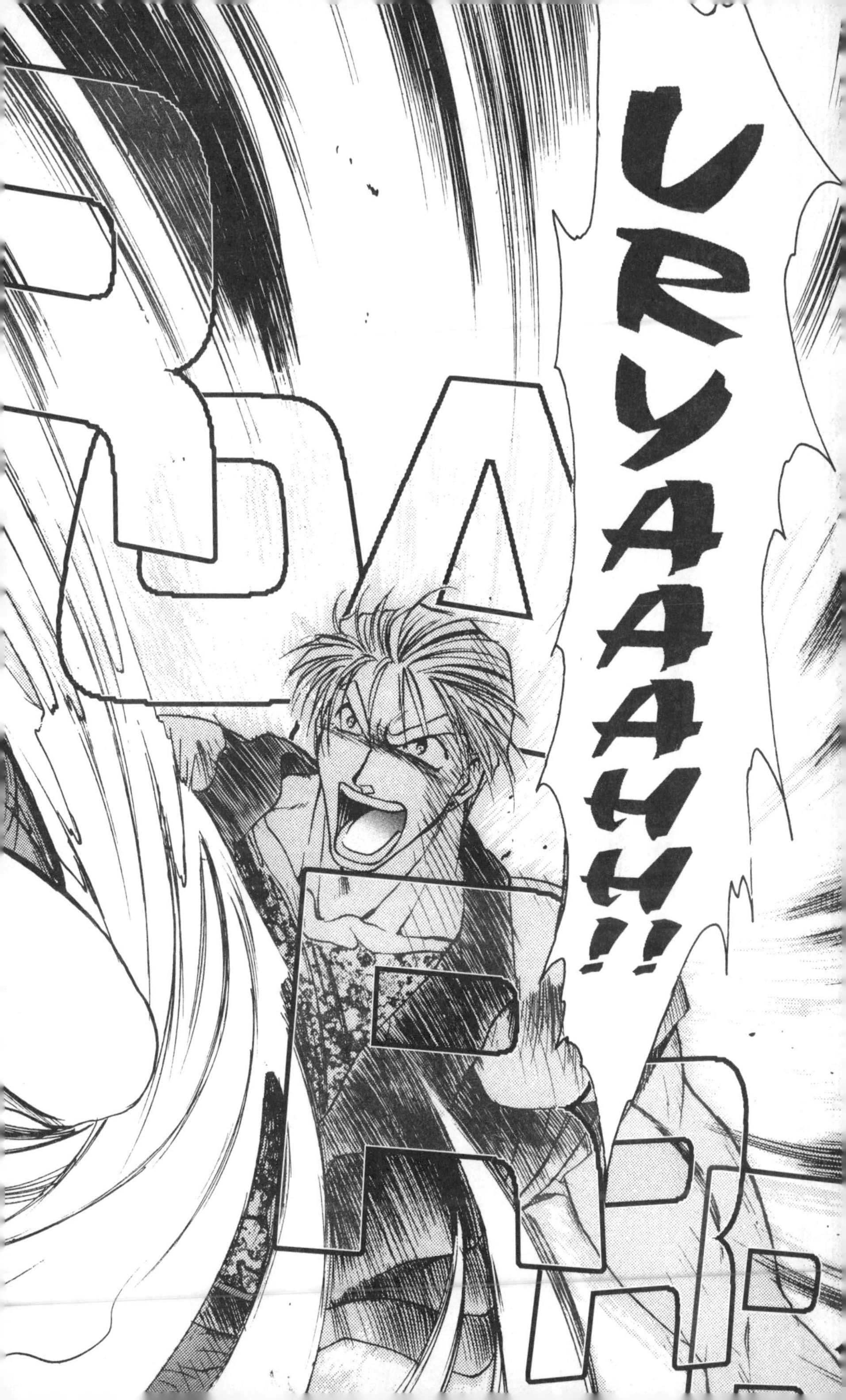
URYAAAHH!!

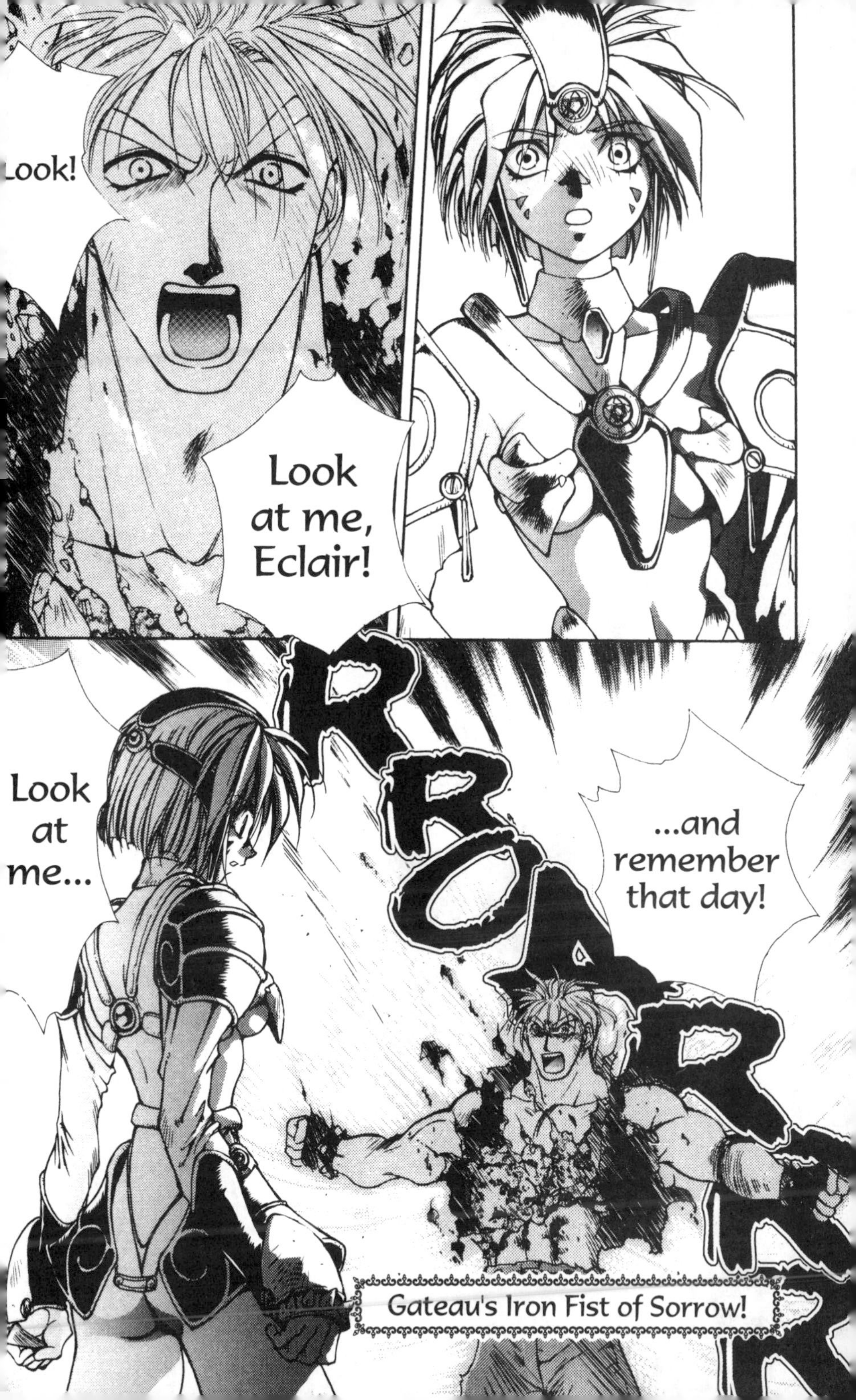

Look!
Look at me, Eclair!
Look at me...
RROARR
...and remember that day!
Gateau's Iron Fist of Sorrow!

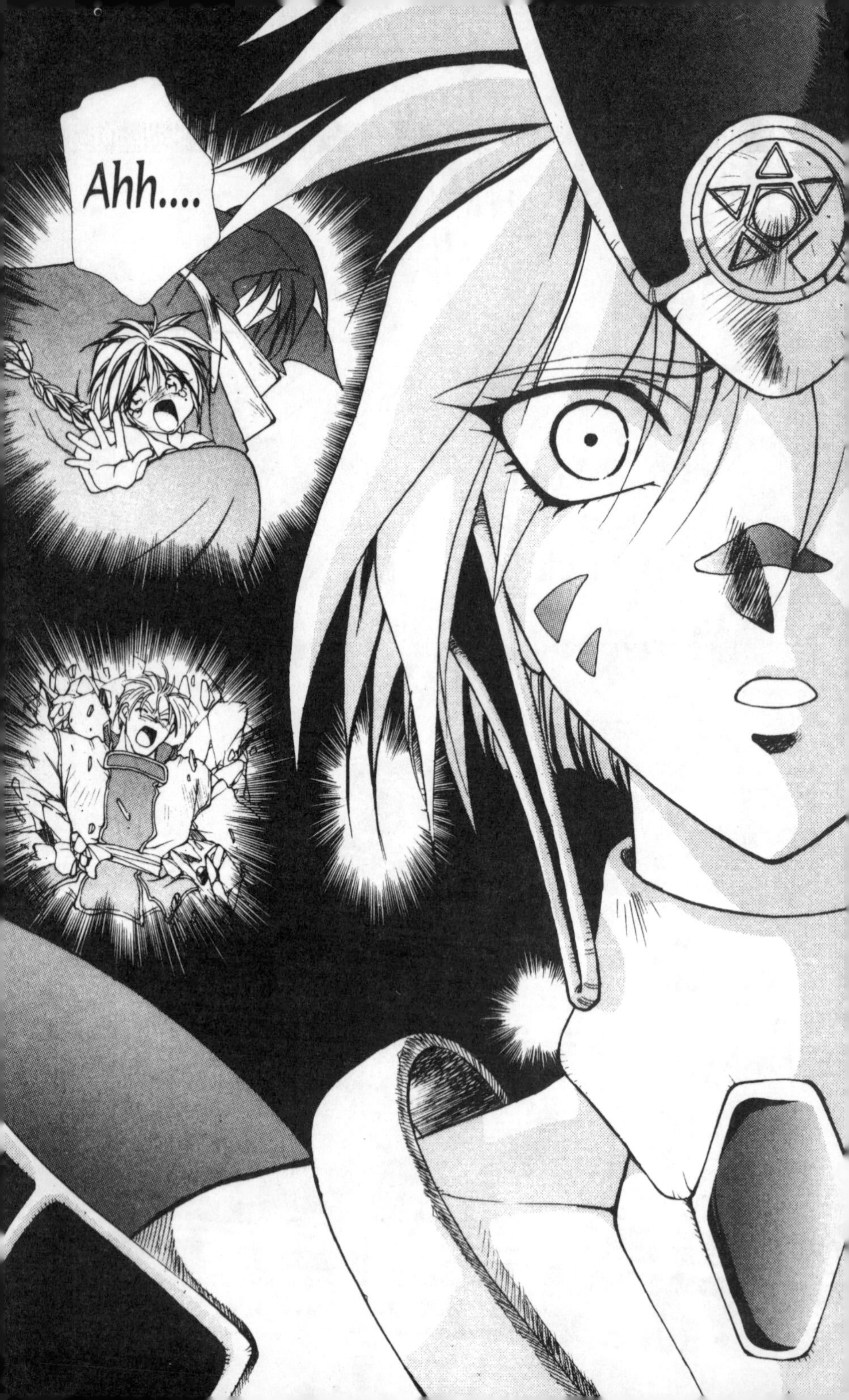
Ahh....

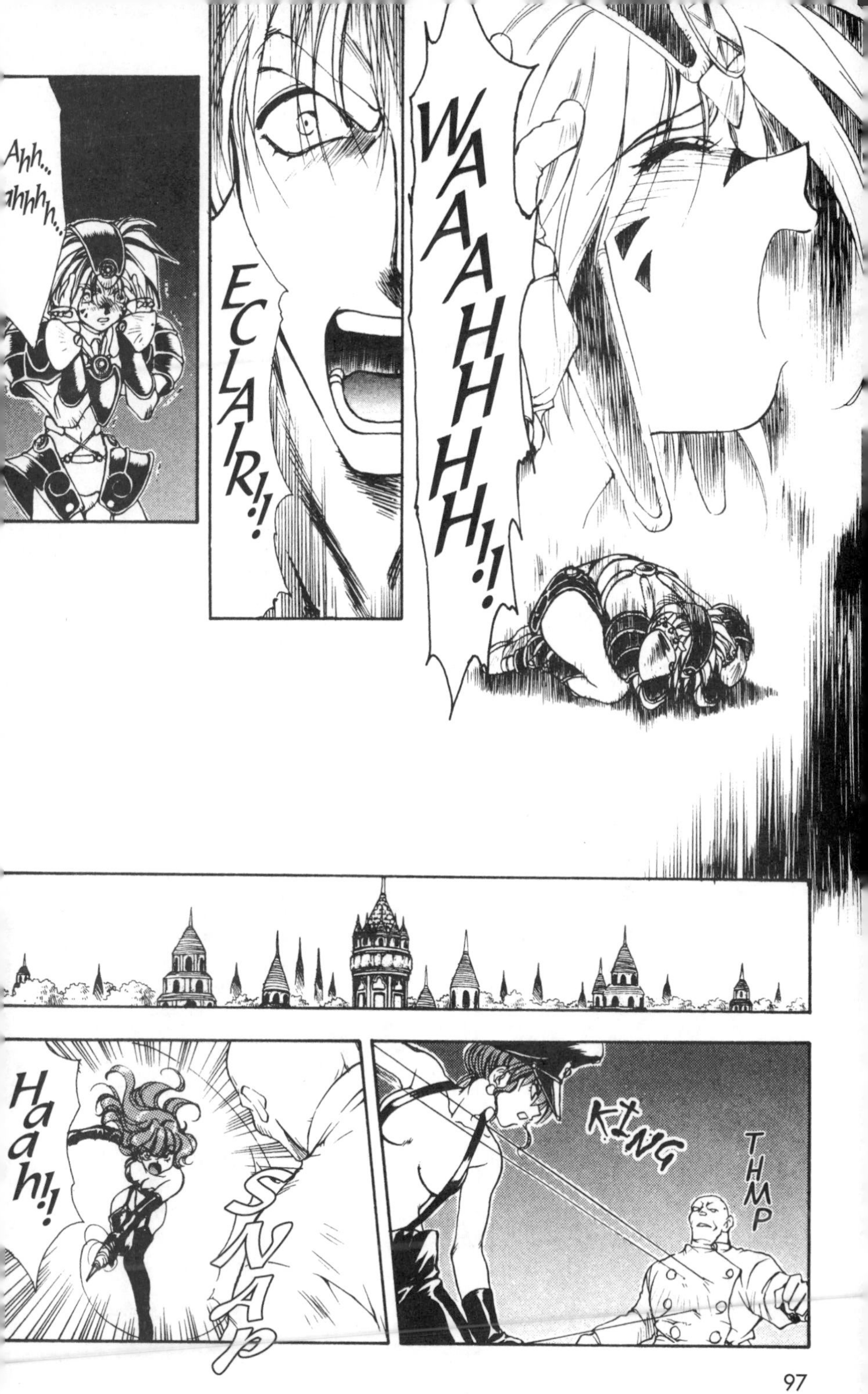
Ahh... ahhhh...
ECLAIR!!
WAAAHHHHHH!!
Haaah!!
SNAP
KING
THMP

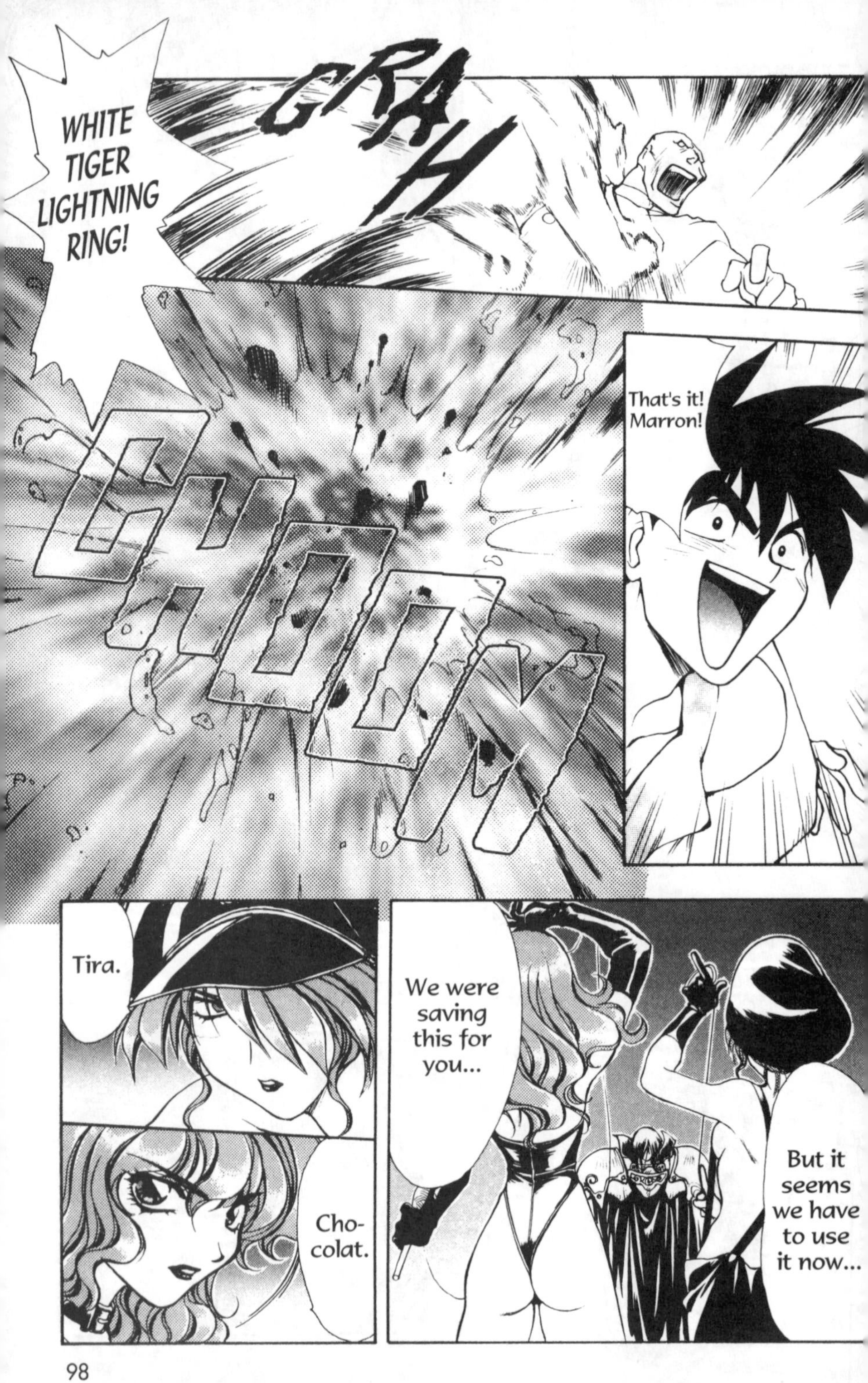

WHITE TIGER LIGHTNING RING!
GRAH
CHOOM
That's it! Marron!
Tira.
Cho-colat.
We were saving this for you...
But it seems we have to use it now...

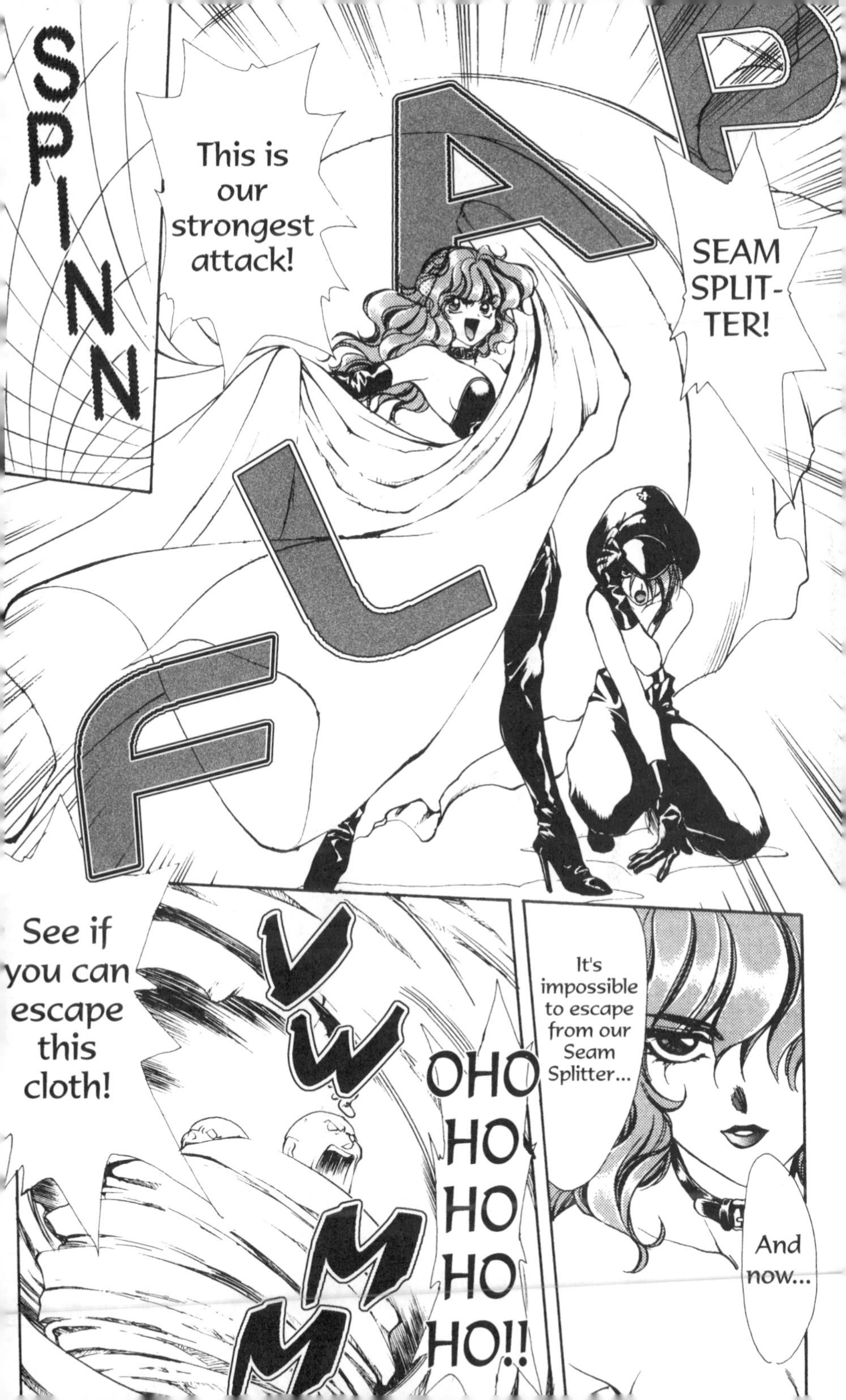
SPINN
This is our strongest attack!
FLAP
SEAM SPLIT-TER!
See if you can escape this cloth!
VWMM
OHO HO HO HO HO HO!!
It's impossible to escape from our Seam Splitter...
And now...

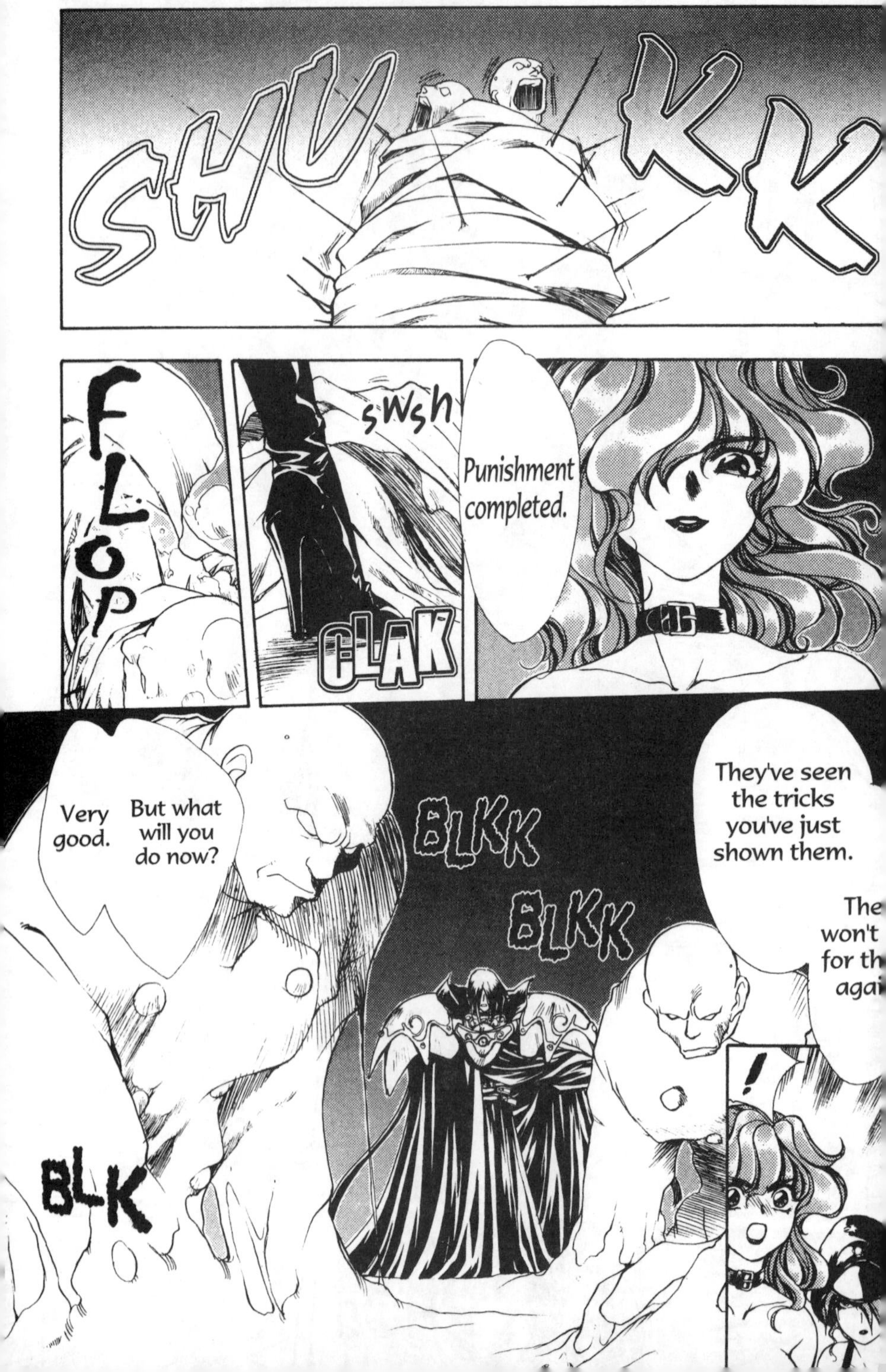
SHUKK
FLOP
swsh
CLAK
Punishment completed.
Very good.
But what will you do now?
BLK
BLKK
BLKK
They've seen the tricks you've just shown them.
The won't for th agai
!

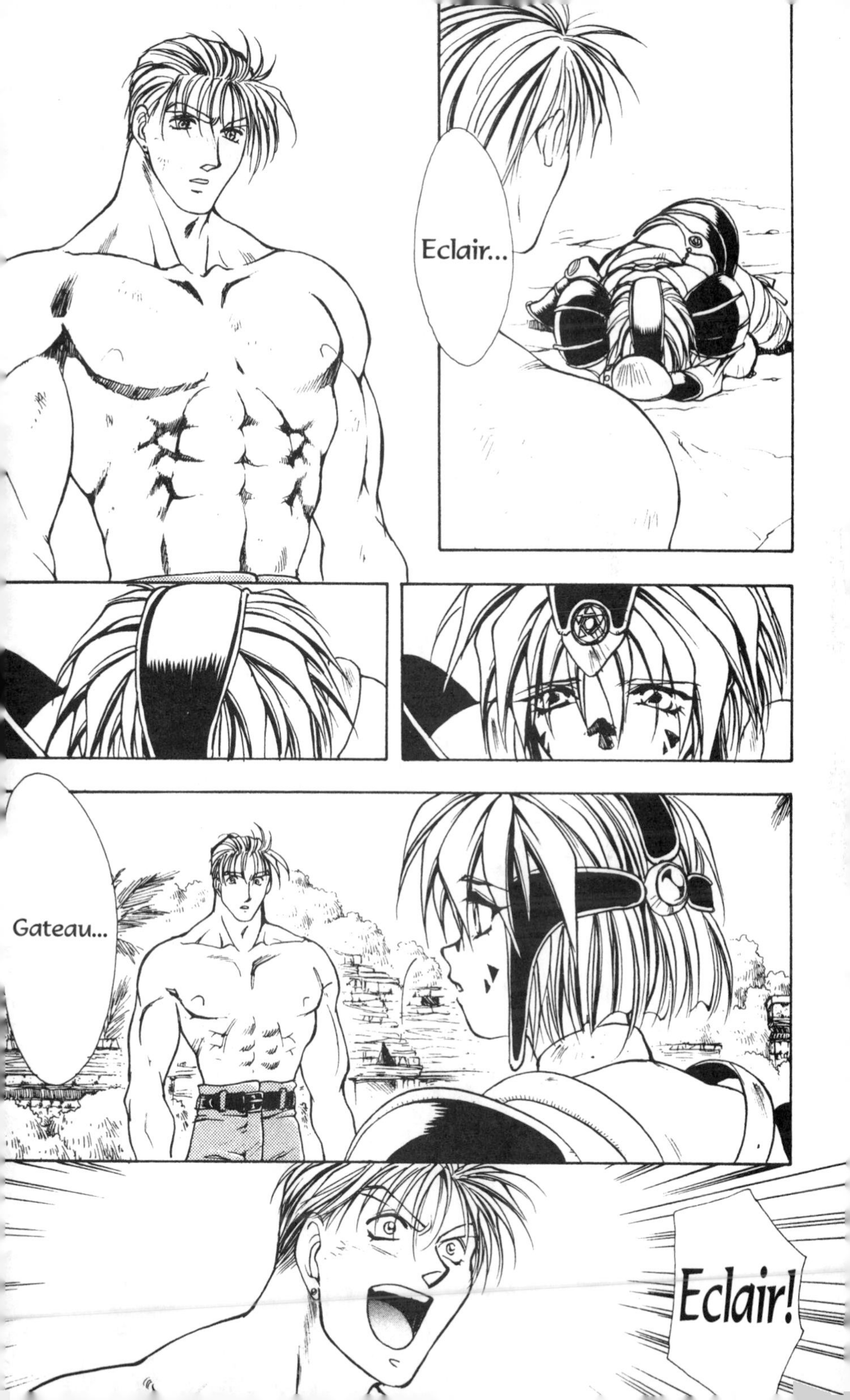
Eclair...
Gateau...
Eclair!

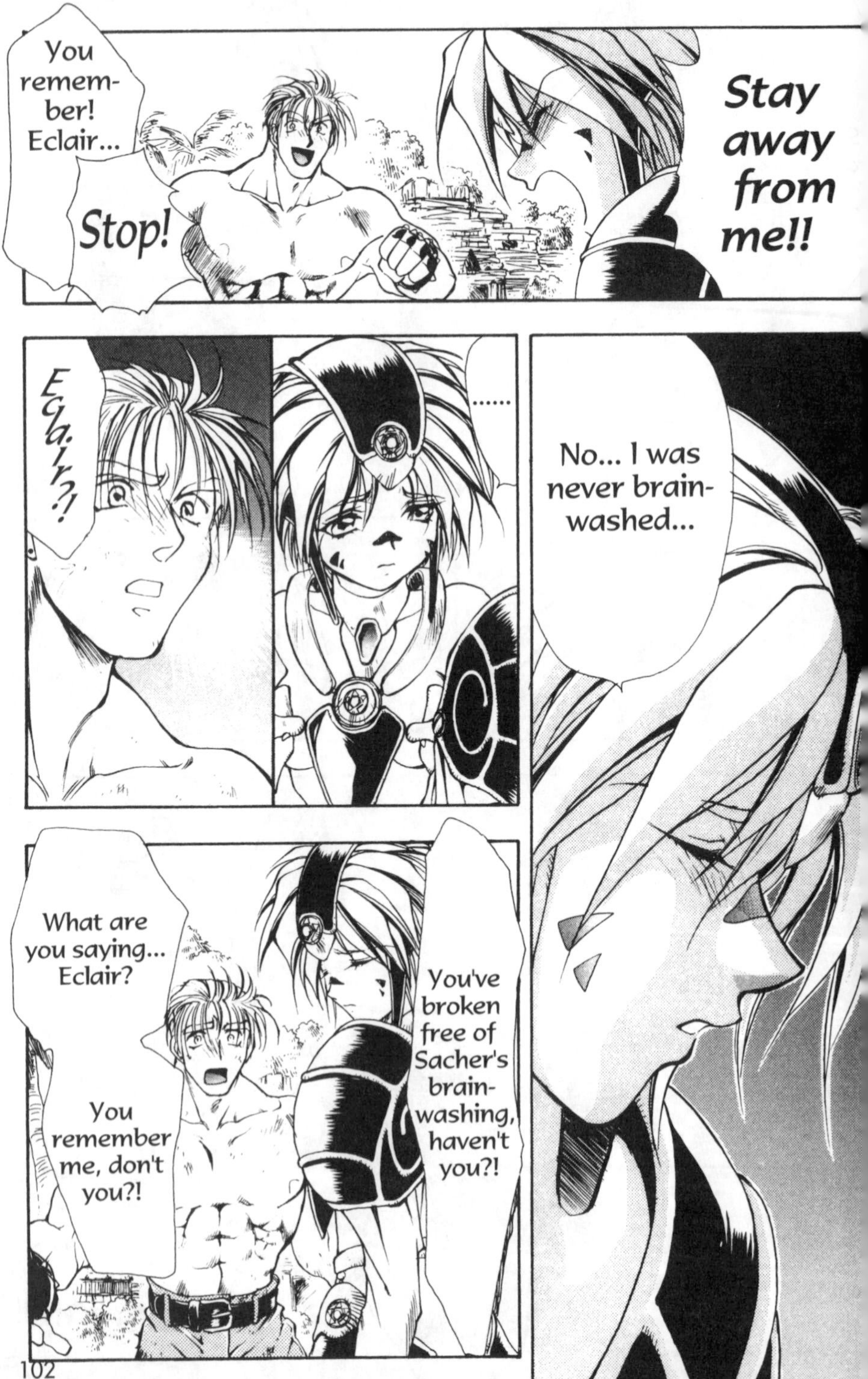
You remember! Eclair...
Stop!
Stay away from me!!
Eclair?!
......
What are you saying... Eclair?
You remember me, don't you?!
You've broken free of Sacher's brainwashing, haven't you?!
No... I was never brainwashed...

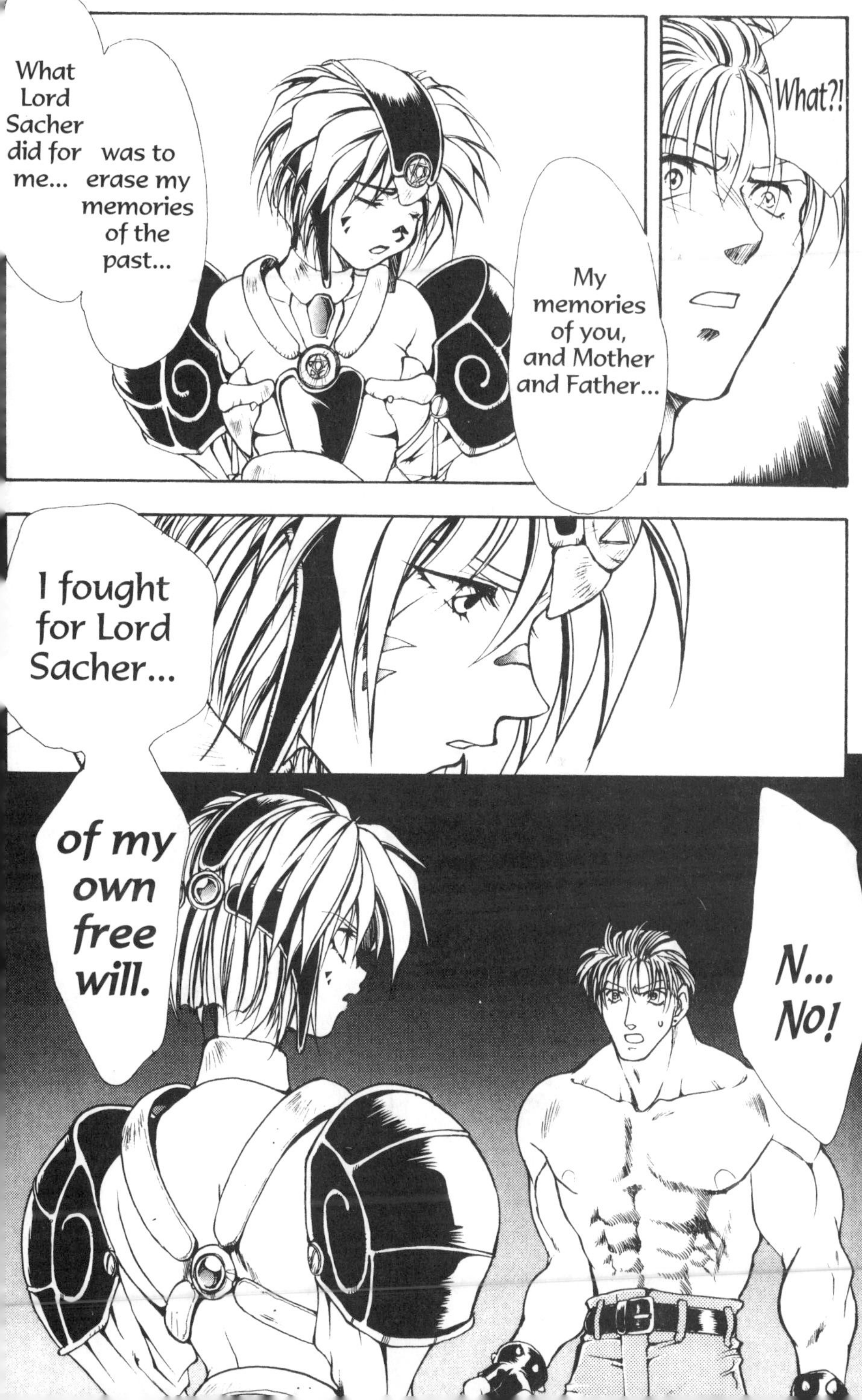
What Lord Sacher did for me... was to erase my memories of the past...
My memories of you, and Mother and Father...
What?!
I fought for Lord Sacher...
of my own free will.
N... No!

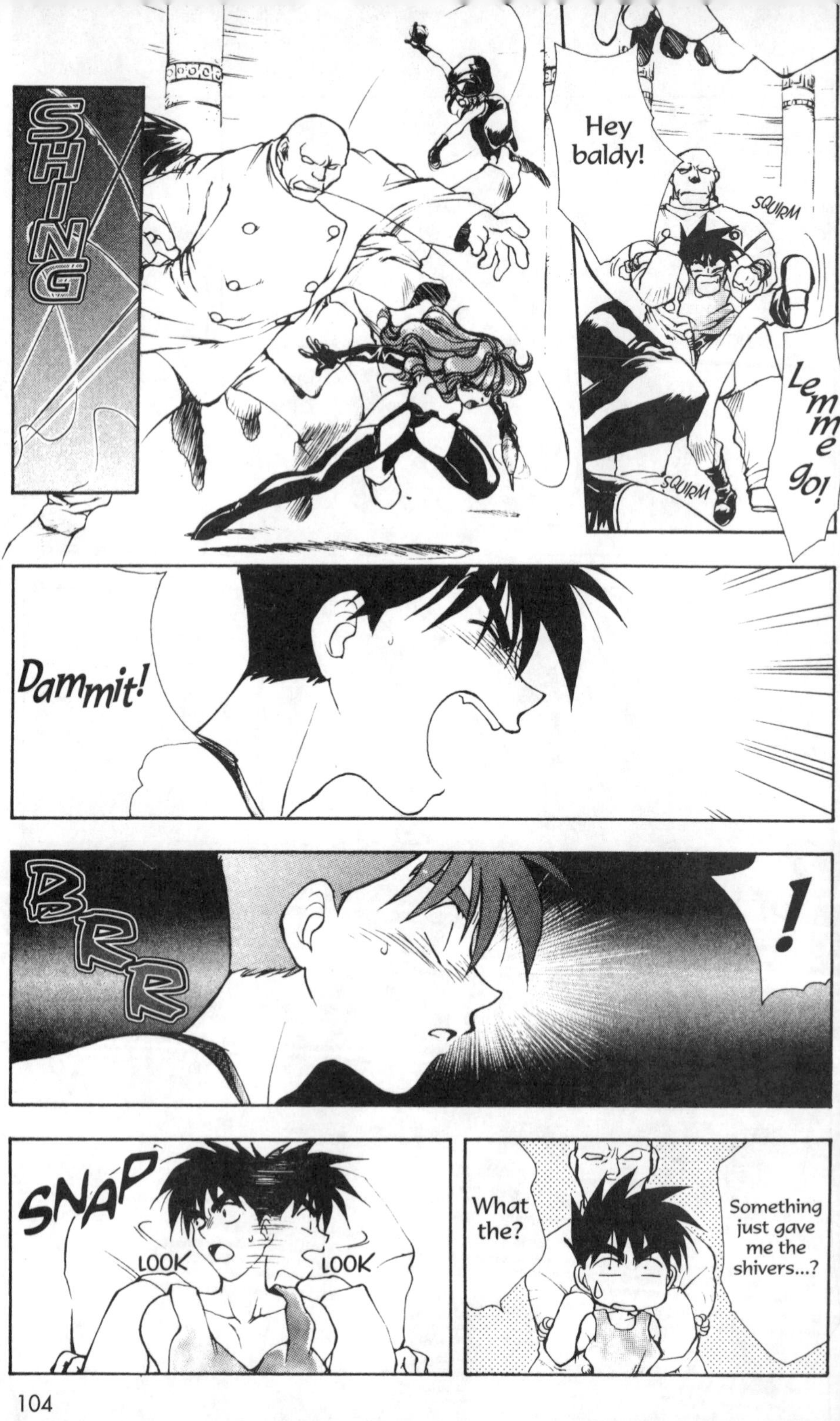
SHING
Hey baldy!
SQUIRM
Lemme go!
SQUIRM
Dammit!
BRRR
!
SNAP
LOOK
LOOK
What the?
Something just gave me the shivers...?

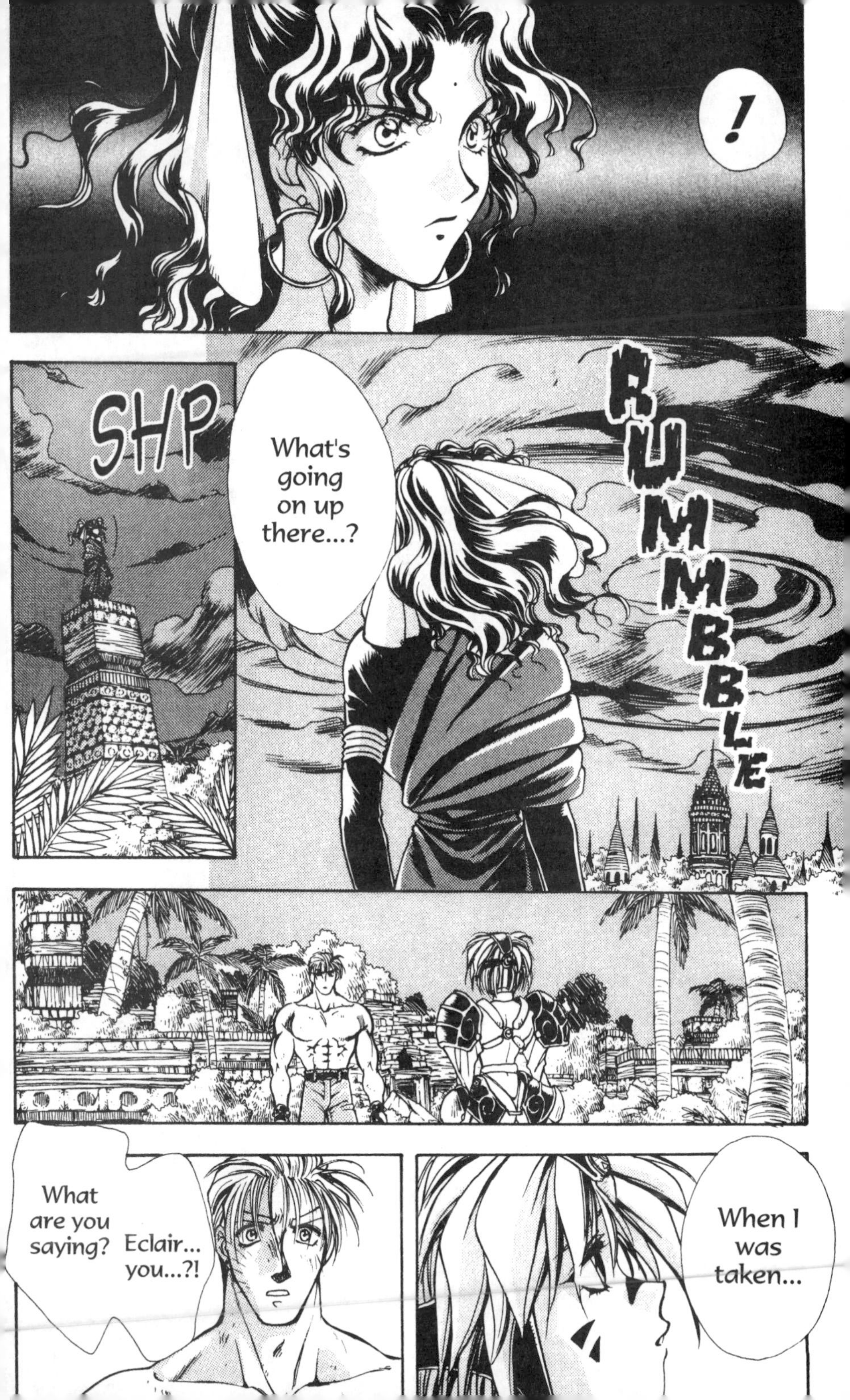
!
SHP
What's going on up there...?
RUMMMBBLE
What are you saying? Eclair... you...?!
When I was taken...

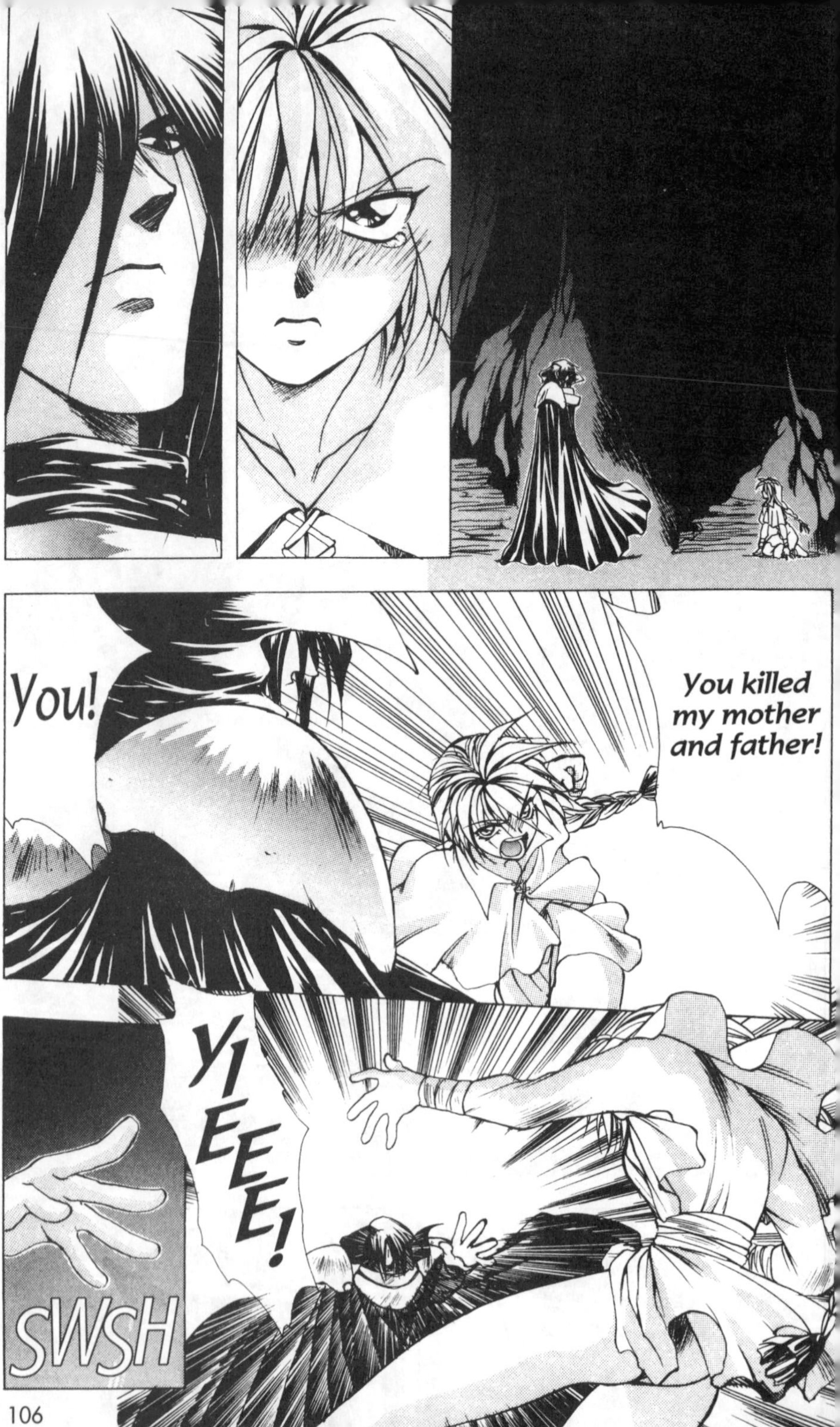
You killed my mother and father!
You!
YIEEEE!
SWSH

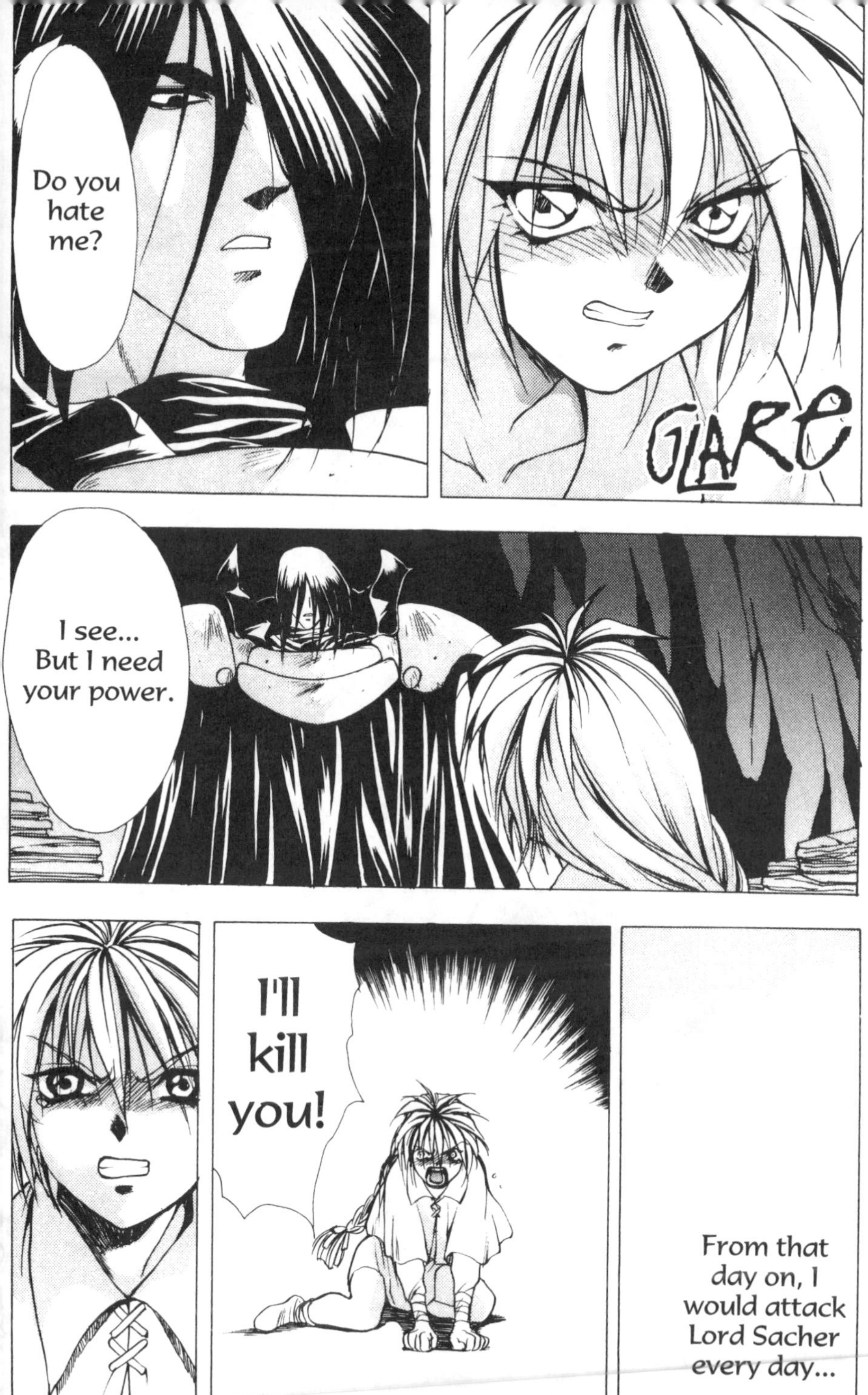
Do you hate me?
GLARE
I see... But I need your power.
I'll kill you!
From that day on, I would attack Lord Sacher every day...

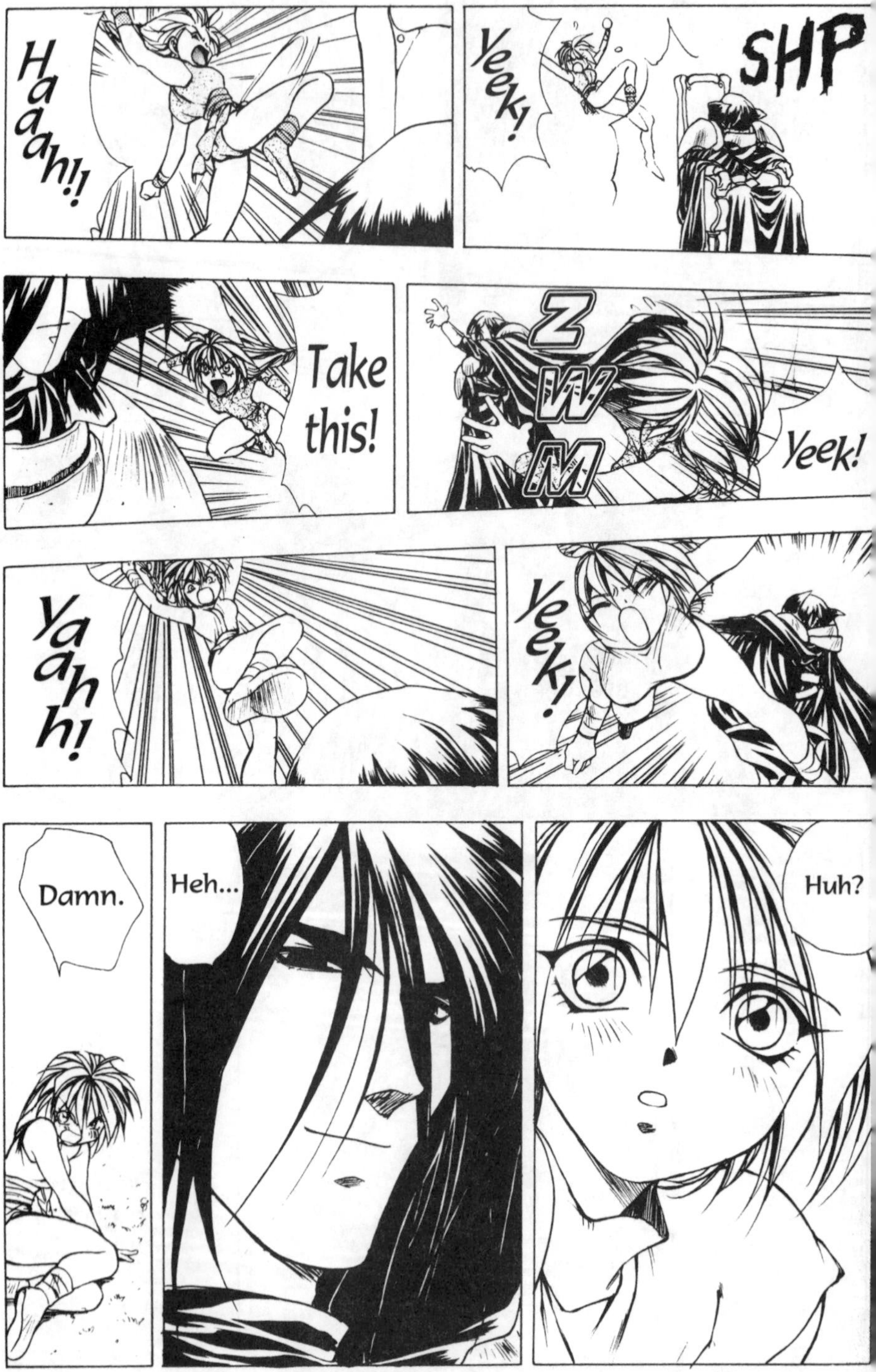
Haaaah!!
Yeek!
SHP
Take this!
ZWM
Yeek!
Yaahh!
Yeek!
Damn.
Heh...
Huh?

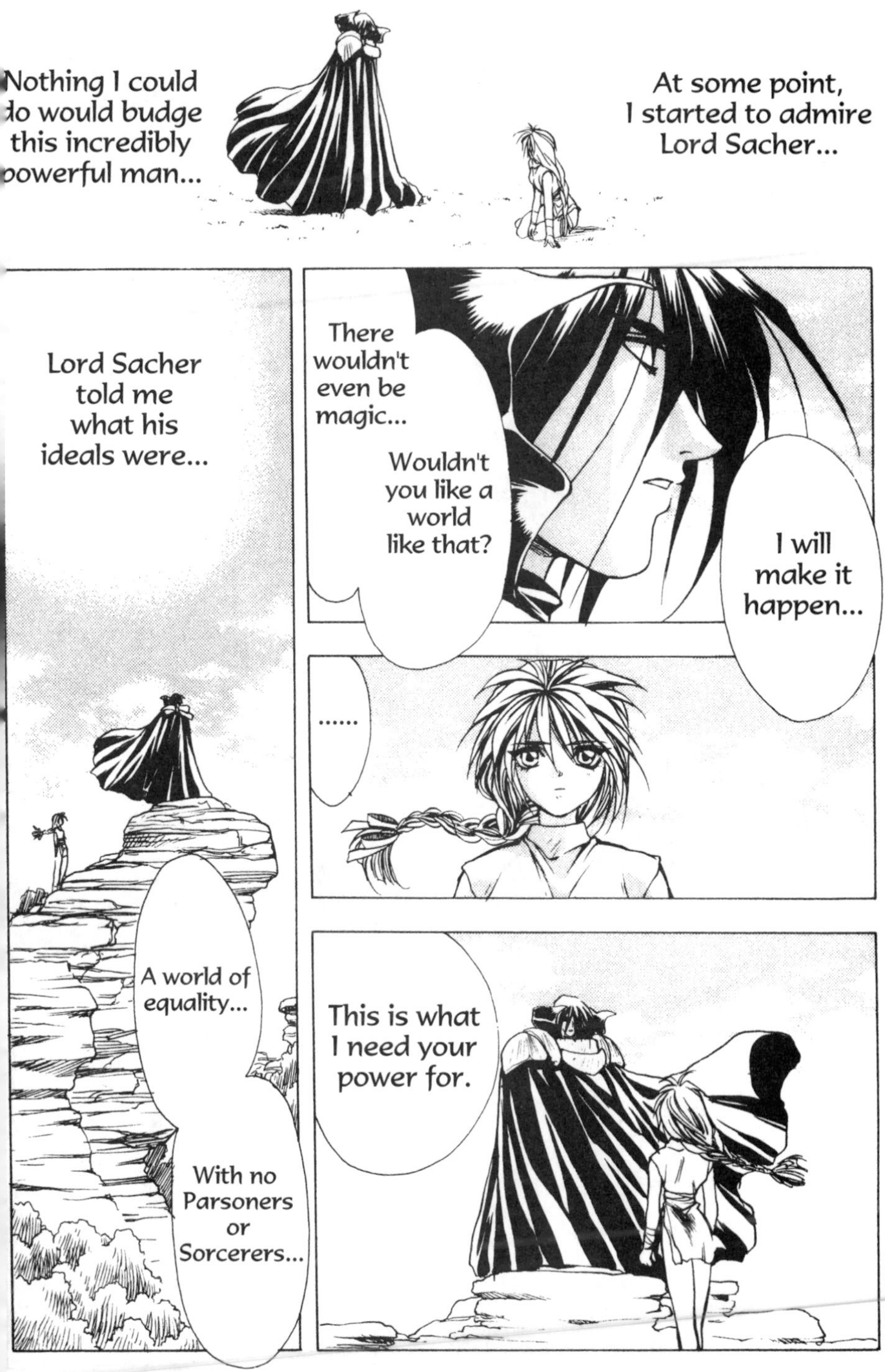
Nothing I could do would budge this incredibly powerful man...
At some point, I started to admire Lord Sacher...
Lord Sacher told me what his ideals were...
A world of equality...
With no Parsoners or Sorcerers...
There wouldn't even be magic...
Wouldn't you like a world like that?
I will make it happen...
......
This is what I need your power for.

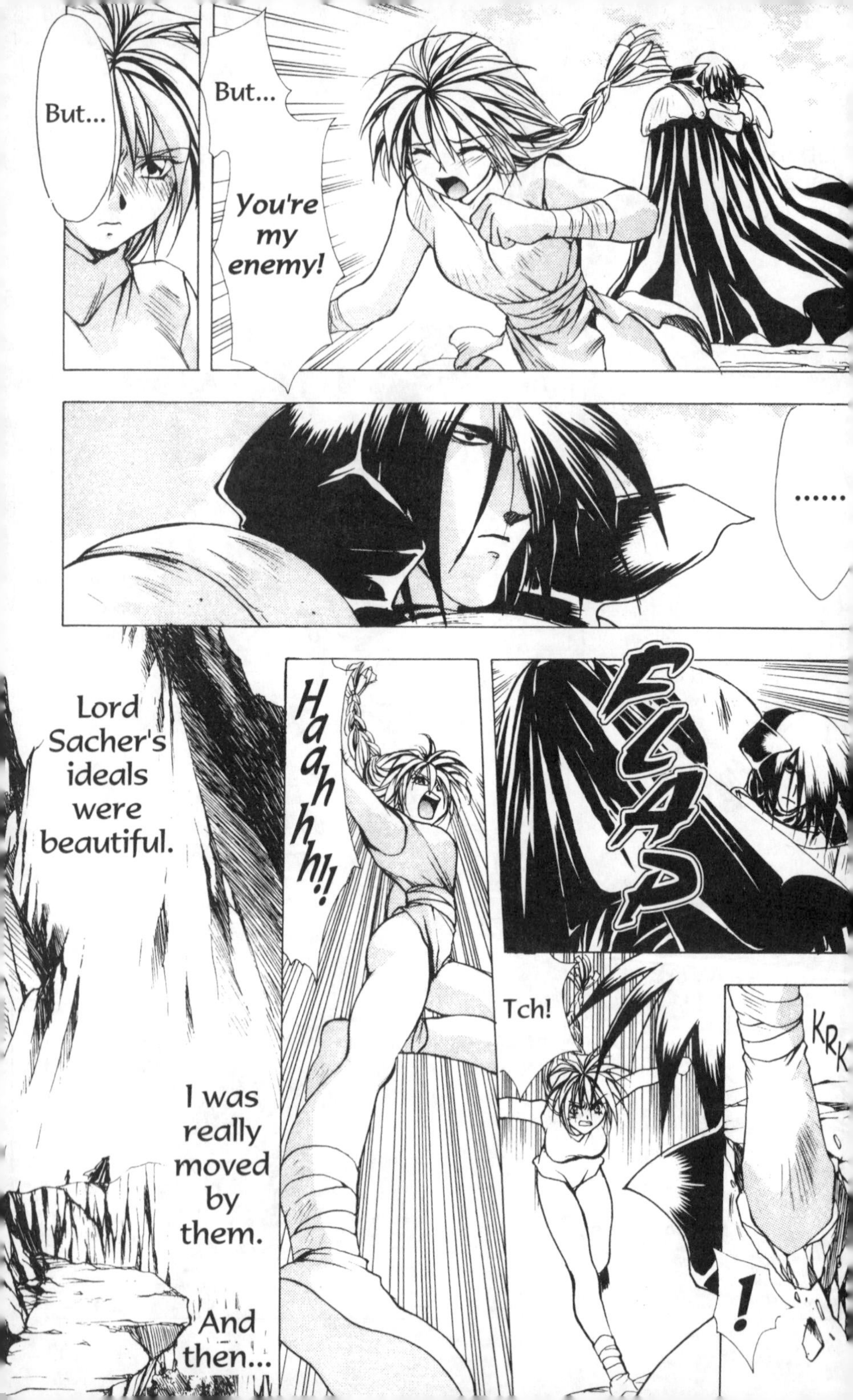
But...
But...
You're my enemy!
......
Lord Sacher's ideals were beautiful.
I was really moved by them.
And then...
Haaahhh!!
FLAP
Tch!
KRK
!

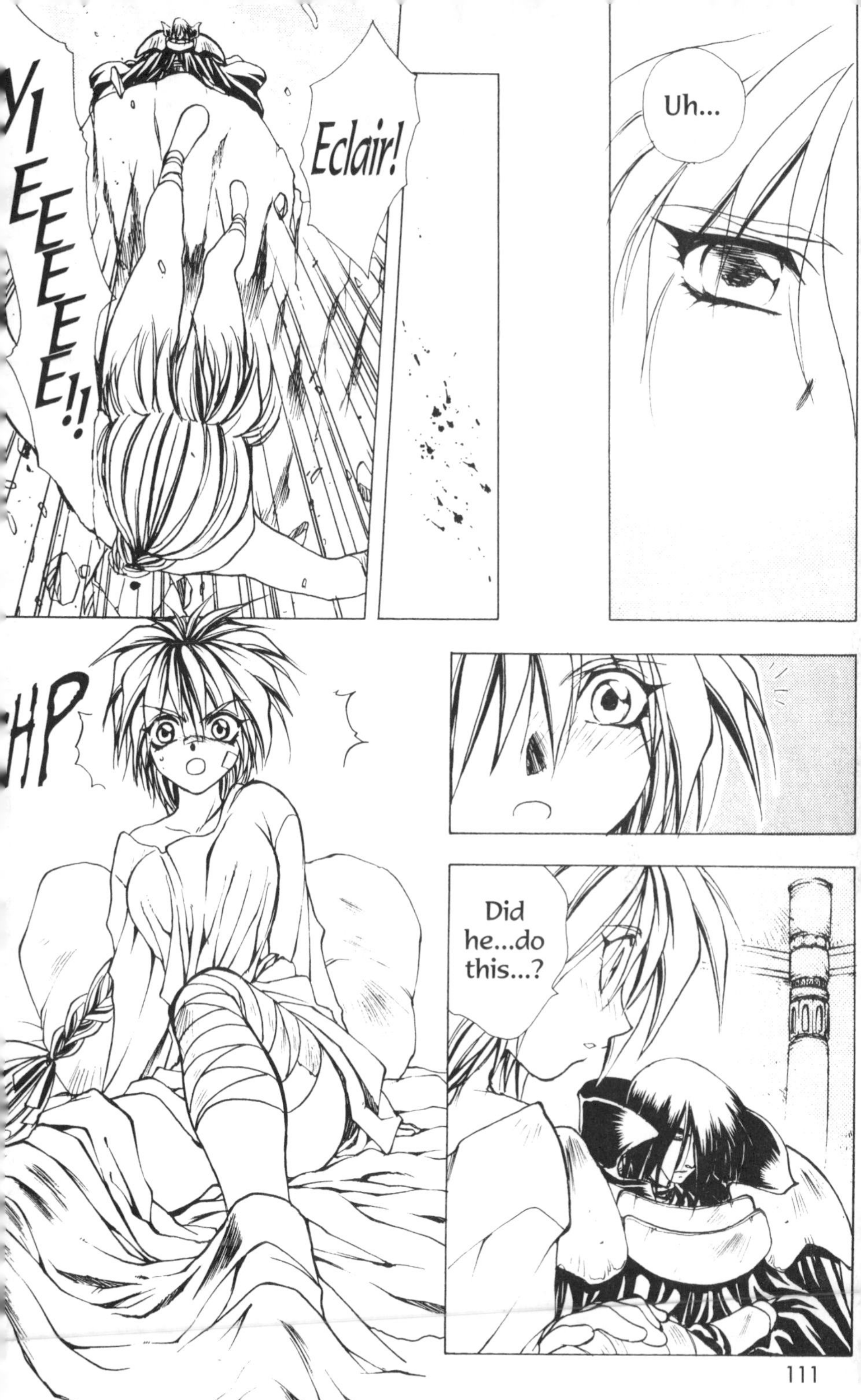
YIEEEEEE!!
Eclair!
Uh...
HP
Did he...do this...?

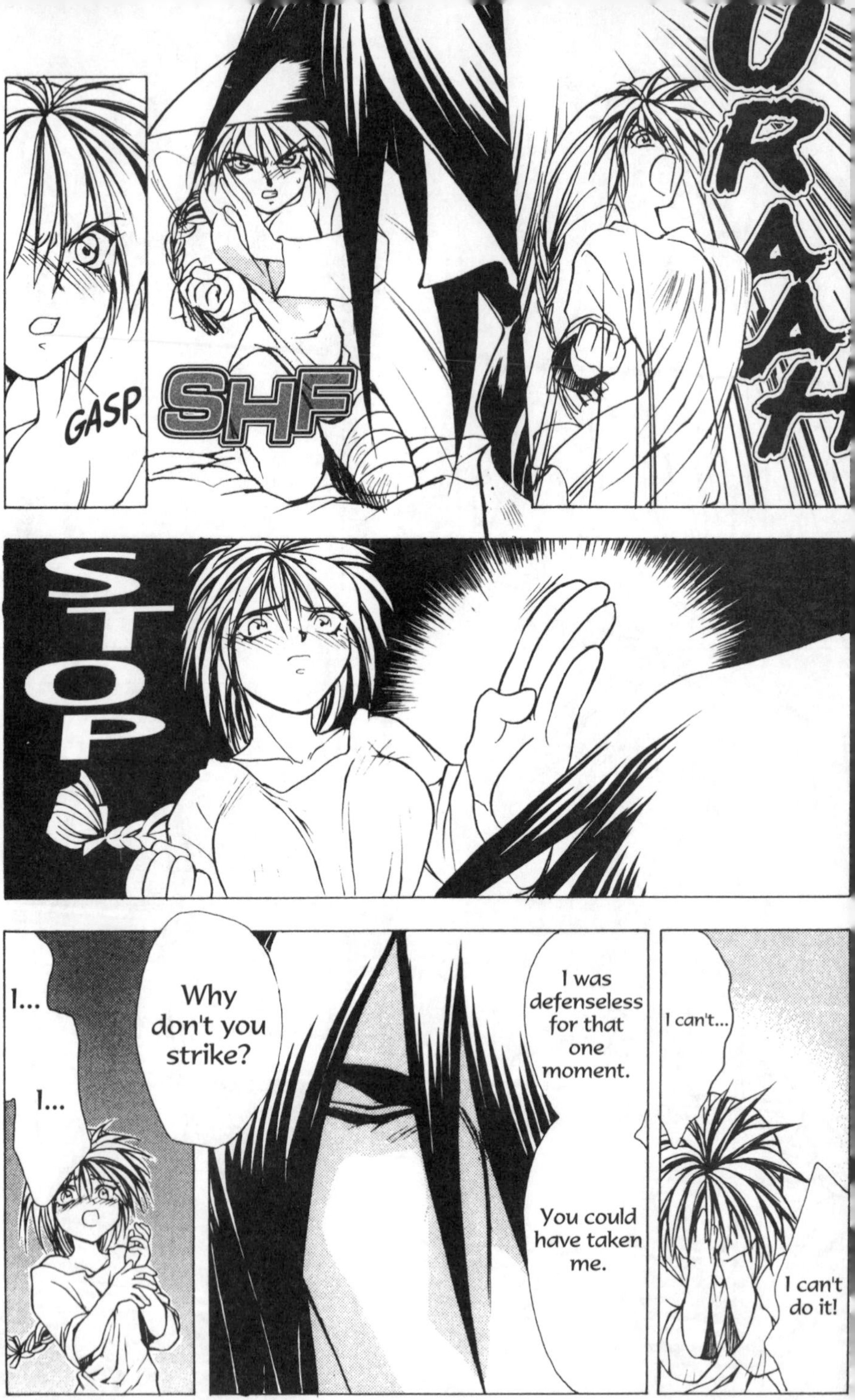
GASP
SHF
ORAH
STOP
I...
I...
Why don't you strike?
I was defenseless for that one moment.
You could have taken me.
I can't...
I can't do it!

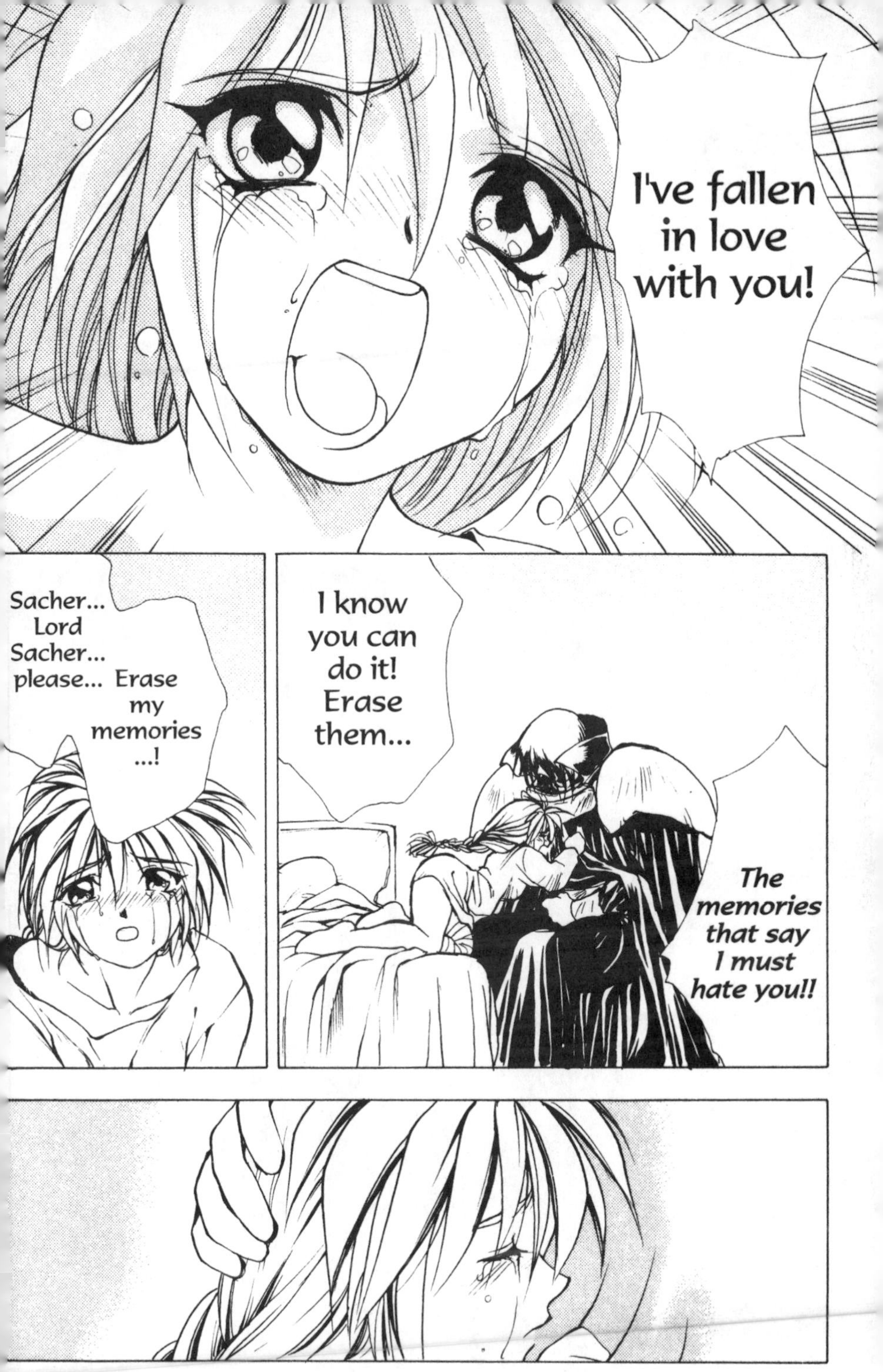
I've fallen in love with you!
Sacher... Lord Sacher... please... Erase my memories ...!
I know you can do it! Erase them...
The memories that say I must hate you!!

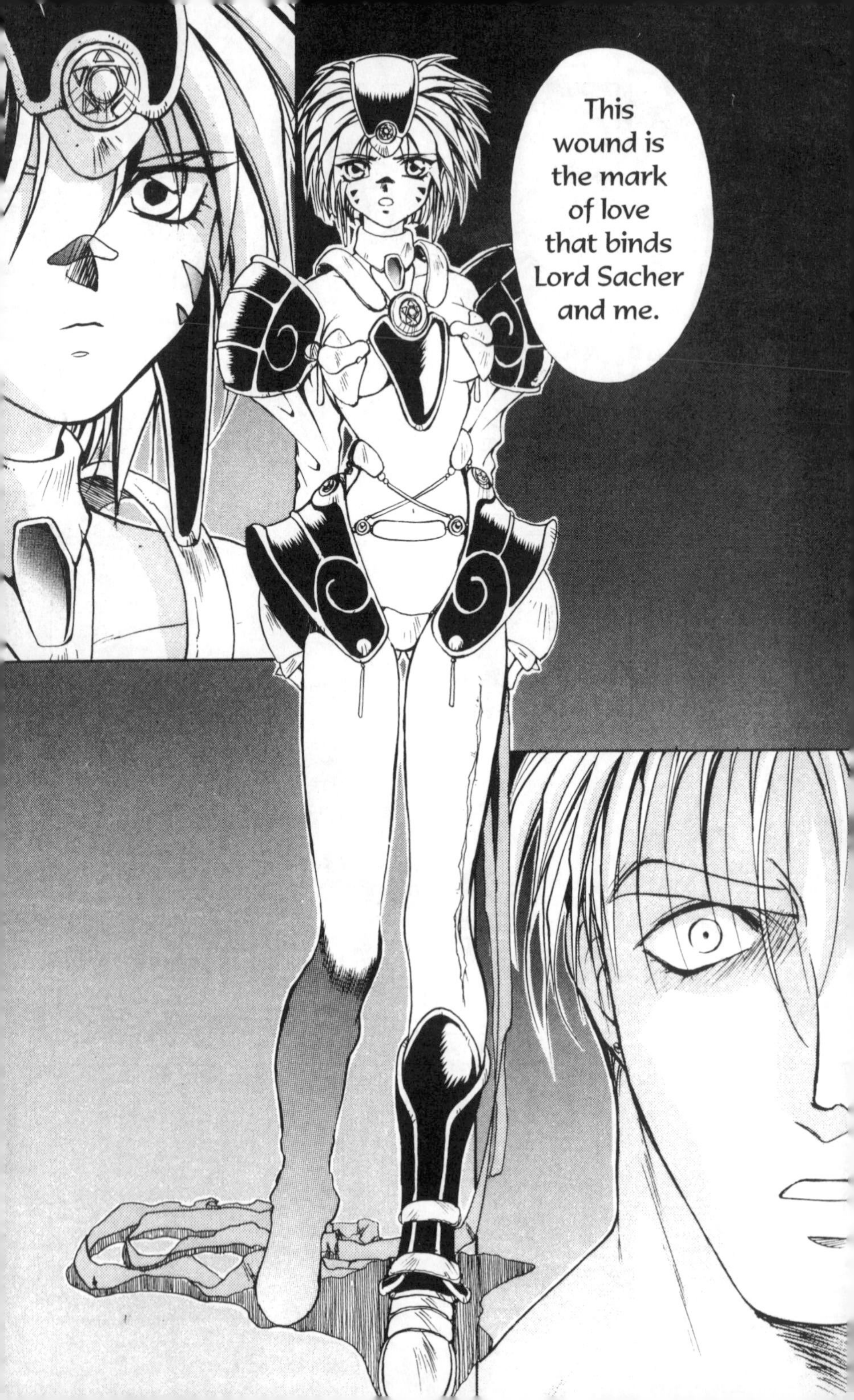
This wound is the mark of love that binds Lord Sacher and me.

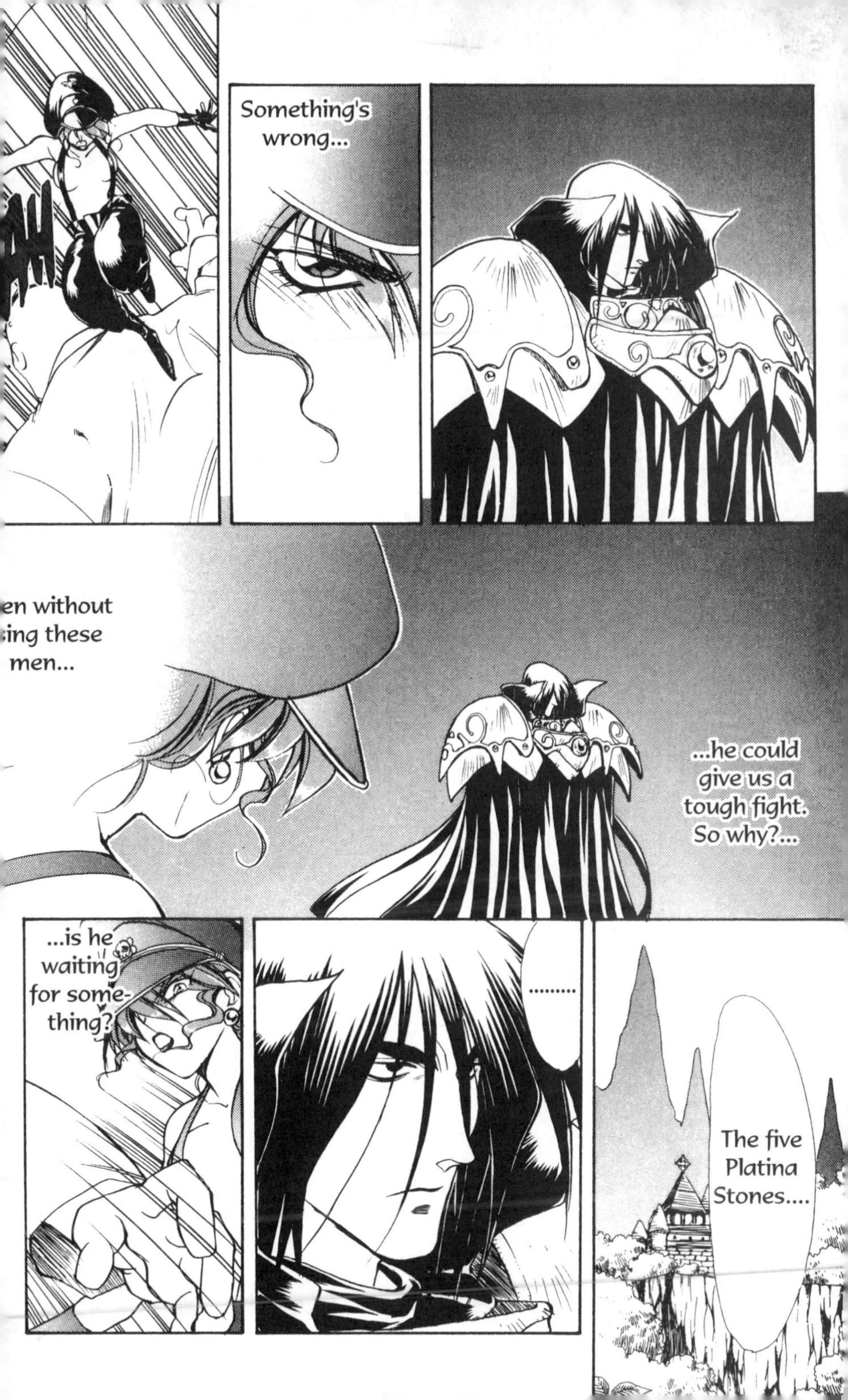
AH
Something's wrong...
en without
ing these
men...
...he could give us a tough fight. So why?...
...is he waiting for some-thing?
....
The five Platina Stones....

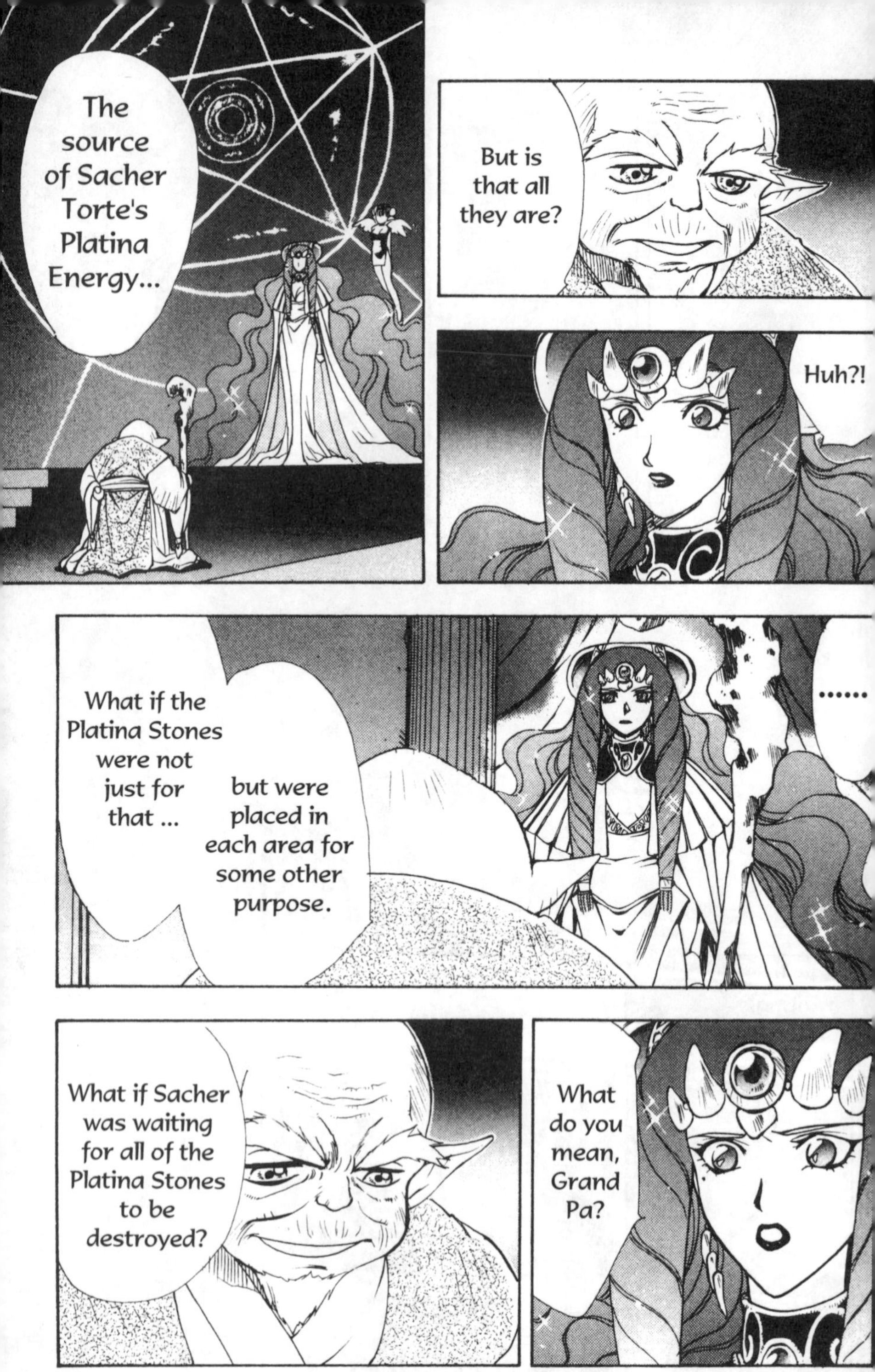

The source of Sacher Torte's Platina Energy...
But is that all they are?
Huh?!
What if the Platina Stones were not just for that ...
but were placed in each area for some other purpose.
......
What if Sacher was waiting for all of the Platina Stones to be destroyed?
What do you mean, Grand Pa?

We were careless.

This world is brimming with magic energy that no longer has a place to go.

The Streams of Magic that traverse the world

have recently been disrupted.

Erk?!

It started when Carrot and the others started destroying the Platina Stones.

......

117

They must have been controlling the Platina Stones

and the Streams of Magic.

But that's where Carrot and the gang are!

......

As each of the Platina Stones were destroyed, the Streams lost control. Now they are all heading toward the last Platina Stone.

When the last Platina Stone is destroyed...

All of the Streams of Magic will collide... then...

Oh no!

My children...!

118

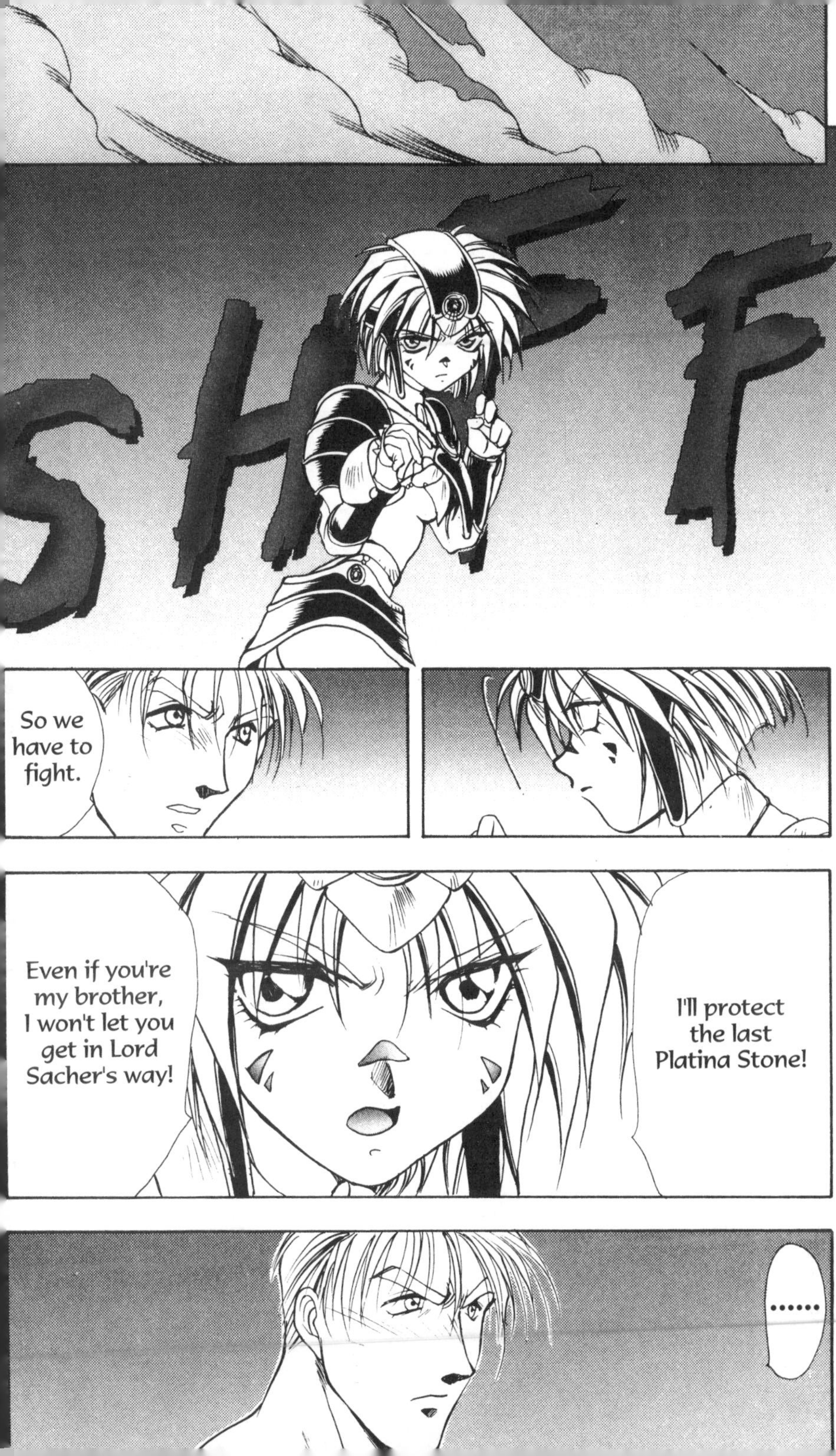
SHFF
So we have to fight.
Even if you're my brother, I won't let you get in Lord Sacher's way!
I'll protect the last Platina Stone!
......

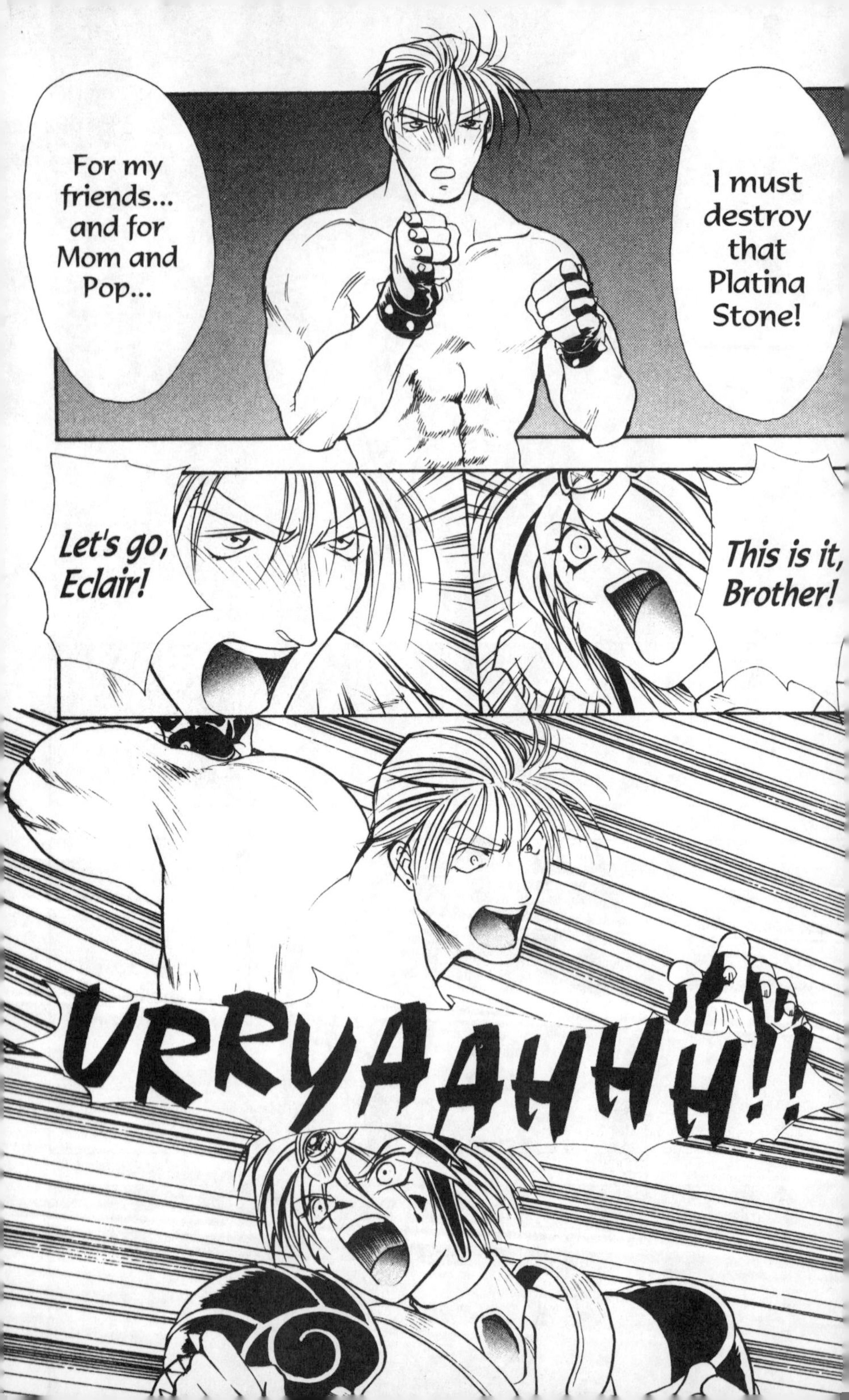
For my friends... and for Mom and Pop...
I must destroy that Platina Stone!
Let's go, Eclair!
This is it, Brother!
URRYAAHHH!!

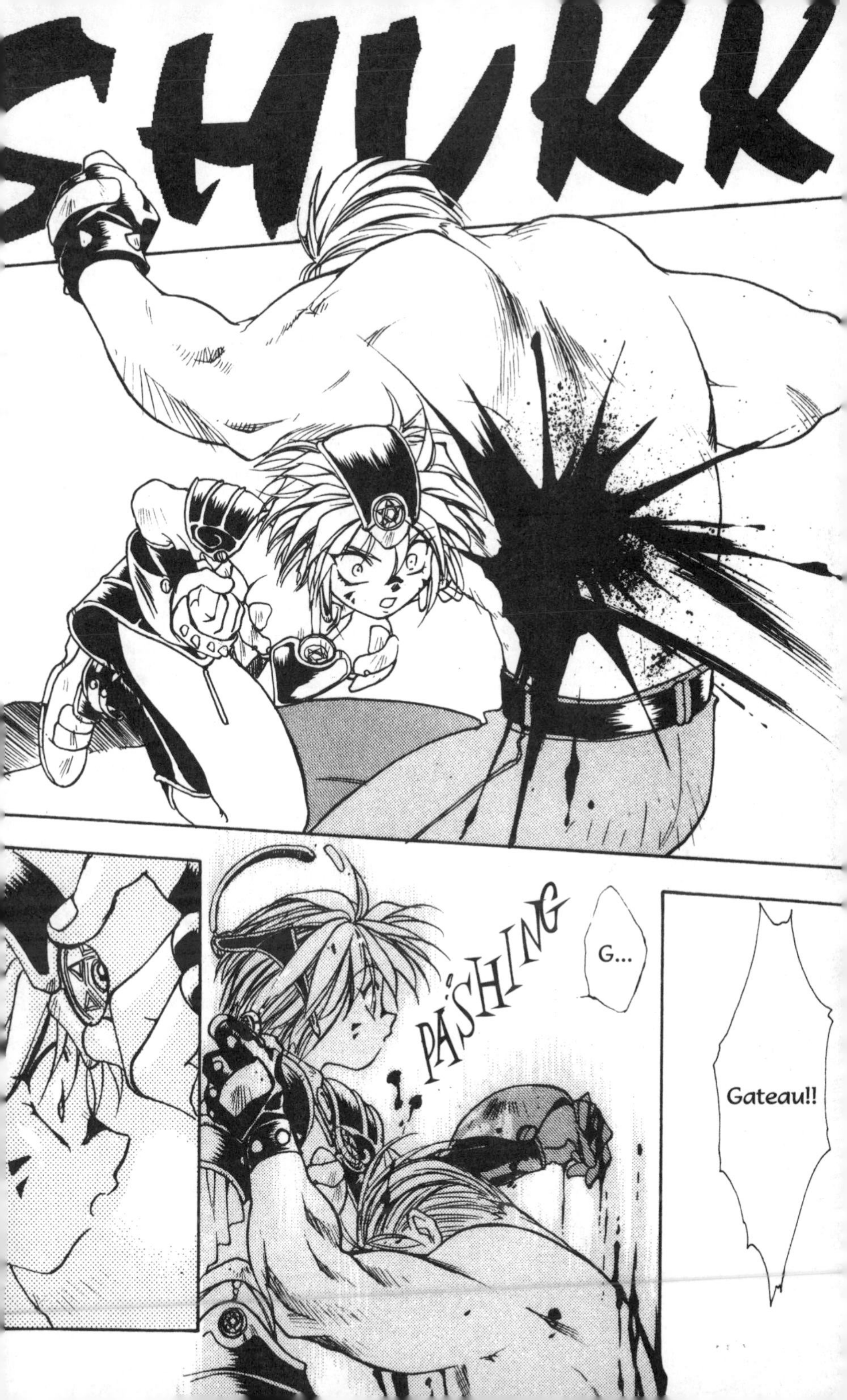
SHUKK
PASHING
G...
Gateau!!

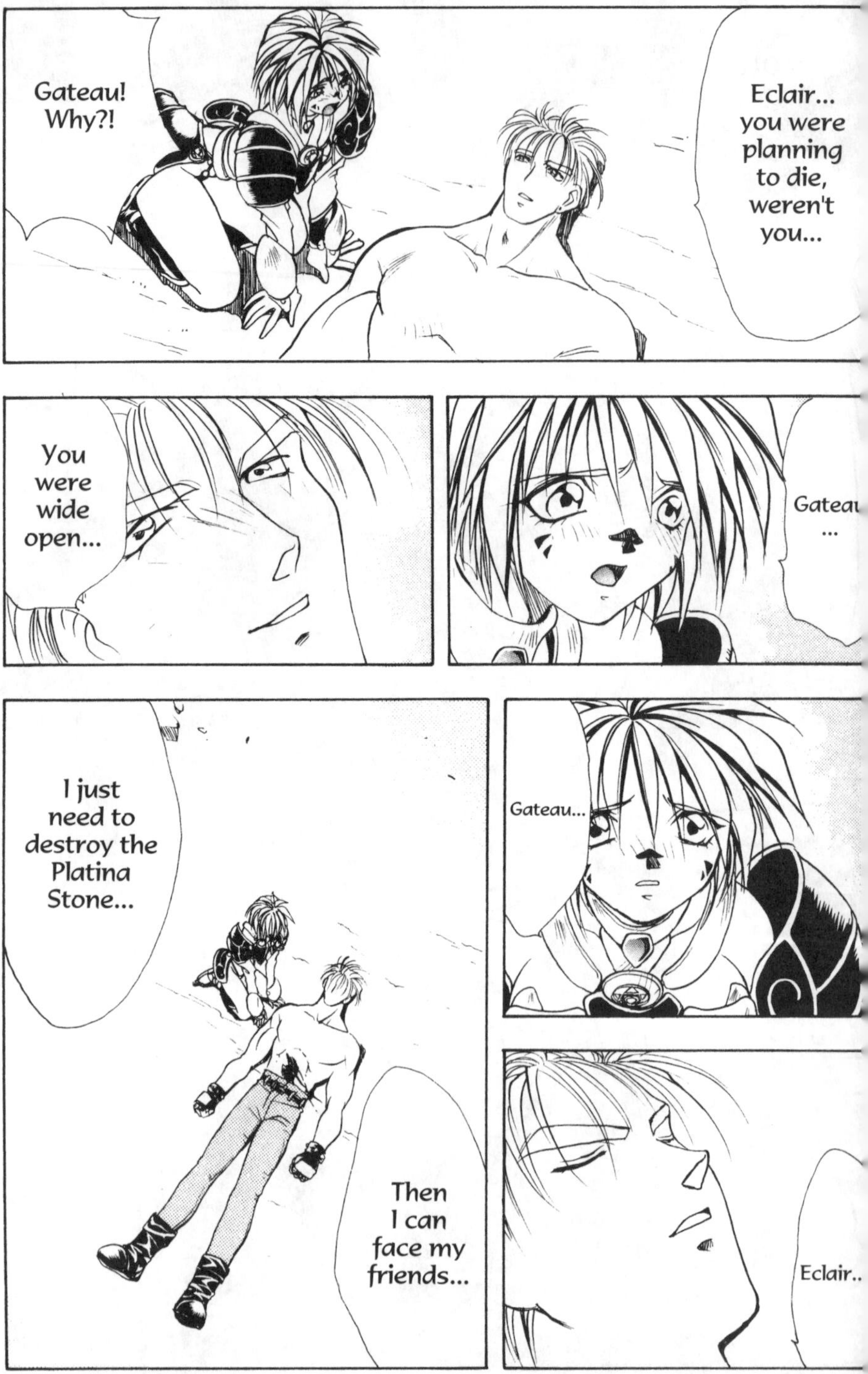
Gateau! Why?!
Eclair... you were planning to die, weren't you...
You were wide open...
Gateau ...
I just need to destroy the Platina Stone...
Gateau...
Then I can face my friends...
Eclair..

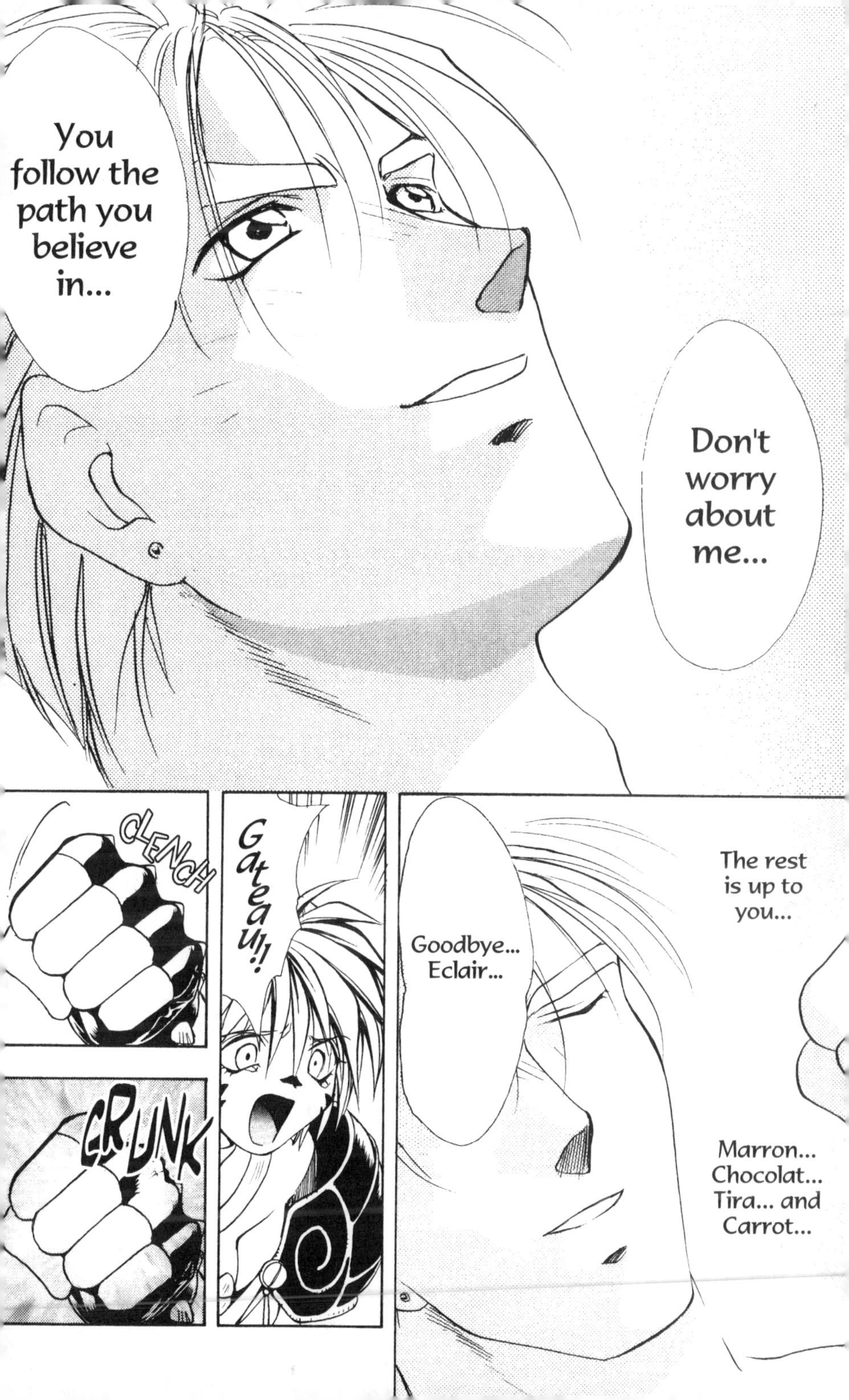
You follow the path you believe in...
Don't worry about me...
CLENCH
CRUNK
Gateau!!
Goodbye... Eclair...
The rest is up to you...
Marron... Chocolat... Tira... and Carrot...

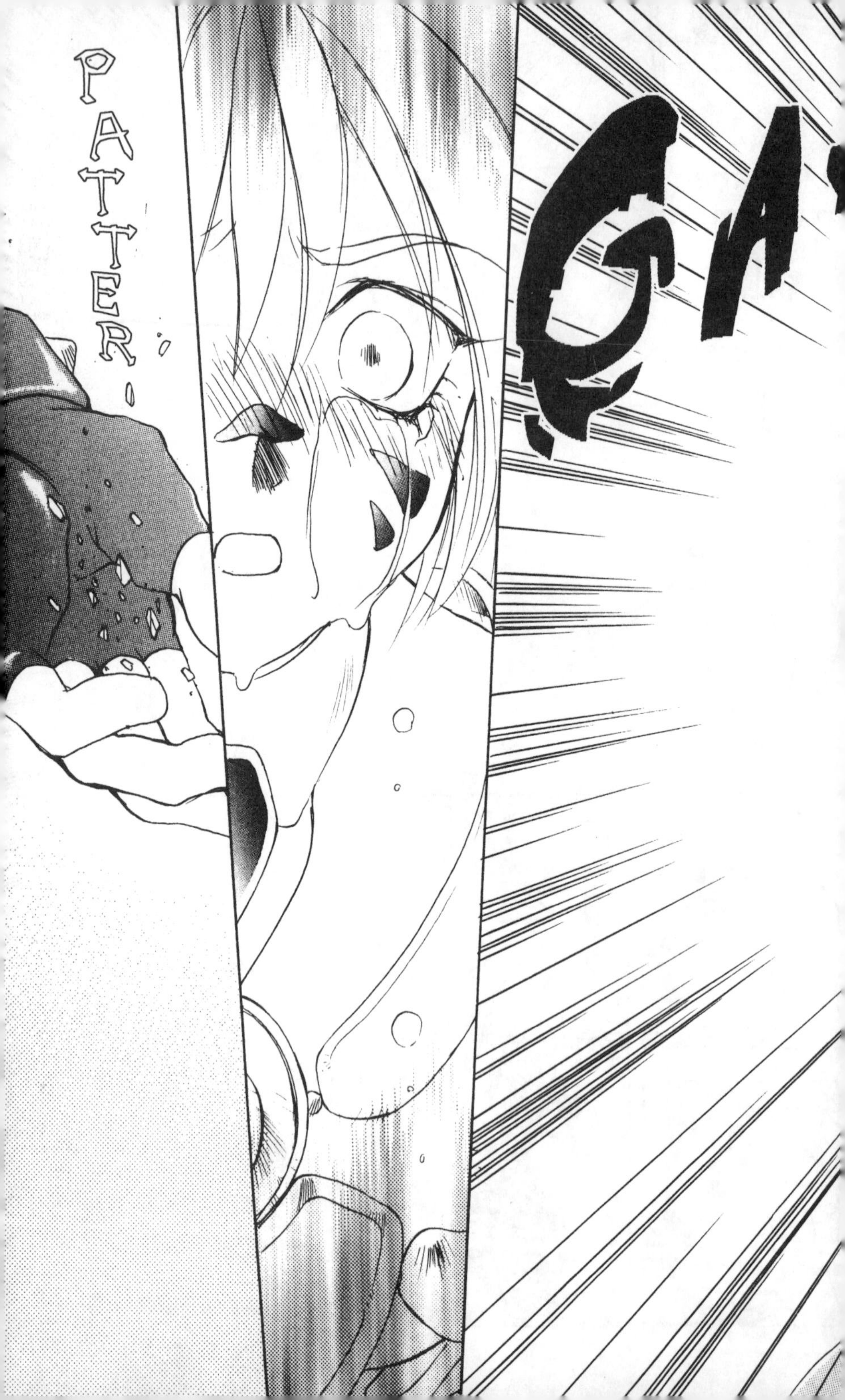
PATTER
GA

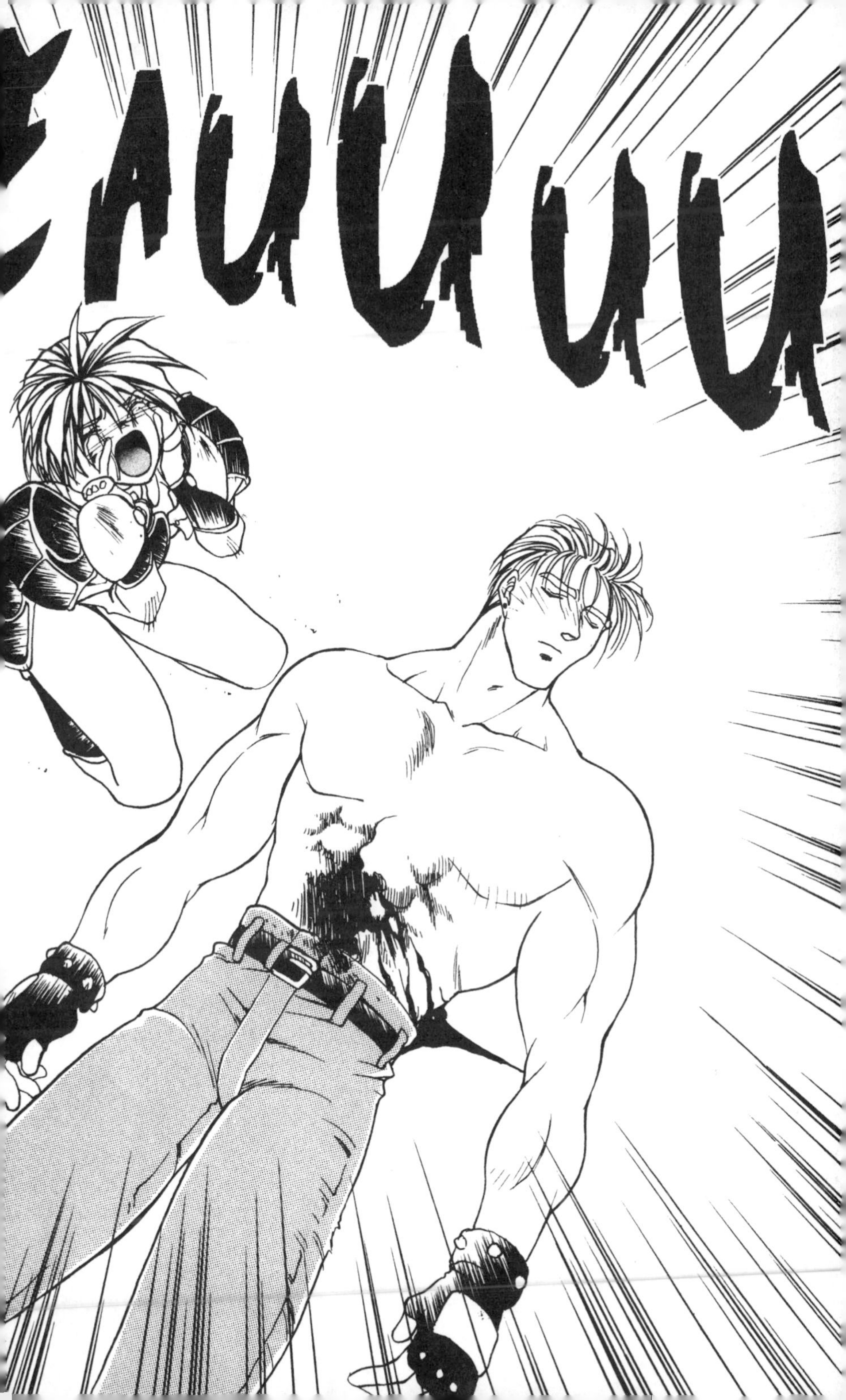
EAUUUUU

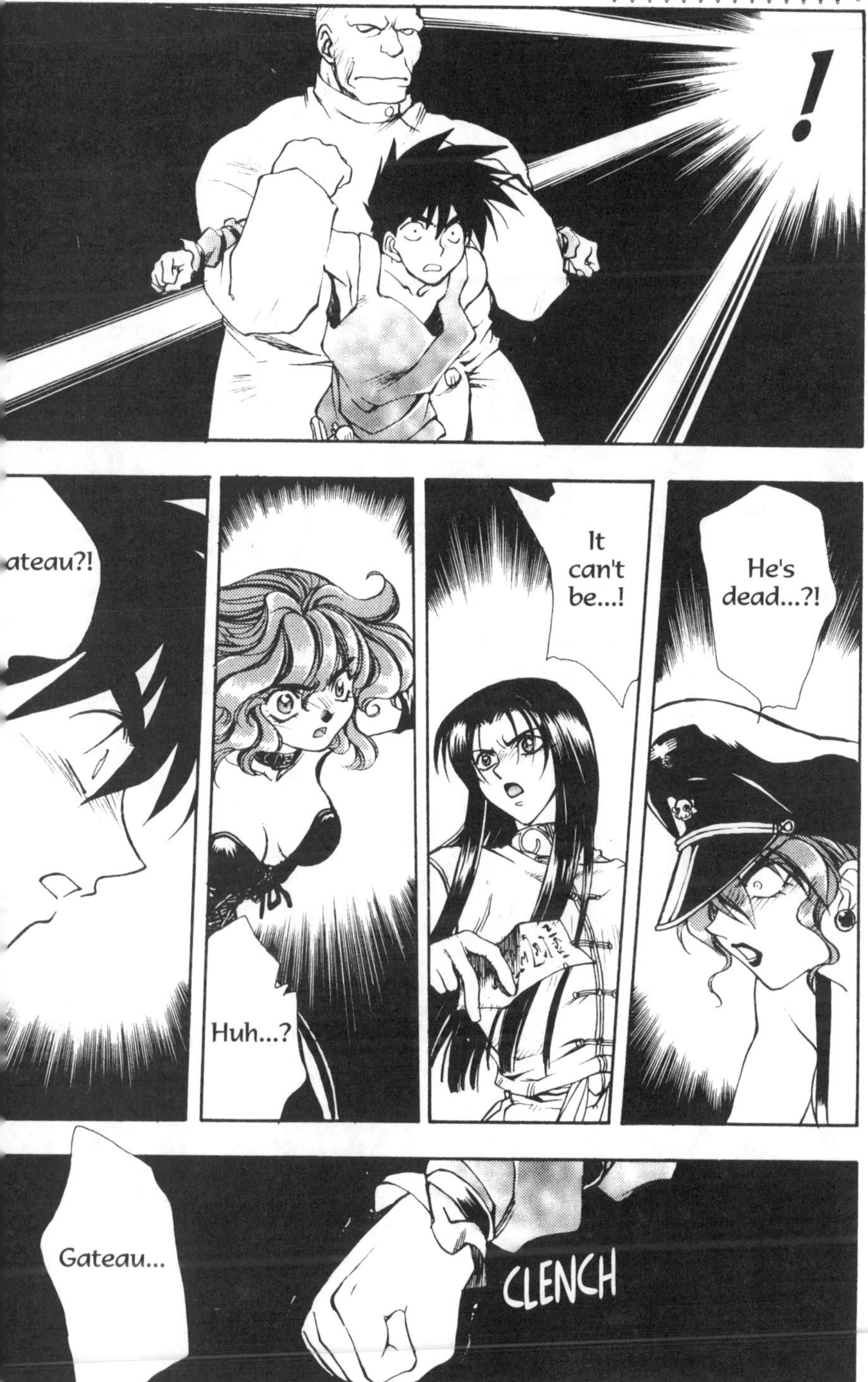
!
ateau?!
Huh...?
It can't be...!
He's dead...?!
Gateau...
CLENCH

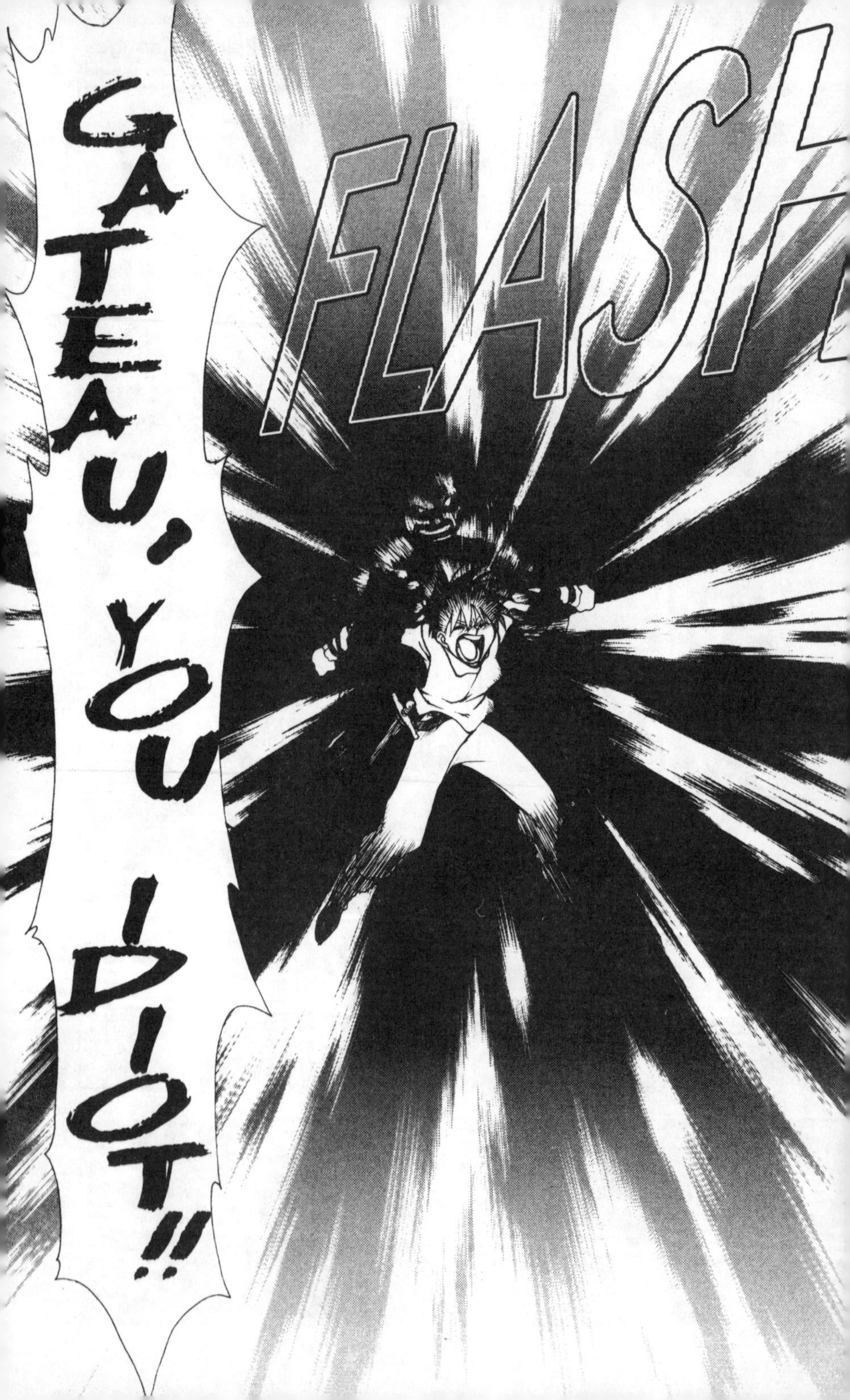
GATEAU, YOU IDIOT!!
FLASH

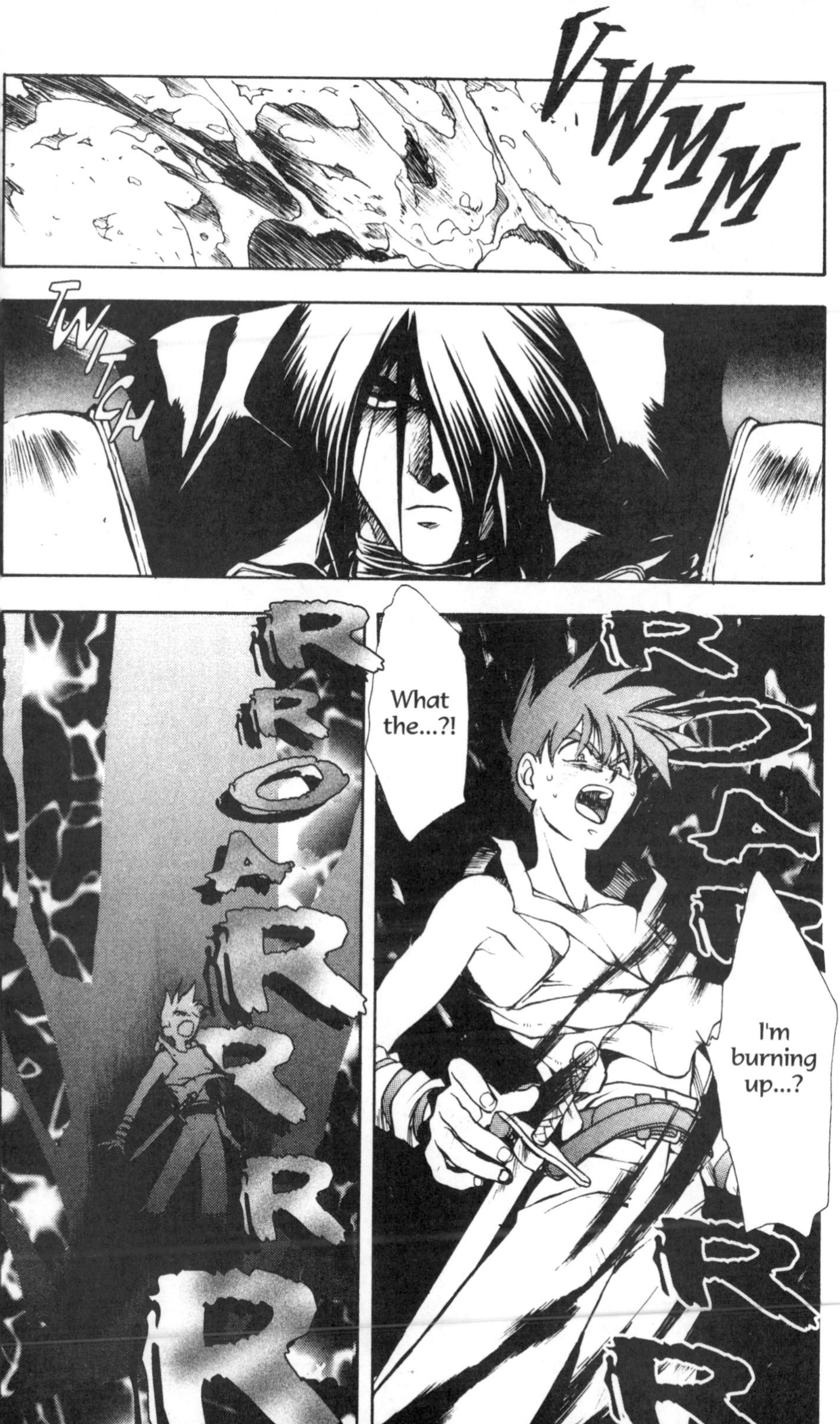

VWMM
TWITCH
RROARRRR
What the...?!
ROARRRR
I'm burning up...?

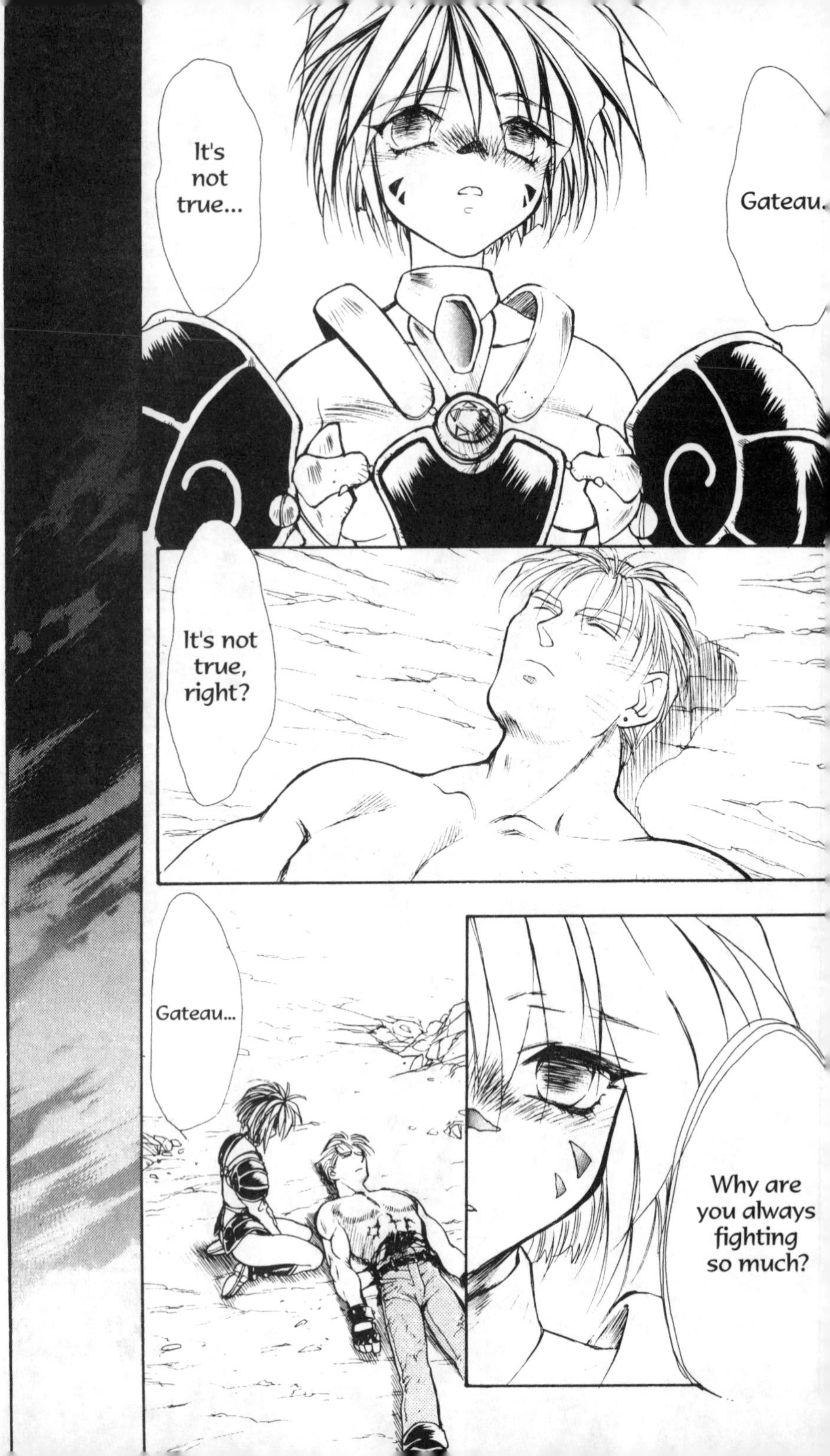
It's not true...
Gateau.
It's not true, right?
Gateau...
Why are you always fighting so much?

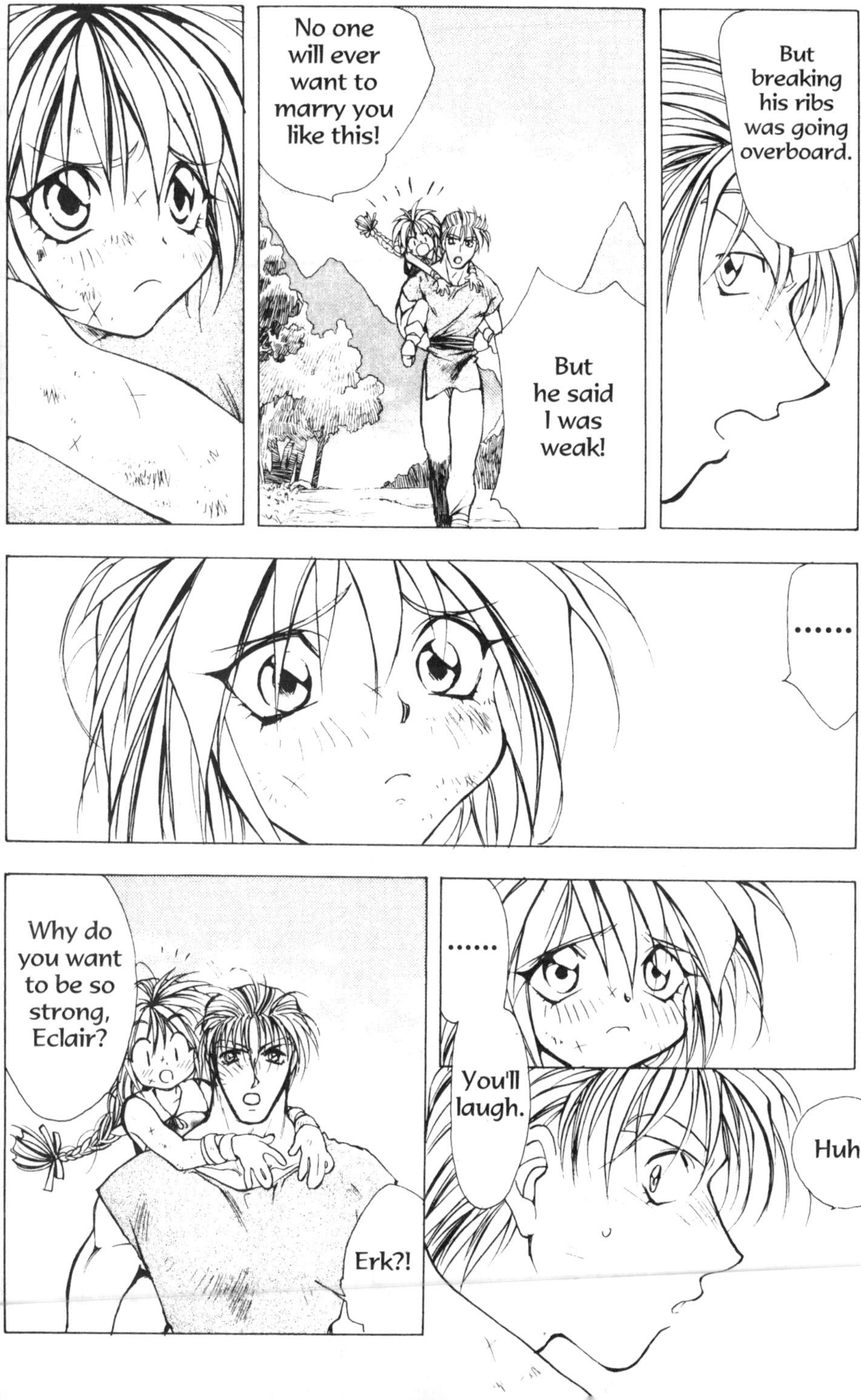
No one will ever want to marry you like this!
But he said I was weak!
But breaking his ribs was going overboard.
......
Why do you want to be so strong, Eclair?
Erk?!
......
You'll laugh.
Huh?

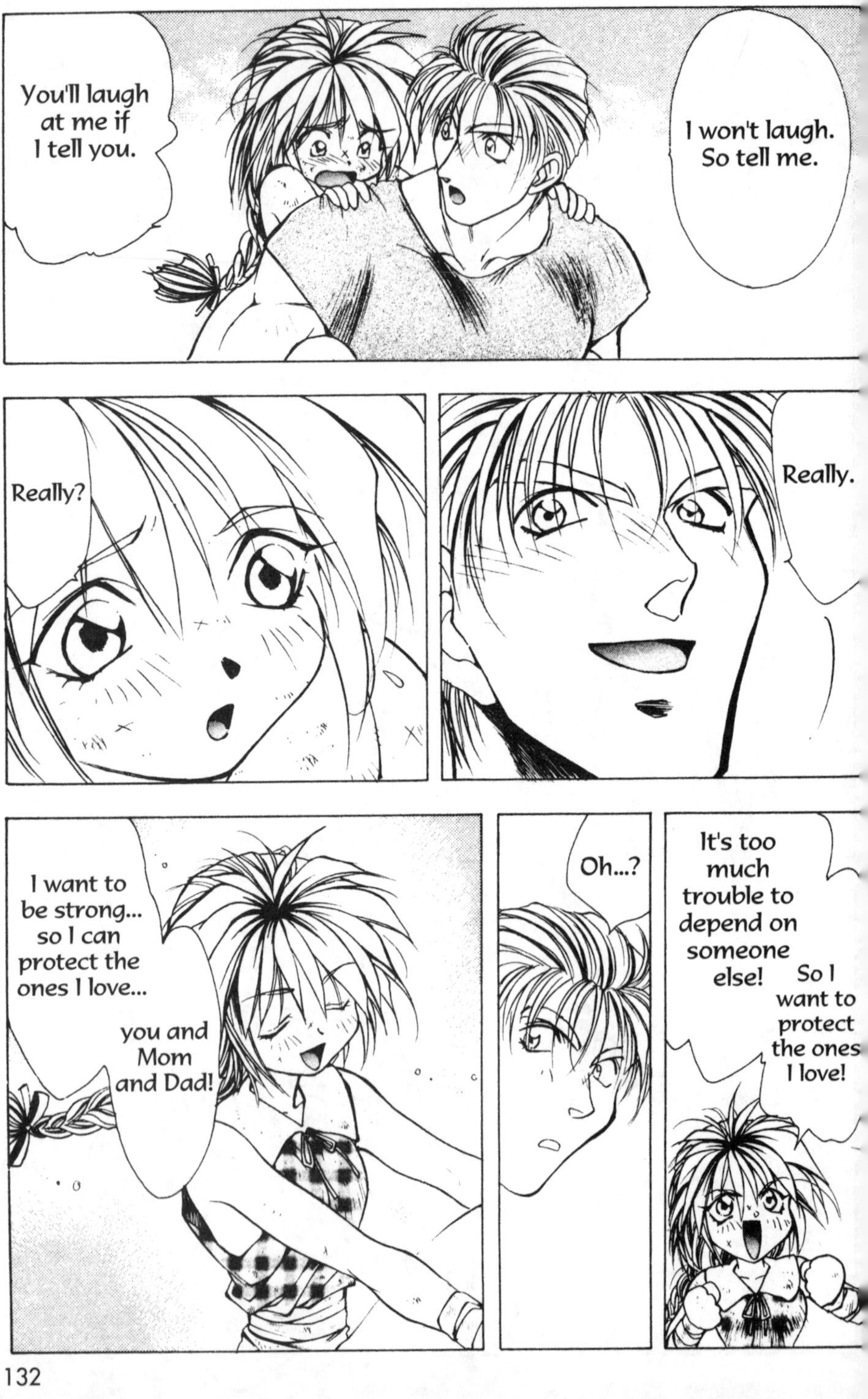
You'll laugh at me if I tell you.
I won't laugh. So tell me.
Really?
Really.
I want to be strong... so I can protect the ones I love...
you and Mom and Dad!
Oh...?
It's too much trouble to depend on someone else!
So I want to protect the ones I love!

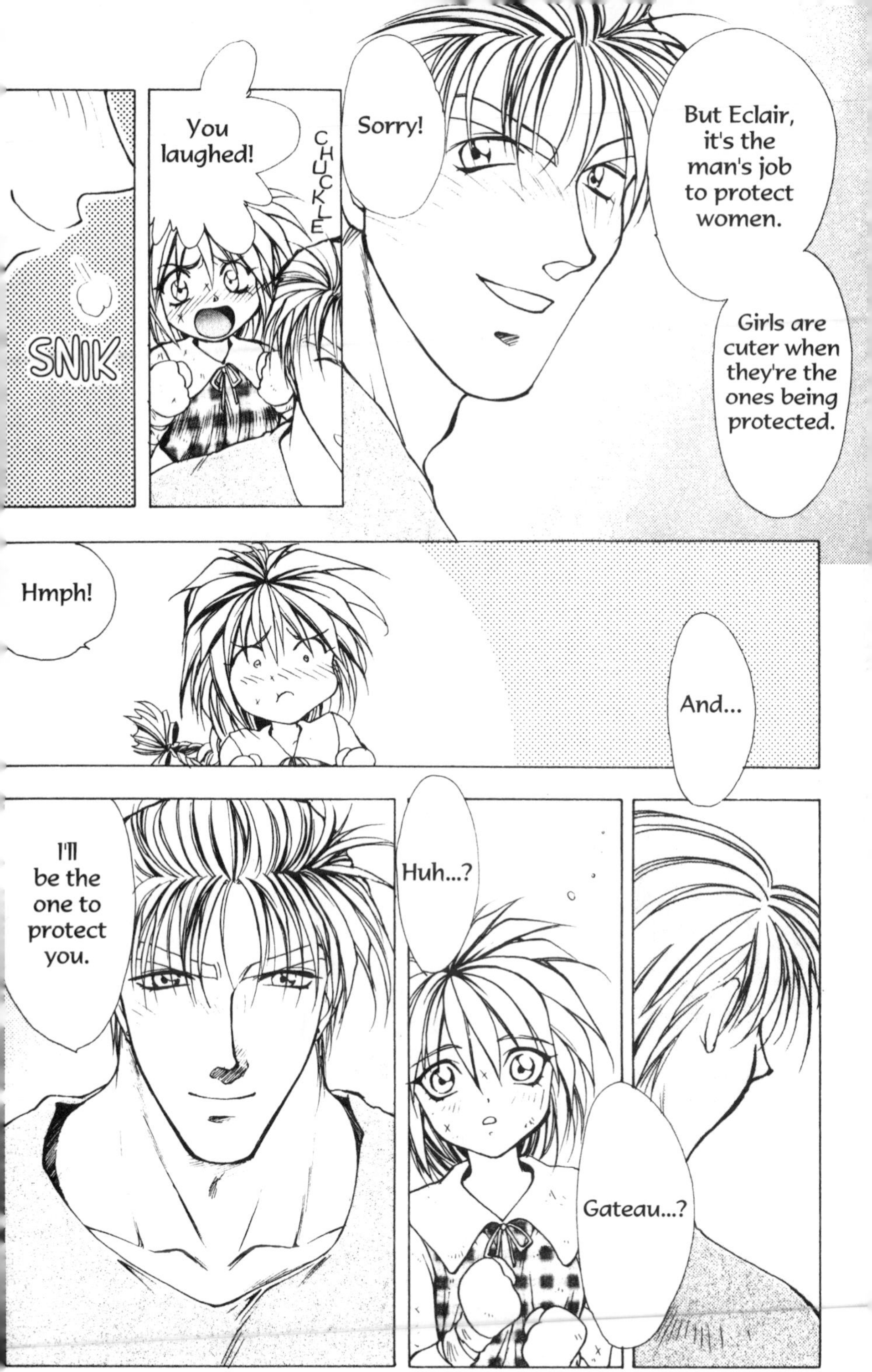
SNIK
You laughed!
CHUCKLE
Sorry!
But Eclair, it's the man's job to protect women.
Girls are cuter when they're the ones being protected.
Hmph!
And...
I'll be the one to protect you.
Huh...?
Gateau...?

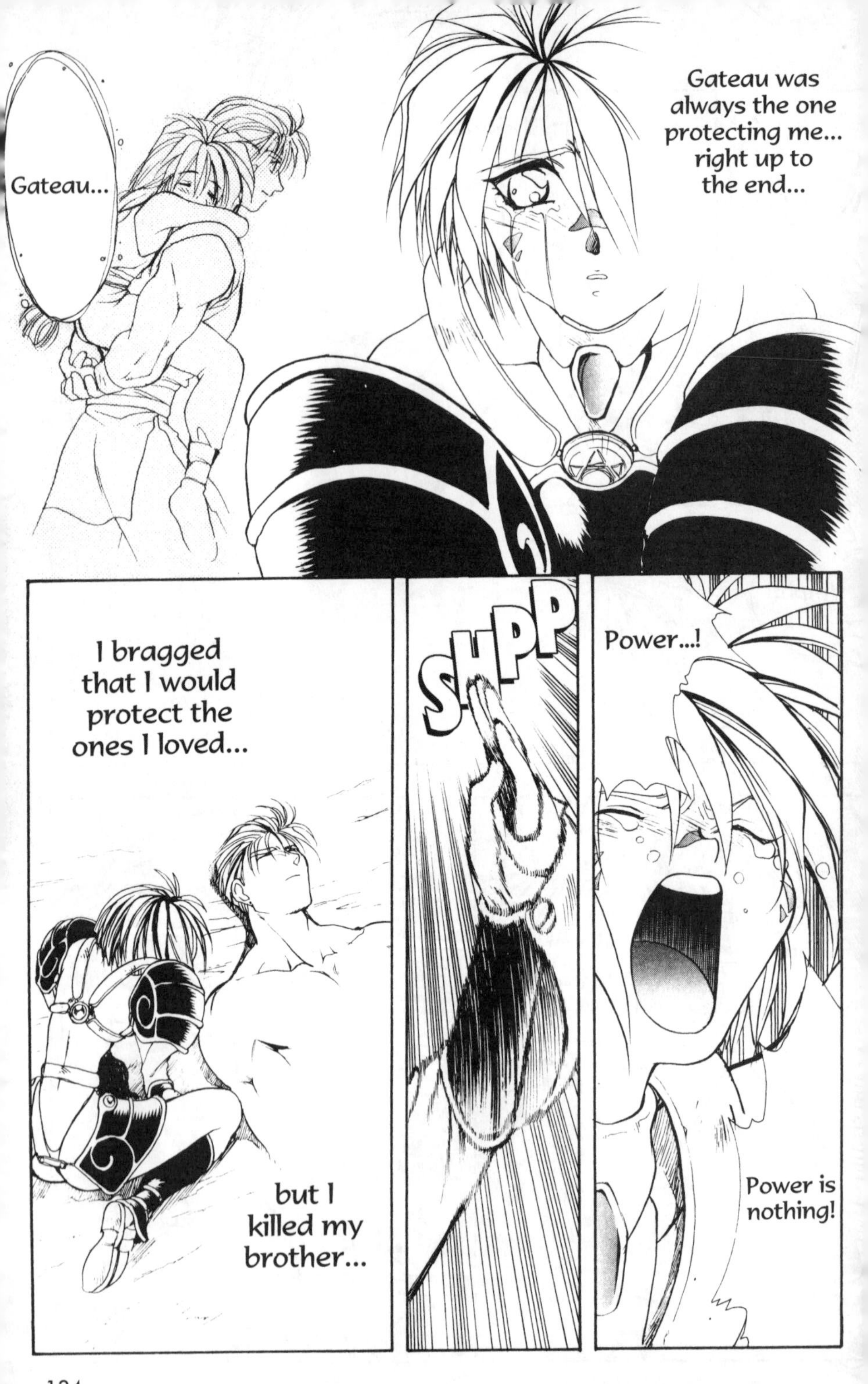
Gateau...
Gateau was always the one protecting me... right up to the end...
I bragged that I would protect the ones I loved...
but I killed my brother...
SHPP
Power...!
Power is nothing!

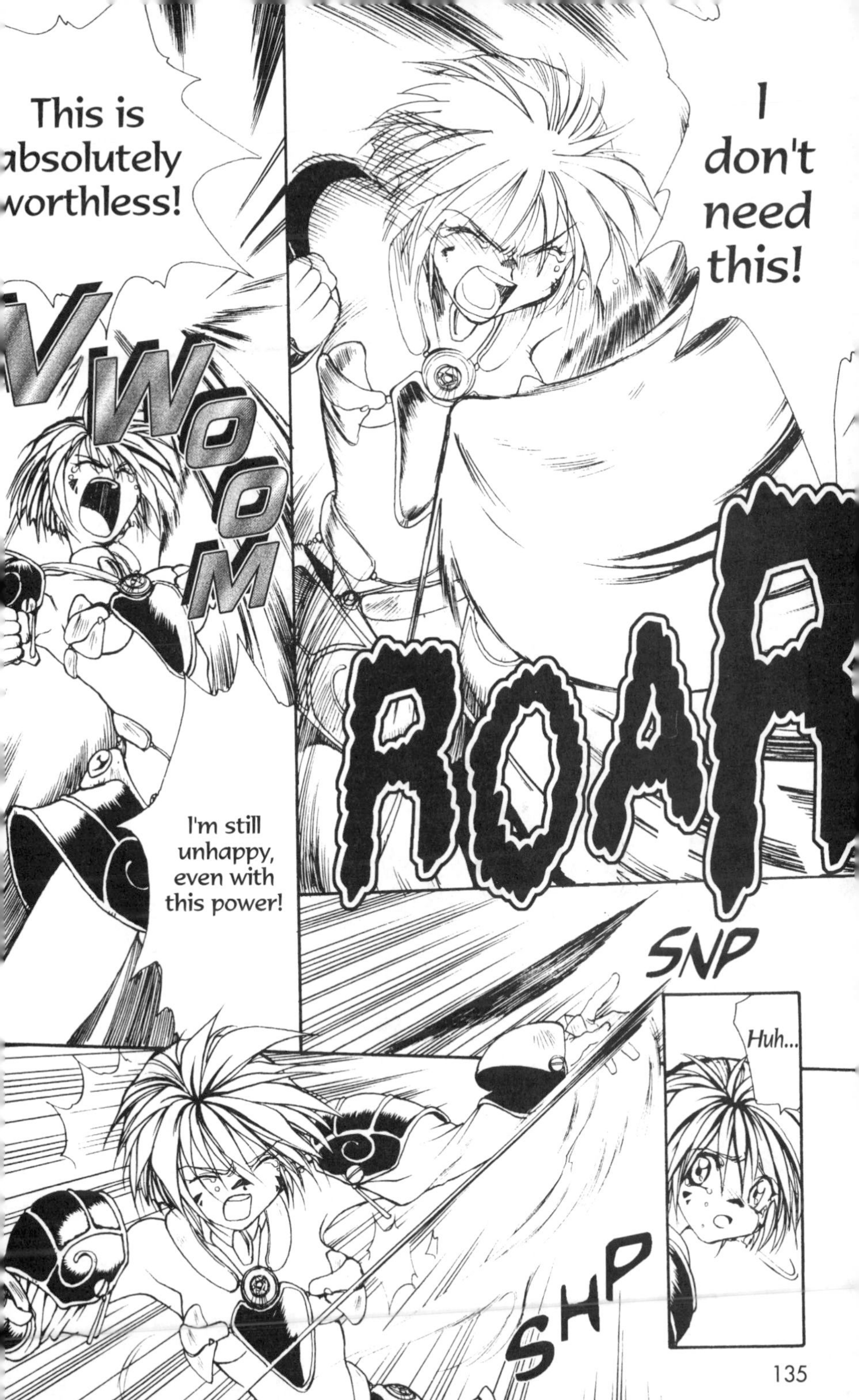

This is absolutely worthless!
VWOOM
I'm still unhappy, even with this power!
I don't need this!
ROAR
SNP
SHP
Huh...

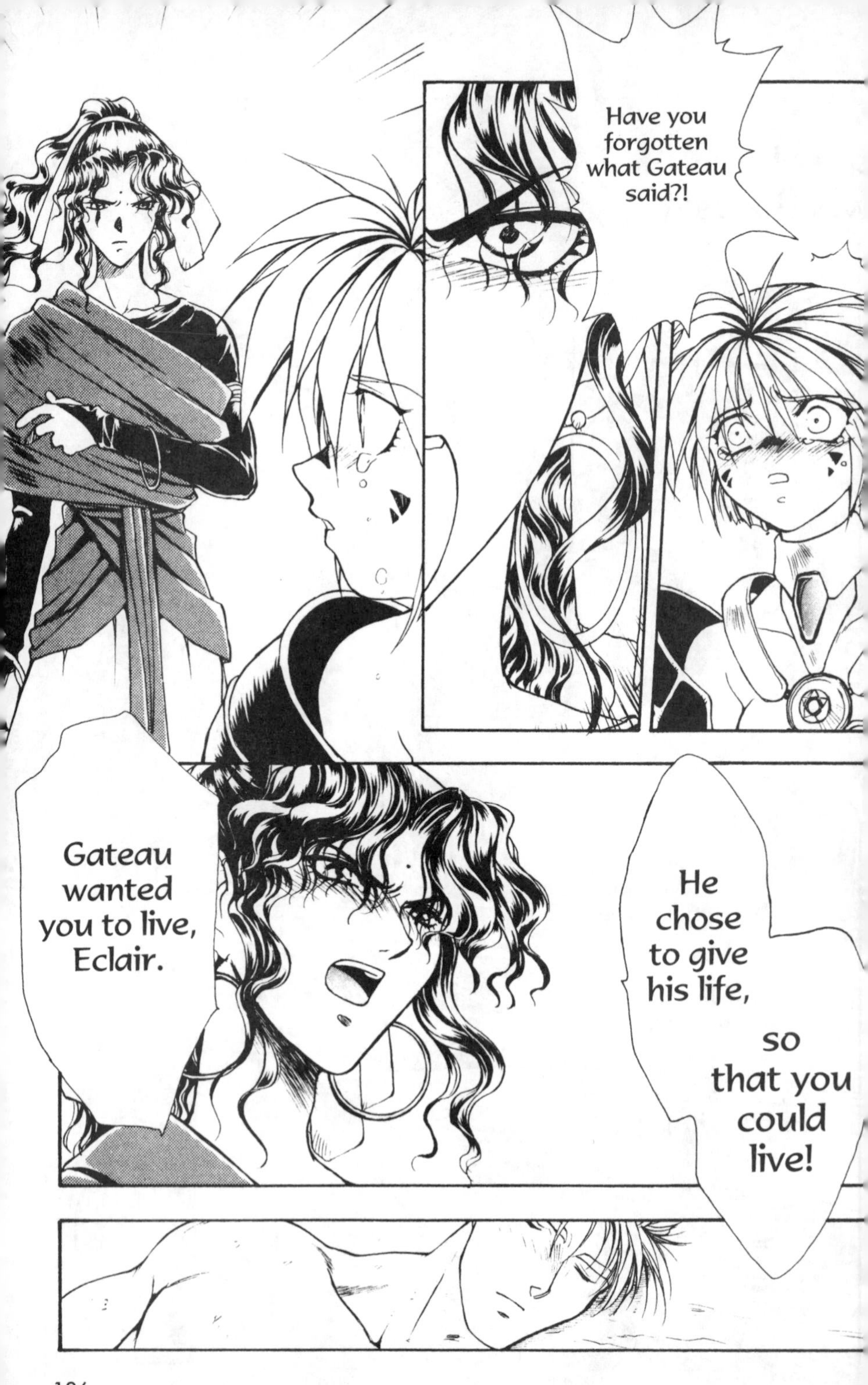
Have you forgotten what Gateau said?!
Gateau wanted you to live, Eclair.
He chose to give his life,
so that you could live!

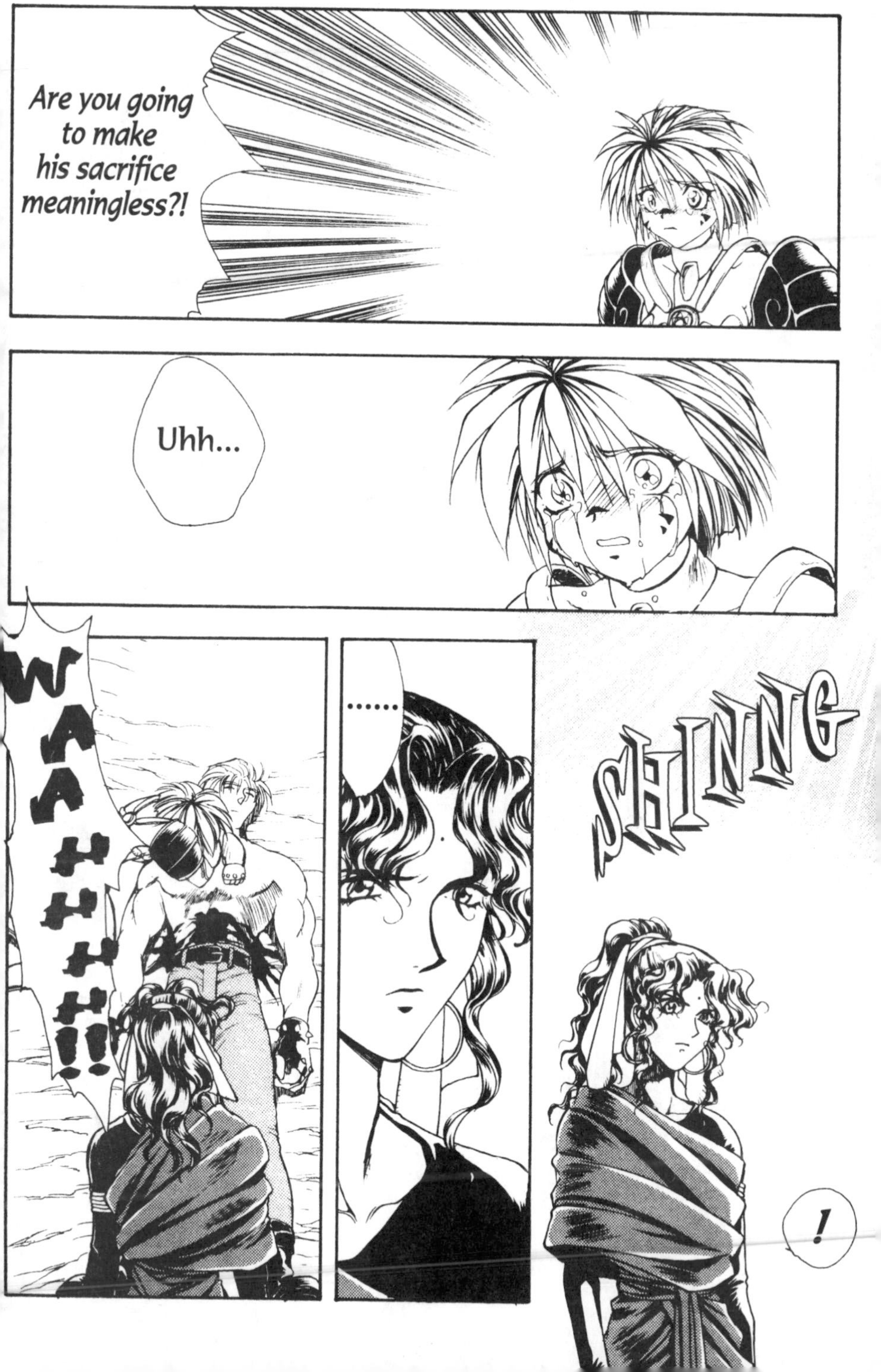

Are you going to make his sacrifice meaningless?!
Uhh...
WAAHHHH!!!
......
SHINNG
!

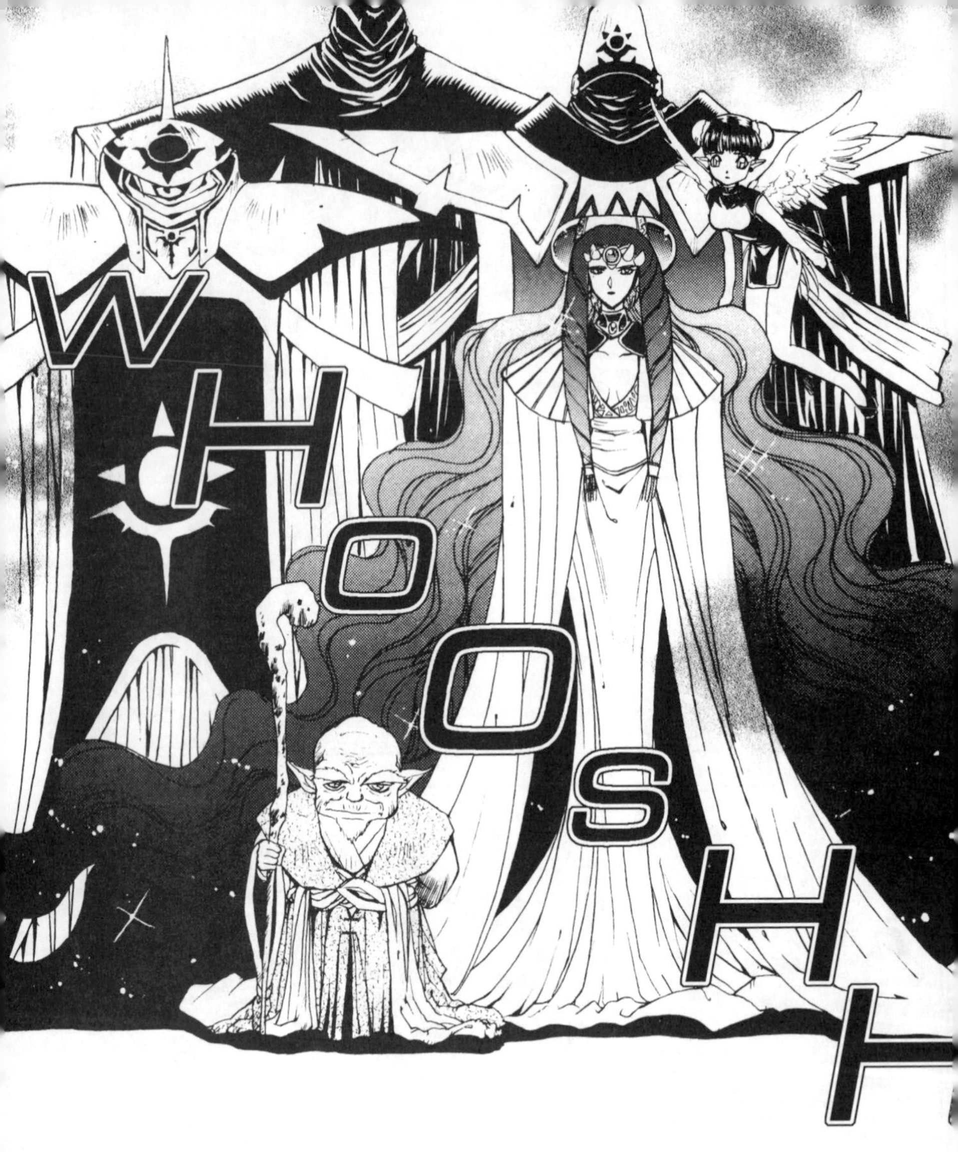
WHOOSH

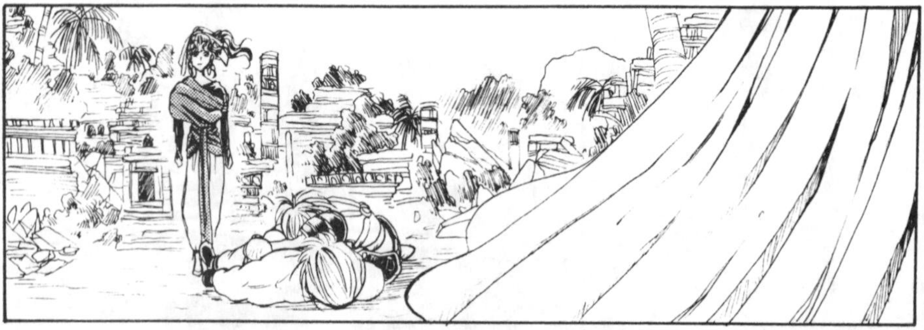

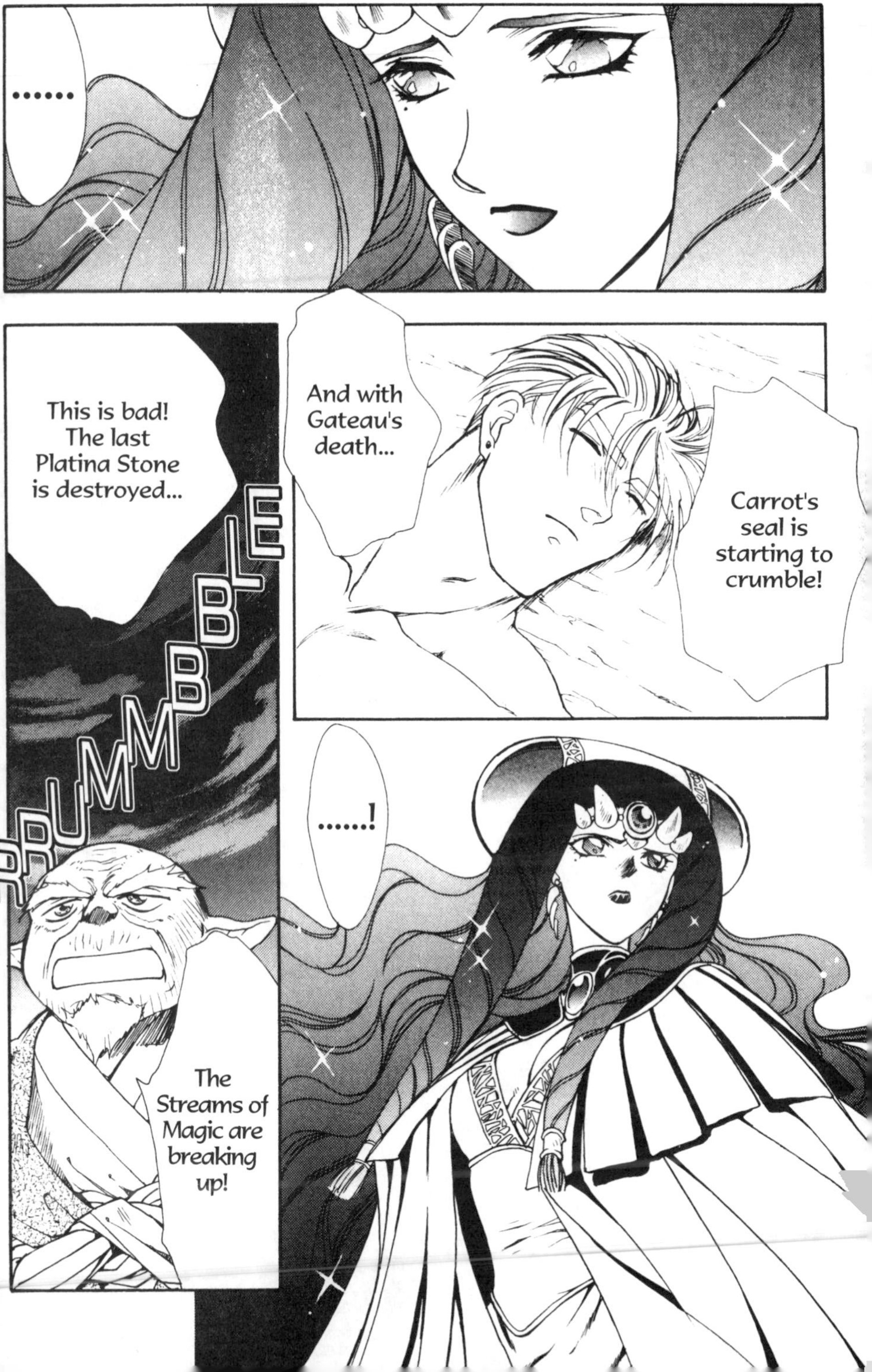
......
This is bad! The last Platina Stone is destroyed...
And with Gateau's death...
Carrot's seal is starting to crumble!
RRUMMMBBLE
The Streams of Magic are breaking up!
......!

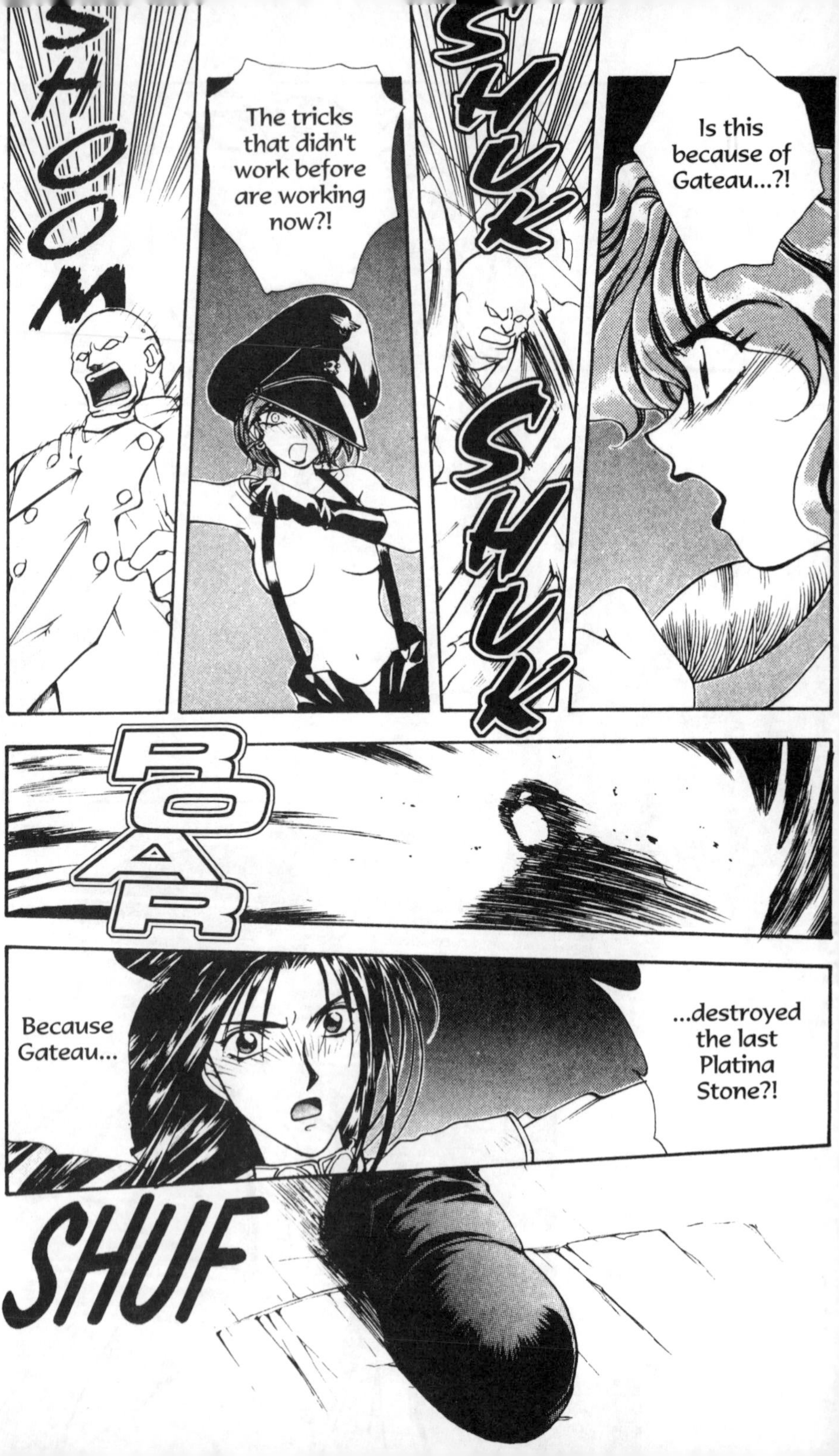
SHOOM
The tricks that didn't work before are working now?!
SHUK
SHUK SHUK
Is this because of Gateau...?!
ROAR
Because Gateau...
...destroyed the last Platina Stone?!
SHUF

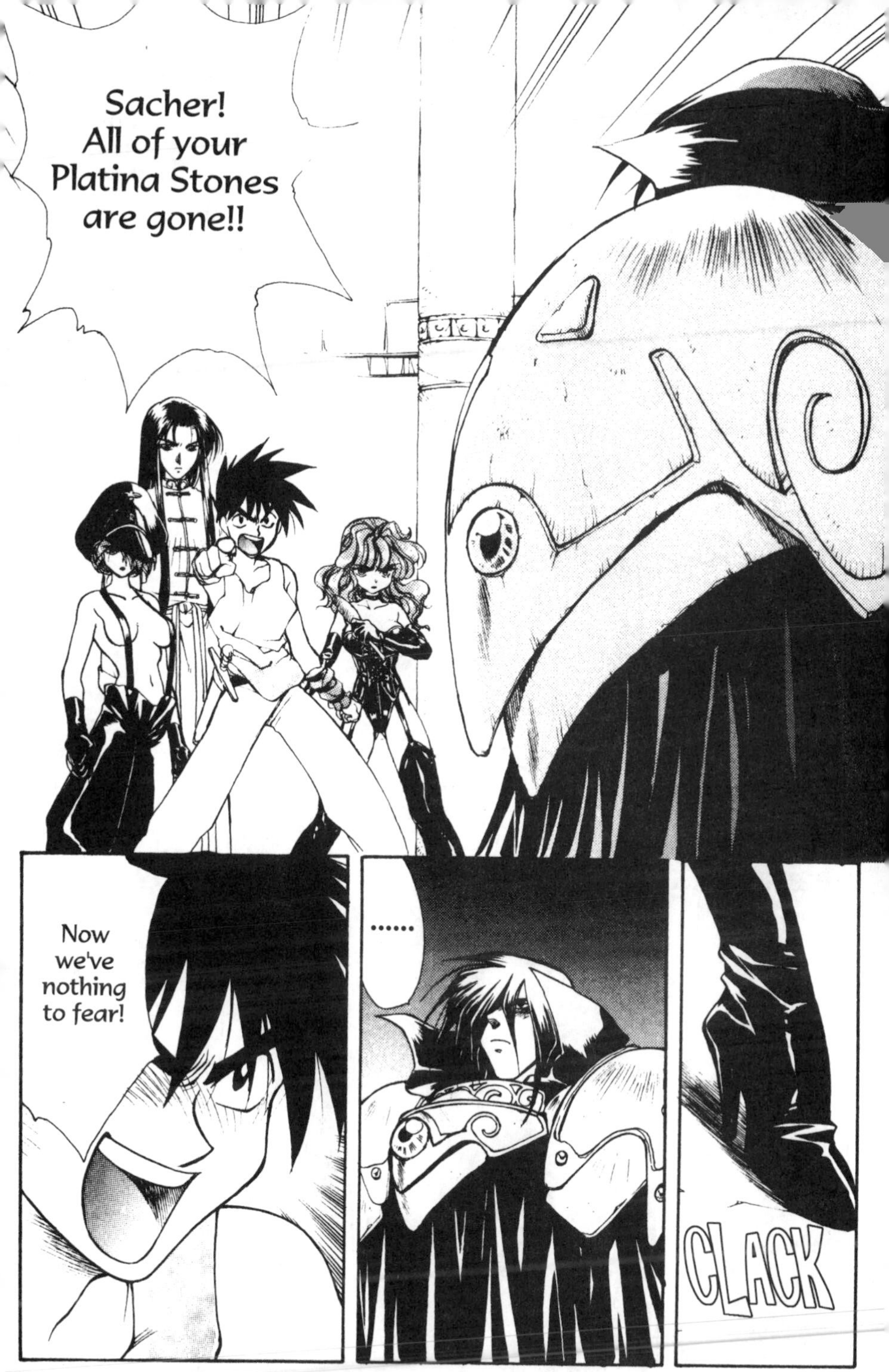
Sacher! All of your Platina Stones are gone!!
Now we've nothing to fear!
......
CLACK

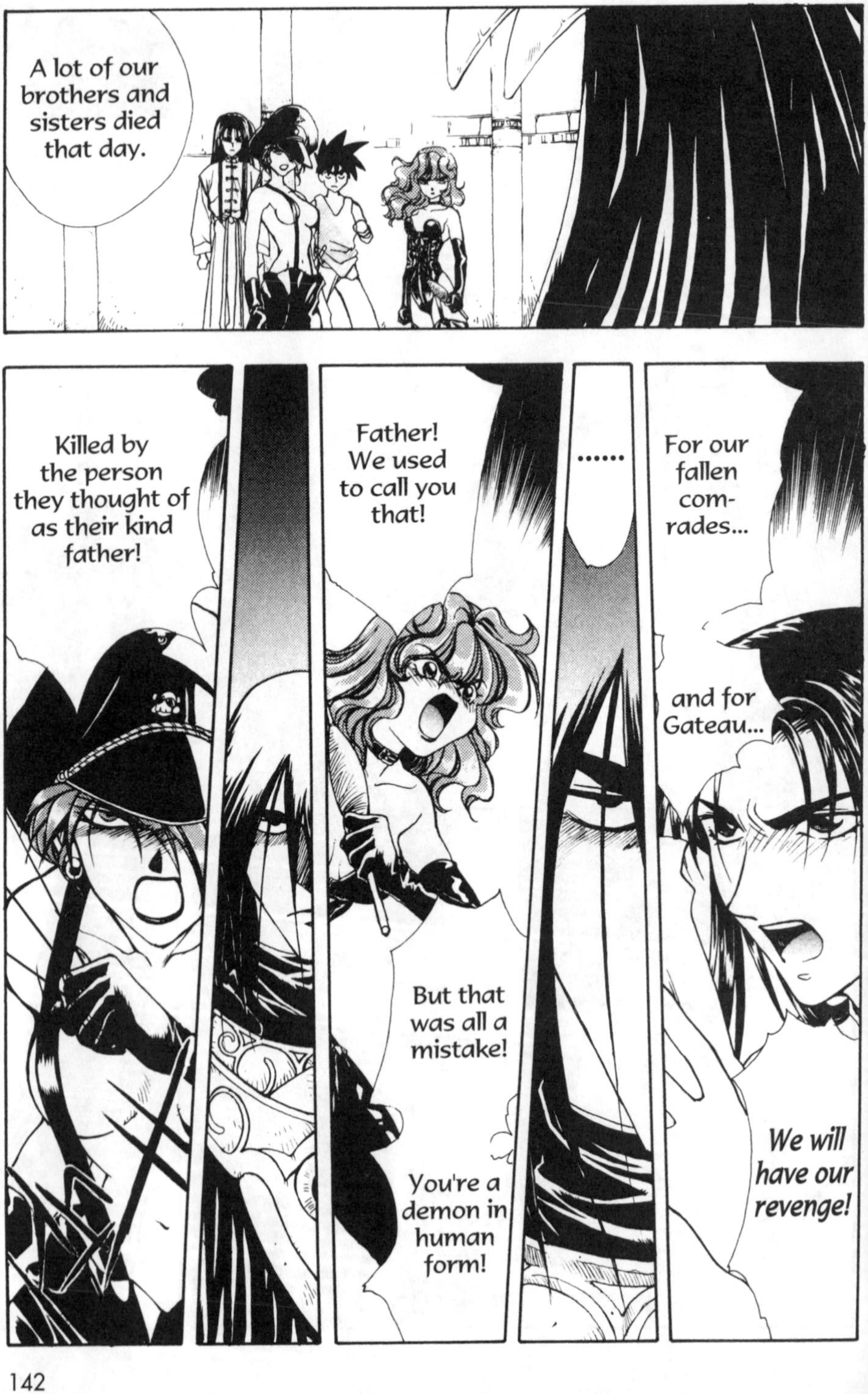
A lot of our brothers and sisters died that day.
Killed by the person they thought of as their kind father!
Father! We used to call you that!
But that was all a mistake!
You're a demon in human form!
......
For our fallen com-rades...
and for Gateau...
We will have our revenge!

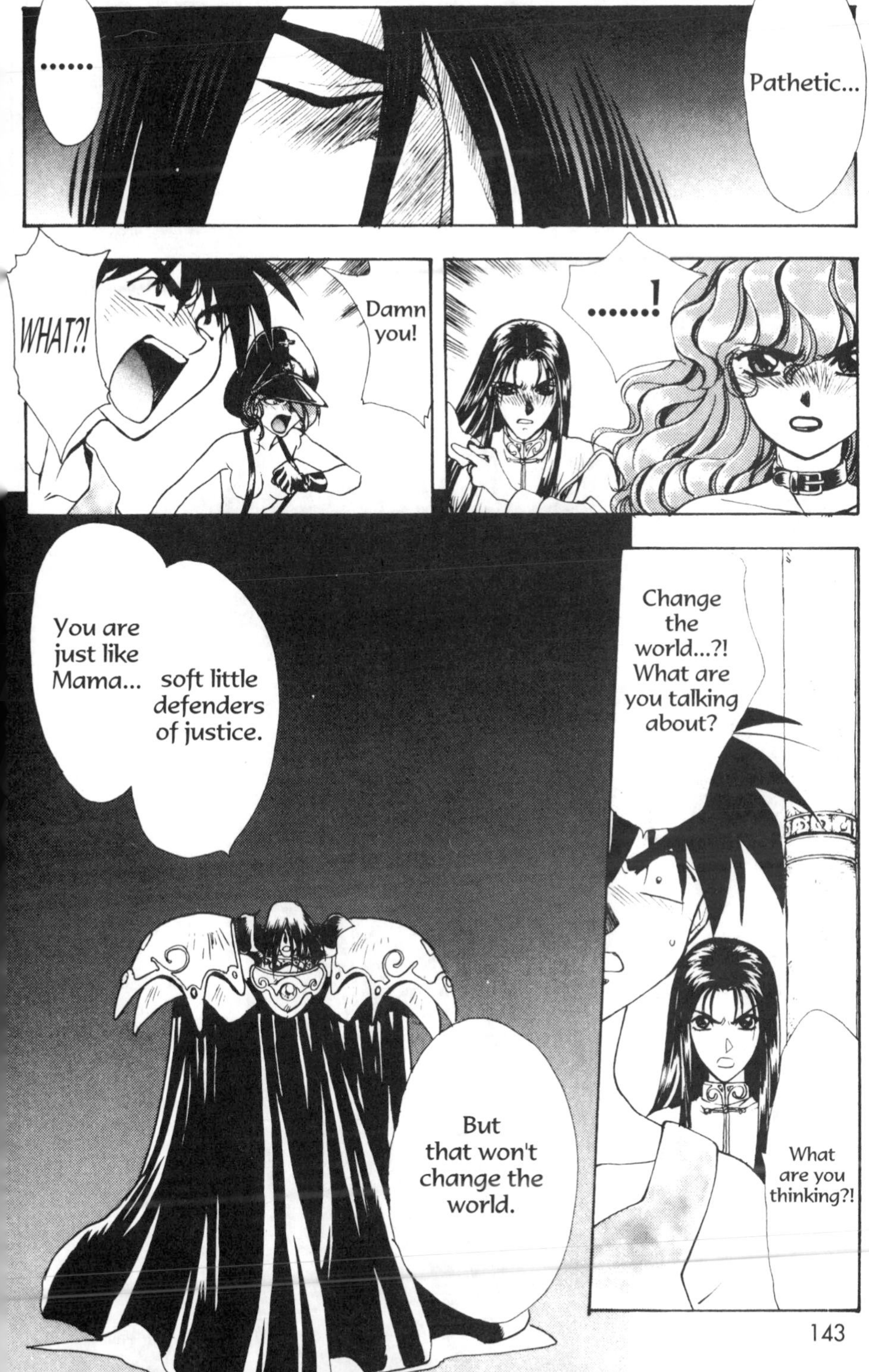

......
Pathetic...
WHAT?!
Damn you!
......!
You are just like Mama... soft little defenders of justice.
But that won't change the world.
Change the world...?! What are you talking about?
What are you thinking?!

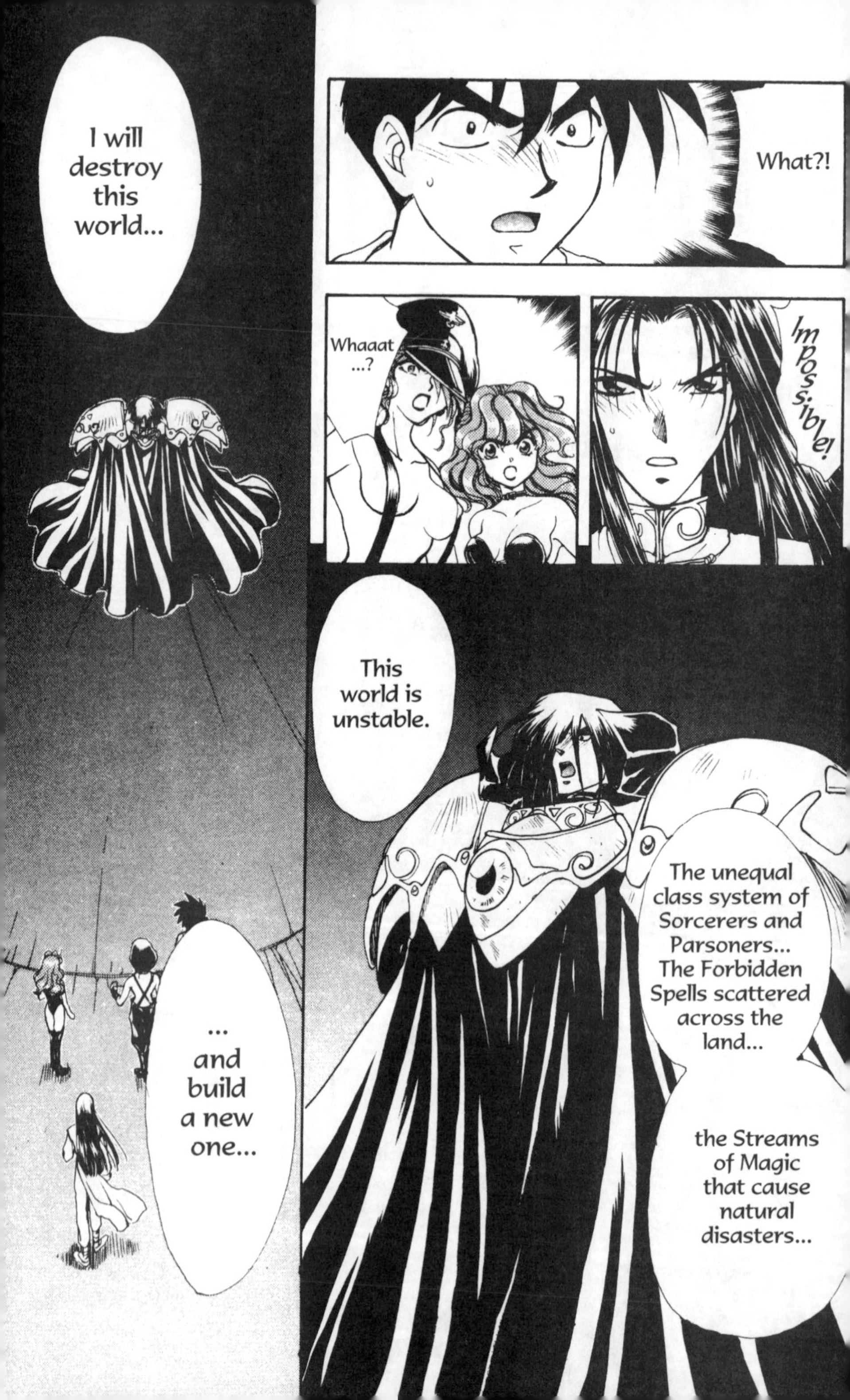
I will destroy this world...
... and build a new one...
What?!
Whaaat ...?
Impossible!
This world is unstable.
The unequal class system of Sorcerers and Parsoners... The Forbidden Spells scattered across the land...
the Streams of Magic that cause natural disasters...

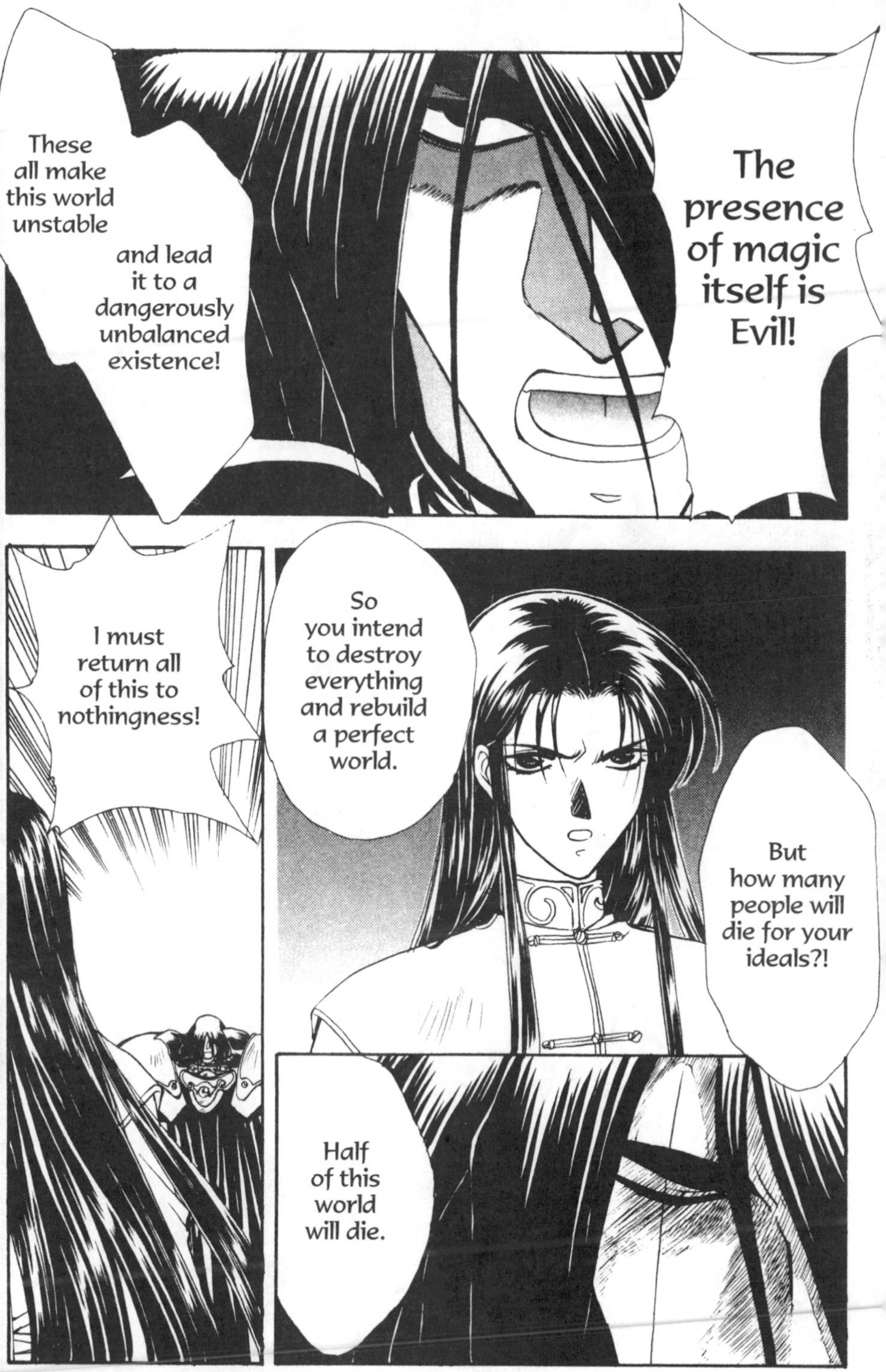
These all make this world unstable
and lead it to a dangerously unbalanced existence!
The presence of magic itself is Evil!
I must return all of this to nothingness!
So you intend to destroy everything and rebuild a perfect world.
But how many people will die for your ideals?!
Half of this world will die.

Whaat?!

You can't...!

You don't care if half the world dies for your ideals?!

Huh! What a joke!

You wouldn't understand.

You haven't watched the endless contradictions of this world since the time of the war.

There can be no progress without sacrifice!

146

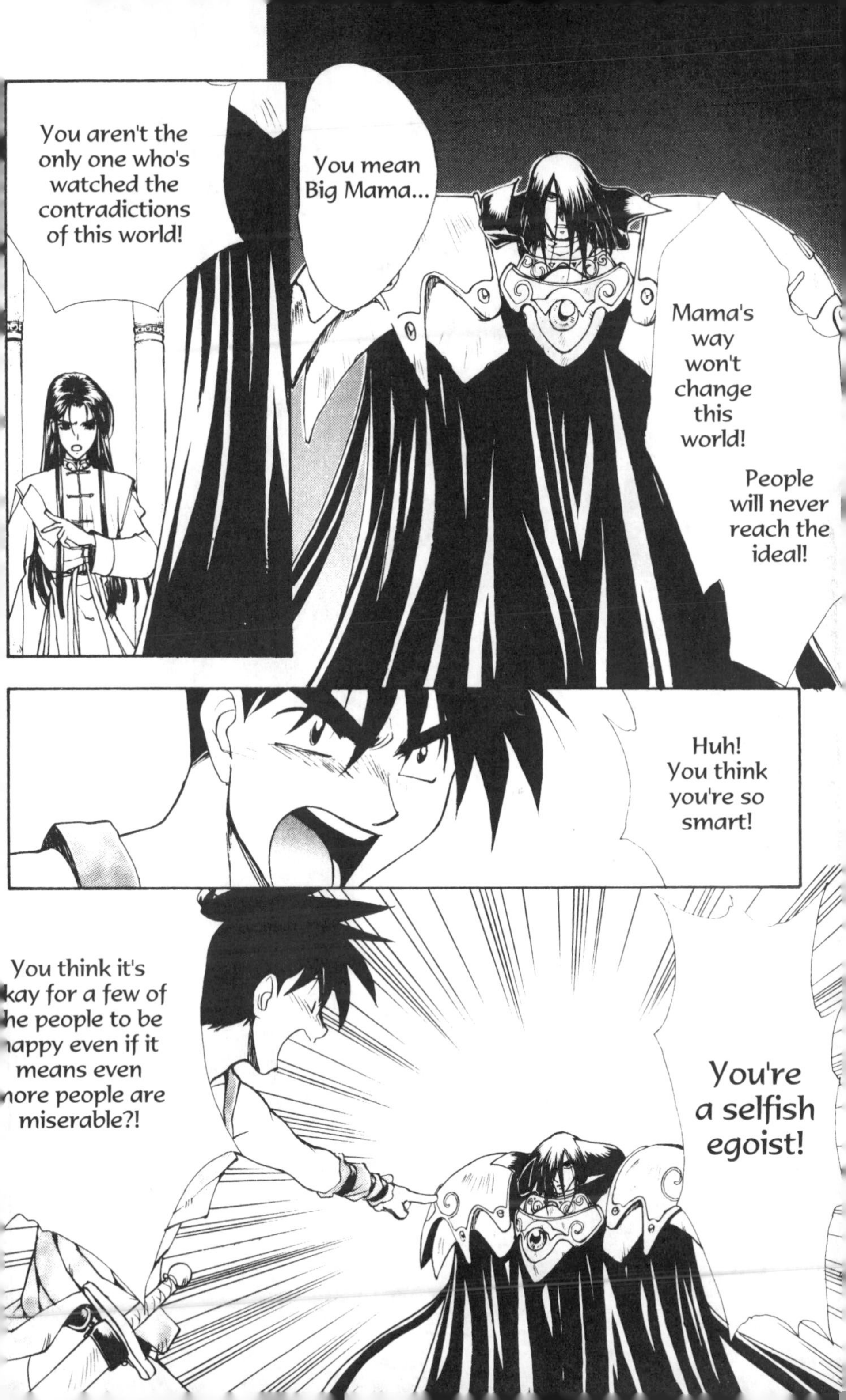
You aren't the only one who's watched the contradictions of this world!
You mean Big Mama...
Mama's way won't change this world!
People will never reach the ideal!
Huh! You think you're so smart!
You think it's kay for a few of he people to be appy even if it means even ore people are miserable?!
You're a selfish egoist!

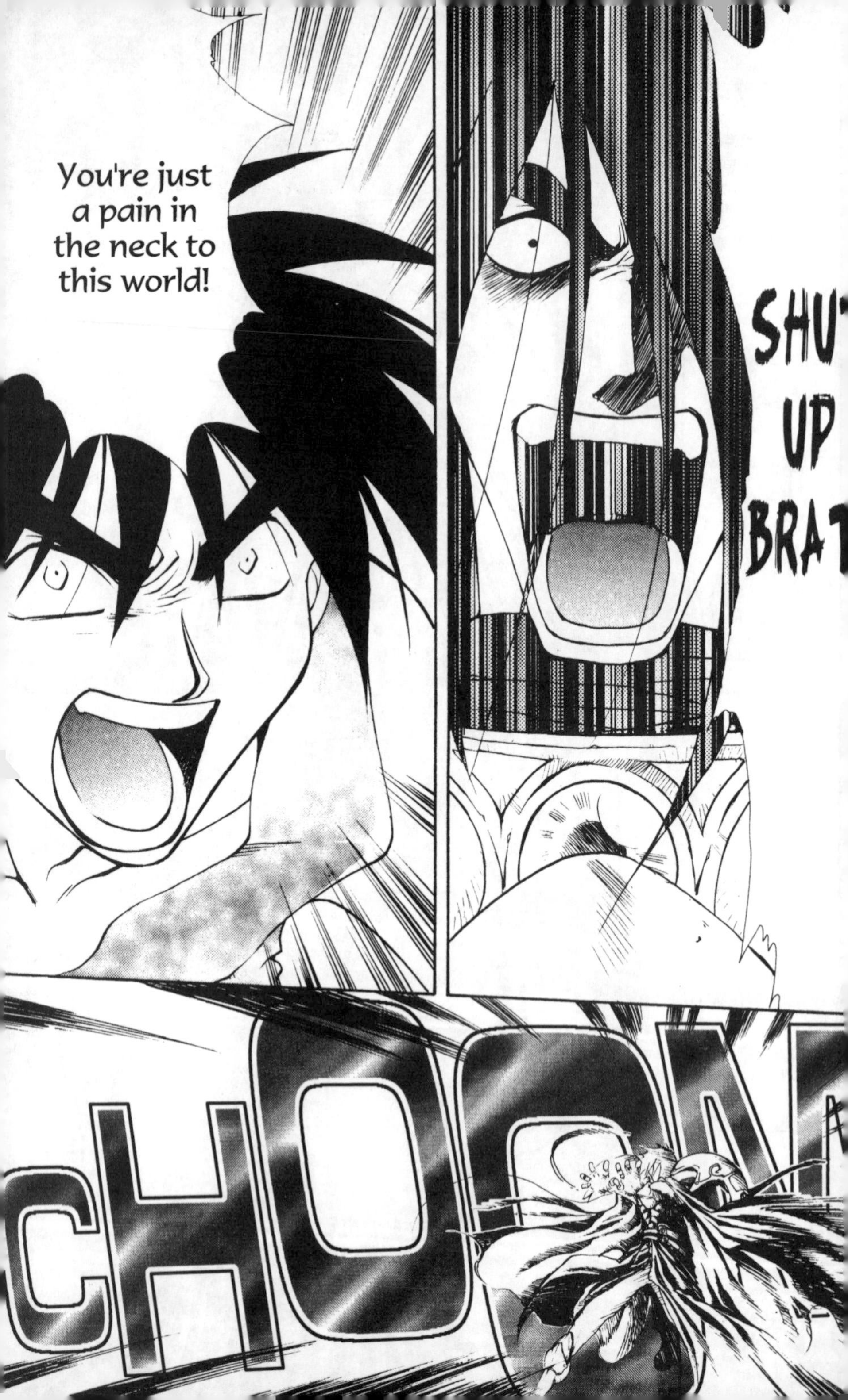
You're just a pain in the neck to this world!
SHUT UP BRAT
CHOOM

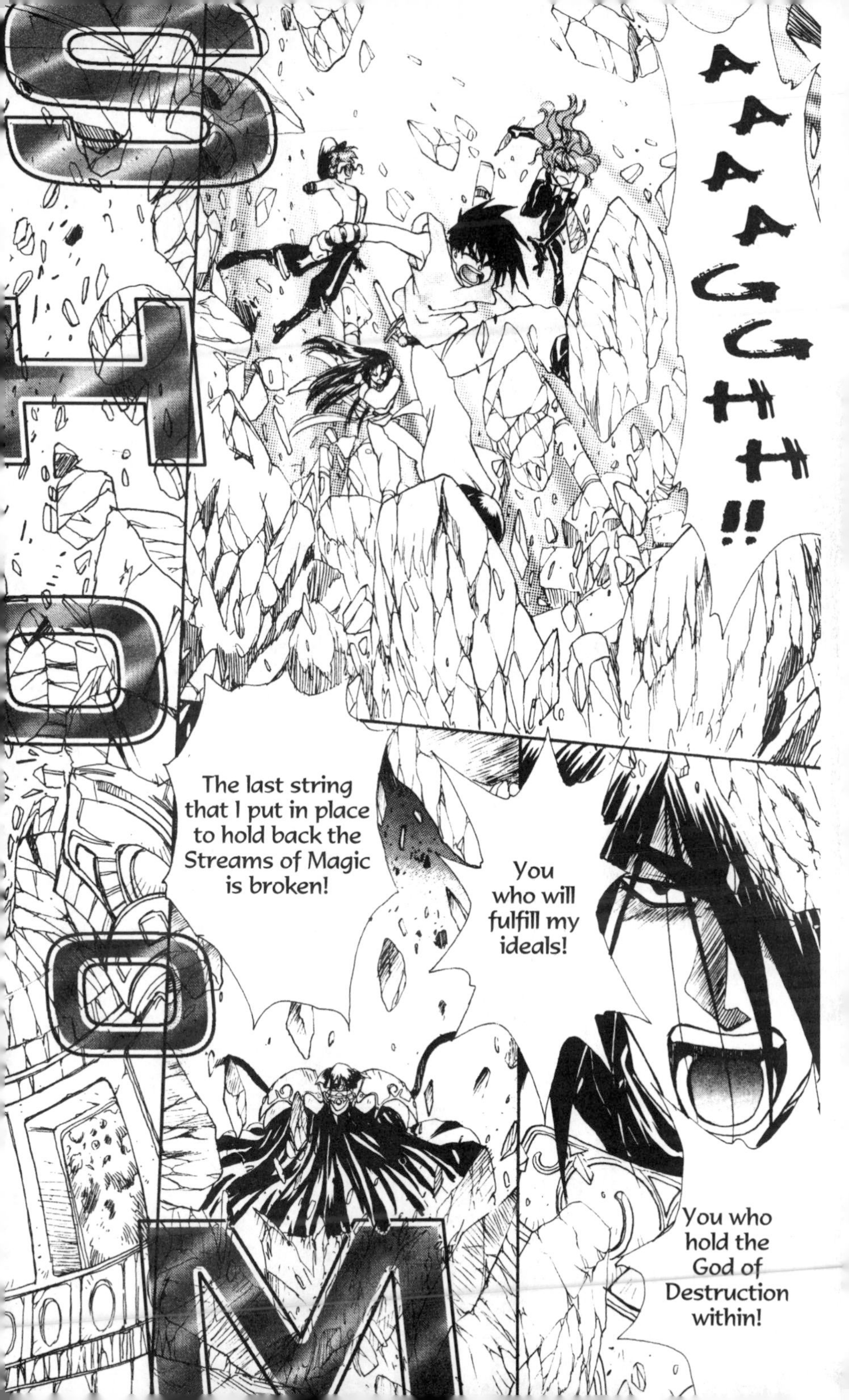
AAAAGGHH!!
The last string that I put in place to hold back the Streams of Magic is broken!
You who will fulfill my ideals!
You who hold the God of Destruction within!

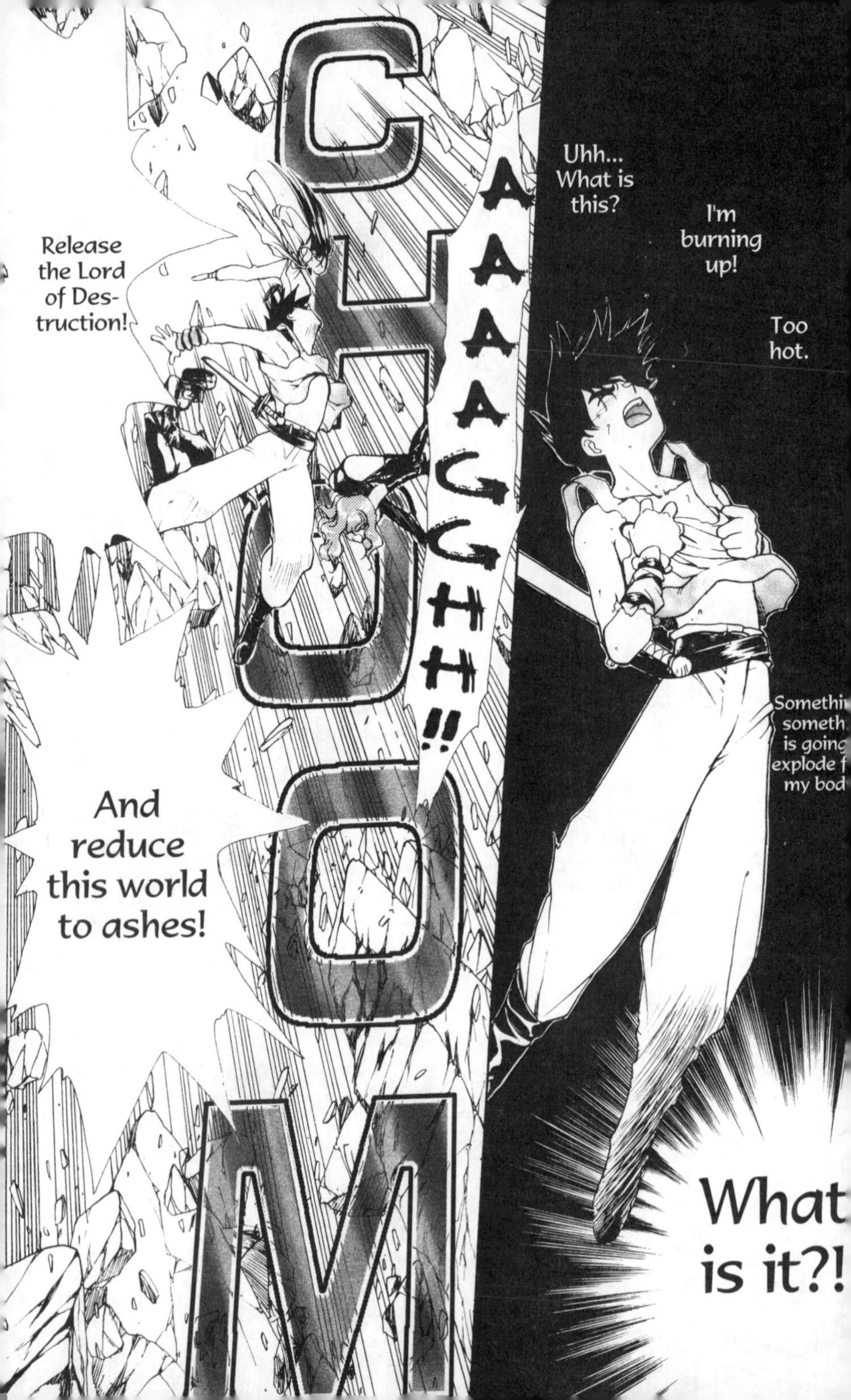
Release the Lord of Des-truction!
And reduce this world to ashes!
CHOOM
AAAAGGHH!!
Uhh... What is this?
I'm burning up!
Too hot.
Somethi someth is goinc explode f my bod
What is it?!

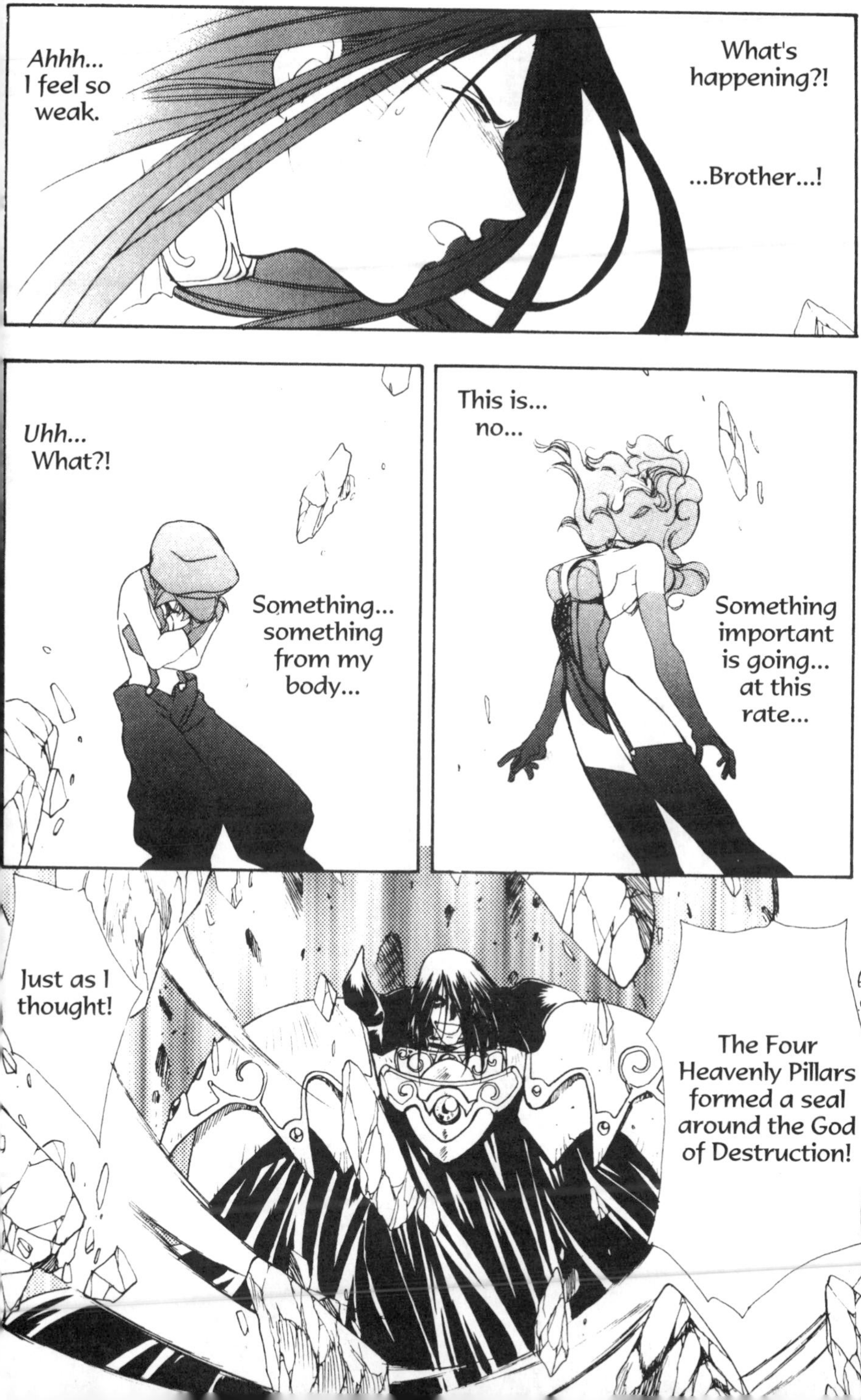

Ahhh... I feel so weak.
What's happening?!
...Brother...!
Uhh... What?!
Something... something from my body...
This is... no...
Something important is going... at this rate...
Just as I thought!
The Four Heavenly Pillars formed a seal around the God of Destruction!

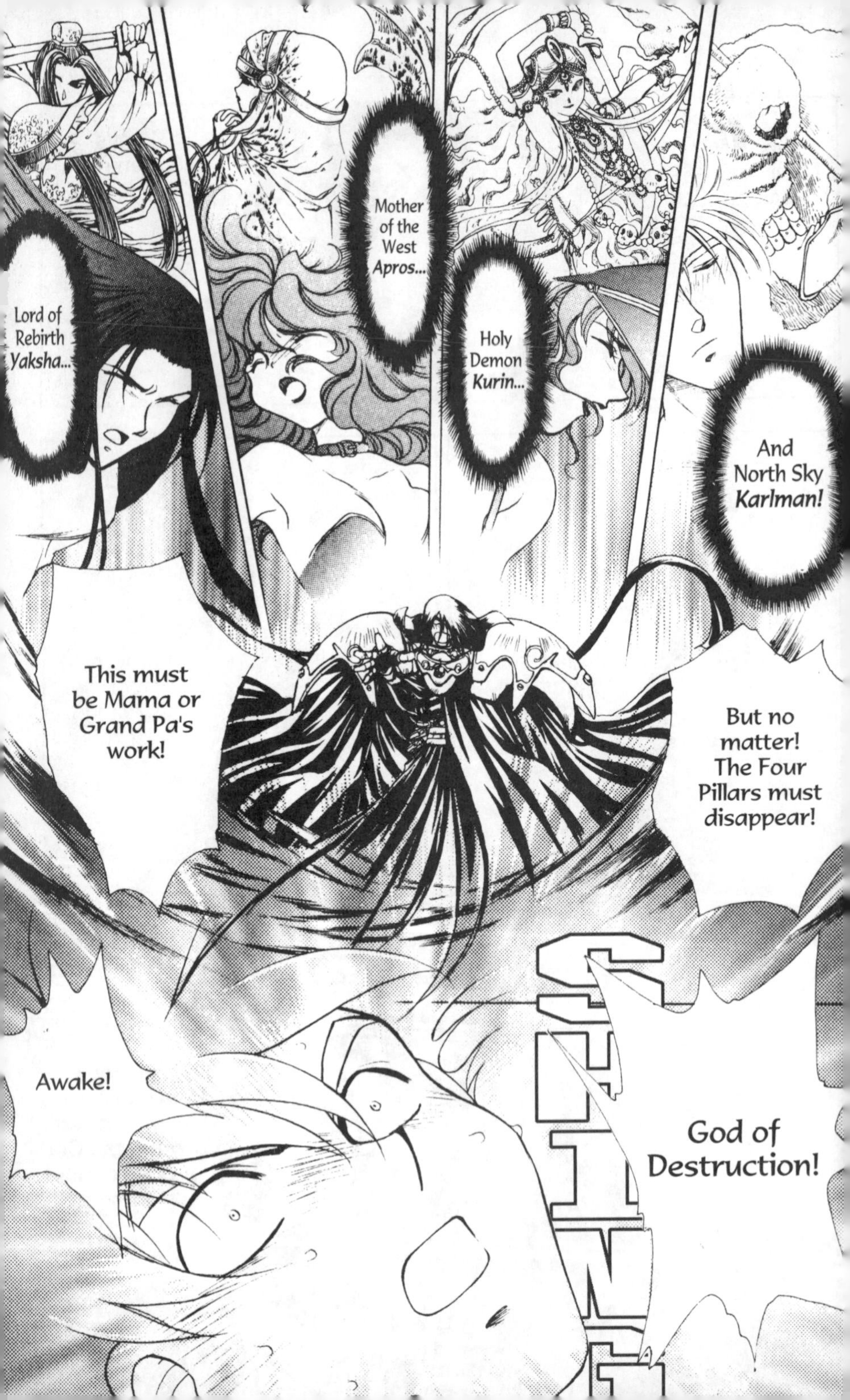
Lord of Rebirth *Yaksha...*
Mother of the West *Apros...*
Holy Demon *Kurin...*
And North Sky **Karlman!**
This must be Mama or Grand Pa's work!
But no matter! The Four Pillars must disappear!
Awake!
God of Destruction!

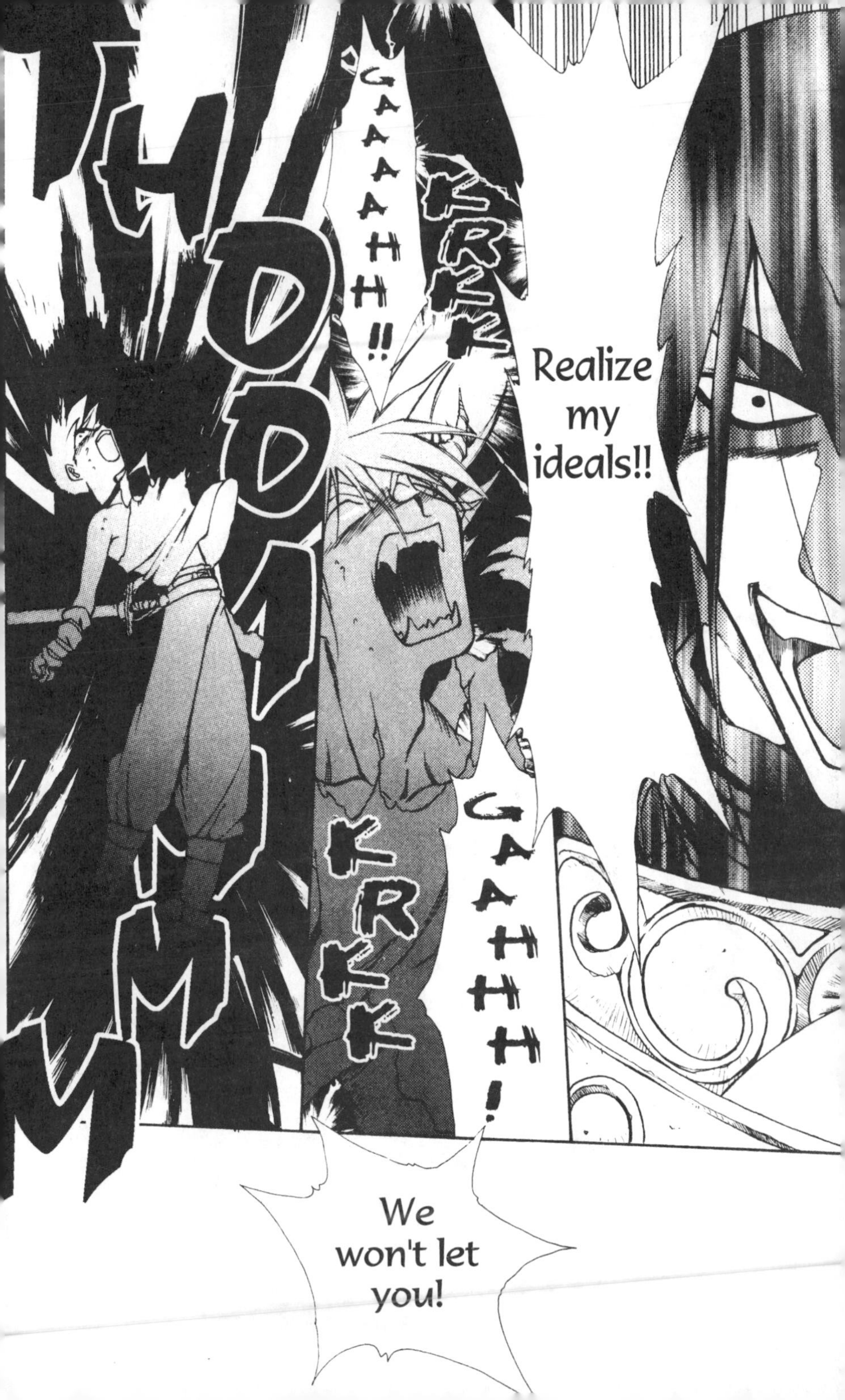
GAAAAAHH!!
Realize my ideals!!
GAAHHH!!
We won't let you!

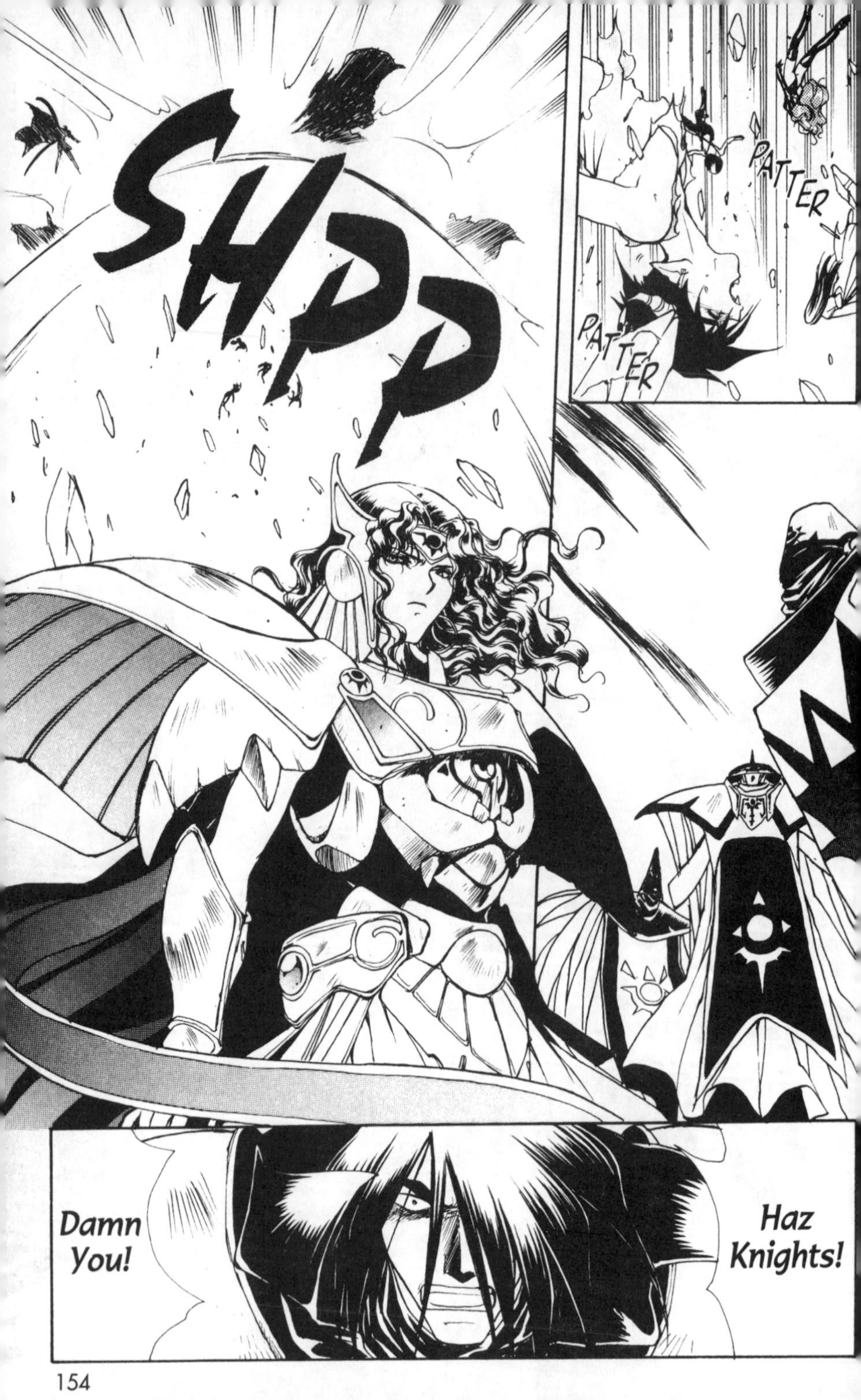
SHPP
PATTER
PATTER
Damn You!
Haz Knights!

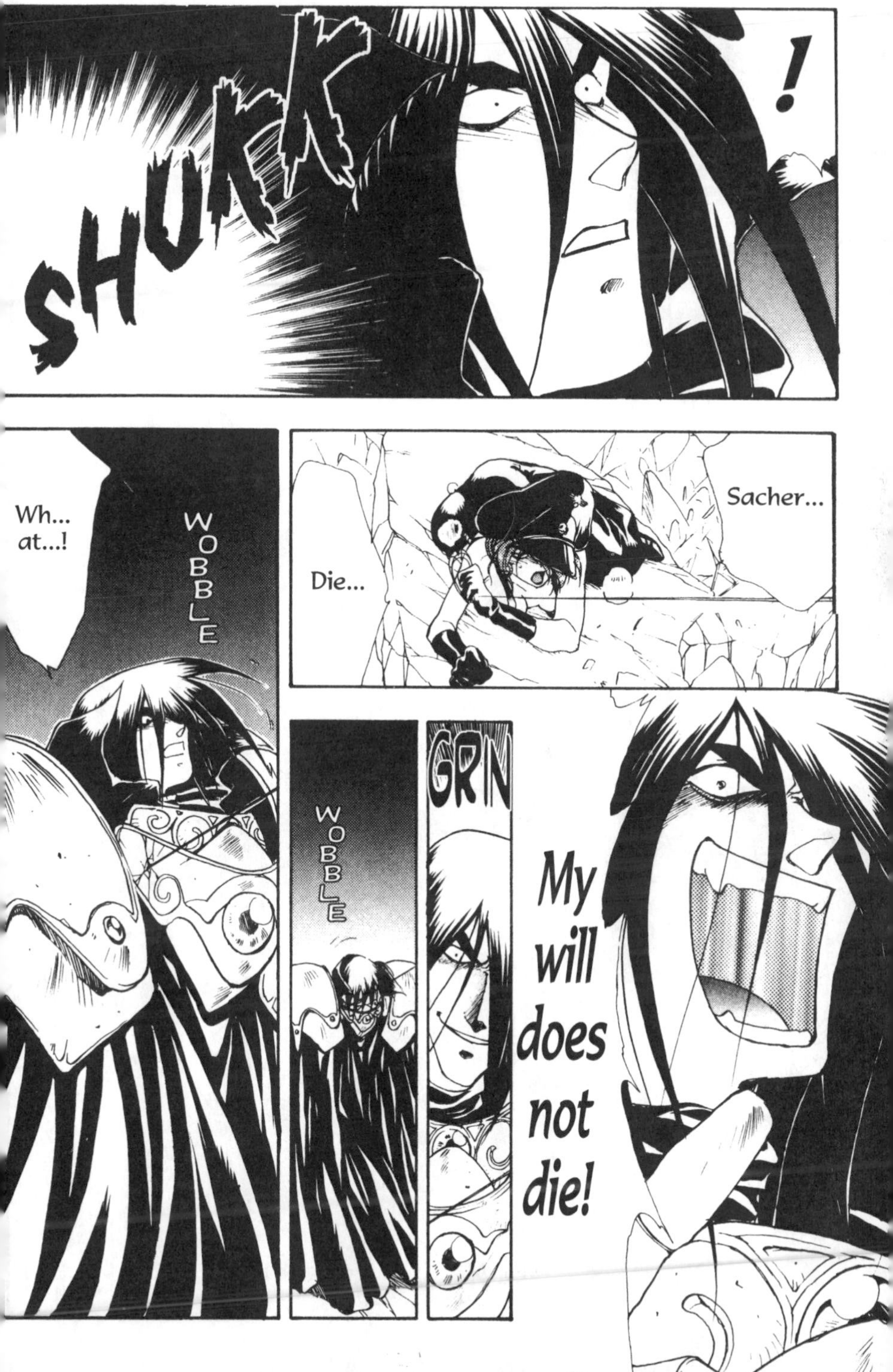
SHUKK
!
Wh... at...!
WOBBLE
Die...
Sacher...
WOBBLE
GRIN
My will does not die!

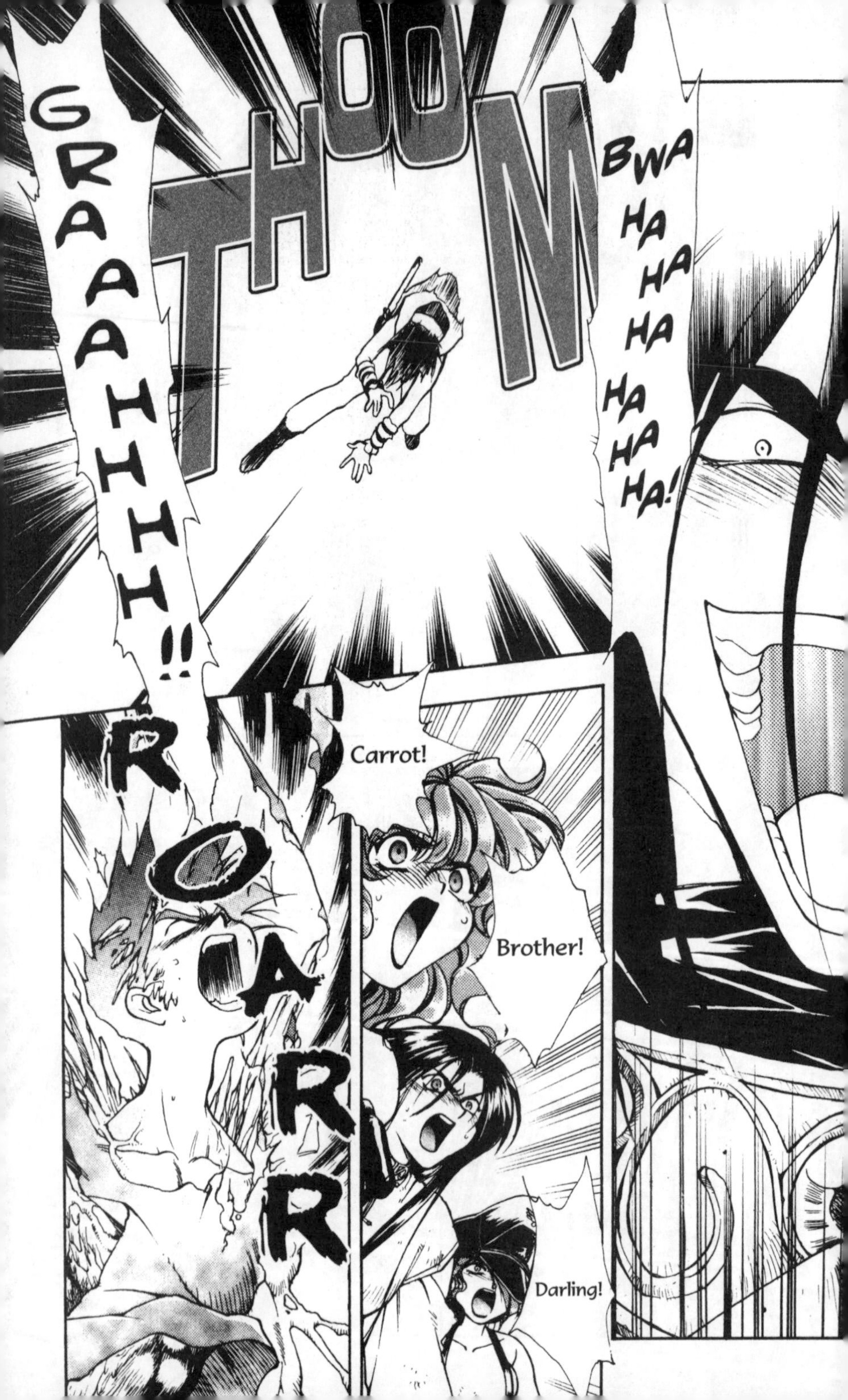
GRAAAHHHH!!
THOOOM
BWAHAHAHAHAHAHAHAHA!
ROARRR
Carrot!
Brother!
Darling!

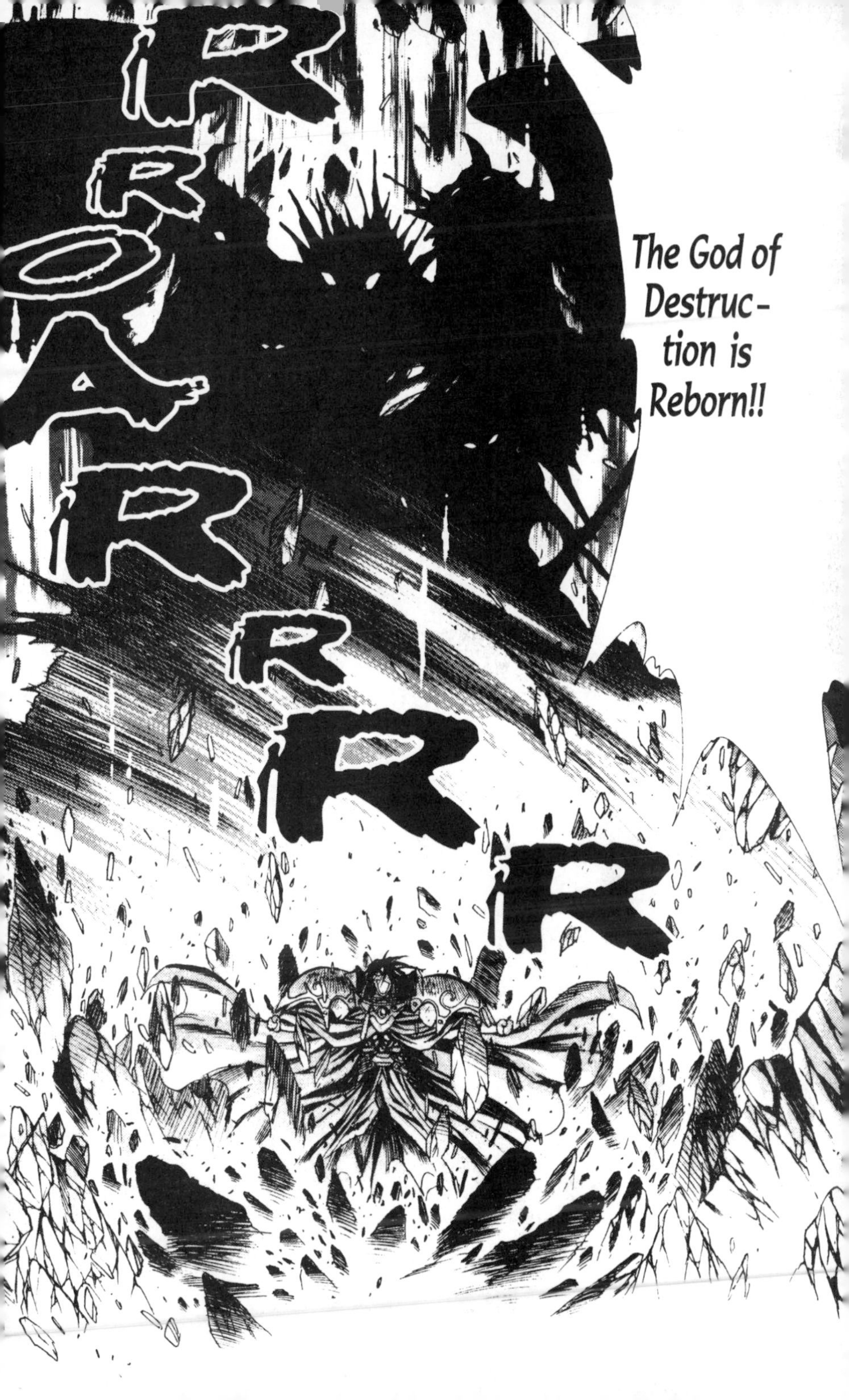
RROARRRRR
The God of Destruc-tion is Reborn!!

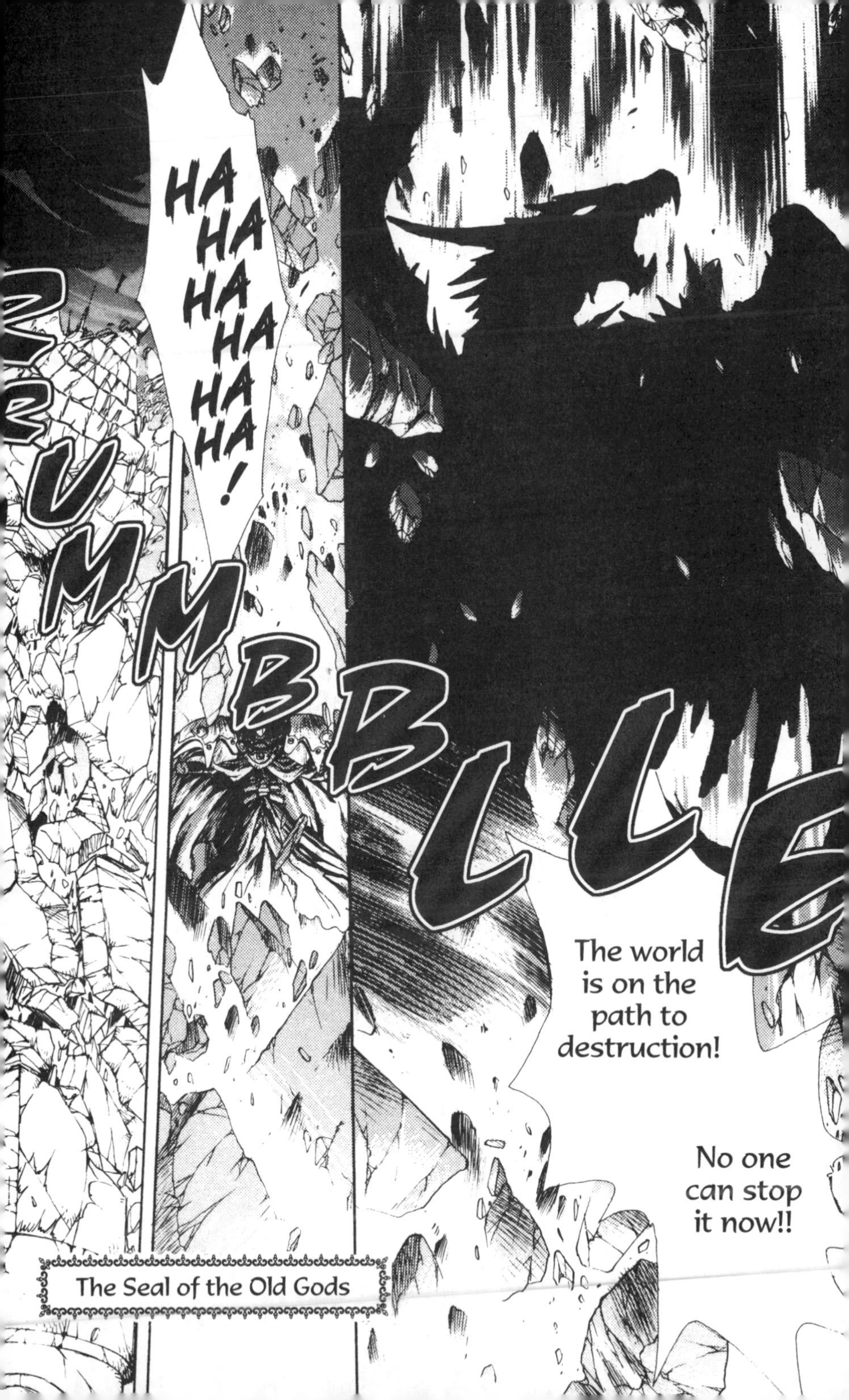
HA HA HA HA HA HA HA HA!
RUMMBBLLE
The world is on the path to destruction!
No one can stop it now!!
The Seal of the Old Gods

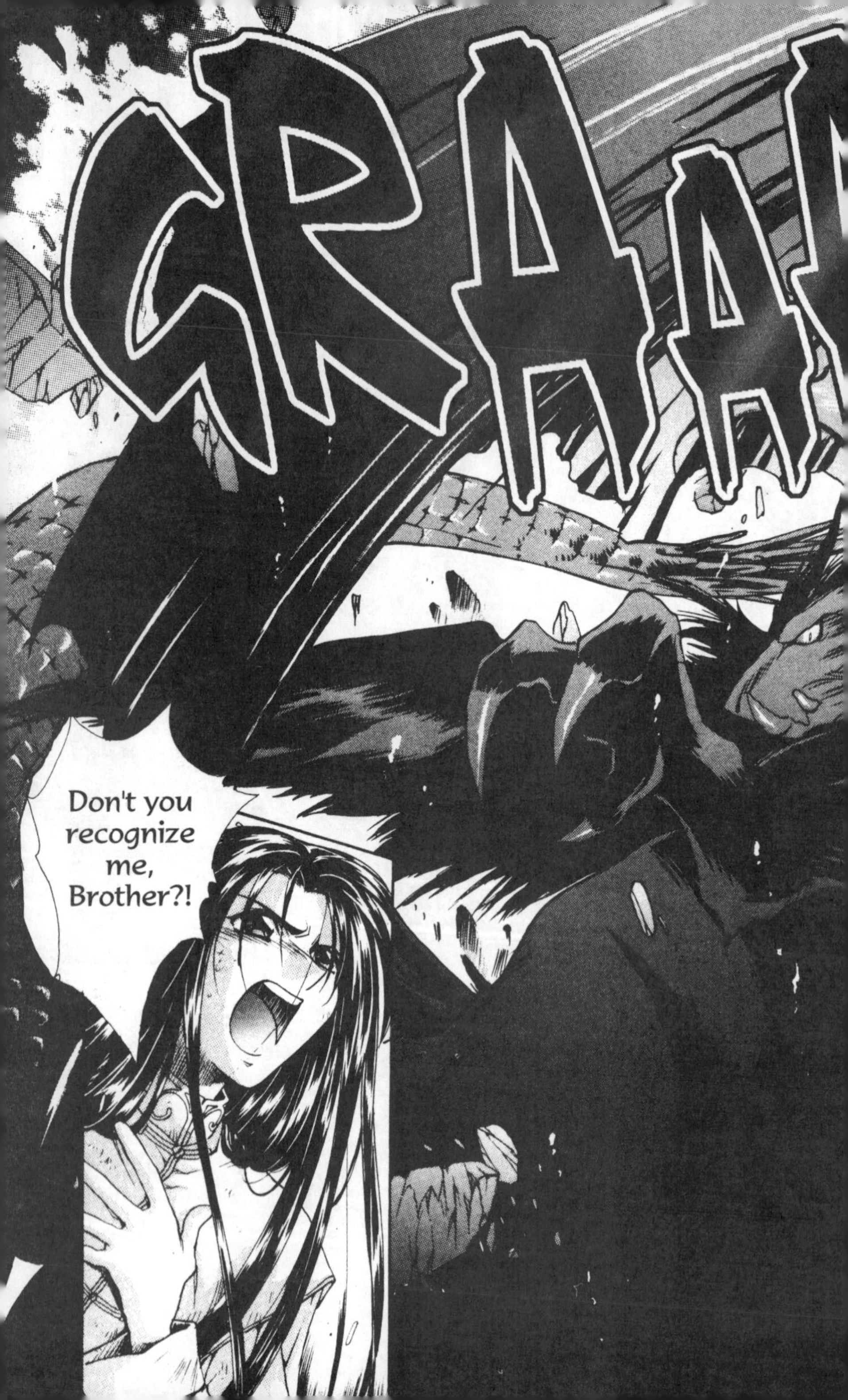
GRAA
Don't you recognize me, Brother?!

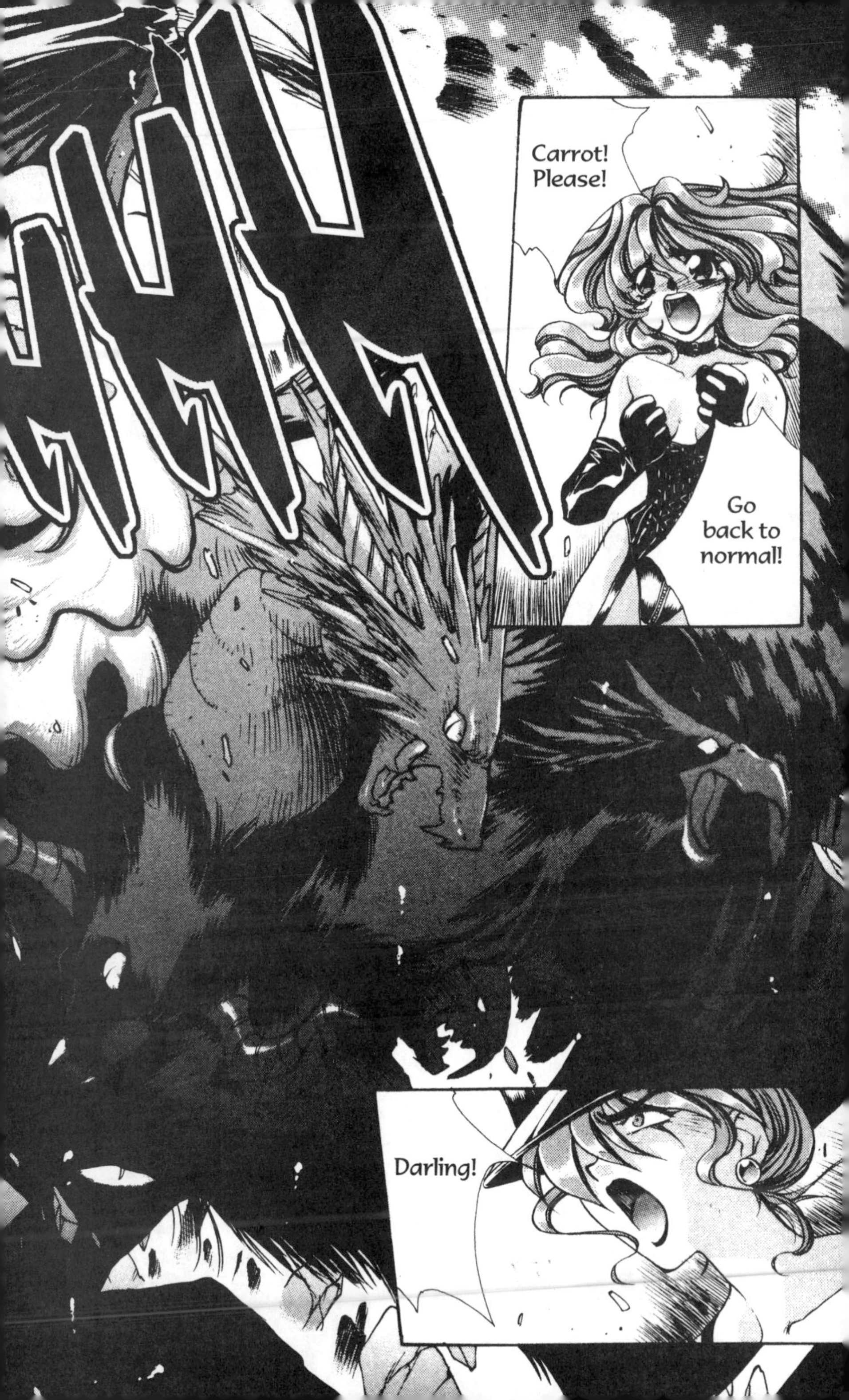
Carrot! Please!
Go back to normal!
Darling!

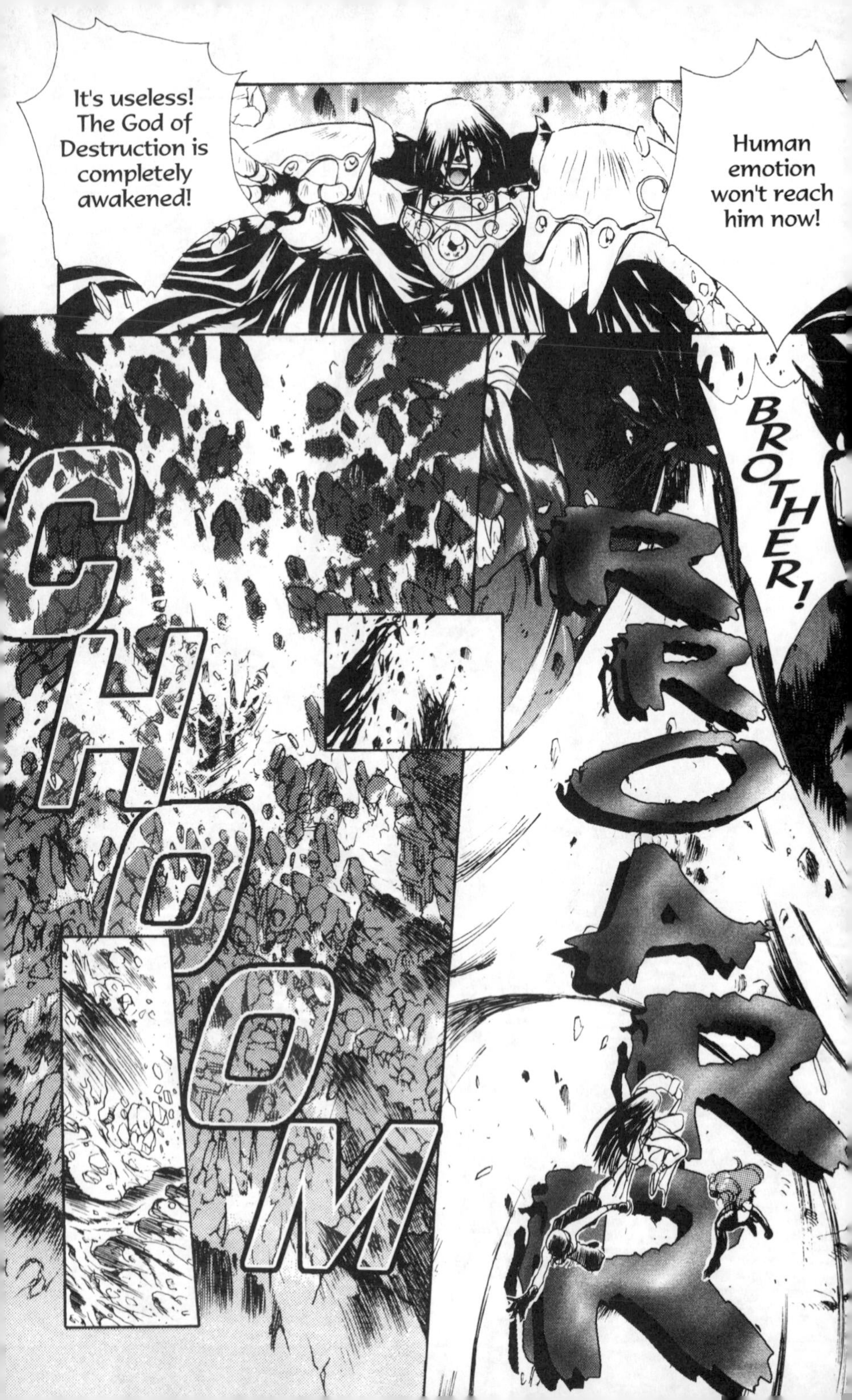
It's useless! The God of Destruction is completely awakened!
Human emotion won't reach him now!
BROTHER!
CHOOM
RROARR

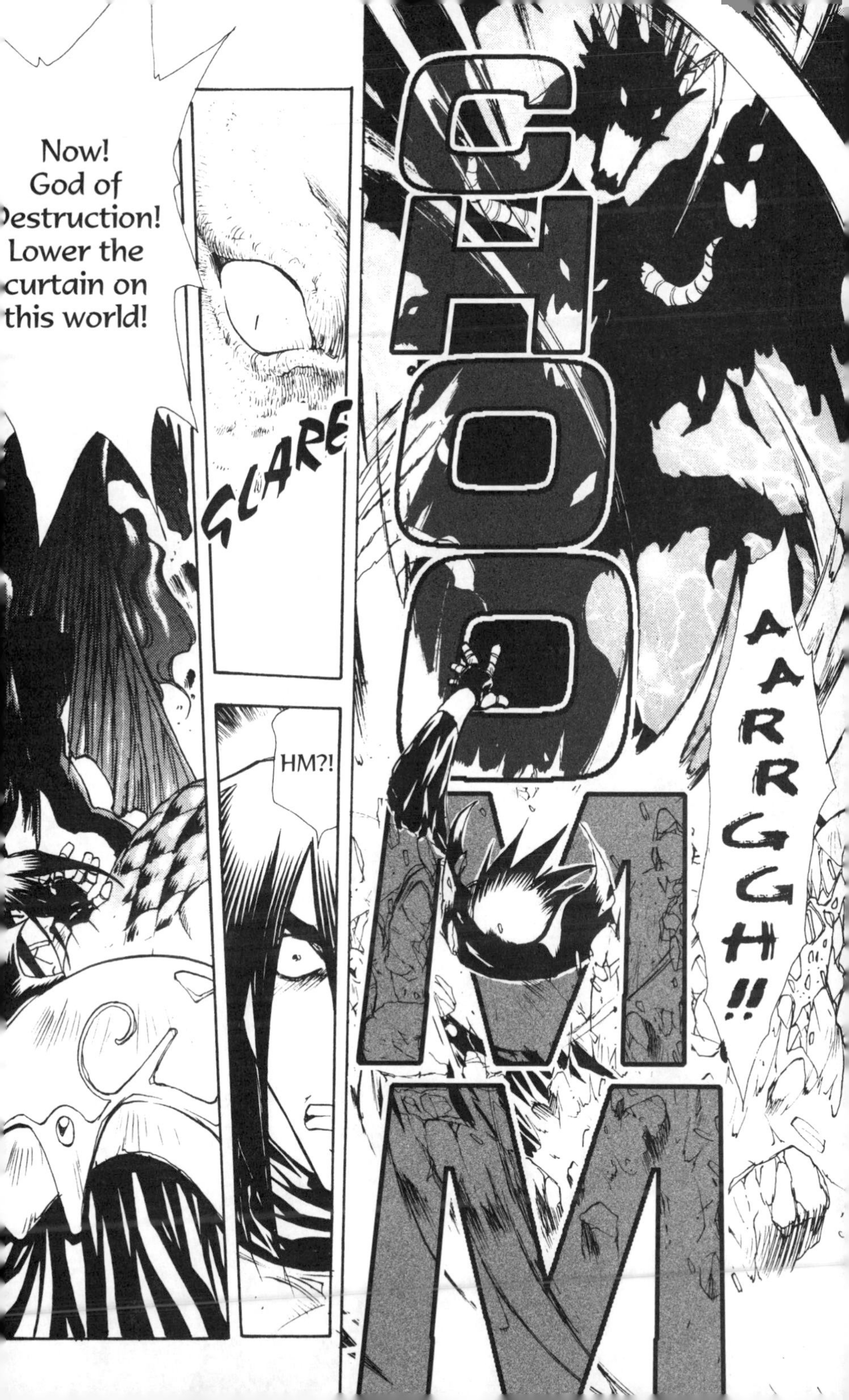
Now! God of Destruction! Lower the curtain on this world!
GLARE
HM?!
CHOOMM
AARRGGH!!

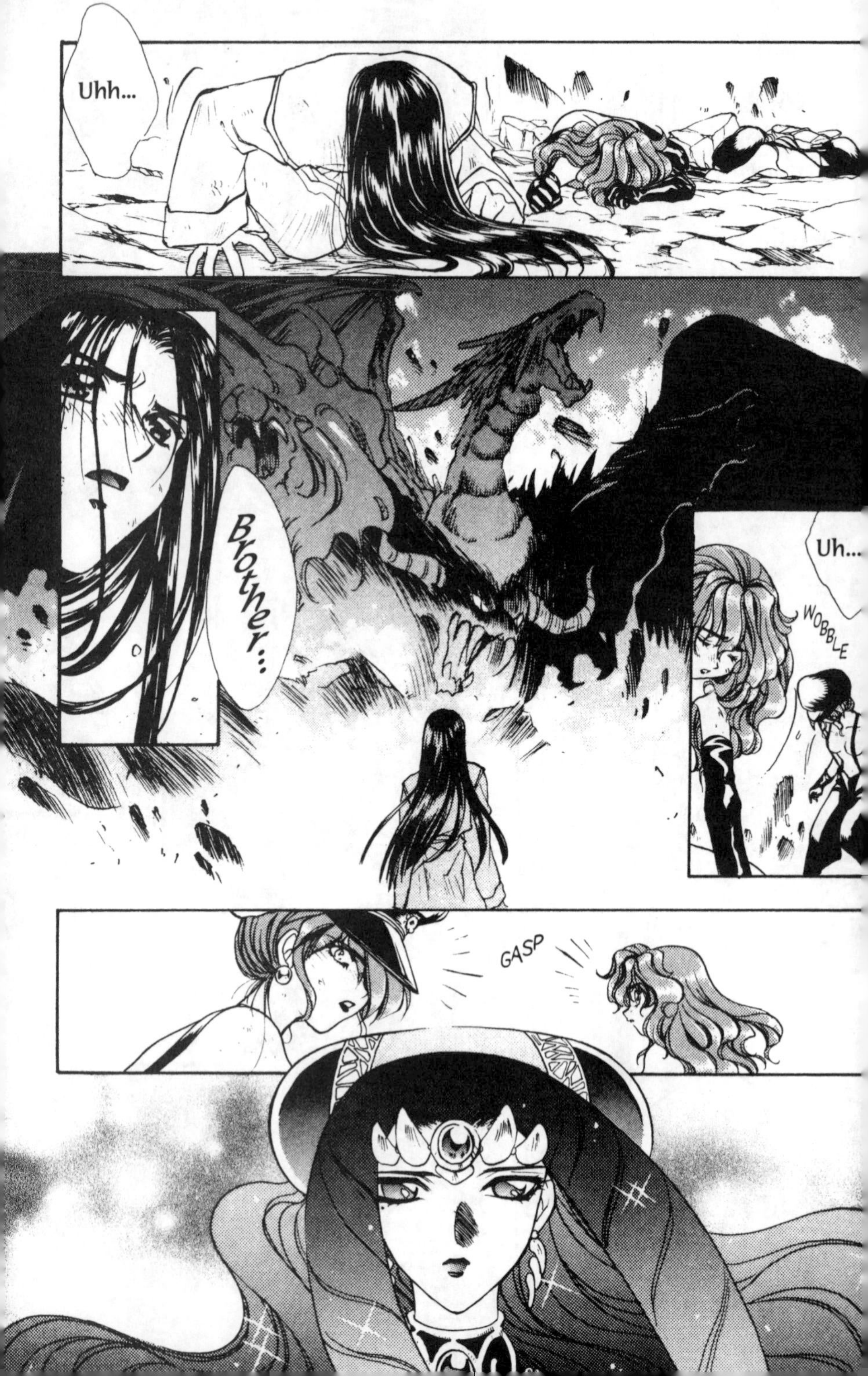
Uhh...
Brother...
Uh...
WOBBLE
GASP

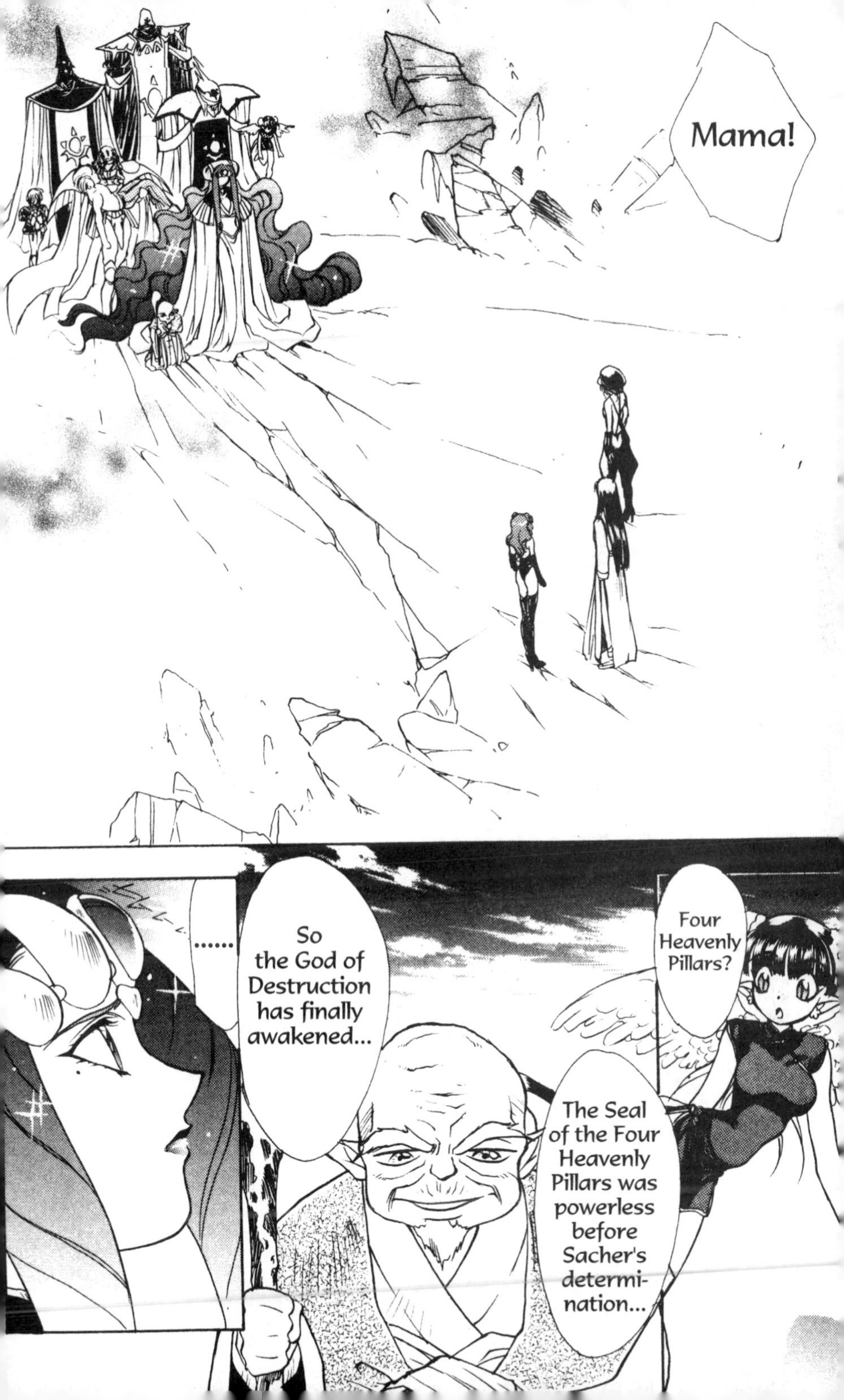
Mama!
......
So the God of Destruction has finally awakened...
The Seal of the Four Heavenly Pillars was powerless before Sacher's determi-nation...
Four Heavenly Pillars?

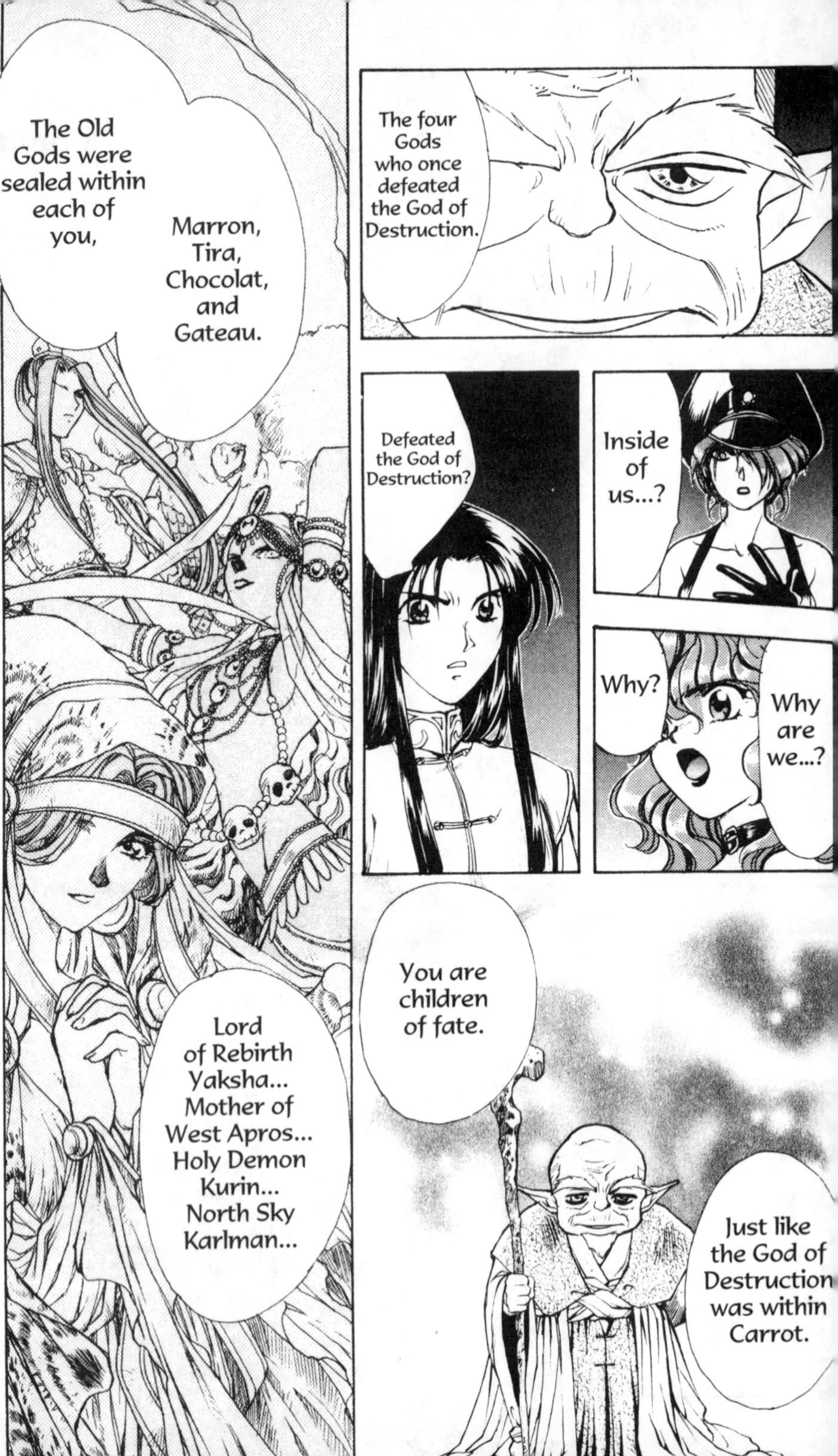
The Old Gods were sealed within each of you,
Marron, Tira, Chocolat, and Gateau.
Lord of Rebirth Yaksha... Mother of West Apros... Holy Demon Kurin... North Sky Karlman...
The four Gods who once defeated the God of Destruction.
Defeated the God of Destruction?
Inside of us...?
Why?
Why are we...?
You are children of fate.
Just like the God of Destruction was within Carrot.

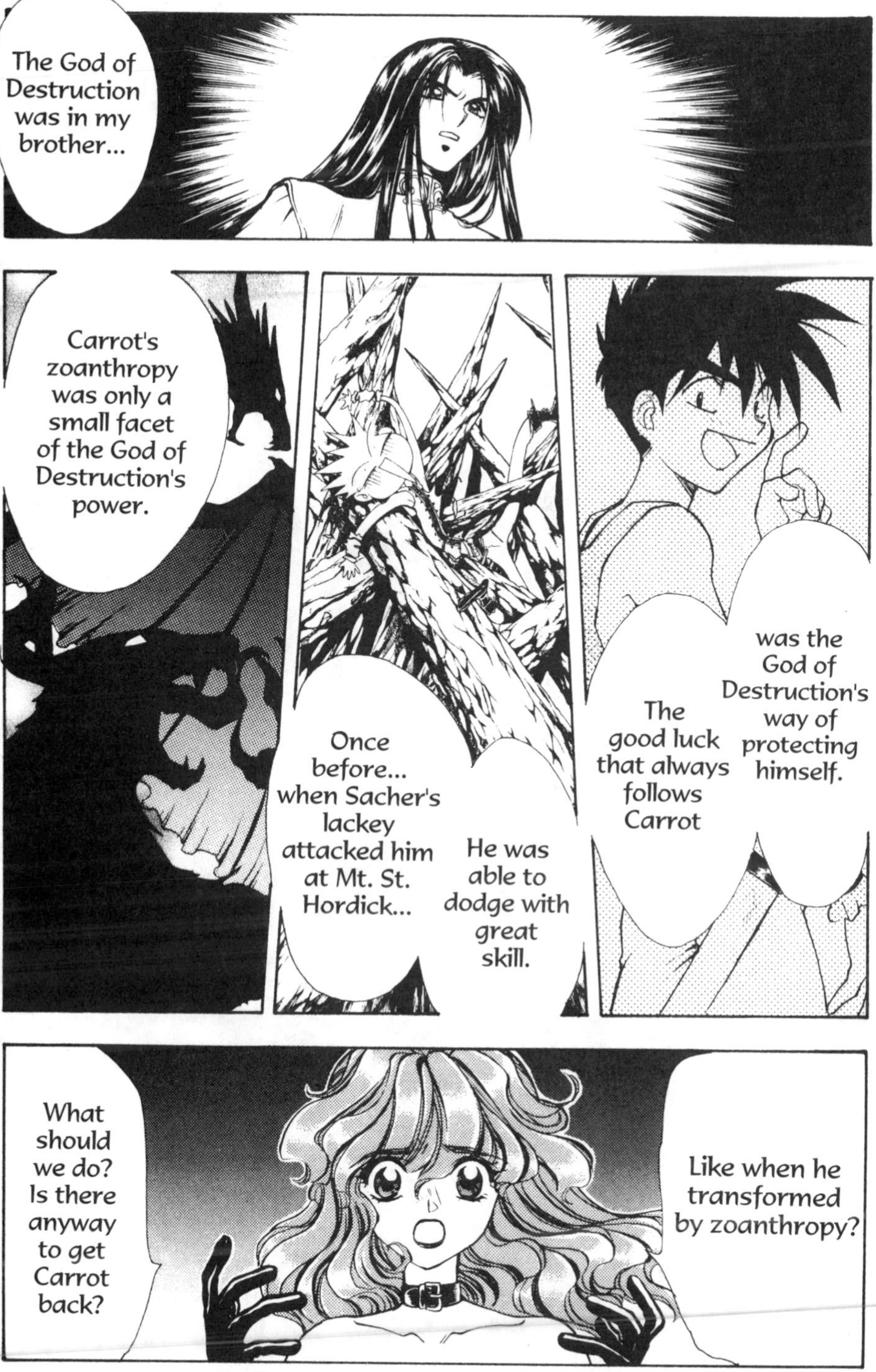

The God of Destruction was in my brother...
Carrot's zoanthropy was only a small facet of the God of Destruction's power.
Once before... when Sacher's lackey attacked him at Mt. St. Hordick...
He was able to dodge with great skill.
The good luck that always follows Carrot
was the God of Destruction's way of protecting himself.
What should we do? Is there anyway to get Carrot back?
Like when he transformed by zoanthropy?

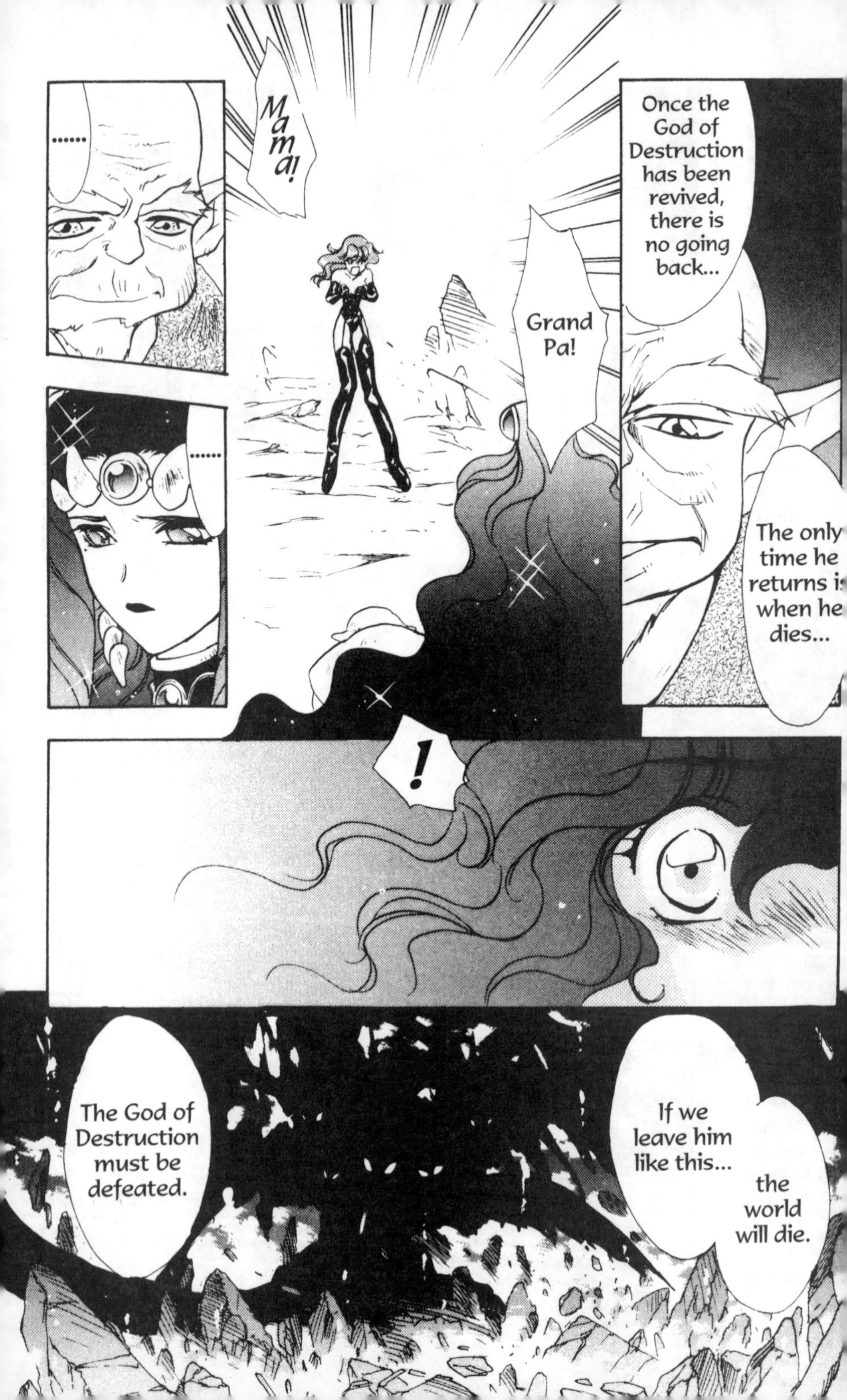
......
......
Mama!
Grand Pa!
Once the God of Destruction has been revived, there is no going back...
The only time he returns is when he dies...
!
The God of Destruction must be defeated.
If we leave him like this...
the world will die.

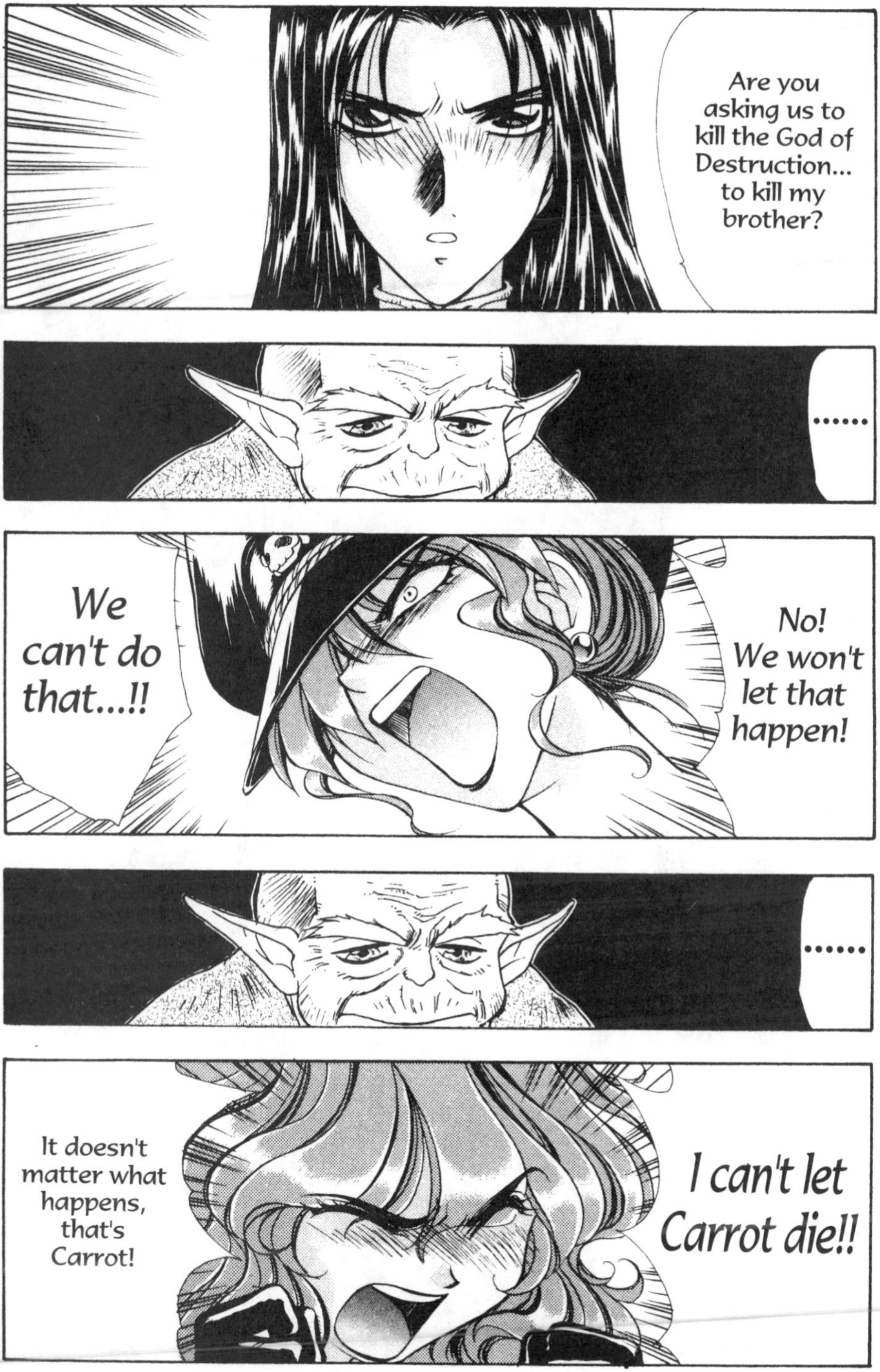

Are you asking us to kill the God of Destruction... to kill my brother?
......
We can't do that...!!
No! We won't let that happen!
......
It doesn't matter what happens, that's Carrot!
I can't let Carrot die!!

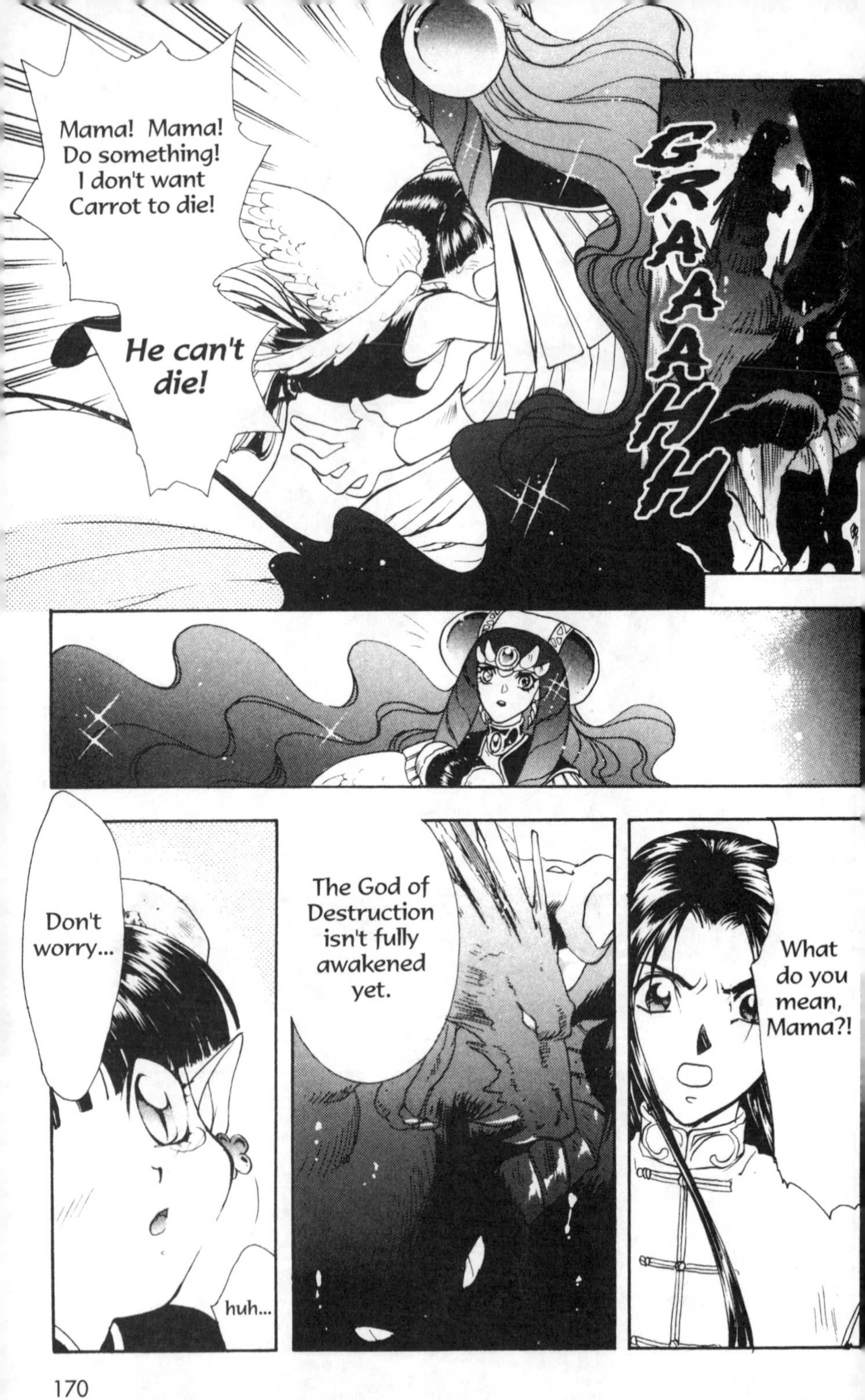
Mama! Mama! Do something! I don't want Carrot to die!
He can't die!
GRAAAHH
Don't worry...
huh...
The God of Destruction isn't fully awakened yet.
What do you mean, Mama?!

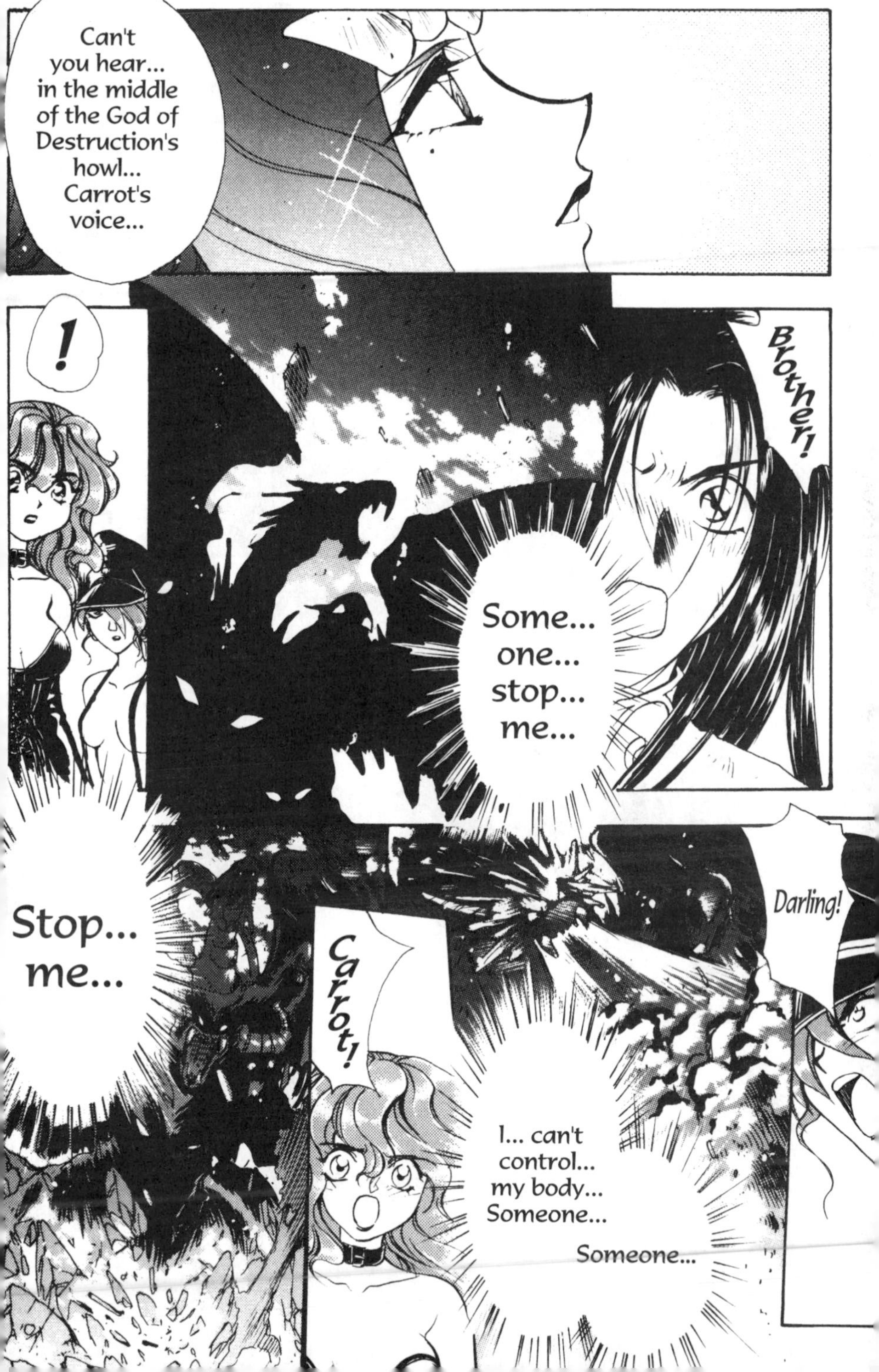
Can't you hear... in the middle of the God of Destruction's howl... Carrot's voice...
!
Brother!
Some... one... stop... me...
Stop... me...
Carrot!
Darling!
I... can't control... my body... Someone...
Someone...

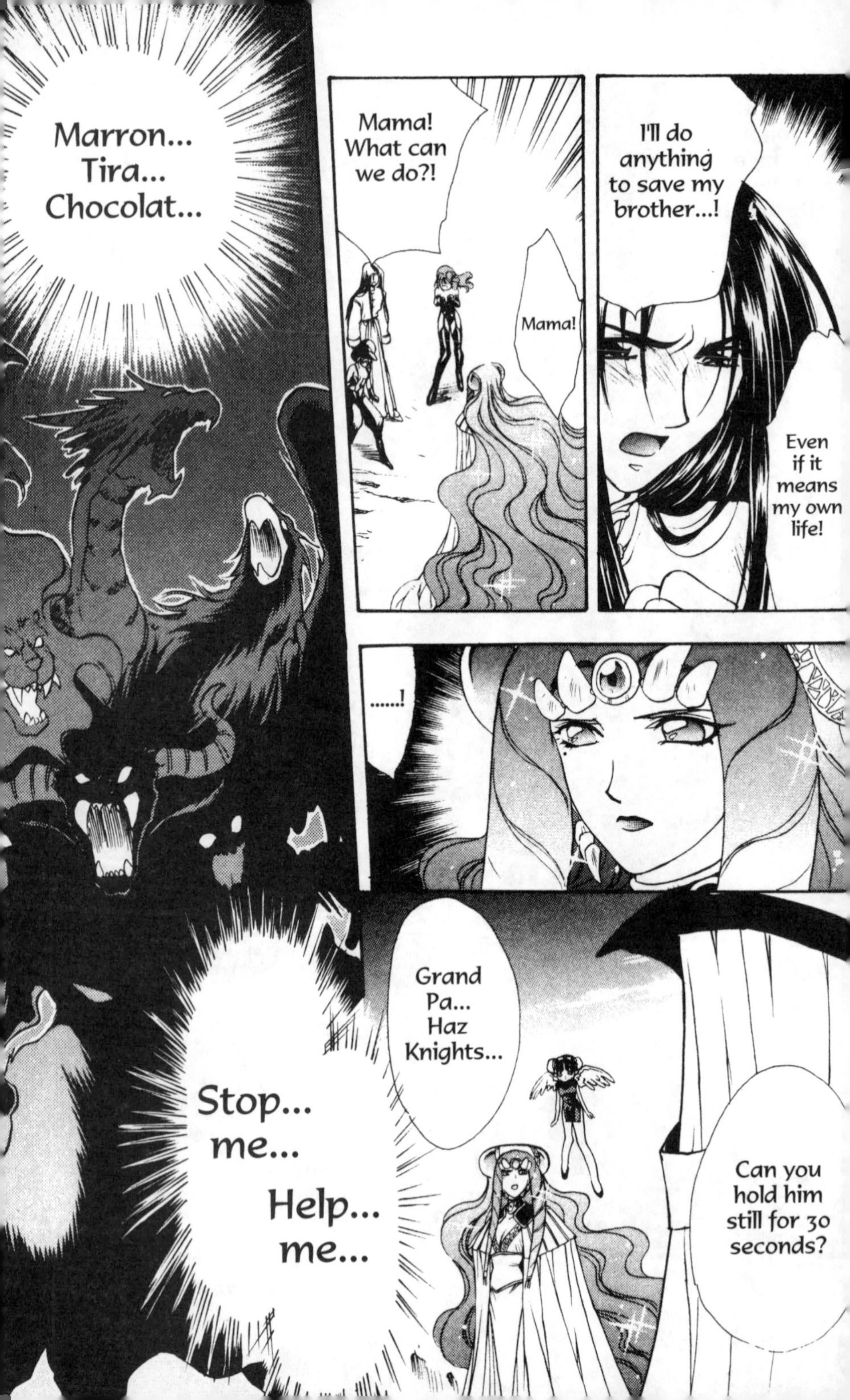
Marron... Tira... Chocolat...
Stop... me... Help... me...
Mama! What can we do?!
Mama!
I'll do anything to save my brother...!
Even if it means my own life!
......!
Grand Pa... Haz Knights...
Can you hold him still for 30 seconds?

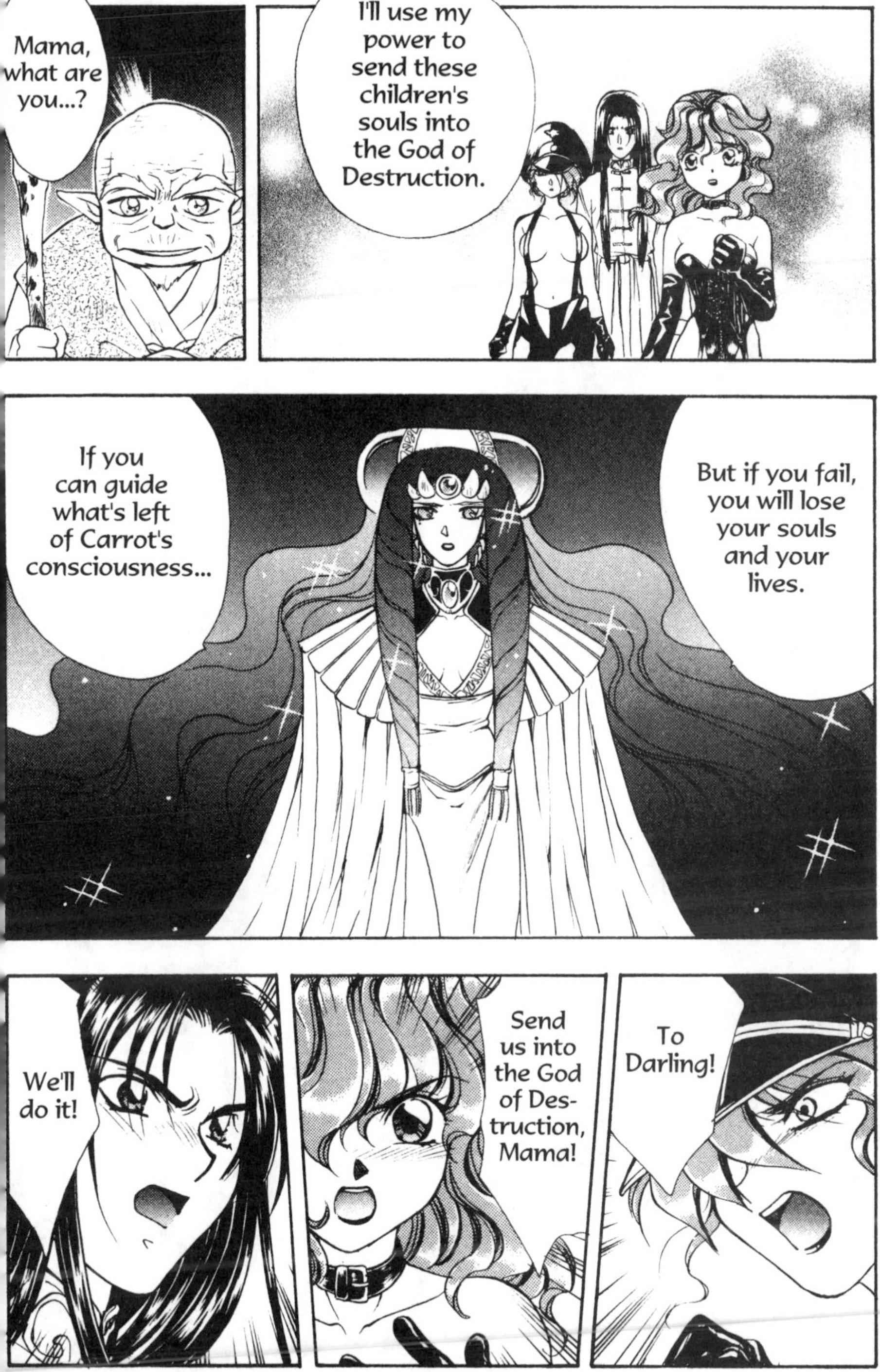
Mama, what are you...?
I'll use my power to send these children's souls into the God of Destruction.
If you can guide what's left of Carrot's consciousness...
But if you fail, you will lose your souls and your lives.
We'll do it!
Send us into the God of Des-truction, Mama!
To Darling!

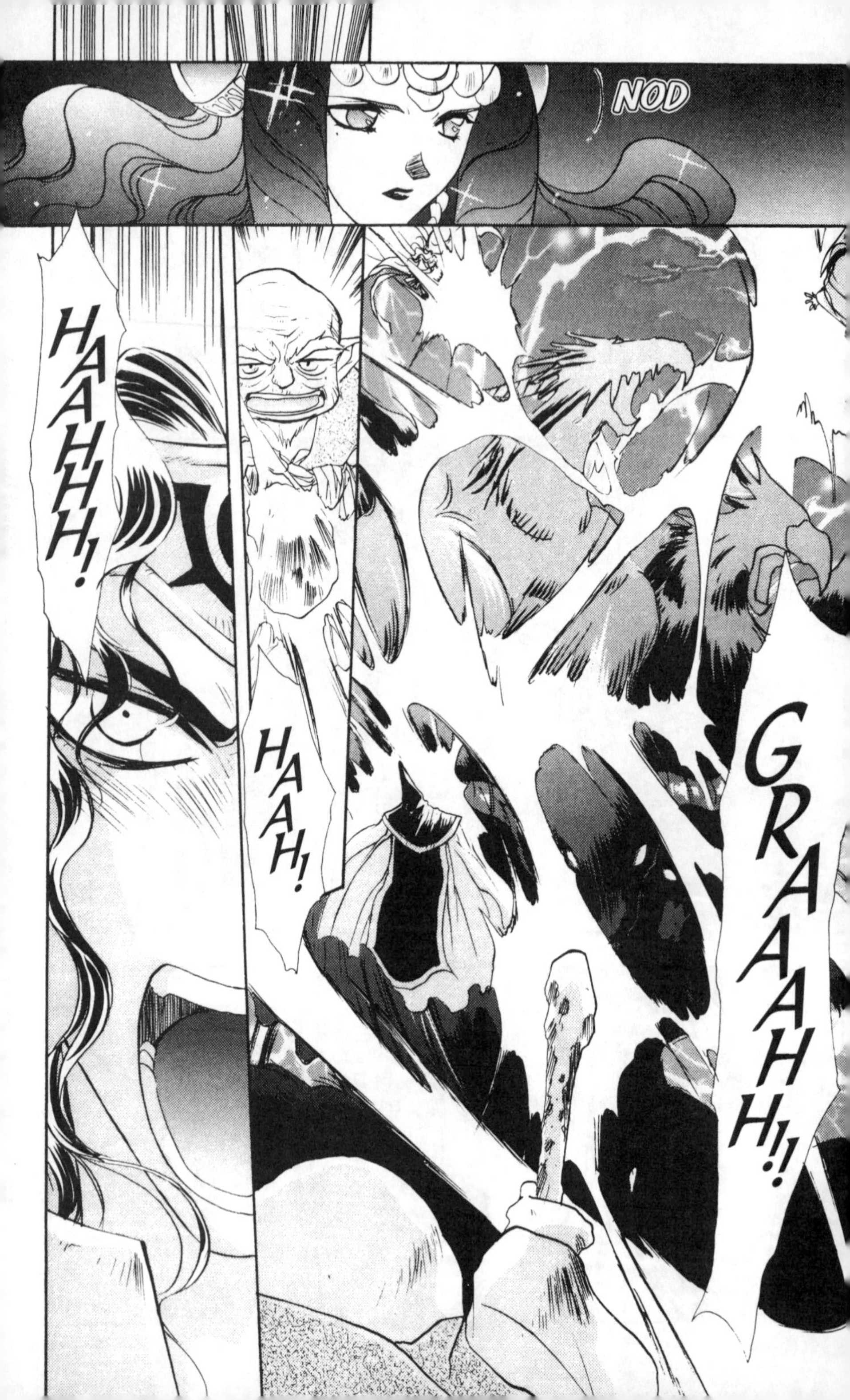
NOD
HAAHHH!
HAAH!
GRAAAHH!!

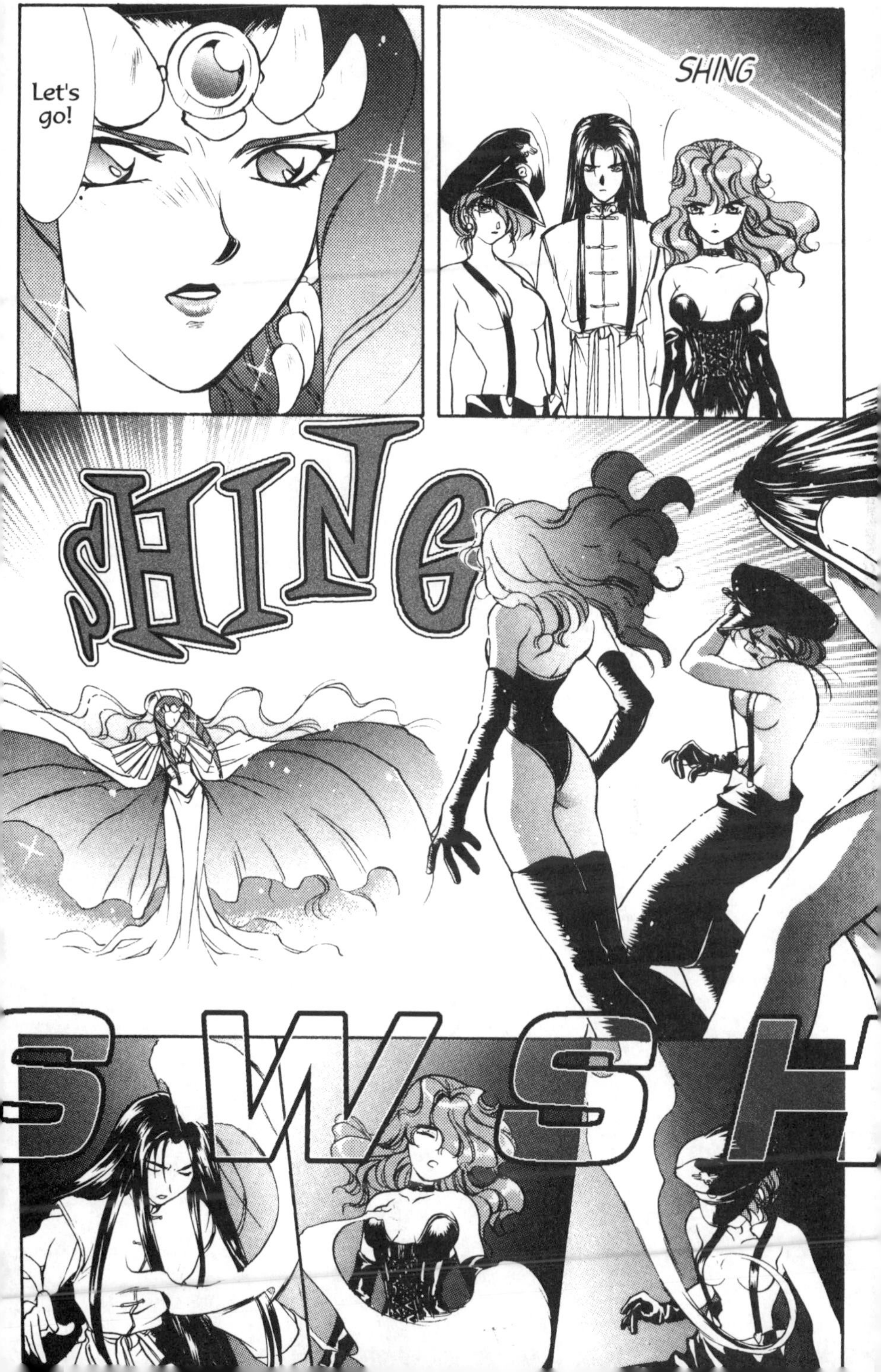
Let's go!
SHING
SHING
SWSH

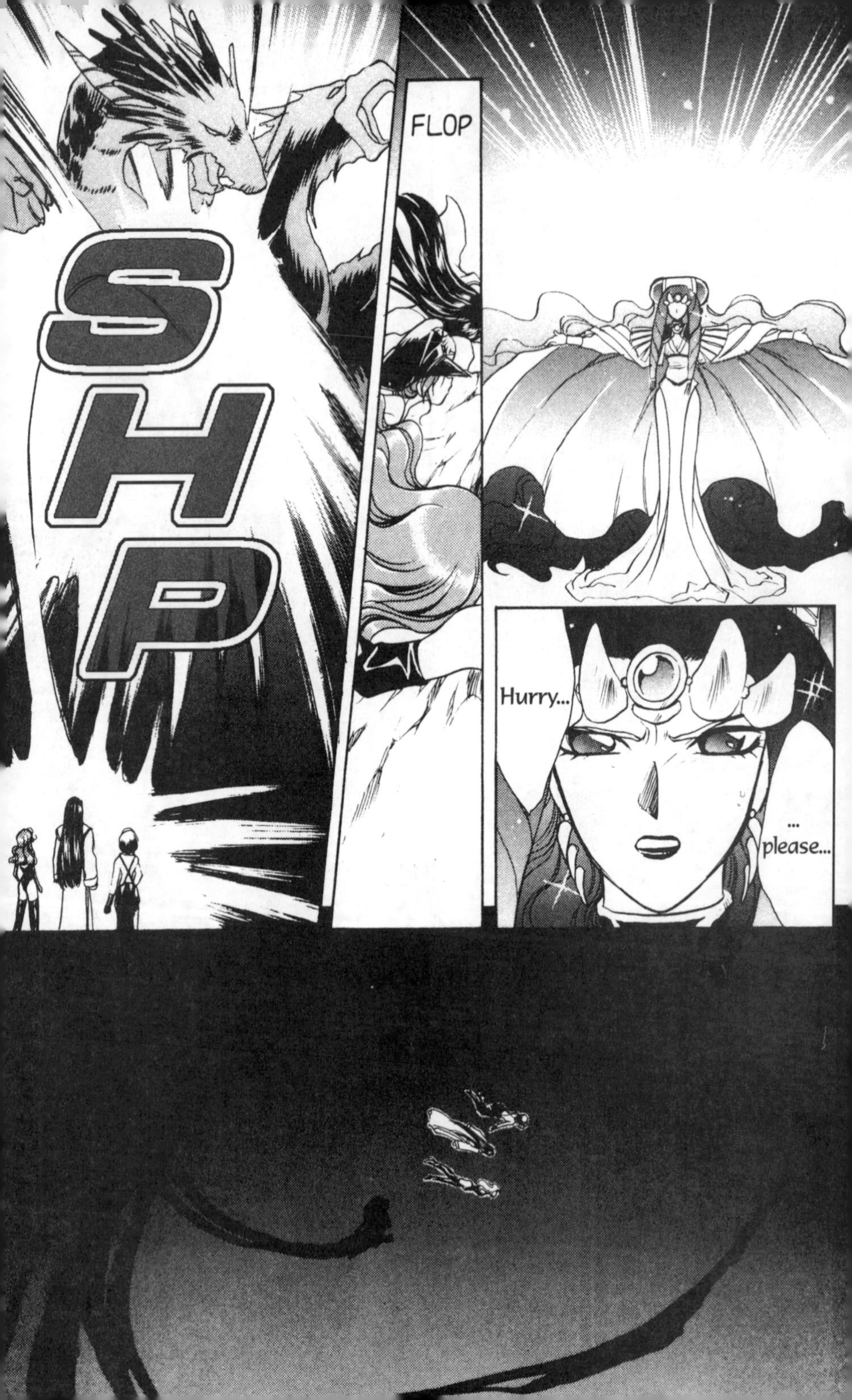
SHP
FLOP
Hurry...
...
please...

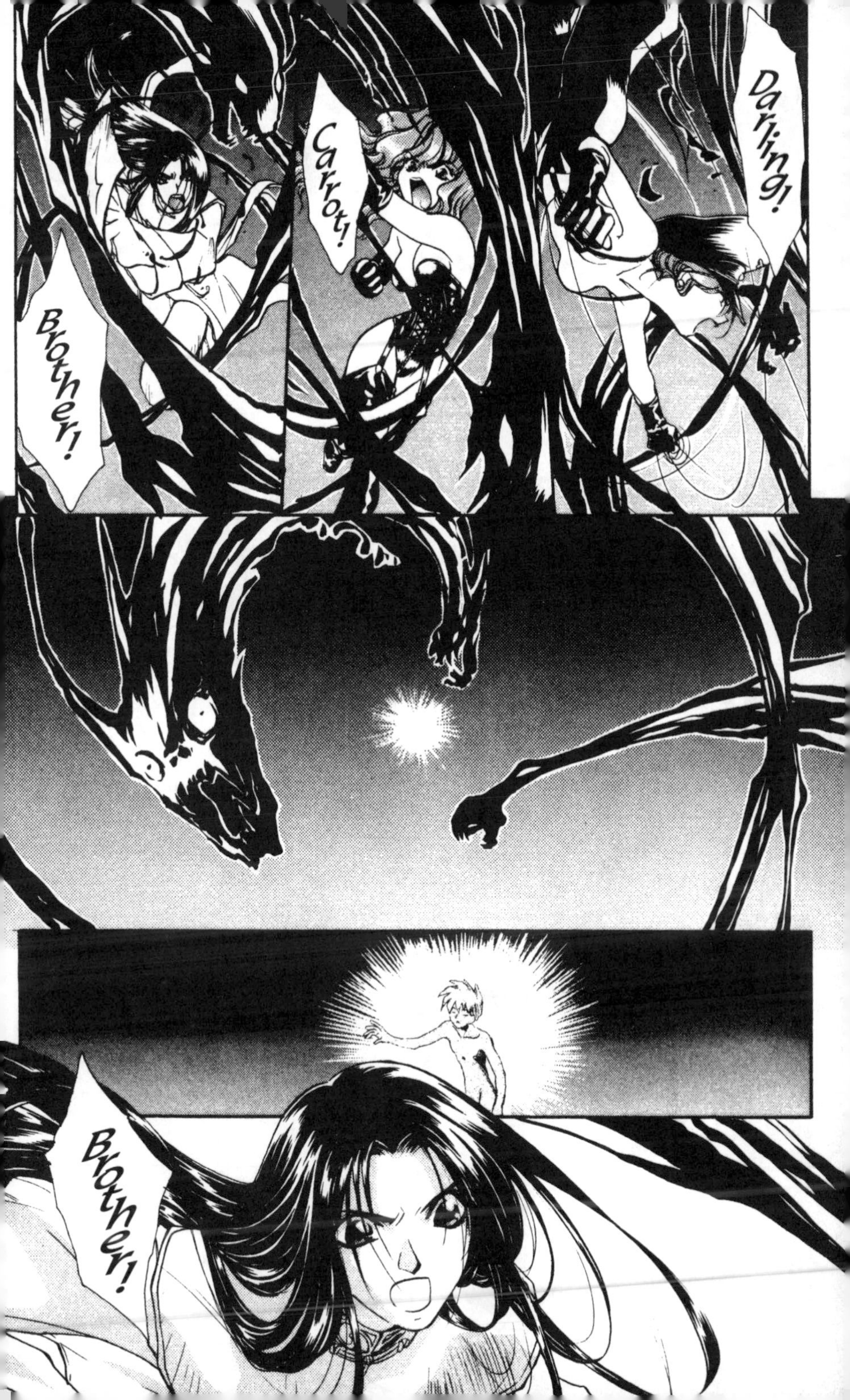
Brother!
Carrot!
Darling!
Brother!

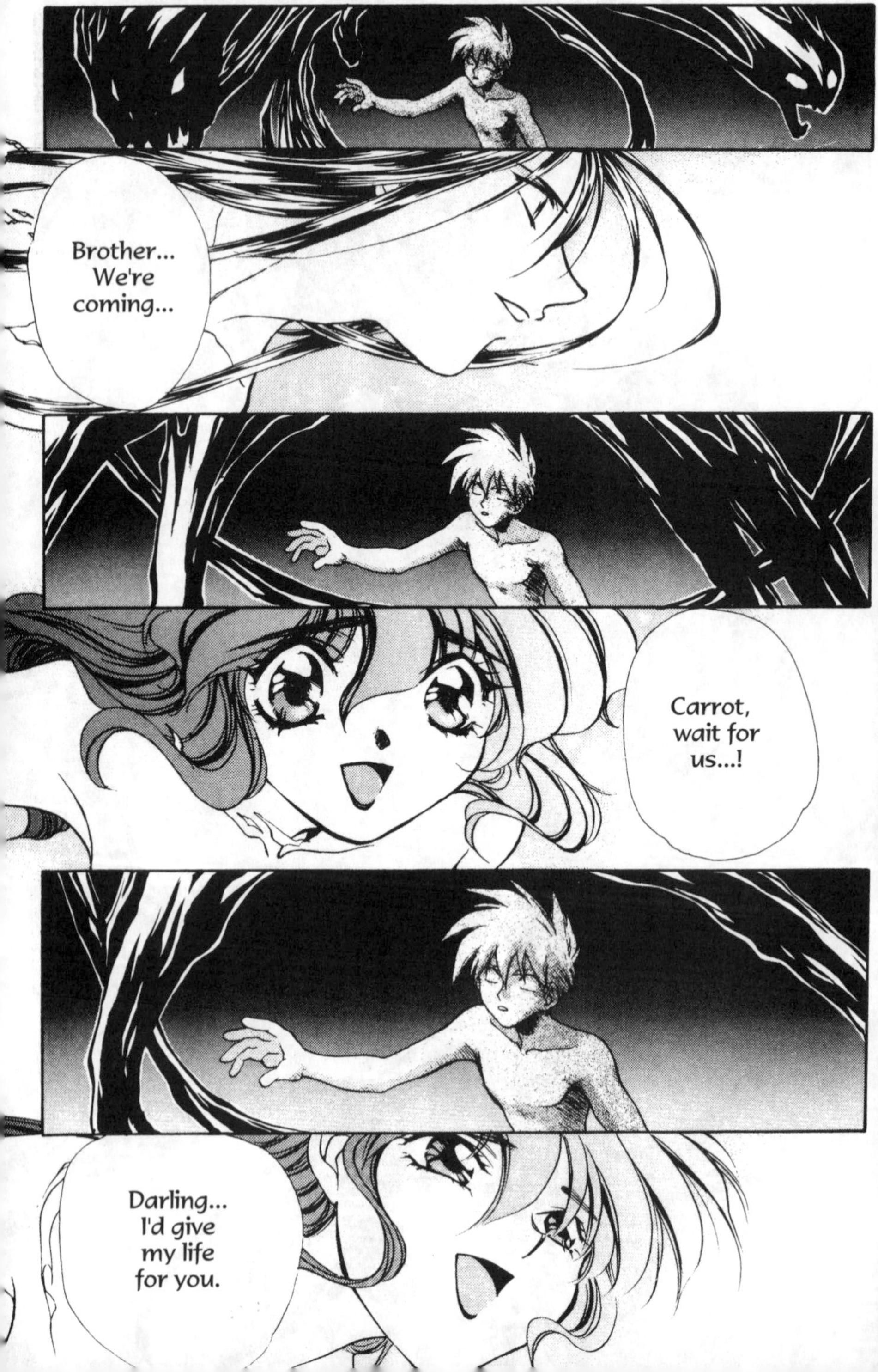
Brother... We're coming...
Carrot, wait for us...!
Darling... I'd give my life for you.

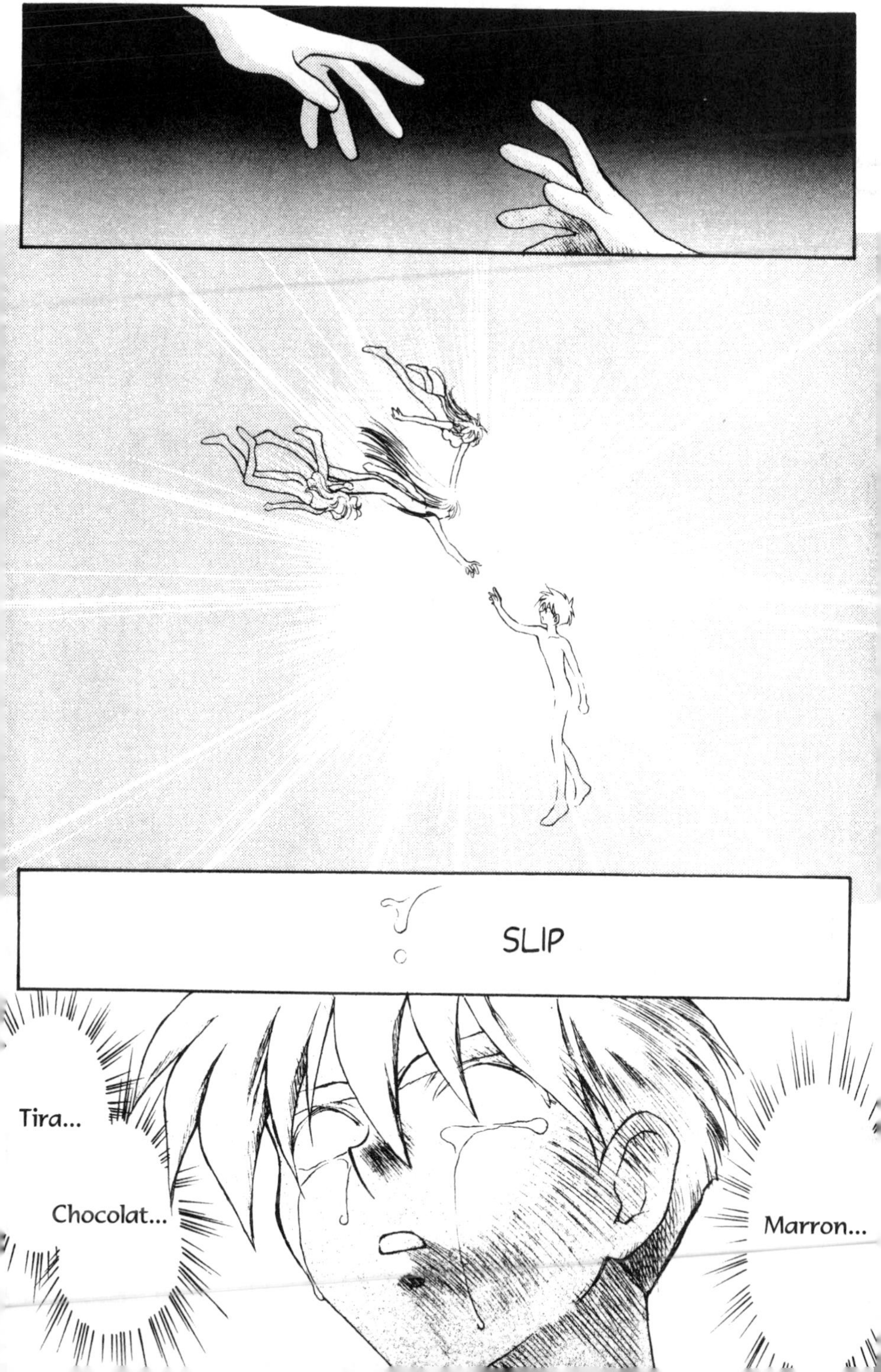
SLIP
Tira...
Chocolat...
Marron...

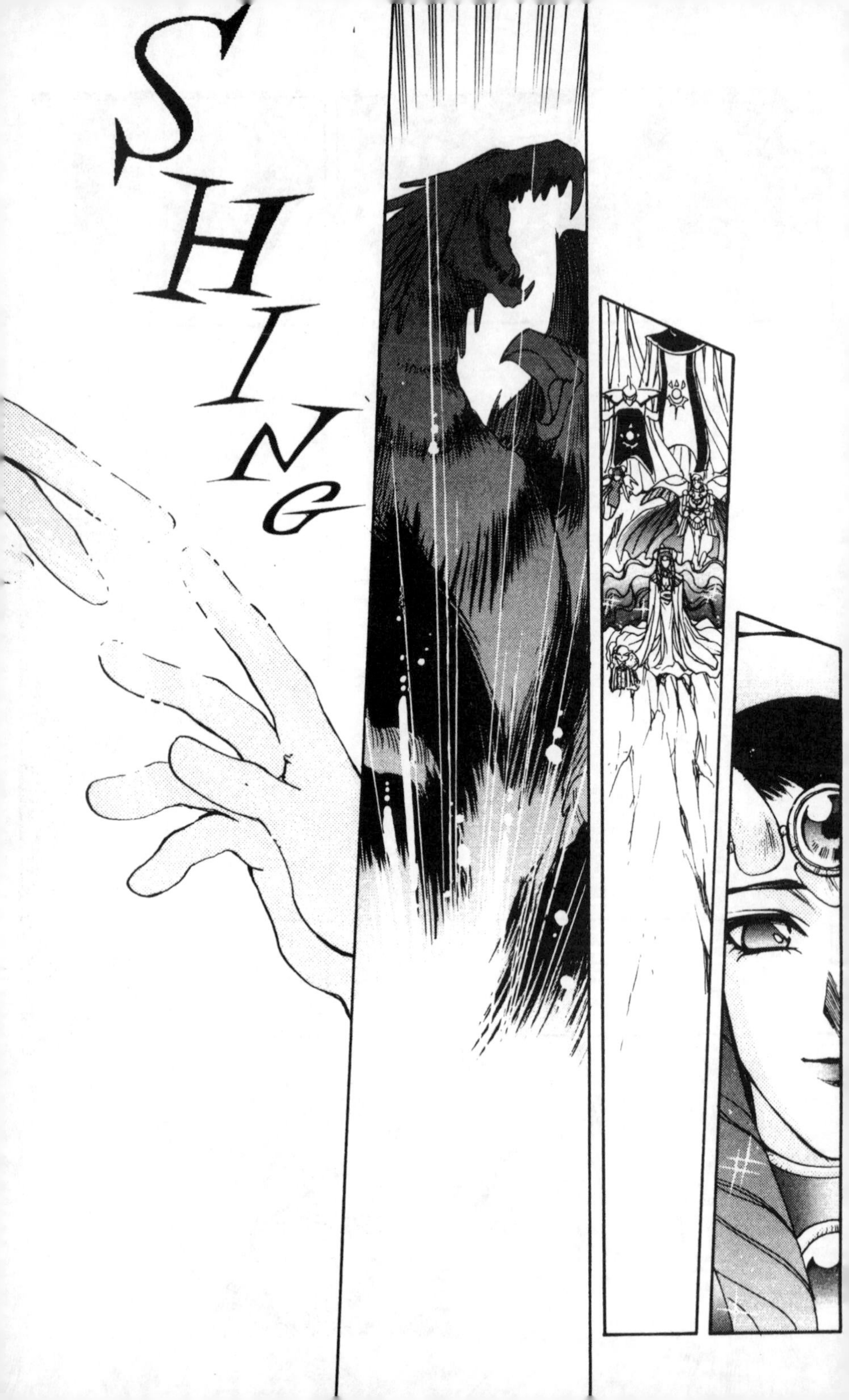
SHING

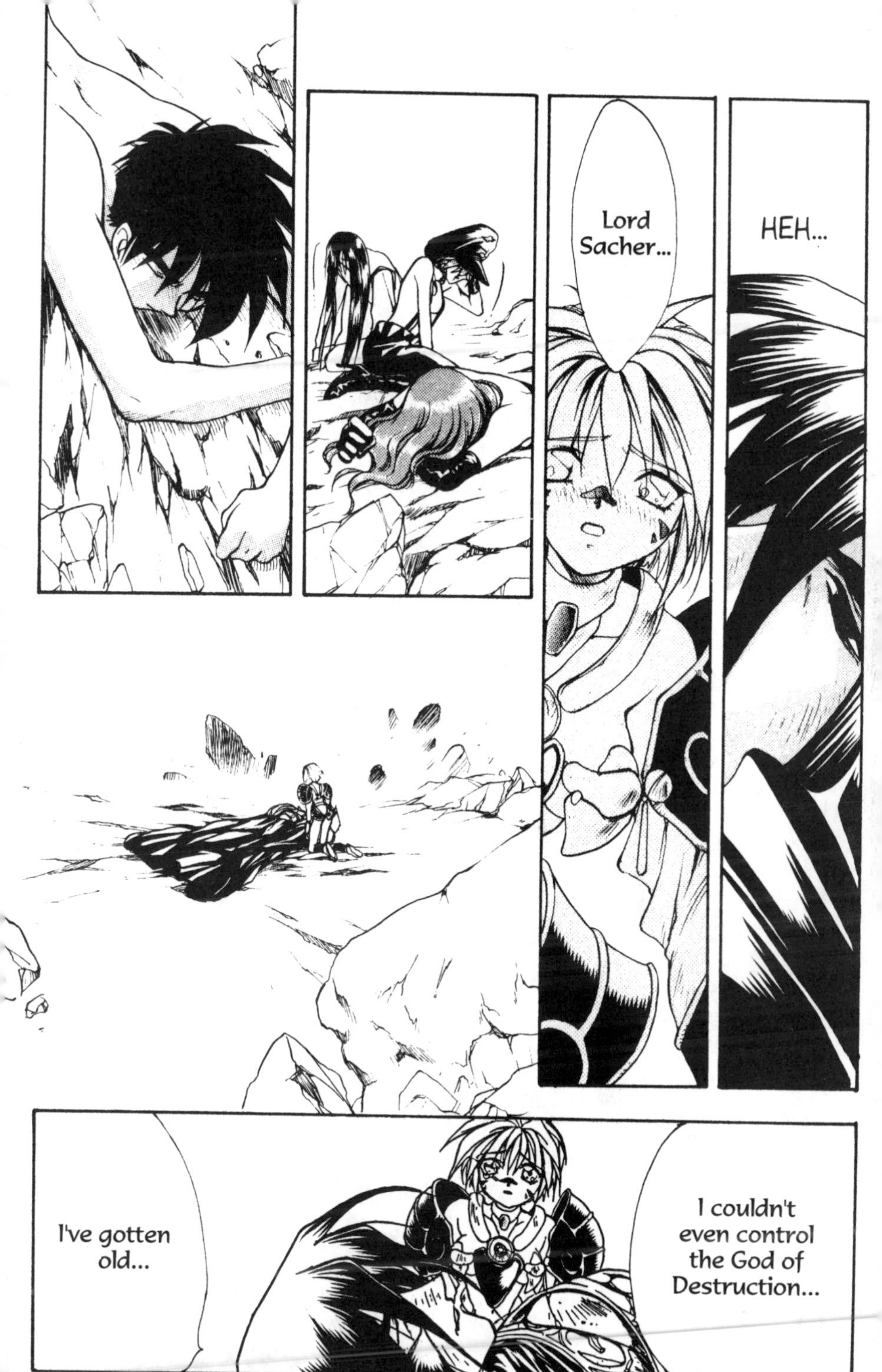
Lord Sacher...
HEH...
I've gotten old...
I couldn't even control the God of Destruction...

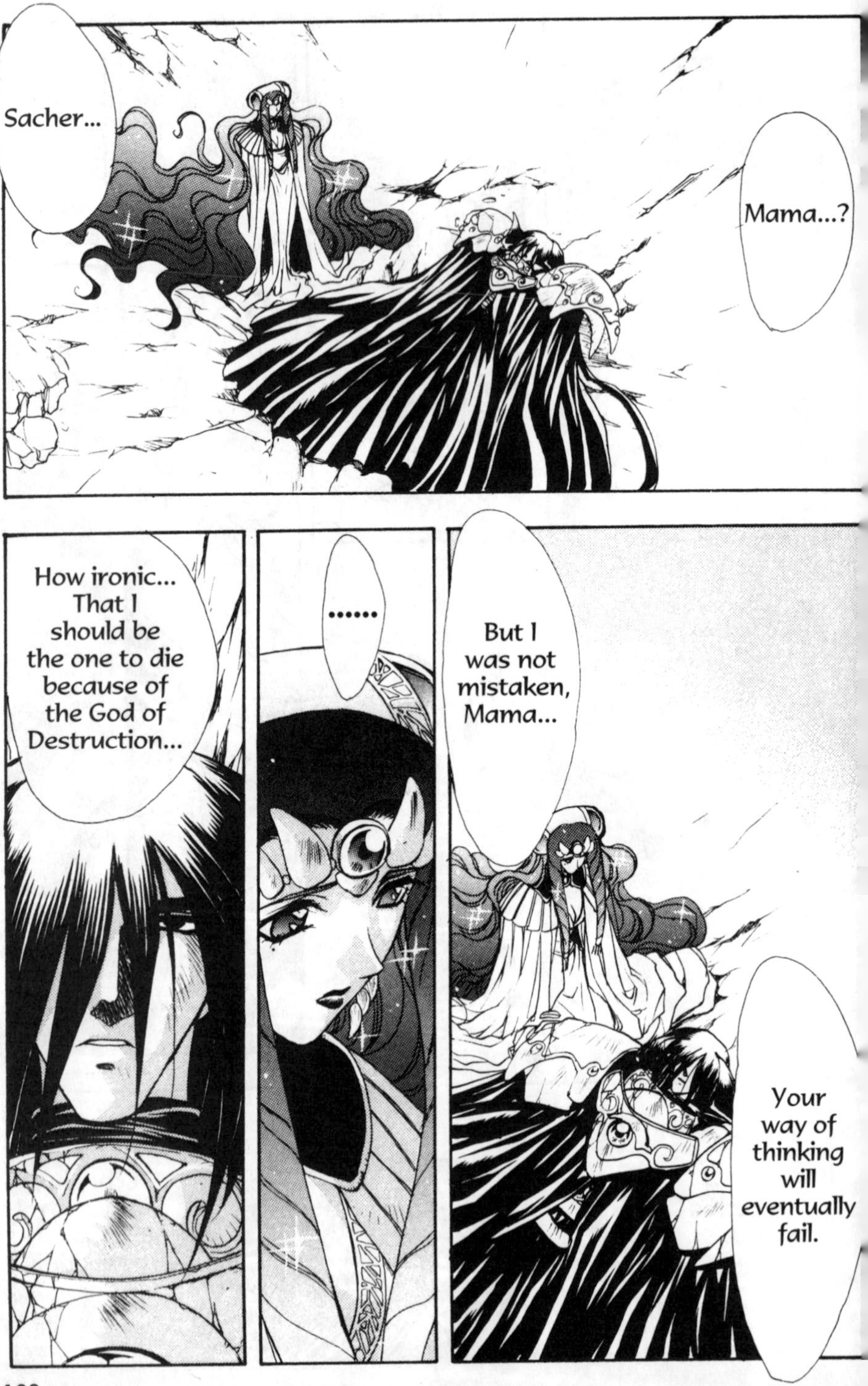
Sacher...
Mama...?
How ironic... That I should be the one to die because of the God of Destruction...
......
But I was not mistaken, Mama...
Your way of thinking will eventually fail.

Even if that time should come, I will still believe in mankind.

People are strong. They can face any difficulty and never lose hope.

Hope...

How soft-hearted...

......

But that's like you...

That heart full of hope will overcome any problem.

Sacher...

Eclair...

You stayed
by my side
until the end...

This
is my
thanks
to you...

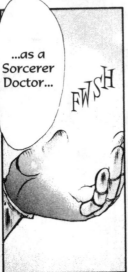

...as a
Sorcerer
Doctor...

FWSH

FWMM

SWSH

BADUM

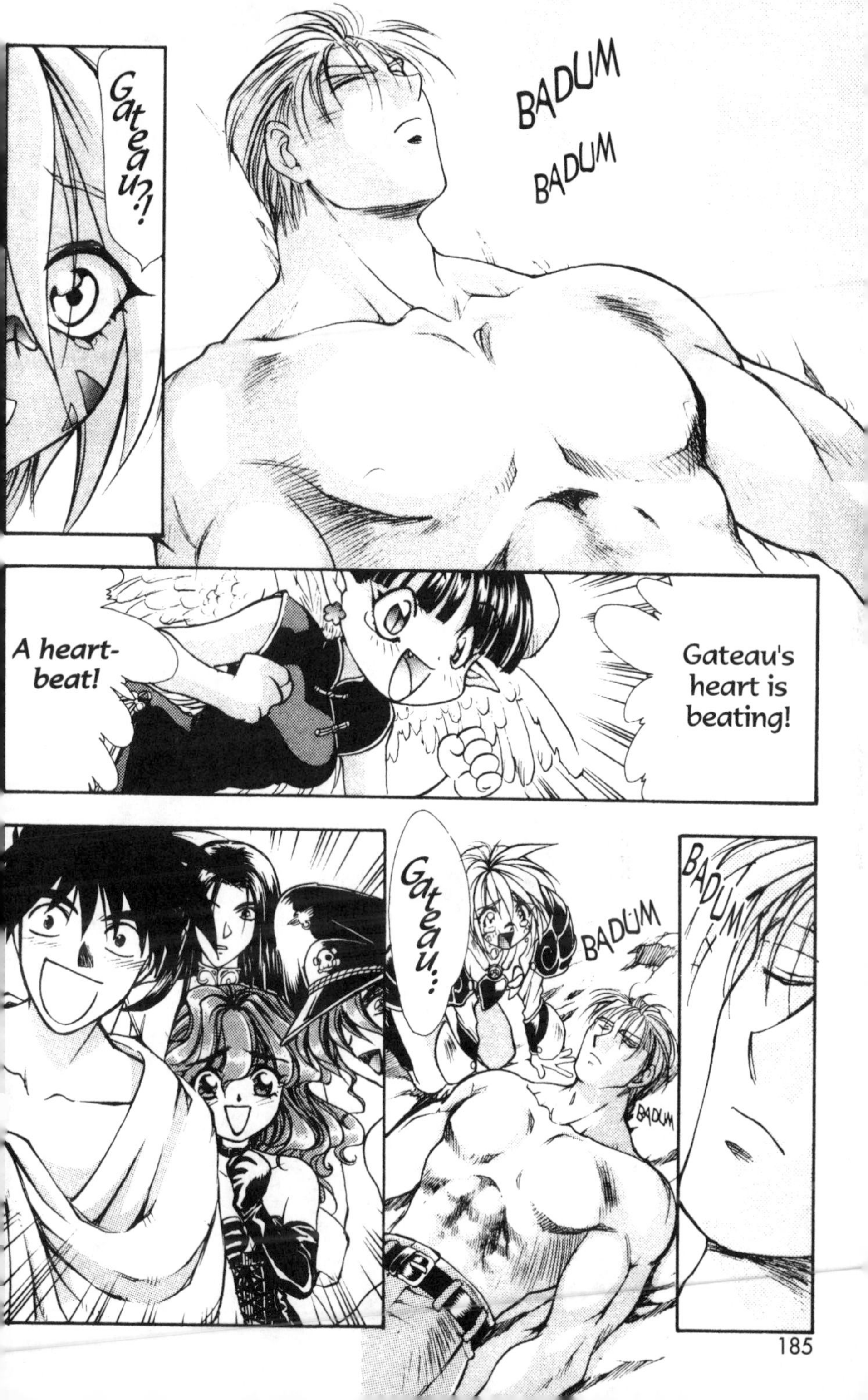

Gateau?!
BADUM
BADUM
A heart-beat!
Gateau's heart is beating!
Gateau...
BADUM
BADUM
BADUM

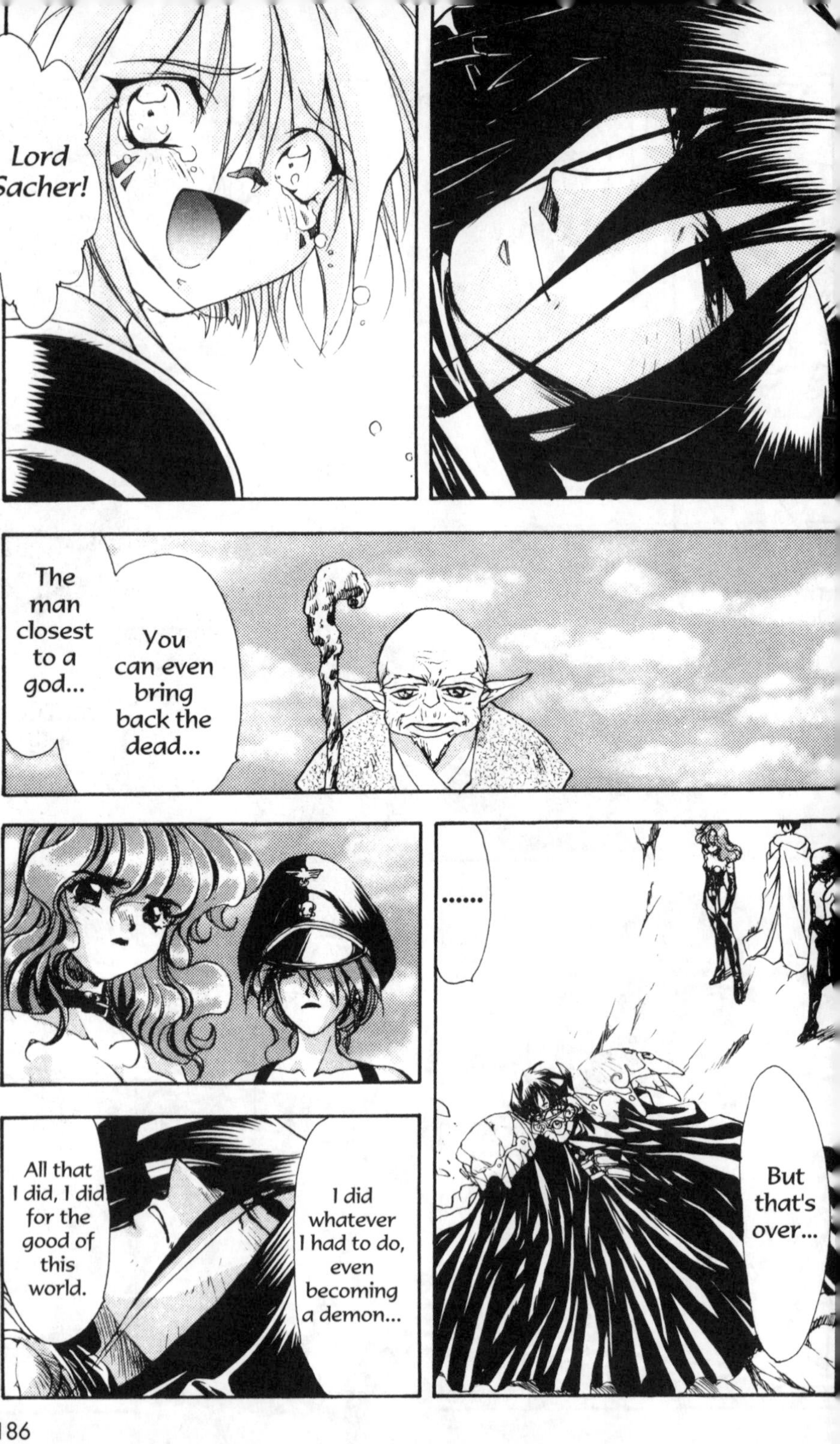
Lord Sacher!
The man closest to a god...
You can even bring back the dead...
......
All that I did, I did for the good of this world.
I did whatever I had to do, even becoming a demon...
But that's over...

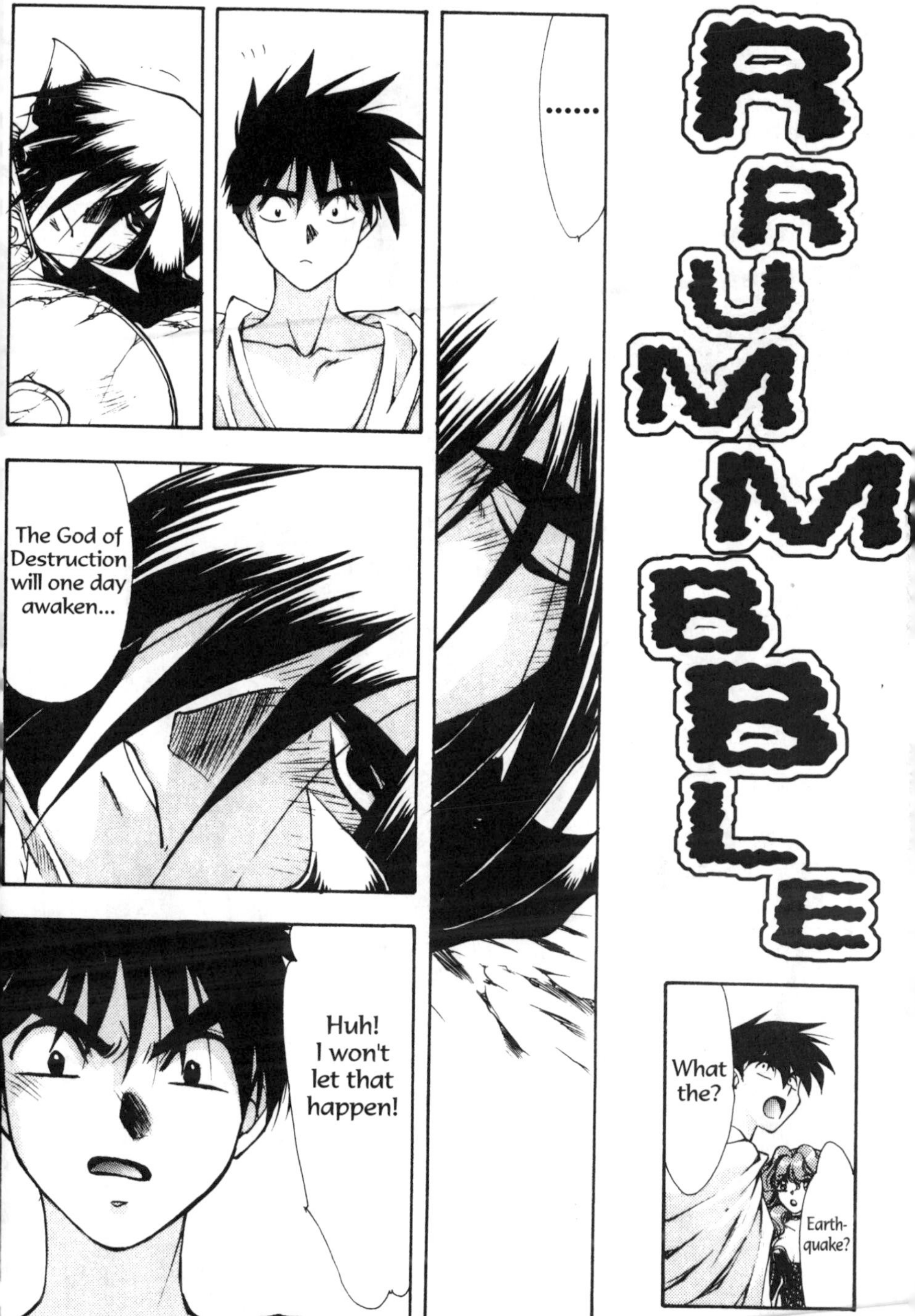
The God of Destruction will one day awaken...
Huh! I won't let that happen!
......
RRUMMBBLE
What the?
Earth-quake?

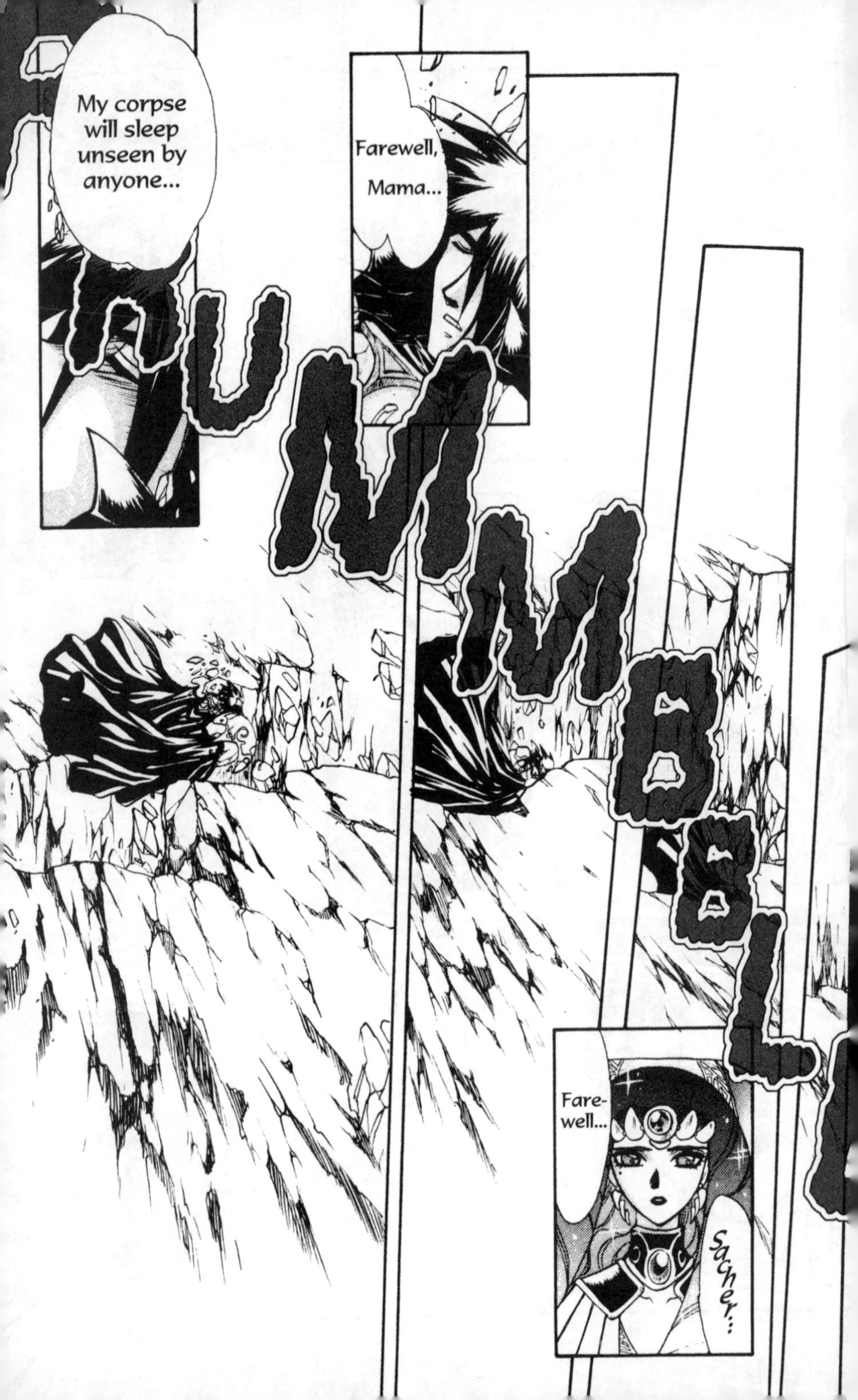
My corpse will sleep unseen by anyone...
Farewell, Mama...
RUMMBBL
Fare-well...
Sacher...

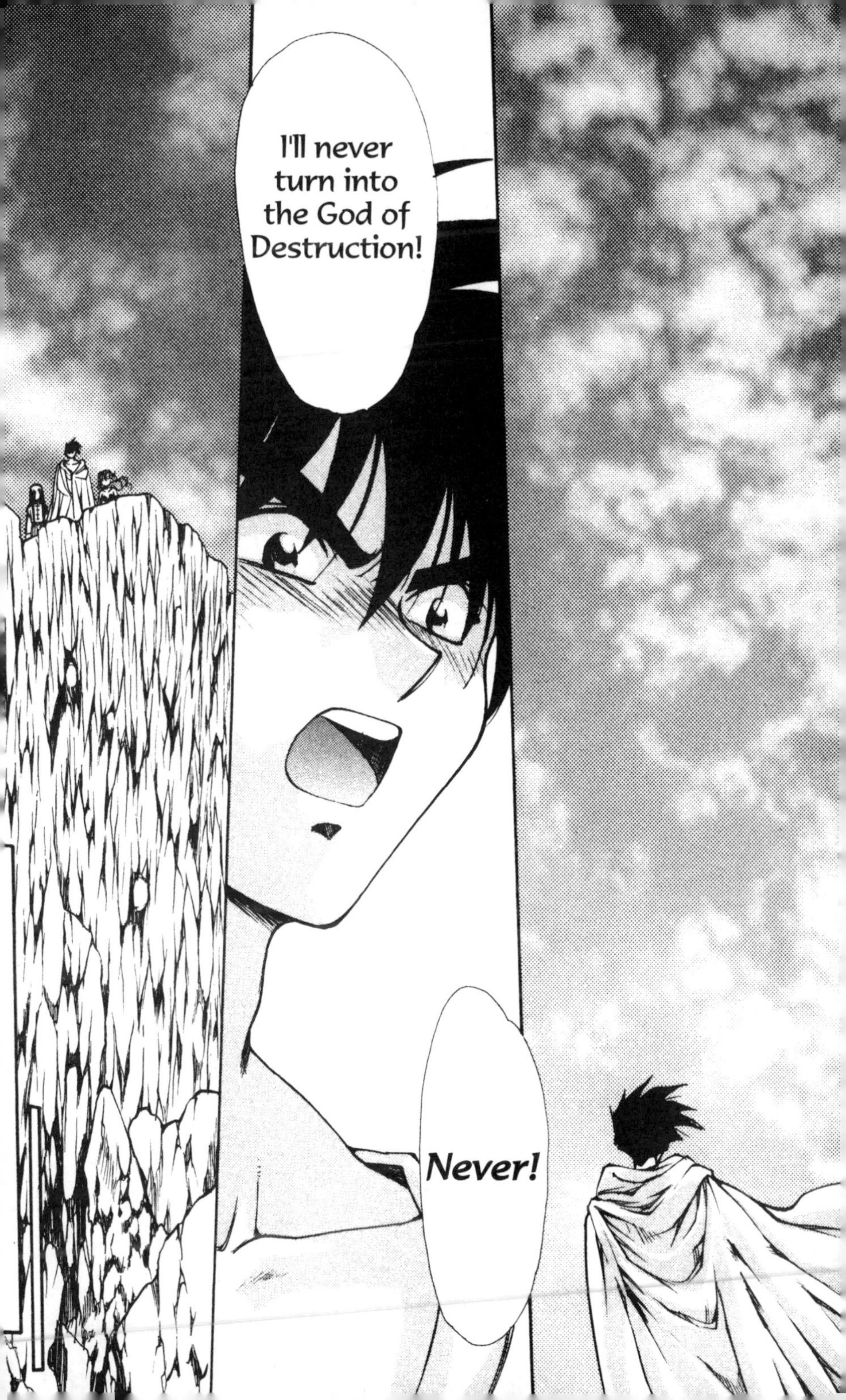
I'll never turn into the God of Destruction!
Never!